FREE THE PRESS

The Death of American Journalism and How to Revive It

BRIAN J. KAREM

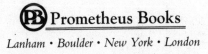 Prometheus Books

Lanham • Boulder • New York • London

Ⓟ Prometheus Books

An imprint of Globe Pequot, the trade division of
The Rowman & Littlefield Publishing Group, Inc.
4501 Forbes Boulevard, Suite 200, Lanham, Maryland 20706
www.rowman.com

Distributed by NATIONAL BOOK NETWORK

British Library Cataloguing in Publication Information Available

Library of Congress Cataloging-in-Publication Data

Names: Karem, Brian J., author.
Title: Free the press : the death of American journalism and how to revive
    it / Brian J. Karem.
Description: Lanham, MD : Prometheus, [2021] | Includes bibliographical
    references. | Summary: "Blending his experiences as a veteran reporter
    with trenchant analysis of the erosion of trust between the press and
    the government in the past 40 years, Free the Press gives readers a
    unique perspective on the challenges facing journalism, as well as the
    rise of hostility between these institutions"—Provided by publisher.
Identifiers: LCCN 2021022479 (print) | LCCN 2021022480 (ebook) | ISBN
    9781633887664 (cloth) | ISBN 9781633887671 (epub)
Subjects: LCSH: Government and the press—United States. | Press and
    politics—United States. | Freedom of the press—United States. |
    Journalism—Political aspects—United States. |
    Journalism—Objectivity—United States. | United States—Politics and
    government.
Classification: LCC PN4751 .K364 2021 (print) | LCC PN4751 (ebook) |
DDC
    070.4/4932—dc23
LC record available at https://lccn.loc.gov/2021022479
LC ebook record available at https://lccn.loc.gov/2021022480

♾ The paper used in this publication meets the minimum requirements of
American National Standard for Information Sciences—Permanence of Paper
for Printed Library Materials, ANSI/NISO Z39.48-1992.

For my parents, my wife, and my children.
"All You Need Is Love."

CONTENTS

FOREWORD

This is a book about the evolution of the news business in the United States from the "good old days" when the public got most of its information about the country and the world from serious news organizations that tried to get it right and report it straight to the days when massive shifts in technology and society along with the unbridled lust for profit spawned thousands of new information avenues that are often wrong and deliberately misleading.

The public used to trust the press by and large and watched approvingly movies like *Good Night and Good Luck*, about Edward R. Murrow's takedown of communist-hunting Senator Joseph McCarthy, and *All the President's Men*, in which the *Washington Post*'s Woodward and Bernstein headed Richard Nixon toward his political downfall.

But today, the cry of "fake news" and denunciation of the press as "enemies of the people" hounds the work of even the most careful and honest of news organizations, and the worst purveyors of off-the-wall conspiracy theories and laugh-out-loud falsehoods are followed with slavish devotion in the name of the First Amendment's freedom of the press.

How did this happen, why, and what can be done about it?

Brian Karem, who entered the news business when it was so much simpler and a whole lot better, has watched it evolve into a hodgepodge of the good, the bad, and the ugly that it too often is today, and he has some answers here to those important questions.

Karem has been a news reporter for four decades, reporting stories both from around the United States and abroad, but is best known these days for his work as a White House correspondent.

He first stepped into the White House press room in 1986 and has covered every president—and most of Washington's best-known politicians—

ever since. He understands, like most good reporters, that the job is to report on the intentions and actions of the powerful men and women who run our government and to question them about matters of public interest—in other words, to hold their feet to the fire, if you will, and to not worry about being liked, just about being fair and right.

I really became an admirer of Karem's work when, in the early days of George H. W. Bush's presidency, he pressed President Bush to answer a question about the work of the administration's "War on Drugs," and the president got annoyed and told him to sit down.

On my report on the ABC News magazine program *Prime Time Live* about the incident, I asked Brian why he kept trying to get an answer in the face of an order from the president of the United States.

Here is his answer in our exchange (as edited):

Donaldson: He asked you to sit down and you persisted.

Karem: I just wanted the question answered.

Donaldson: Well, Brian. He's responsible to the people of the United States, but is he really responsible to you, Brian Karem?

Karem: Well, I'm a reporter and the public's representative at the meeting, and I'm sorry, but I'm not in a popularity contest.

Of course, in those days, such exchanges were sometimes sharp and direct but always civil—neither the press, the presidents, nor their press secretaries called each other names or publicly denounced each other.

But during the presidency of Donald J. Trump, that changed. Lying to the press and attacking reporters was the order of the day for Mr. Trump and his press staff. Running against the press has always been a favorite tactic of public office holders who get in trouble, but the Trump White House raised it to a high art.

Once after a public presidential event in the White House Rose Garden had ended and President Trump had departed, Karem and a guest who was a Trump supporter got into a verbal fight. The Trump supporter was not reprimanded, as far as we know, for his part in the altercation, but the White House press secretary ordered Karem's pass suspended for what she called *his failure* to maintain decorum.

Fortunately, the federal courts disagreed with her action and ordered Karem's pass restored.

The press is certainly not above criticism. And it is understandable that public officials and their fans don't want to hear uncomfortable questions from reporters.

The news business that I was in for fifty-two years in Washington and that Karem is in today, while different in so many ways, has had the same basic objective—get the facts right and tell it straight.

It was one of our founding fathers—John Adams—who pointed out to the jury while representing British soldiers who had defended themselves in a fight with American colonists that "facts matter" and by presenting the facts of what happened overcame the colonists' emotional hatred of the British. He won the freedom of the British soldiers.

Let us hope that today, in another emotional time, the work of gathering and relaying facts by serious journalists like Brian Karem will again prevail.

Otherwise, our country and its democracy are lost.

Sam Donaldson
Former White House Correspondent
ABC News

INTRODUCTION

This is a cautionary tale I hope and not a postmortem—though it may seem like one.

I also hope to present solutions to the problems written about here. You may or may not agree with them, but I hope you think about them—at least a little more than we think about the clickbait that passes as journalism on a variety of platforms these days. The tale is about the apparent death of independent journalism. After thirty-seven years in this business, I can tell you that reviving it will take a herculean effort. Considering who got elected president in 2016 and how the 2020 election turned out, it has become more difficult to do so, but I retain faith that it can be done.

For four years, the Donald Trump administration promoted lies daily in press releases, in appearances on television, and from the bully pulpit available to his staffers in the James S. Brady Press Briefing Room or on the macadam drive outside of the West Wing. But Trump also did so through a number of social media platforms—especially Twitter. Those lies bounced around inside informational silos like Fox News, OAN, Newsmax, and more. The more they bounced, the more attention they got and the more believable they became to millions of Americans. Even when CNN, the *New York Times*, or other large media outlets point out the lies, they did so by repeating the lies first. There seems to be no way to avoid this cancerous invasion of our news with lies, half-truths, and bad fiction.

But Donald Trump is merely a symptom. He's the result of forty years of the government and corporate media owners engaged in a systemic destruction of the First Amendment and free press.

As the story goes, in the summer of 1962, President John F. Kennedy arrived for a visit in Louisville, Kentucky. My dad, a dedicated Catholic and Democrat, watched him land, and, with me in his arms (I was approximately a year and a half old), he pushed to the front of the crowd of well-wishers gathered at the airport to see the president.

A former football player and at the time a spry twenty-two years old, Dad had no problem getting to the front of the line, thereby getting a chance to see the president, and in the process, he unknowingly showed me my future purpose.

As he reached out to shake the president's hand, "he put you down to do so," my mother later wrote in my baby book.

I don't know where Dad intended to put me down—perhaps on the tarmac. But mom also said as Dad did, so the "president picked you up and held you and asked you what your name was."

My response? Well, according to my father, I urinated in my wonderful cloth diaper and consequently all over the president.

And as my father later told me, "You've been pissing on politicians ever since."

The truth is politicians have been pissing on us since before I was born. But they really picked up their pace when Richard Nixon got into office. He tried to leverage a foreign government to the bargaining table during the Vietnam War in order to secure his election. He was notorious for trying to manipulate the media, and when he couldn't do it to his satisfaction, he put some of his minions, including Roger Ailes, the future architect of Fox News, to the task of reinventing the media to his liking. Nixon resigned. Roger Ailes stuck around.

Ailes found his success with two key politicians in the 1980s—Ronald Reagan and Kentucky senator Mitch McConnell. His main media accomplice became Rupert Murdoch.

With Reagan, Ailes found a man who would systematically deconstruct the media, allowing multiple media ownership, deregulating the airwaves, and ultimately getting rid of the fairness doctrine. Reagan, in turn, credited Murdoch and the *New York Post* for his 1980 victory in the presidential election. Reagan later waived a prohibition against owning a television station and a newspaper in the same market so Murdoch could continue to control the *Post* and the *Boston Herald* while he expanded his television presence in both markets.

With McConnell, Ailes found the key political ally who would put party over country and, as planned, would help out friends like Murdoch and eventually Sinclair broadcasting.

I joined the rank of professional reporters shortly after Reagan got into office—at a time when afternoon newspapers were dying because television news was taking the audience—and I've remained in the profession through never-ending downsizing, constriction in the business, and the rise of the internet.

Most of the places I have worked during the past thirty-five years have been bought, sold, or closed. The first newspaper I worked for while still in college was the *Kingdom-Daily Sun Gazette* in Fulton, Missouri—a town made famous by the book *Kings Row* and also famous for being the site of Winston Churchill's "Iron Curtain" speech. That newspaper no longer exists.

The newspaper I joined when I left college, in Conroe, Texas, the *Conroe Courier*, is a shell of its former itself. I recently visited the offices. They are closed. Gone. That newspaper was bought and is run from outside of Conroe. Consequently, it has little presence in the local community. The newspaper and television stations I worked at in Laredo, Texas, the *Laredo News* and KLDO-TV, are no longer around. WKYT-TV in Lexington, Kentucky, which afforded me my first chance to go to the White House briefing room, is the only place I worked that hasn't changed dramatically. Both the *Courier Journal* and the *Louisville Times*, the latter of which was routinely listed as one of the top ten newspapers in the country some forty years ago, are dramatically different. The *Times* closed, and Gannett bought the *Courier Journal* after Barry Bingham sold it because of a family dispute. Gannett consequently turned a great newspaper into a gastrointestinal statement.

There are many causes for the collapse of these newspapers and television stations. Arguments can be made for cultural, economic, and a variety of political factors leading to their downfall. These are all relevant and will be explored at length. But many of these factors are merely symptomatic of an overriding cause—government intervention. Although the press was set up to be independent and the public's best chance of holding politicians accountable to the public, during the past 200 years, governmental contempt for the press and economic pressures have led to thousands of tiny cuts in press revenue and transparency and ultimately have lessened the ability to hold government accountable—making many papers, at times, almost unreadable.

The government has removed requirements for public notice ads. It has made public information inaccessible except through expensive litigation or cost-prohibitive reproduction charges. It ended the fairness doctrine. It sold the public on that move by claiming government action would assist free speech. That was the real coup. In the end, the government turned around and blamed the media owners for the problems—though it was the owners that bought the government con—or helped spread it for the sake of their own bottom line.

Thirty years of this governmental manipulation finally led to Donald Trump's proclamation that reporters are the enemy of the people—and a sizable number of Americans believed him then and still do now. Far from being the enemy of the people—we are the people. True, a press pass allows access to the front seat of the theater, but the price of that front-row seat has heretofore been to hold politicians accountable by asking them the hard questions.

The government has hobbled these efforts by legislation, by regulation, and by bribery. Holding out access like a journalistic carrot on a stick, presidents have silenced individual journalists, while legislative and regulatory efforts have reduced the number of independent media companies and thus the overall number of reporters.

Journalism has long attracted young professionals with good minds and an independent nature, but keeping them in the past four decades of constriction is difficult. Institutional knowledge is not what it was when I first became a reporter.

I've watched young children die. In covering crime, I've seen hundreds of dead bodies in various states of decomposition that would make horror movie special effects wizards vomit. By my count, I witnessed twenty-two people take their last breath on this planet. I still remember their faces. They were police officers, criminals, old people, car accident victims, and one eight-month-old baby boy whose face and bare feet still haunt me to this day.

I've covered professional sports, wars, politics, county fairs, city council meetings, Congress, every president since Ronald Reagan, NASA, weird and big weather, earthquakes, fires, famine, and stand-up comedy.

I've worked in television, radio, and newspaper; on the internet; and for magazines. My life has been reporting on multiple platforms and on a variety of beats and has taken me across the world and back—and luckily on someone else's nickel because working reporters still do not make squat.

I'm not the only reporter to have done this, but the constriction of the news business has led to far fewer of us—and thus far less institutional knowledge and as a consequence less comprehensive reporting. It used to be that you had to have a great deal of experience in order to be assigned the White House press beat. Today, kids are hired right out of college and paid low wages to handle what is one of the most important beats in the world—covering the president of the United States. Is it any wonder the institution is looked on with such disdain?

Today, reporters professionally survive by being little more than stenographers—and without experience or mentors to guide young reporters, it is a hellish existence.

Mentors on my journey include Sam Donaldson, Helen Thomas, Barry Bingham Sr., and many more hardworking, innovative, exceptional reporters and writers. Through my travels and my work, one thing has become breathtakingly clear to me:

From the moment I became a reporter, the government has systematically tried to destroy independent reporting. The government's intended rise of corporate journalism—as Ben Bagdikian told us in *The Media Monopoly*—has assisted in destroying the Fourth Estate and free speech.

Today, there are fewer reporters to cover more people than at any time in my life. The prime example is in Laredo. When I moved there in 1984 to be a county reporter for the *Laredo News*, earning my first chance to cover a presidential race, there were two daily newspapers, three network-affiliated television stations, and several radio stations servicing a population of 100,000 people. Since it was on the Texas–Mexico border, there were also two Spanish-speaking newspapers and one Hispanic television station.

Today? One newspaper, one television station, and 300,000 people.

The federal, state, and local governments that accomplished this task have opened us up to fascism and sowed seeds of doubt into our most cherished democratic foundations. A lack of education isn't a new story—but the federal government's promotion of it is. It has left people providing and believing "alternate facts." It leaves every reporter from a small-town Iowa community newspaper to a reporter for a network or the *New York Times* being labeled "fake news" or the "enemy of the people."

In a country where press freedom is guaranteed in the First Amendment to the Constitution, we are today, according to Reporters Without Borders, ranked just forty-fourth in press freedom. Peaceful protesters are gassed outside of the White House while reporters are beaten and threatened. Our press freedom continues to erode, and no one, it seems, wants to address why or how this happened. It seems we only want to attack each other.

That's the problem.

There is a solution.

1

JUSTICE TO ALL,
PARTIALITY TO NONE

It was a typical day in the Donald Trump administration—which means it would have been an atypical day in the life of any other administration.

The president was talking about sending American troops to the southern U.S. border to help stop a "crisis" that we were told included roving caravans of marauding illegal immigrants intent on looting the countryside, engaging in criminal activities, and stealing American jobs while also in the process of sapping our infrastructure and human services by collecting unemployment.

To send U.S. troops to the border, Trump had to get authorization from Congress because such a move violated the Posse Comitatus Act.[1] The act limits the powers of the U.S. military to enforce domestic policies within the United States.

Republicans have long supported this legislation, but the Trump administration seemed to be unaware of it. On the day in question, John Bennett, who at the time was Roll Call's White House reporter, and I walked back behind the James S. Brady Press Briefing Room in the West Wing to the lower press offices to ask a member of Trump's staff how the president was going to get around the act and if he planned to ask Congress to give him a waiver. At the time, the GOP ran the House and the Senate—so opposition was unlikely. And Congress has given presidential waivers in the past.

Bennett was a few steps ahead of me and had already cornered Deputy Press Secretary Hogan Gidley in his office. Gidley was once considered for the top job Sarah Huckabee Sanders and later Stephanie Grisham and Kayleigh McEnany held, but he was never chosen. Gidley was a dapper dresser, prone to drinking muscle milk, which he kept stored in his office and which was often given as gifts from staff members.

He was energetic and for the most part friendly. He tried to help out the press, often muttering and jotting things down in a notebook and promising to get back to us—which he seldom did—but he tried. Some of the president's staff joked about his boundless energy and how he always seemed to be on the go. One assistant vowed to put a bell on his neck so we would know where he was.

Bennett asked Gidley about the Posse Comitatus Act. Hogan stared at him and then me and then said, "Is that some kind of rule or something?"

Bennett and I stared at each other, and we seemed to say in unison. "It's a law," and I added, "Republicans are usually supportive of it." Hogan nodded as if he understood and then went on to answer a few other questions.

At the end, Bennett circled back around to the first question, and Gidley nodded vigorously, telling us both that he'd get back to us about "that Hakuna Matata thing" before shooing us out his door.

"Hakuna Matata?" Bennett said when we got back to the basement cubicles that served as office space for reporters. "He called the Posse Comitatus Act 'that Hakuna Matata thing,' what the fuck? He quoted the Lion King*?"*

That brand of lunacy was indicative of the Trump years at the White House. But it wasn't the reaction we got from Gidley that surprised me. Like Bennett, I couldn't help but chuckle.

Later, when we recounted this story to others, I was surprised there were reporters who had no idea what the Posse Comitatus Act is. "Why would I need to know that?" one reporter asked me.

Another younger reporter said it wasn't important, and that reporter also asked me how to keep a press secretary from asking a reporter a question in response to a question.

Suddenly, I felt as if I were in that scene in Broadcast News *where Albert Brook's character chides William Hurt's character about his lack of knowledge of government. Only it was worse. I questioned some of the young reporters and found the White House beat was only their second (sometimes their first) job in the business. One reporter told me, "I just got thrown into it."*

Journalism sure has changed. Or maybe not.

The American journalistic trek through time that led us to Donald J. Trump began in 1690. That year, Benjamin Harris, an Englishman living in Boston, published the first multiple-page newspaper in what would later become the United States. Living and working in Boston, the erstwhile journalist introduced to the world *Publick Occurrences Both Forreign and Domestick* in September. The newspaper had three pages of text, and the fourth page was left blank for others to write in pieces of news they could in turn hand out to others—an early example of social media.[2] The publication contained local news, gossip, and a piece on King William's war. The British government closed it down after one issue, Harris was jailed, and the colonies didn't get another multipage newspaper until 1704, when John Campbell published *Boston News-Letter*.

Newspapers were cutting-edge technology. Unlike word-of-mouth communications and later the internet and television, newspapers also represented an unchangeable foundation on which political and social issues could be discussed. Anyone who's ever played the "telephone game" knows how easily the spoken word can change—even without intent. Anyone who's ever read the news on the internet or seen "deep fake" videos knows how ephemeral those methods of communication are. Newspapers were and are different. Once printed, the word doesn't change unless amended in further print issues. This enabled then and does now a voluminous amount of people to read the *same thing*. When Alexander Hamilton, James Madison, and John Jay united to produce the Federalist essays, they chose to publish them in *The Independent Journal* and *The Daily Advertiser*, from which those essays were copied by practically every paper in America long before they were made into a book.

Until then, the most widely spread printed material was the Bible.

From the beginning of our republic, the government and the *independent* press were contentious players on the public scene. Journalists by nature are antagonistic toward those in power. "And what is a journalist without energy, enthusiasm, and integrity, plus insatiable curiosity and courage," Helen Thomas wrote.[3]

Thomas noted, as H. L. Mencken did before her, that journalists rarely encourage friendship among those they cover—and often do not even encourage such feelings among their competitive peers. The craft has never been among the higher-paid professions, though some of the richer talking heads on networks make a barrel full of cash. The rewards in such a lifestyle come in a proximity to events and the ability to then communicate facts of those events to the rest of us. The firsthand seat at historic events and the ability to directly question those in power and to tell everyone what is actually going on is a powerful draw to people with a certain independent mind-set. Journalism has always attracted those types, but it is hard to hold on to them.

In the beginning, it was all about the politics. Newspapers owed allegiance to politicians and parties. Competing factions had competing newspapers.

The founding fathers were well aware of the problems of the emerging Fourth Estate, and Thomas Jefferson, for one, never hesitated to call reporters and publications on the carpet for perceived transgressions and inaccurate reporting. And while Jefferson was a staunch critic, he was an even larger supporter of the free press. His quotes are often taken out of context, but the fact remains free speech is guaranteed in the *First* Amendment and was seen as a cornerstone of democracy by our founding fathers.

In the first years of the republic, the U.S. Postal Service Act provided substantial subsidies: newspapers were delivered up to 100 miles for a penny and beyond for 1.5 cents, when first-class postage ranged from six cents to a quarter.[4] As a result, the growing population of the United States stayed informed and literate, and that, in turn, helped to drive economics and the engine of democracy.

As the country got its footing, the press started feeling its oats. George Washington became upset with the competing press, particularly the part the press played in bitter acrimony between John Adams and Thomas Jefferson.

One of the most acrimonious criticisms occurred in the *Connecticut Courant*, the weekly precursor of the *Hartford Courant*, the oldest continuously published newspaper as of March 2021. It has gone through a long history of sales and acquisitions but began as a weekly called the *Connecticut Courant* on October 29, 1764, becoming daily in 1837. In 1979, it was bought by the Times Mirror Company. In 2000, Times Mirror became owned by the Tribune Company, which later combined the paper's management and facilities with those of a Tribune-owned Hartford television station. In 2014, the *Courant* and other Tribune print properties were spun off to a new corporate parent, Tribune Publishing, separate from the station.

Jefferson, who said he still supported a free press, also encouraged court packing and investigations against those in the press he didn't like—stirring up animosity from Federalists. Jefferson even sued the *Courant* for criminal libel and took it a step farther.

The Reverend Azel Backus was charged with libeling the president from his Bethlehem pulpit. Backus had called Jefferson a "liar, whoremaster, debaucher, drunkard, gambler."

He also made references to Jefferson's using slaves for immoral purposes.[5]

In *The Opposition Press of the Federalist Period*, Donald H. Stewart noted the decline of the Federalists and the rise of Jefferson's Democratic-Republican Party. He said much of it came to pass because Jefferson was very good at manipulating and driving press coverage, which helped him spread the word and gave rise to his power. Not until Lincoln's plurality in 1860 did a "victorious electoral machine" arise from nothing within less than a decade. "With all their gifts for leadership and all the popular topics that arose, Madison, Jefferson and their companions could not possibly have worked this miracle without the aid of the newspapers."[6]

As newspapers began printing on pulp, replacing more expensive cloth-laden paper, printing prices fell, and the Penny Press was born. Advertising freed the press from its political overlords and for many years helped to drive the independence that marked the supposed "golden age" of journalism.

Some, of course, never believed there was a golden age. Critics point out that newspapers traded one overlord—politicians—for another—advertisers (who often influenced and were influenced by politicians). Newspaper owners and editors thought they had an independence from those factors, with few or no sacred cows. However, Ambrose Bierce described a reporter as a "writer who guesses his way to the truth and dispels it with a tempest of words."[7]

H. L. Mencken decried the institution in his day, saying, "Every other American city of that era was full of such papers—dreadful little rags, venal, vulnerable and vile."[8]

There was no stopping the press, however. As the nation grew, so did its newspapers. In 1775, there were but a handful of newspapers. By the Civil War, there were more than a thousand.

The Pony Express and the expansion west of railroads and the telegraph led to increasing competition for news and increased speed in news reporting. Special editions of newspapers or quickly printed "extras" informed the citizenry of breaking news.

One of my favorite stories, told to me by the late Barry Bingham Sr., had to do with the country's westward expansion. While it is probably nothing more than an apocryphal tale, Bingham told it with a zeal. A Pony Express rider on the frontier stopped into a post to drop off the mail and other dispatches. The dispatch recipient, being an important man of reputation, was quite pleased until the rider explained he'd left the man's newspaper at his previous post—at which time the recipient of the dispatches became angry. "Don't you think you'd better go back and get it?" The previous post was some 25 miles away.

"That's the power of the press!" Bingham told me.

As the country became smaller, press partnerships grew, and those eventually became wire services.

The Associated Press helped drive the demand and delivered to readers who craved the latest news from faraway places readers might otherwise not have seen. The Associated Press also helped to free newspapers from the New York and Washington markets by providing independent reporting.

A few selections from different newspapers show how the press changed and did so very quickly.

On June 9, 1813, the *New York Spectator*'s lead story was about the loss of the Chesapeake during the War of 1812. The paper featured several correspondents, news from Congress on other issues, and a story reprinted from the *Portland Gazette* (Maine) about a lost boy. The stories didn't pretend to be impartial.

On the date of the Lincoln assassination, the *New York Observer*'s front page was dominated with featured letters from politicians expressing their grief along with a tick-tock of the events of the day that are still far more in depth than some history books.

By 1876, when Custer faced his last stand, the press had changed. Now there were ads on the front page of newspapers and claims of fairness and justice. The *Daily Critic* in Washington, D.C., had a banner motto, "Justice to All, Partiality to None." There were ads on the front page that included special notices, cigar ads, and a listing for a house for rent blocks away from the White House for $50 a month. The rental was lauded as the "best in town."

Advertising freed newspapers from politicians—or at least gave the appearance of such—but their accuracy, as in any age, was only as good as the reporters and editors who used the means to report the news. In the *Los Angeles Express* on April 15, 1912, telegraphs and advanced communications allowed the paper to publish a front-page story on the sinking of *Titanic*, which had occurred a few days earlier. But the newspaper erroneously reported that "everyone is safe" in the sinking.

Two days later, the *New York World* reported the number of dead and missing closer to reality, but not until April 23 in a Swedish newspaper, the *Swedish Tribune-News*, would the numbers be reported accurately.

Today, Donald Trump and others would call this "fake news," but back then, it was accepted that while the newspapers represented the first draft of history, the first headlines weren't the last draft—and we anxiously awaited getting updates without the prejudice we all seem to embrace today. And while we all seem to live in an accelerated news cycle where a story a day old is now history, back then, we were more patient with getting the facts because our means of dissemination of the facts was not much faster than the time it took to get those facts. Today, we want it now, and we want to produce it first. When we get things wrong, which we often do, today, we often ascribe dirty motives to getting things wrong—when such motives usually don't exist.

That's not to say crusading journalism and attitudes didn't exist. They did indeed. Henry Watterson, Horace Greeley, and Henry Raymond stand out as some of the outstanding editors of the newspapers from the nineteenth and early twentieth centuries. Yellow journalism and the muckrakers helped influence politics, including Teddy Roosevelt, who read Upton Sinclair's *The Jungle* and advocated the reforms in the meatpacking industry that led to healthier supplies of meat for millions.

Of course, Roosevelt didn't like the press either. In 1906, he coined the term "muckraker" and said of journalists, "There are, in the body politic, economic and social, many and grave evils, and there is urgent necessity for the sternest war upon them. There should be relentless exposure of and attack upon every evil man whether politician or business man, every evil practice, whether in politics, in business, or in social life. I hail as a benefactor every writer or speaker, every man who, on the platform, or in book, magazine, or newspaper, with merciless severity makes such attack, provided always that he in his turn remembers that the attack is of use only if it is absolutely truthful."[9]

The truth has always been in the eye of the beholder—or in the eye of the guy who buys ink by the barrel. There remains the apocryphal story of William Randolph Hearst saying, "You furnish the pictures and I'll furnish the war."

Whether or not that is true, Hearst, the founder of the Hearst newspaper chain (the largest newspaper chain in the country while Hearst was alive), and Joseph Pulitzer (the publisher for whom the Pulitzer Prize is named) were at the turn of the twentieth century two of the most powerful men in journalism and had a dramatic effect on government and our lives.

The competition among newspapers led to sensationalism—then and today—though today, it is seen mostly on talking-head panel shows on cable networks, viral videos on TikTok, Instagram, Twitter, or spurious claims from dubious online publications that are replacing older sources of information because of the ease of the online app.

At the beginning of the twentieth century, competition and sensationalism led to newsboys on street corners hawking breaking news. "Extra. Extra. Read all about it!" was a familiar and clichéd cry from street corners across the country. The newsboy strike of 1899 led to a movie, *Newsies*, which depicted this lifestyle. By World War II, the fight for control of news sales led to an emphasis on home delivery. The "Newsies" were no more.

It wasn't, as Sean Spicer would say in the Brady Briefing Room one day in 2017, "all unicorns and rainbows" either when it came to the press and government. A century before Spicer and President Donald Trump went after the press, in 1917, the postmaster general revoked the mailing privileges of the newspaper the *Milwaukee Leader* because he felt that some of its articles impeded the war effort and the draft. Articles called the president an aristocrat and called the draft oppressive. Over dissents by Justices Brandeis and Holmes, the Supreme Court upheld the action.[10]

E. W. Scripps was the founder of the first newspaper chain in the United States, and it was the founding of the chains that led to the downfall of independent journalism and today's constriction of ownership and influence. It is the mistaken belief, fostered by government promotion and prodding, as well as the lobbyists for the large chains, that larger newspapers have a better chance of survival. This has effectively destroyed journalism. While chain-store journalism does technically help large newspapers survive, it also kills the independent publisher who cannot attract large advertisers who thrive on the immense circulation numbers of the chain newspapers. As a result, most of the local coverage that attracts viewers, listeners, and readers has died. It is replaced by cookie-cutter reporting by a small number of reporters who, by their proximity to those they cover, often come to believe they are as important as the issues and people they cover. Elitism and ignorance abound in today's journalism.

"As a result of the application of chain-store methods to journalism by these amiable Vandals there are fewer papers than there used to be, and the individual journalist is less important. All the multitudinous Hearts papers are substantially identical, and so are all the Scripps-Howard papers," H. L. Mencken observed in 1927. "Two thirds of their contents are produced in great factories, and what remains is chiefly a highly standardized bilge."[11]

By the time Franklin Delano Roosevelt came to power, newspapers had solidified their influence. But there was a new competitor on the scene—radio. Nothing revolutionized news coverage as radio did. Not before and not after.

Radio shortened the length of time in the news cycle as nothing else had before it—not even television was as radical in bringing breaking news before the general public. The internet is merely the latest act in the revolution sparked by the instantaneous effect of radio.

WHAS radio in Louisville, Kentucky, owned by the Bingham family, who also owned the independent *Courier-Journal* and *Louisville Times*, was an example of the new power in news. WHAS was designated by the federal government a "clear channel" radio station. That status allowed the station to broadcast a more powerful signal than other stations that could be heard by more people, and it also meant no other radio station in the United States could broadcast on the same frequency. During the disastrous

1937 Ohio River valley flood that ravaged communities from Pittsburgh, Pennsylvania, to Cairo, Illinois, this enabled WHAS radio along with WLW, "The Nation's Station," in Cincinnati to assist millions of listeners. In a flood that lasted from late January into February, 385 people died, and more than a million were left homeless.

WHAS, part of the fledgling CBS radio network at the time—which had been in existence less than a decade—was in the right place at the right time. WHAS quickly went to nonstop news coverage, transmitting commercial free for weeks. The broadcasts were mostly messages relayed to rescue crews. When the floodwaters threatened to cut off the WHAS broadcast, Nashville's WSM picked up WHAS's broadcasts for three days. This natural disaster cemented the need to broadcast breaking news.

Newspapers could not compete with this immediacy, and the 1937 flood set the stage for profitable radio and television networking going forward. When CNN went wall-to-wall with coverage of the *Challenger* disaster or during the Gulf War, they were paying homage to the valiant efforts of radio reporters in 1937. The immediacy of radio was a bellwether for the newspaper industry. As early as the 1930s, journalists such as H. L. Mencken noted that acquisitions made newspapers stronger but also took away some independence. While, with advertising, the newspapers could push back stronger against politicians and were less corrupt, they also began sacrificing the local coverage that made them relevant. And no newspaper reporter could ever hope to compete with radio news when it took hours to post a newspaper story versus mere moments when a radio station could go "live" from a breaking event. Newspapers could provide context and nuance, but radio drove you to the story—and inevitably the ability to break a story led to sacrificing nuance and context for availability. Newspapers had the day-to-day job of holding government accountable, but radio and, later, television reporters got to be "stars" by covering breaking news, and that also led to the decline of newspapers.

As television entered the fray, newspapers lost even more of their audience. Morning shows, noon shows, late afternoon, and 11 p.m. or 10 p.m. newscasts overthrew the morning and afternoon papers—and the joy was, with free television on the airwaves, no viewer had to pay for television news. Advertisers picked up all of the cost. So newspapers, which sold subscriptions, began to lose readers *and* advertisers.

The big turnaround in news came because of President John F. Kennedy. He enjoyed a close relationship with reporters. They felt they were a part of Camelot. Then Kennedy got assassinated, and television came into its own with wall-to-wall coverage. We saw Jack Ruby gun down Lee

Harvey Oswald. We saw Lyndon Baines Johnson take the oath of office on an airplane. We saw Jackie Kennedy walk off a plane with bloodstains on her dress. It was one of my earliest memories, and I remember my mother crying. On our little black-and-white television set, it looked like chocolate stains, and I distinctly remember thinking, "Mommy's crying because that woman has chocolate stains on her dress."

We saw the caissons. We saw the funeral. We watched Walter Cronkite pronounce the president dead and smoke a cigarette on set while he did it.

Reporters in the field, like Dan Rather, became well known to millions of Americans for covering the Kennedy assassination. Rather had joined the ranks of CBS after showing Houston television viewers who watched KHOU the first radar pictures of a hurricane. He also gained fame for risking his life during the hurricane, wading into the floodwaters of Hurricane Carla in 1961. Rather was made for television, and his Kennedy assassination coverage helped make viewers solid believers in television news. From that point on, television news dominated and became the primary source for informing Americans. It continues to this day with ongoing challenges from Twitter, Instagram, Facebook, and TikTok.

In the beginning of its news domination, television benefited from newspapers and radio. Many of the best-known television reporters and anchors had print or radio backgrounds. They were beat reporters who developed sources and were familiar with the nuances of city hall and Congress. When Walter Cronkite spoke out against the Vietnam War, Lyndon Johnson knew he was done—not because Cronkite was a popular talking head but because he was an experienced reporter who had covered World War II and had the gravitas of a wide variety of experience and depth of coverage that could not be denied.

Soon, Cronkite and the others of his generation were replaced by a new kid in town—the television reporter who never worked a beat, never worried about sourcing, and was driven purely by looks and ratings. They would help tank reporting. The owners who hired them and promoted them were at fault. But they didn't care. Access, proximity, live shots—those began to matter in the television world, and it drove out more in-depth coverage as ratings increased. We began to give our viewers what they wanted—and not necessarily what they needed to know.

Newspapers, which had already begun to buy each other out during Mencken's time, accelerated this move during the middle and late twentieth century. Far from being owned by politicians, newspapers, radio stations, television networks, and local stations became subservient to advertisers. Advertising freed journalism from politicians. But nothing could free journalism from the needs of the marketplace. Journalism, though not compatible with capitalism, became tethered to it.

Investigative journalism, the heart of any good reporting, is expensive and timely and invariably is going to aggravate businesses or politicians—especially if those investigations uncover serious wrongdoing. By the mid-1970s at the University of Missouri, some intrepid reporters founded Investigative Reporters and Editors, an organization that came into being in the aftermath of Nixon's Watergate scandal. Its goal is to help investigative reporters like Bob Woodward and Carl Bernstein who spearheaded the work exposing Watergate.

That was a heady time for young journalists. Everyone wanted to be the next Woodward and Bernstein. Fewer wanted to be or knew about Ben Bagdikian, who worked at the *Washington Post* and helped publish the *Pentagon Papers*.

The *New York Times* broke the story of those papers, released publicly by Daniel Ellsberg. That led Ellsberg to being prosecuted under the espionage act by the Nixon administration. At first, Nixon didn't mind the release of sensitive information that showed John F. Kennedy and Lyndon Johnson had lied to the American public. But Secretary of State Henry Kissinger convinced Nixon it was a bad precedent should Nixon want to hide anything or lie to the public, so Nixon had U.S. Attorney General William Rehnquist intervene. After Ben Bradlee and Bagdikian began to publish their own stories in mid-June 1971, based on the information Ellsberg leaked, Rehnquist sought an injunction in U.S. district court. Judge Murray Gurfein declined to issue the injunction, writing that the "security of the Nation is not at the ramparts alone. Security also lies in the value of our free institutions. A cantankerous press, an obstinate press, a ubiquitous press must be suffered by those in authority to preserve the even greater values of freedom of expression and the right of the people to know."[12]

Nixon, of course, appealed this decision and lost at the Supreme Court, 6–3. All nine justices penned opinions on the vote. Justice Hugo Black wrote, "Only a free and unrestrained press can effectively expose deception in government. And paramount among the responsibilities of a free press is the duty to prevent any part of the government from deceiving the people."[13]

The Supreme Court decision was seen as a mixed bag in courtrooms across the country. For 15 days, major newspapers had been stifled while the case was considered before the Supreme Court, and while the free press ultimately prevailed, it was Bagdikian who saw the media landscape for what it was. Bagdikian once went undercover in a prison to expose the harsh living conditions there. He was a Peabody and Pulitzer Prize–winning editor. Later in life, he famously told his college students, "Never forget that your obligation is to the people. It is not at heart, to those people who pay you, or to your editor, or to your sources, or to your friends, or to the advancement of your career. It is to the public."[14]

Bagdikian also penned *The Media Monopoly*, a book that highlighted the problem of media ownership resting in a mere handful of corporations. In the last edition before he died, Bagdikian wrote that the number of corporations controlling most of the media decreased to five: Disney, News Corporation, Time Warner, Viacom, and Bertelsmann.[15]

The power, Bagdikian warned us, "gives each of the five corporations and their leaders more communications power than was exercised by any despot or dictatorship in history."

Interestingly enough, it was the government itself and, in particular, people like Mark S. Fowler, Roger Ailes, and Rupert Murdoch who aided and abetted the consolidation effort.

Those in government knew by Nixon's time as president that an unfettered and unfriendly press could utterly destroy the wants of nefarious and less-than-honest politicians.

Both Edward R. Murrow, the most famous news broadcaster of the early television news era, and William Paley, who built CBS into one of the foremost radio and television network operations in the United States, played roles in waking government to what a free press could do to a corrupt politician.

Paley, according to *60 Minutes* creator Don Hewitt, was the man who put "Edward R. Murrow on the radio and 60 minutes on television."[16]

Murrow is famous for roasting and bringing low "Tailgunner Joe," Senator Joseph McCarthy, who was responsible for a "Red Scare" in the United States. Murrow exposed him as a bigot and a liar, and what Murrow did to him on *Face the Nation* is unforgettable. That broadcast and Murrow's life work led to Murrow laying bare what faced journalists in a speech before the Radio, Television, News Directors Association annual meeting in 1958.

"There is a great and perhaps decisive battle to be fought against ignorance, intolerance, and indifference. This weapon of television could be useful," Murrow began. "Of course, to undertake an editorial policy; overt, clearly labeled, and obviously unsponsored; requires a station or a network to be responsible. Most stations today probably do not have the manpower to assume this responsibility, but the manpower could be recruited. Editorials, of course, would not be profitable. If they had a cutting edge, they might even offend. It is much easier, much less troublesome, to use this money-making machine of television and radio merely as a conduit through which to channel anything that will be paid for that is not libelous, obscene or defamatory. In that way one has the illusion of power without responsibility."

Murrow was angry because, as he saw it, broadcasting corporations wouldn't even defend their own interests—but instead kowtowed to the politicians in power. And he was very skeptical of the top network brass. "The top management of the networks with a few notable exceptions, has been trained in advertising, research, sales or show business. But by the nature of the corporate structure, they also make the final and crucial decisions having to do with news and public affairs. Frequently they have neither the time nor the competence to do this."

Murrow and others at the time were rightly concerned that if broadcasting corporations always reached for the largest possible audience, they would continue to defend giving the public what it wanted at the cost of information the electorate needed in order to survive. He saw it right and understood from the very beginning that large corporations and self-serving governments had a vested interest in corrupting the nature of a free press and worried what would happen if there was no intervention to divorce the news business from big business.

"But this nation is now in competition with malignant forces of evil who are using every instrument at their command to empty the minds of their subjects and fill those minds with slogans, determination and faith in the future. If we go on as we are, we are protecting the mind of the American public from any real contact with the menacing world that squeezes in upon us. We are engaged in a great experiment to discover whether a free public opinion can devise and direct methods of managing the affairs of the nation. We may fail. But in terms of information, we are handicapping ourselves needlessly."

While Murrow couldn't foresee the rise of the internet, he did predict accurately the decline of the influence of television from the problems:

"It may be that this present system, with no modifications and no experiments, can survive. Perhaps the money-making machine has some kind of built-in perpetual motion, but I do not think so. To a very considerable extent, the media of mass communications in a given country reflects the political, economic and social climate in which it grows and flourishes. That is the reason our system differs from the British and the French, and also from the Russian and the Chinese. We are currently wealthy, fat, comfortable, and complacent. We have currently a built-in allergy to unpleasant or disturbing information. And our mass media reflect this. But unless we get up off our fat surpluses and recognize that television in the main is being used to distract, delude, amuse and insulate us, then television and those who finance it, those who look at it and those who work at it, may see a totally different picture too late."

And he closed with this:

"We are to a large extent an imitative society. If one or two or three corporations would undertake to devote just a small fraction of their advertising appropriation along the lines that I have suggested, the procedure might well grow by contagion; the economic burden would be bearable, and there might ensue a most exciting adventure—exposure to ideas and the bringing of reality into the homes of the nation."[17]

Thus, the problem was laid out graphically and dramatically more than 60 years ago. Advertisers had given journalism freedom from the politicians, but journalism had become enslaved to its advertisers. Certain restraints, like the fairness doctrine and limited ownership, which prevented media monopolies, managed to keep the press, more or less, where the founders wanted us—unfettered and untouched by politics.

However, large advertisers working hand in hand with politicians, and their influence, as Murrow pointed out in 1958 and as Mencken pointed out 20 years before him, were limiting the independence of the press.

It was an uneasy relationship. Large corporations could still turn on the government, easily, since they owned and operated companies that broadcast over the airwaves to millions of people and owned companies that bought ink by the barrel. With so many newspapers and a growing number of local television stations, the government seemingly could do little. But the large broadcasters and newspaper companies helped bring about their own destruction. Some critical of the media say the government and the large corporations worked hand in hand to destroy the free press—others say it was mere happenstance and the confluence of interests helped to do it. But the results are indisputable.

To effectively control the media, government had to limit the number of reporters and the number of companies interacting with the government. Conservatives loathed the "liberal" media from the moment the Penny Papers separated themselves from direct government influence. To sell newspapers and to get listeners or viewers, media managers were far more inclusive than the federal government. Where they weren't, alternative media and minority media properties popped up that were sustained, some easily and some not so easily, by the communities those niche organizations served.

The fairness doctrine became law in 1949 during the Truman administration. The doctrine was a policy that required the holders of broadcast licenses to both present controversial issues of public importance and to do so in a manner that was—in the view of the Federal Communications Commission—honest, equitable, and balanced. The commission eliminated the policy in 1987 and removed the rule that implemented the policy from the *Federal Register* in August 2011.[18]

Some viewed it as unnecessary restrictions on broadcasters that newspapers didn't have to abide by, and thus the doctrine limited free speech. But it did have the virtue of making sure that everyone had a voice and that both sides of a controversy got consideration. When the Reagan administration moved to eliminate the doctrine in 1987, it was universally hailed by big government and big business as a move to enhance free speech, but it had the opposite effect. It guaranteed one-sided coverage, increased division in the country, and led us to the point today where audiences choose which network to watch based on their own beliefs rather than being exposed—even briefly—to the beliefs of others. In short, it narrowed and did not expand free speech. The dominant view on events, whether factual or not, could be carried on a network, and if viewers who agreed with that point of view were the majority of viewers, then that network could increase its fees for advertising, sucking up valuable resources and ensuring those outside of that viewpoint would have a harder row to hoe in presenting competing views.

After Nixon fell in the mid-1970s, one man would lead the charge to remove limitations on broadcasters and simultaneously make sure that there would be fewer reporters around to cause problems. Roger Ailes, aided and abetted by Murdoch and Fowler, did it. How he did that is up next.

2

HEAR THE FOOTSTEPS, SAM?

Richard Nixon was, according to Louisville publisher Barry Bingham Sr., "one of the vilest men" he ever had the "displeasure of covering or knowing professionally." Hunter S. Thompson, another Louisville native of some fame, was upset when Nixon released his "enemies list" and, finding he wasn't on it, vowed to do better to make the cut. There are many things to be said about Richard Nixon: most of them are negative, and most of them have already been said. But it was Nixon's chance meeting in 1967 with a young producer of the *Mike Douglas Show* (before it became a nationwide network show) that may have done more damage to the United States than any of the crimes Nixon committed and for which he was later pardoned.

That year, as he explored his options in a run for the Oval Office, Nixon met Roger Ailes. The young producer (at the time Ailes was twenty-seven) made an impression on Nixon as they discussed politics and television. During his 1968 presidential campaign, Nixon began to rely on Ailes for advice on how to position the lighting and the lectern for his TV appearances, on what clothes to wear, and on how to cut his hair and had Ailes write memos prescribing what his long-term media strategy should be and much more.[1]

Nixon needed someone to help him deal with the press because he hated and feared reporters in a manner that bordered paranoia. His antipathy was calculated. His reactions were visceral. After the 1952 presidential campaign, when the revelation of his secret slush fund nearly led Dwight Eisenhower to drop him as his running mate, Nixon rarely trusted reporters.[2]

On September 23, 1952, sixty-eight years to the date before Donald Trump would answer my question about the peaceful transfer of power in a presidential election, Nixon made his infamous "Checkers" speech. On that day, Nixon traveled to Los Angeles and delivered a half-hour television address in which he attacked his opponents and accused them of inappropriate use of campaign funds as he defended himself against accusations he had inappropriately received funds to reimburse himself for his political expenses. It was a vintage Nixon speech and a template for all future Trump attacks—reverse the pressure. Deflect or attack to defend. The speech became famous, however, not for his withering attacks on those who leveled accusations against his inappropriate behavior but because Nixon said, whatever happened, his family was going to keep a black-and-white dog that had been given to him that his children had named Checkers. Thus, we have the Checkers speech.

It worked. Nixon stayed on Eisenhower's ticket as his running mate and sixteen years later became our president. He never forgot how reporters covered the Checkers story. The press apparently found out about Nixon's slush fund two months after he had been chosen as the GOP vice presidential nominee. The story grew exponentially, and Nixon saw conspiracy. He rarely trusted reporters afterward, and that caused him problems. After he lost his bid for the California' governorship in 1962, he called more than 100 reporters to the Beverly Hilton Hotel and furiously proclaimed, "You don't have Nixon to kick around anymore, because, gentlemen, this is my last press conference."[3]

Nixon blamed the press for his loss, and Governor Pat Brown, who won reelection, later said, "That's something Nixon's going to regret all his life. The press is never going to let him forget it."[4] Nixon was a sore loser.

However, the press also inadvertently led to Nixon's rehabilitation. A short time after the 1962 defeat, Howard K. Smith hosted the documentary *The Political Obituary of Richard Nixon* on ABC. It was seen as a partisan cheap shot against Nixon, and angry callers plagued ABC after the documentary aired. Former GOP presidential candidate Thomas Dewey wrote to Nixon, saying, "It seems to me that Howard K. Smith has been quite helpful, unwittingly . . . Smith has proved you were right in your comments about the press."[5]

By the time Nixon decided to run for president in 1968, he was looking for someone to help him deal with a press corps he loathed. He found himself a friend in Ailes, and on the urging of confidant and future chief of staff H. R. Haldeman, Nixon hired Ailes to be his "executive producer for television." Ailes, propelled into the national spotlight with this move, would later act as a political consultant for Ronald Reagan. He helped Ronald Reagan and Mitch McConnell win in 1984 and helped run an infamously negative campaign to get George H. W. Bush into the White

House in 1988 before he would go on to Fox News, sex scandals, and everlasting infamy.

Nixon saw something in an argumentative and energetic Ailes in 1967 that drew the two of them together. "The Press is your enemy," Richard Nixon infamously told the chairman of the Joint Chiefs of Staff. In Ailes, he found someone who would fight back against what Nixon saw as a "left-wing" media empire. As most presidents before him and after him, Nixon firmly believed the "media elite" were out to get him. This was rooted in Nixon's feelings of paranoia but also because of the actions Nixon took as president, which were dutifully and sometimes exuberantly reported by the press. Nixon, like Trump after him, never could accept responsibility for his actions and was perhaps the first chief executive who didn't mind breaking the Constitution in order to protect himself.

While he hated the press, in truth, he received nearly nine months of an informal "honeymoon" period from reporters before people began looking seriously at some of the more questionable actions he took as president.

As Richard Harris noted in a 1973 article for *The New Yorker*, "Probably no other President has been as widely supported by the press and has then as bitterly and publicly criticized by that institution as Richard Nixon. In 1960, Nixon was endorsed over Kennedy by seventy-eight percent of the country's newspapers that took a position on the election; in 1968, Nixon got eighty percent of whatever editorial support was expressed; and in 1972 he got ninety-three percent."[6]

In truth, with a few notable exceptions, the press was very easy on Richard Nixon. Of course, by the beginning of the 1972 campaign, the press had been partially silenced by direct and implied threats from the administration. A constant barrage of insults from Vice President Spiro Agnew helped. "Nattering Nabobs of Negativism" still resounds today in the shouts of "fake news." But the Justice Department also prosecuted reporters who refused to reveal confidential sources to prosecutors, judges, and juries.[7]

Reporters went easy on Nixon during the 1972 campaign and instead concentrated on his challenger, Democratic Senator George McGovern's supposed unprofessional and obsequious conduct—he was an easier mark for many tepid yet seemingly professional reporters who lacked the wherewithal to challenge an incumbent president. Following the Watergate break-in, only fourteen of the 2,200 members of the Washington press corps made an effort to investigate or report on it to any extent—though it was the largest political scandal of its day.[8]

James Reston wrote in the *New York Times*, "The main charge against the press in general, though not against the few newspapers that exposed the deceptions of Vietnam and Watergate, is not that the press was too aggressive but that it was too timid or lenient or lazy."[9]

Hindsight reveals the laziness or lack of courage among reporters, but at the time, Nixon did not see things that way.

What Nixon desperately wanted—and what he lacked—was a way to publish his propaganda without media interference. He didn't have Twitter. He didn't have social media. What he wanted was a friendly, pliable broadcast network. Protests and anger against the Vietnam War were reaching a crescendo. President Johnson had refused to even run for a second term after Walter Cronkite announced the Vietnam War to be unwinnable. Nixon wanted none of that. He desperately wanted to control his message in hopes of securing his second term—and at the same time silencing his critics, who were many.

Roger Ailes was way ahead of Nixon.

Halfway through his first term and apparently with the blessing, backing, and energy of Ailes, an unsigned memo in the Nixon Library, reported by *Business Insider* in 2011, shows that Ailes already had the idea that was "Fox News" firmly in mind. Called "A Plan for Putting the GOP on TV News," it is an unsigned, undated memo calling for a partisan, pro-GOP news operation to be potentially paid for and run out of the White House. Aimed at sidelining the "censorship" of the liberal mainstream media and delivering prepackaged pro-Nixon news to local television stations, it reads today like a detailed blueprint for a Fox News prototype. From context provided by other memos, it's apparent that the plan was hatched during the summer of 1970. And though it's not clear who wrote it, the copy provided by the Nixon Library literally has Ailes's handwriting all over it—it appears he was routed the memo by Haldeman and wrote back his enthusiastic endorsement, refinements, and a request to run the project in the margins of the memo.

Newton Minow, the former head of the Federal Communications Commission under President John Kennedy, was famous for making a speech calling television a "vast wasteland." His assessment of Ailes has remained steady over the course of five decades. "Roger Ailes sought not to reach all viewers, only those who agreed with his views."[10]

Ailes insisted the best way to achieve those ends had to focus on television and not on print. "Today television news is watched more often than people read newspapers, than people listen to the radio, than people read or gather any other form of communication. The reason: People are lazy. With television you just sit—watch—listen. The thinking is done for you."

Ailes wanted the Nixon administration to create its own network "to provide pro-administration, videotape, hard news actualities to the major cities of the United States."[11] Other television news outlets, such as NBC News, ABC News, CBS News, and PBS News, are the "enemy," he wrote, and suggested going around them by creating packaged, edited news stories and interviews directly to local television stations.

World events, Nixon's paranoia, and the Watergate scandal overcame Nixon before he could move on this idea. But the seeds Nixon planted would sprout and bear a nasty, foul fruit. The gardener who would ensure that was Roger Ailes.

The infamous Roger Ailes grew up in Warren, Ohio, the son of a factory maintenance foreman. He graduated from Ohio University in Athens, majoring in radio and television, and served as the student station manager of WOUB for two years.[12] He began his career as a production assistant and worked at KYW-TV, where he produced a local talk-variety show, *The Mike Douglas Show*, before it went national. Meeting Nixon pushed Ailes into the spotlight—not just because he had an abundant amount of energy but also because he had ideas. Television was a shallow medium, and Ailes intended to take political advantage of that fact. He favored exploitation of the medium rather than reformation. "Television rarely, if ever, tells the whole story," Ailes said in a 1971 speech he titled "Candidate + Money + Media = Votes." "It is imperative that we begin to understand what TV can and cannot do."[13]

He told journalist Joe McGinniss shortly before Nixon's first presidential election, "This is it. . . . This is the way they'll be elected forevermore. The next guys up will have to be performers."[14]

McGinniss would later chronicle these efforts in *The Selling of the President 1968*.

Ailes choreographed everything. What appeared to be real was merely a reality show. Makeup, camera angles, and other moves Nixon called gimmicks, thanks to Ailes, did indeed become standard for politicians everywhere. Further, Ailes proved he wasn't above creating scandals to aid his cause. Like the yellow journalists who seemingly invented the Spanish-American War, Ailes operated under the theory that news was whatever people wanted to watch—even if it were unfounded rumors or wild conspiracies. It didn't matter. The idea of alternative facts began with Roger Ailes, though it would take many more years before Kellyanne Conway would give the fiction a name as she stood in the driveway of the North Lawn of the White House.

Ailes had immediate success in getting politicians that he supported elected, but there were two key obstacles that kept Ailes from realizing his dream for media degeneration and domination. The fairness doctrine and rules governing media ownership were huge obstacles. The fairness doctrine dictated that any story of controversy carried with it the need for contrary and competing coverage. There were no real teeth to the doctrine and few proscribed remedies other than losing a broadcast license—a fate no major network ever suffered. Far from a perfect plan to deal with providing equal time, what the fairness doctrine did was effectively build a philosophical buffer into the news. News organizations could not play exclusively in one philosophical or political lane. The fairness doctrine worked because it got broadcasters into the habit of providing competing ideas. Ailes, as former Federal Communications Commission chairman Minow pointed out, didn't want that. He wanted to dominate the airwaves with companies that thought like he did.

The fairness doctrine hobbled that idea, but so did a large number of diverse companies owning broadcast and print media outlets. A smaller number was easier to control. That was the very reason newspaper and television ownership had long been heavily regulated—under the fear media monopolies would destroy free speech. But to Ailes's point of view, it kept news and information in the hands of the "media elite" and the liberals.

Ailes's first attempt to capitalize on what he outlined in his memo to President Nixon in 1970 came a year after Nixon left office. In *Dark Genius*, a biography of Ailes, Kerwin Swint revisits the dawn (1973) and early demise (1975) of the news service funded by conservative brewer Joseph Coors to counter the "liberal" TV networks. Coors, a profligate donor to conservative candidates, causes, and institutions, thought the media needed an ameliorating conservative voice, too. TVN was less a network than a video wire service, producing and distributing segments to network and independent TV stations. The Coors brain trust hoped ultimately to leverage the service into a fourth network, one based on emerging satellite technology.[15]

Ailes joined TVN in 1974 as its news director, and while he later tried to distance himself from the project, maintaining he was only a consultant, he bragged in the *Columbia Journalism Review* in 1974 of his power to hire, fire, and program the news service.

At its height, TVN employed fifty people and claimed to feed nearly two dozen news segments to about 80 broadcasting subscribers in North

America. Former employees said the service tried to tilt coverage to the right. It never really caught on. But Ailes walked away from the endeavor with bigger ideas. After the collapse, Ailes went back to being a political consultant, and in 1979, the stars would align: he would find a vehicle through which he could make his dreams of a conservative news network come true in Ronald Reagan.

Ailes, working with Reagan and his acolytes, systematically destroyed ownership rules and laws that protected and guided the press. Under Ronald Reagan, both the fairness doctrine and media ownership rules dissolved. Reagan controlled most of the destruction, but Ailes and Reagan needed a strong-handed ally in Congress—preferably in the Senate—who could cement the changes Ailes wanted on the media and cultural landscape. Ailes went shopping to find a malleable and power-hungry representative who wasn't too worried about equal time, ethics, or fair play. What he found was Mitch McConnell.

Mitch McConnell was the only Republican gain made in the Senate in the 1984 election. One commercial, produced and masterminded by Roger Ailes, gave McConnell a seat in the Senate and successfully changed the course of history. All McConnell had to do was sell out his moderate tendencies that got him elected to the county judge/executive post in Jefferson County, Kentucky. More than a million people call Jefferson County, which includes Louisville, home. Louisville is the birthplace of Muhammad Ali, Diane Sawyer, and Hunter S. Thompson. It is a progressive city that Thompson once described for *Scanlan's Magazine* as a "Southern City with Northern problems." McConnell, who was born in Mississippi and moved to Kentucky as a child, came to embrace civil rights and a variety of other progressive causes to get elected in Louisville. Edmund "Pete" Karem, my uncle and a McConnell contemporary, is the former chief justice of the circuit court, and as a former Republican, he worked side by side with McConnell in McConnell's early career. "Mitch McConnell is about one thing," Pete told me many times. "Mitch McConnell." In short, there is no great story arc in Mitch McConnell's life. He's always used people and events to further his own cause. My other uncle, David Karem, the former Kentucky Senate majority leader, quoting former U.S. House speaker Tip O'Neill, said he held McConnell "in the highest minimum regard."

McConnell's desire for power and malleability made him and Ailes excellent partners.

In his autobiography *The Long Game*, McConnell called hiring Ailes "one of the smartest moves I made." He wasn't so sure at first. Ailes had an unconventional idea for an attack ad.

McConnell was seen as having virtually no chance of beating Walter "D." Huddleston, the incumbent U.S. senator. Huddleston had a sterling reputation and a 94 percent attendance and voting record.

Ailes didn't care. He wanted to attack Huddleston with an ad that humorously made fun of Huddleston's attendance. Featuring a hunter with a bunch of coonhounds roaming the countryside looking for Kentucky's junior senator, it galvanized opposition and catapulted McConnell into power. It is a commercial so memorable anyone still alive in the Bluegrass State who had attained the age of reasoning in 1984 can often recall it with a laugh—even if they find McConnell detestable.

In his autobiography, McConnell said he initially thought the ad campaign was "insane" and was destined to be a failure—though he gave it a green light. "Ailes was particularly nervous about the scene he had to film at the U.S. Capitol. His plan was to unleash the pack of dogs, and turn them loose on the steps of the Capitol. 'We may get arrested for this one,' Ailes told his small crew. 'So we gotta do this in one shot.' He placed a pile of hamburger meat at the top of the steps and some in [actor] Snarfy's pant cuff so the dogs would stay close to him until they were unleashed," McConnell wrote.[16]

Al Cross, working for the *Courier Journal* and *Louisville Times*, covered McConnell and later recalled the impact the ads had on the race. "He was 40 points behind with two months to go," Cross said. "But then they put up this hound dog ad and it made people laugh."

By 1984, I joined the ranks of professional reporters and began to witness the changes on the media landscape brought about by Ailes, McConnell, and Reagan—firsthand. I left college to report for the *Conroe Courier*, a newspaper in suburban Houston. My wife worked at the neighboring *Woodland Sun*. It was suburban suburbia, and neither of us was quite ready for that. I started as a sports reporter, and within a few months, I was the sports editor. My wife covered local politics. In less than a year, we moved to the Texas–Mexico border in Laredo. Pam became a television producer and a radio reporter. I was the county beat reporter for the *Laredo News*, a local publication owned by a business magnate who once dedicated the front page of the newspaper to his daughter's wedding. Within a few months, with the possibility of getting a raise of the extravagant sum of $2,500 a year, I became a television reporter at KLDO-TV.

By that time, Reagan had already initiated the changes that would ultimately destroy newspaper and television competition and lead to the consolidation of the industry that has hobbled both. But that was hard to see as two newlyweds scraping together a weekly budget that included a lot of liver and onions or tuna and noodles. Both newspapers I worked for up to that point had healthy competition. In Conroe, I worked for the established newspaper and competed against an upstart publication. In Laredo, I worked for the upstart. Less than a year later, I would be paid the fantastic sum of $16,000 a year to work for a new television affiliate in Laredo as its lead reporter.

I met Sam Donaldson, ABC News anchor and foreword writer of this book, that same year. Covering a Walter Mondale appearance in South Texas on the campaign trail leading up to the 1984 election, I was stationed in the back of a group of reporters trying to ask Mondale questions. Shouting, raising hands, whatever it took, we all tried to get our questions answered by the candidate. This was and remains in many places standard operating procedure. Those who traveled with Mondale had the decided advantage. He knew them. He was familiar with them. Me? I remember I caught his eye as I smiled at him, but he didn't know me from any of the microphones in the aircraft hangar where he held his press conference, much less the reporters. As I heard the question-and-answer session progress, I decided to jump in with a question of my own. I don't remember what the question was, but I do remember Donaldson spoke up to ask a question at the same time I did, and suddenly I found myself trying to out-shout Donaldson. Mondale heard me and answered my question. I had attended the press conference with a fellow reporter from our newspaper. He chuckled when he saw I had managed to get my question in above the din of the man whom Gary Trudeau once dubbed the "human megaphone" in a *Doonesbury* comic strip.

"Hear the footsteps Sam?" my friend joked.

Afterward, I was formally introduced to Donaldson. I found him to be helpful and supportive of a young reporter. Years later, I would remember this and try to be as supportive of young reporters as Sam had been of me. As a young reporter, many in the profession did not necessarily find other, more experienced reporters to be as helpful. Access to those in power can often taint those near it. Some experienced reporters felt themselves privileged and often looked down on young reporters. This was and still can be a major problem. Those with access also tend to be less likely to rock the boat. The White House press corps is famous for being a citadel of stenographers—those who smile and pretend they are protecting democracy when in fact they are only serving themselves and their corporate managers.

Donaldson, Helen Thomas, Tom Brokaw, Bill Plante, Peter Jennings, and a few others never treated me that way and were all about their work, and I was appreciative of that fact. Two years into Reagan's first term,

Donaldson asked him to comment on the perception that "disarray is here in the White House, that you have been out of touch, that you have had to be dragged back by your staff and friends on Capitol Hill to make realistic decisions on the budget. There was even a newspaper column saying that your presidency is failing."

Reagan was a minor god to the conservatives, and Donaldson got a great deal of grief for his actions. "I suppose neither man liked hearing those things," Donaldson said in his autobiography, *Hold On, Mr. President!*, "but those things were being said about them and it was legitimate to ask them to respond."[17]

Being popular with whomever you're covering should never be the goal of any reporter. When I first met Helen Thomas, she told me if I was looking for popularity or friendship, then I should seek another way of making a living. Donaldson told me nearly the same thing, adding that one of his biggest concerns were reporters who were "too timid" to ask a decent question.

Both also acknowledged that true independence was derived from the ability to ask the hard questions without fearing you'd lose your job if you did so. A healthy and robust press is necessary to push the envelope and ask any question necessary of those in power—but it is difficult to do so when those who own the media are friends with or otherwise compromised by those in power. "I'm not advocating rudeness," Donaldson once explained to me, "but I'm far more concerned about the reporters who are either too afraid or too disinclined to ask a question."

On my podcast "Just Ask the Question," Donaldson told me about a time when he thought his aggressive style might just cost him his job. He and Thomas showed up at the christening of the new ABC bureau in Washington, D.C., at the same time as President Reagan. It was a private affair, but of course, being the ABC White House reporter, Donaldson showed up. Helen Thomas was of course Helen Thomas and could show up anywhere. The rumor was, when I was a young reporter, she was the one person in Washington who never had to worry about getting an invitation to anything. She assumed she was welcome and no one would tell her otherwise.

As Reagan made his way into the new offices, Thomas and Donaldson began peppering him with questions. Larry Speakes, Reagan's deputy press secretary (James Brady retained the title of press secretary out of respect even after he was shot along with Reagan in a failed assassination attempt) got angry and thought the invitation had been a way to mousetrap Reagan into answering some questions.

Roone Arledge, the head of ABC News, also there for the event, was apparently embarrassed and a bit angry about the exchange. Donaldson remembered saying something smart to Speakes in front of Reagan and Arledge—something like, "Well what are you going to do, fire me?"

To his shock, Arledge said something to the effect of "that's not a bad idea" when Reagan spoke up and dismissed the whole thing. "That's just Sam being Sam," he said. Reagan never broke a sweat. Donaldson didn't lose his job, and the rest is history. Despite their contentious relationship, Reagan knew Donaldson was doing his job, and having someone who recognized the need for reporters to be present and ask the hard questions rather than calling them "fake news" and the "enemy of the people" also went a long way to ensuring the public respected those in power. Although Reagan arguably made future rancor between reporters and those in power possible with his actions, he never personally stooped to the denigrating, rancorous personal attacks of some of his successors over the years.

But make no mistake: despite Reagan's defense of Sam Donaldson, the end of a free press began in earnest when Reagan stepped into the White House.

3

NO DIFFERENT THAN TOASTERS

When Ronald Reagan became president at the end of 1980, there was a new behemoth on the horizon that would affect all television viewing. Ted Turner already created "Super Station WTSB" in Atlanta. It began broadcasting a twenty-four-hour news channel in June 1980. Turner and his creation, CNN, would lead a revolution in news. Where it had taken a quarter of a century for television news to establish its unarguable dominance over the public in providing news, it would take CNN just six years to show that we lived in a twenty-four-hour news cycle, and CNN unquestionably became the initial platform on which that news would be delivered.

On January 28, 1986, CNN was the only media company broadcasting live when the space shuttle *Challenger* exploded seventy-three seconds into its flight and killed all seven crew members aboard—including Christa McAuliffe—who would've been the first teacher in space. The national tragedy propelled CNN to the forefront of news as it provided an immediacy heretofore unseen anywhere. CNN began the 1980s having a hard time getting into the pool rotation at the White House with other broadcasting companies—by the end of the 1980s, it was a full-fledged stakeholder in covering national and international news.

The Reagan administration initially ignored the impact of CNN while remaining antagonistic toward most of the mainstream corporate media and taking actions that Donald Trump would mimic later.

As *Editor and Publisher* reported on October 24, 1987, "President Reagan accused the American press and Congress of being influenced by Communists disinformation just days before a congressional report accused his administration of waging its own cover propaganda campaign involving U.S. newspapers and other media."[1] Congress, even members of the GOP at the time, accused Reagan of running an essentially secret propaganda operation promoting the administration-backed war against the Nicaraguan government. Reagan, Deputy Press Secretary Larry Speakes, Vice President Bush, and all the other president's men didn't like having those secrets spilled all over the airwaves or in news print. They took action to see that things would change.

At the time, some 80 percent of the media were controlled by a mere twenty or so companies. "That was too many," as noted author and journalism professor Steve Weinberg said. "It's a small group, but still too many to effectively control what the media reports." Control is exactly what Reagan wanted and what the corporate ownership craved. A State Department unit, according to the Government Accounting Office, had in 1983 set up a covert operation engaged in "prohibited, covert propaganda activities designed to influence the media and the public."

This type of media disinformation wasn't exactly new, but it was extensive and was driven by the executive branch. Reagan took the Richard Nixon "rat fucking" schemes from Watergate to a new level. The propaganda efforts were outlined in a memo written by Jonathan S. Miller to Pat Buchanan, the White House communications director, and included placing pro-Contra op-ed pieces in the *Washington Post* and *New York Times*, among other papers. Miller's memo also claimed credit for a television news story on NBC in March 1985 based in part on consultations with State Department "contractors" who visited the Contras—according to *Editor and Publisher*.[2]

It alluded to tips to television news operations and to "cut outs" arranging for Contra leaders to visit news organizations including Hearst, *Newsweek*, Scripps-Howard, the *Washington Post*, and *USA Today*. Representative Jack Brooks (D-TX) said the "illegal operation represented an important cog in the administration's effort to manipulate public opinion and congressional actions." A government spokesman from the State Department called the charges by the Government Accounting Office "so far out of line as to be ridiculous."

At the same time this was going on, the Newspaper Guild and other newspaper-related unions were planning to introduce in Congress legislation that would limit the size of newspaper chains to thirty newspapers or 3 million total circulation. Newspaper owners, far ahead of the administration and television owners, recognized the future. "We think it's bad for America and bad for our membership to see so many newspapers fall into the hands of so few people," Charles Perlik told *Editor and Publisher*.

Reagan had other ideas. He wanted to deregulate all of the media. He had already used newspaper ownership as an example to justify the deregulation of television media ownership. Mark S. Fowler, as head of the Federal Communications Commission (FCC), wasn't done. He would leave in April 1987, and behind him, he would leave an incredible wake of destruction that culminated in the death of the fairness doctrine.

According to *Congressional Quarterly*, "The Reagan administration's deregulation drive in television was led by communications lawyer Mark S. Fowler, who served as FCC chairman from May 1981 until April 1987. Arguing that television was merely a 'toaster with pictures,' Fowler sought to make the broadcasting industry as free from government control as the appliance industry—and the print media. In the space of a few years, the commission abolished limits on what stations could show, such as the number of commercials, as well as requirements on what they had to broadcast, such as news coverage. In addition, relatively liberal FCC policies allowed a substantial increase in the amount of sexually oriented material being broadcast."[3]

From 1981 going forward, Fowler, as the head of the FCC, would oversee the destruction of the traditional views of news media ownership. Fowler's idea, according to those who were there at the time, was to create an environment that would allow television stations and networks to make money and grow larger—supposedly strengthening the television news industry. It did make the networks and corporate media ownership stronger, but it also had a fatal side effect. The networks grew larger, and without making television owners treat their property as a trusteeship with responsibilities to protect the commonwealth instead of preying on it, greed and avarice took over. Thus, as first broadcast television news and later cable television news overwhelmingly dominated the marketplace, they hastened the shrinking contribution of newspapers, and, as contrition occurred, real reporting suffered.

With just one sentence, in 1981, Fowler summed up the administration's feelings about the television medium. It's a "toaster with pictures," Fowler said. This was a direct rebuttal of Newton Minow, the FCC chairman under President John F. Kennedy, who argued that government needed to play an intimate role in serving the public interest as charged in the Communications Act of 1934.

Newton was himself a controversial figure. The SS *Minnow* of *Gilligan's Island* was sarcastically named after the FCC chairman following a speech he gave to the National Association of Broadcasters in their annual convention on May 9, 1961. "When television is good, nothing—not the theater, not the magazines or newspapers—nothing is better. But when television is bad, nothing is worse. I invite each of you to sit down in front of your television set when your station goes on the air and stay there for a day without a book, without a magazine, without a newspaper, without a profit and loss sheet or a rating book to distract you. Keep your eyes glued to that set until the station signs off. I can assure you that what you will observe is a vast wasteland," Minow said.[4]

Some fifty years later, Minow said in a Harvard speech he believed television news was an important public service but also said, "Too much deals with covering controversy, crimes, fires, and not enough with the country's great issues." Presidential campaigns, he said, were obsessed with trivial concerns.[5]

When Reagan entered the White House and appointed Fowler as the head of the FCC, the idea of the airwaves being a trusteeship was gone. At the time, cable news was in its infancy. Newspapers were slowly declining as television news—on the rise since the Kennedy assassination in 1963—was riding the crest of its highest wave. In 1986, Sam Donaldson and Helen Thomas cheered the longevity of the press corps and the institutional knowledge inside the White House of the reporters covering the president. "But if deregulation continues unabated," Donaldson and Thomas warned, "it will mean the end of an independent press."

Ben Bagdikian, the stalwart reporter who helped break the *Pentagon Papers* story at the *Washington Post*, warned against increasing corporate ownership at that time. He preached for a diversity of ownership, but Reagan was having none of that type of common sense.

Broadcasters, according to the FCC's fairness doctrine, had to present opposing views on controversial issues. Reagan, using the rise of CNN and cable programming much as he had used newspaper ownership to justify deregulating television, said there was simply no way to require cable providers to comply with the same rules as broadcasters. It would stifle the First Amendment. Bill Clinton would also later use Reagan's reasoning on the 1996 telecommunications act to address the World Wide Web.

But Reagan set the table. By 1987, amid growing criticism, Reagan's FCC came to believe the fairness doctrine should be abandoned because it believed that the "doctrine chilled the speech of broadcasters and inhibited free and open debate on the public airwaves," as the Congressional Research Service put it. In an effort to preempt such a repeal, Democratic Senator Fritz Hollings introduced the Fairness in Broadcasting Act in March 1987, which would have fully enshrined the fairness doctrine in law. The Senate was split, 55–45, in favor of the Democrats at the time, and the bill passed the Senate, 59–31. A similar bill was passed, 302–102, in the Democrat-controlled House in June, but President Reagan vetoed it.

As the *Los Angeles Times* reported, "The doctrine, instituted by the Federal Communications Commission as public policy in 1949, requires the nation's radio and television stations to 'afford reasonable opportunity for the discussion of conflicting views on issues of public importance.'"

Reagan chimed in. "This type of content-based regulation by the federal government is, in my judgment, antagonistic to the freedom of expression guaranteed by the First Amendment," Reagan said in his veto message. "In any other medium besides broadcasting, such federal policing of the editorial judgment of journalists would be unthinkable."[6]

By trumpeting the First Amendment, Reagan and others in effect began to kill it. He took a variety of moves during his time in office that began the slide in news gathering that culminated with cries of "fake news" and the "enemy of the people." Those deregulatory moves, some also made by Congress, included in 1981 extending television licenses to five years from three. The administration also expanded the number of television stations any single person or company could own from seven to twelve in 1985. Reagan abolished guidelines for minimal amounts of nonentertainment programming in 1985. In 1985, the FCC dropped guidelines for how much advertising could be carried. By deregulating the industry, he allowed fewer owners to make greater decisions, ensuring a survival-of-the-richest scenario.

But the coup de grâce was in 1985 when FCC Chairman Fowler, a former communications attorney who served on Reagan's presidential campaign staff in 1976 and 1980, *began* dismantling the fairness doctrine. That year, the FCC released a report on general fairness doctrine obligations that stated that being fair hurt the public interest and violated free speech rights guaranteed by the First Amendment.[7]

Two years of court decisions, public input, and congressional action finally led to the dismantling of the fairness doctrine. On August 5, 1987, under new FCC Chairman Dennis R. Patrick, the FCC abolished the doctrine by a 4–0 vote. Afterward, Patrick affirmed what Fowler had said before him—the fairness doctrine was eliminated to guarantee free speech.[8]

The decision was controversial at the time and remains so to this day. Among those angered with it was Massachusetts Democrat and House Speaker Tip O'Neill. Speaker O'Neill said in his autobiography that he could relax off hours and enjoy Reagan's company but also called Reagan "Herbert Hoover with a smile" and claimed Reagan was a cheerleader for selfishness.[9] O'Neill did not enjoy Reagan's friendship with the large

corporations—especially those that owned media properties. The owners of these behemoths had an agenda to push: kill the fairness doctrine,
deregulate the industry, and let's have some fun. Their goals dovetailed
nicely with Reagan's supply-side, or "voodoo," economics as it was called
by Reagan's vice president, George H. W. Bush, when Bush was running
against Reagan.

The four pillars of Reagan's economic policy were to reduce the
growth of government spending, reduce the federal income tax and capital
gains tax, reduce government regulation, and tighten the money supply to
reduce inflation.[10]

The results of Reaganomics are still debated. Supporters point to
the end of stagflation, stronger growth in gross domestic product, and an
entrepreneurial revolution in the decades that followed.[11] Critics point to
the widening income gap, an atmosphere of greed, and the national debt
tripling in eight years, which ultimately reversed the post–World War II
trend of a shrinking national debt as a percentage of gross domestic product.

Whatever else you think about Reagan's plans, his supply-side economics did effectively serve as the beginning of the end for the media business as it was known at the time. Reagan, who had greatly benefited by
his looks and telegenic manner, was also not a particular fan of the media,
even as anchors and reporters anointed him the "Teflon president." Nothing stuck to Reagan, and Reagan didn't stick with the media that made
his telegenic presidency possible. He bought into Roger Ailes's view of
the media; he saw television more as a tool to be used to his own ends
rather than as a means to provide factual information to the populace—
particularly if that information was unfavorable to Ronald Reagan.

At a debate appearance at the Center for the Performing Arts in Louisville, Kentucky, on October 7, 1984, Reagan was blasted by the media
with rumors of declining mental capacity after his performance against
Democrat Walter Mondale. Barbara Walters of ABC moderated the debate,
while James Wieghart of the *New York Daily News*, Diane Sawyer of ABC
(a fellow graduate of Seneca High School in Louisville), and Fred Barnes
of *The New Republic* served as panelists. More than 65.1 million people, according to Nielsen Media Research, watched the debate.

According to news reports at the time, for much of the debate, Reagan appeared less confident than he customarily did on television. Later,
Mondale's advisers, clearly pleased, asserted that the former vice president
had rejuvenated his candidacy. Reagan aides were noticeably subdued. A
senior White House official, speaking on condition that he not be named,

told the *New York Times* the president had been "more tentative" in his closing statements than he was in the 1980 campaign debates.

Mondale summed up the first Reagan administration this way: "Can we say, really say, that we will be better off when we pull away from sort of that basic American instinct of decency and fairness?" Mondale asked, sounding a theme "that irritated Mr. Reagan noticeably through the debate," the *Times* noted.[12]

Reagan's people knew that he had stumbled badly and after the debate headed out to the filing room where reporters were busy with live shots and penning their narratives for the early morning newspapers. Reagan's campaigners told a different story to anyone and everyone who would listen, and thus the "spin room" at national debates was born. Presidential debates haven't been the same since.

Reagan ultimately survived Walter Mondale, but his coattails were not excessively long—though luckily for Roger Ailes, it included his protégé Mitch McConnell. Most of the major damage done to the free press would occur in Reagan's second term, which would certainly be remembered for gutting the fairness doctrine and Congress's ineffective attempt to pass a law supporting it. Reagan had the last laugh. His deputy press secretary, Larry Speakes, often told reporters, "Don't tell us how to stage the news and we won't tell you how to report it."

Reagan's eight years in office seemed at times dedicated to destroying the independence of the media. Reagan took advantage of preexisting conditions to be sure. As television news grew into a profitable business, particularly following the assassination of John F. Kennedy, afternoon newspapers slowly but surely disappeared. By the mid-1980s, in Louisville, for example, the venerable *Louisville Times* simply ceased to exist—just a few short years after the reelection in February 1987. It wasn't the only afternoon newspaper to go. According to the Pew Research Center, in 1965, there were 1,444 afternoon newspapers in the United States. In 1985, there were 1,220, and by 2005, there were just 645 left in the country.[13]

The influence of the daily newspaper, long king of providing news content to the general public, began eroding in the 1960s and by the middle of the 1980s had been supplanted by local and national nightly newscasts. Oddly enough, to this day, television and the internet still rely heavily on the diminished newspaper staffs across the country to provide news they in turn use as sources for their own content. Even in 2018, local television seemed to be in an enviable position. The average local TV station "now has more news employees than the average American newspaper, profits are strong and local TV news remains the dominant news source for Americans," according to a 2018 Knight Foundation study.[14]

The Ronald Reagan era led to the position we find ourselves in today. Overnight, it seemed that newsrooms began downsizing as corporations bought each other out and as the elimination of some guardrails enabled corporations to become more profitable at the risk of not providing needed information to the public. If you were born after 1984, you'd never know what it was like beforehand. If you were an adult with a lot of experience like Walter Cronkite, Dan Rather, Sam Donaldson, Helen Thomas, and scores of others who warned us, you knew, but your concerns were rarely noticed and even more rarely acted on. If you were a young professional, like me, who joined the ranks of reporting at the time, you saw the changes occur in real time. All of us in the business saw where it was going, but there was precious little we could do about it—and in the beginning, few cared to listen. Many who sounded the alarm were merely dismissed as being "alarmists."

Today, there are reporters and politicians who have no idea how we got to where we are in this country regarding the free press. While many news consumers know there's something wrong, they have no idea of the inside game played by rich corporations, lobbyists, and the presidential administrations of Democrats and Republicans since 1980 that have effectively destroyed free speech. We live inside the eye of a hurricane.

In my case, my career literally began in the aftermath of one. Hurricane Alicia struck in Galveston, Texas, in August 1983 just as my fiancée and I were driving to Conroe, north of Houston, so that I could take my first full-time job in "the business."

I came of age in the aftermath of Watergate and wanted to ferret out corruption and malfeasance like Woodward and Bernstein had done. I found myself at home in county clerk offices going over property deeds and other legal documents. I wanted to wear myself out as romance has it, doing something good for my country and my family and friends—even if no one appreciated it. Of course, that's the other part of how I romanticized reporting. Mostly, I confess I loved thumbing my nose at authority and do to this day. But I entered my chosen profession as a huge paradigm shift was occurring that would destroy the foundations of a free press and keep reporters in the business fighting for survival—whether it was facing down police, rioters, legislators, or lawyers; a small paycheck; or covering a war.

My first job was far from an ideal job opportunity. While I spent the previous two years managing a Paul Revere's Pizza parlor, making about $15,000 a year doing so while I went to school, I was headed to Conroe to become a sports reporter. It wasn't my dream job—I wanted to cover politics—but it was a job. And for the mere joy of being a reporter, I was going to take a $6,000 cut in pay. For the first month, I lived with the sports editor and his wife until I found an apartment that I could rent for $400 a month. My fiancée and I then tied the knot one week before Christmas in 1983, and after a rollicking honeymoon in St. Louis at a hotel that lacked heat for some reason, we traveled together back to Conroe, where we learned to exist on liver and onions, tuna and noodles, and the occasional roast beef that we would make last for several days.

After driving through the remnants of Hurricane Alicia to make it to Conroe, it took only a few weeks after my arrival to get someone in a position of authority pissed off at me. To me, covering local sports was tedious, boring, and even patronizing—not to mention demeaning. But I had no experience outside of a part-time job at the *Kingdom Daily Sun-Gazette* in Fulton, Missouri, where I laid out ads most days and worked as a weekend reporter on occasion when I wasn't attending school. The highlight to my part-time employment came when my city editor told me to call one day and get a comment from a bank vice president's wife after he apparently committed suicide.

I was the low man on the totem pole and couldn't avoid making the call. I did it and got yelled at by the wife, cursed at, threatened and had a few insults hurled my way that would make Donald Trump proud. But I did the job. I knew then I needed to be in the thick of things. I wanted that seat that made me an eyewitness to history.

So, when I went to visit my sister who was stationed at Fort Sam Houston in San Antonio, I thumbed through the pages of the *San Antonio Light* and found an opening for a sports reporter in Conroe.

One of the perks of the job was writing a column about local sports. I wrote one of my first that fall after watching a high school running back—who normally played defense—rush the ball for ninety-three yards from the line of scrimmage on one play to cement a victory for the local team. I questioned why the coach didn't play him more often on offense. I said he cut through defenses like a "hot knife through butter." The kid was African American, but I flatly refused to believe it had anything to do with race. Every coach I ever met, including every coach I ever played for, merely wanted to win. "You may not like the kid next to you, but you will respect him and will learn to work with him," one of my coaches told me. I was naive to the lack of advancement in civil rights in the Houston area despite it being more than twenty years since the Civil Rights Act.

So, when I was summoned into the coach's office, I had no idea why I was there. For a second, I entertained the thought the coach might congratulate me for my insight, tell me what a great job I did, and promote his defensive back to starting running back. He did not. When I got to his office, there were half a dozen of his assistant football coaches inside. The head coach, Mike Barber, had read my column.

"A hot knife through butter," he said disdainfully as he read it back to me. "What gives you the right to say that?" he asked. "What do you know about football?"

"Well, I played it. My dad coached it . . ." I started to say.

A guy named "Tex," who was the defensive coordinator, spoke up. "Where?"

"Huh?" I asked.

"Where did you play football?"

"Kentucky," I said.

Tex actually spat on the floor. "What the hell do they know about football in Kentucky? This here is Texas boy." I couldn't help but wonder if Tex often spit on the floor and why couldn't he at least spit into the nearby garbage can. Barber was a little more consolatory. "You see, the way we look at it, the Conroe sports reporter should kind of be a Conroe fan. You understand."

I smiled. "Well coach, when you pay my salary, you can tell me how to write any way you want. But until then, I'll write what I want."

My run-in with the coaches was later followed by a few run-ins with newspaper management as I was told to be more "amiable" or "amenable to suggestions" from the teams I covered. The publisher, Barbara Fredrickson, was a former cheerleader, I was told, and was mindful of advertising money from car dealerships and other local businesses that loved Conroe football. The stadium seated thousands more than my high school stadium did, and I was told season tickets were often willed to family and friends on the death of the ticket holder. They all bought newspapers, and I often heard people who said they read the paper opine about the need to see "some good news" in the local paper.

As a young reporter, I was at first unaware of the market pressures being brought to bear against the journalism world, though, to be honest, this type of pressure—to be a cheerleader for a high school sports team or the local city council—was historically part of being part of a press that purchased its independence from politicians by getting in bed with advertisers—who often rented or bought the politicians.

In this case, however, other factors added to the pressure. A second newspaper was opening up locally, and television news was cutting into afternoon newspaper circulation. So, advertisers were increasingly putting more money into radio and television while putting fewer dollars into newspapers. Two daily newspapers in the same small Houston bedroom community promised to make the profit margins thinner and the ass kissing to advertisers more pronounced.

Meanwhile, at the top of the food chain, Ronald Reagan had been in office for four years, and the consolidation in our industry he initiated had begun. Chain newspaper ownership, encouraged to ensure sharing costs and hopefully to keep newspapers alive, meant fewer independent newspapers. The Reagan administration actions to deregulate the industry meant television stations had also recently begun to buy each other out. Cable television domination was right around the corner. Soon, staffs would be cut drastically. Salaries already had been.

I didn't know that. I only knew that I was asked to "play nice" and do more as a young sports reporter. Soon, I began picking up the odd general assignment story when I could, covering county council or any outlying news story that our news reporters couldn't handle. I didn't mind it. I wanted it since I wanted to cover politics and hard news. I had no idea newspaper managers would use my own desires against me. I was just happy to cover news that enabled me to meet people like T. Bone Pickens, T. J. Peale, a Miss U.S.A. who hailed from Cut N' Shoot, Texas, several members of the Bush family, and other local politicians.

Peale was among the funniest. I met him at a county council meeting where he sat in the back of the room and eagerly ate powdered coffee cream from a container while he fiddled with his oversized cowboy boots. "Hi lovely lady," he said to my wife, who had tagged along for the evening meeting. For all the world, he reminded me of Jackie Gleason in *Smokey and the Bandit*. He looked the part. He also proudly claimed to own the council I was covering and told me if I wanted the real "good news," I should talk to him. "Your paper couldn't exist without me," I was told.

After just a few months at the paper, our sports editor left for the new paper (underfunded as it turns out) that opened in town, taking his wife— who was our city editor—with him. I took over the reins as the sports editor and guided a staff of half a dozen full-time or part-time reporters.

It was a time of change in news. Gone were the days of typing stories on an IBM Selectric typewriter with carbonless copies three sheets thick and copy editors with bright red markers. We were cutting-edge baby. We had TRS-80 Tandy computers with 5¼-inch floppy discs. Copyediting was easier, and production times were shorter. We were told the streamlined production would save the company money, but we didn't see it put back into the company anywhere except with the "Trash 80" computers. Well, okay, we also had a Tandy 100—a primitive laptop that allowed us to file stories on-site. So, for example, when I went to cover a Houston Rockets game, I could type my story and actually view three or four lines of copy. After typing up the story, I could then use a 300-baud modem that, when coupled to a telephone, would allow me to send my story back to the newspaper in about ten minutes rather than having to take my notes, drive the hour or so back to the newspaper, and type my story up and have it marked up and rewritten.

The computerization of the newsroom was a great aid in making newspapers more cost efficient and competitive. But salaries didn't increase, and more reporters weren't hired. Production assistants were laid off as newspapers found they no longer needed them and copy editors found themselves beginning to be superfluous as well. Most newspaper owners pocketed the funds they saved by laying off staff, and rare has it been in the past forty years that an owner reinvested those funds by either raising salaries of news staffs or hiring more reporters or editors.

At the *Conroe Courier*, the production department was led by an old woman named Maxine, who we used to joke had been around since Guttenberg made the first printing press. She was an irascible woman with a thick Texas drawl and a need to take frequent cigarette breaks, and many suspected she had a thermos filled with her favorite distilled libation for when times were tough. Naturally, I loved her. She gave me grief. I was young and arrogant, but she taught me a lot, and there wasn't a night that went by as she looked over my sports pages for production where her keen eye didn't catch a mistake. She was very good, and I learned then the need to put as many eyes on a page before it was produced as possible. That, I learned, was the real difference between being a working reporter and— years later when the term became well known—a blogger. My sports pages routinely went from a reporter to a copy editor to me and were sent back to production, where they were printed on wax-backed paper and laid out on large "photo blue" thick pages, where Maxine, her crew, and myself would look them over yet again before they were photographed and turned into flexible printing plates. No fewer than four different eyes checked copy for grammar, spelling, and fact errors before a page was printed.

Maxine was a stubborn woman, and I rarely won an argument with her. That's because most times she was right and I was wrong. I got her one time, though. I had traveled to the Astrodome to write up a game between the Houston Oilers and the Green Bay Packers. It was the opening game of the 1983 season in the final season Hall of Famer Bart Starr coached the Packers. I grew up a Packers fan. Paul Hornung had been a friend of the family and worked at my cousin's meat market in Louisville. My grandfather was a Jesuit and friend of Vince Lombardi. Naturally, the local connection made the family lifelong fans.

Lynn Dickey squared off against Archie Manning that day. Dickey threw for 333 yards and five touchdowns in a game the Packers won in overtime, 41–38. Manning threw for 348 yards and one touchdown. Earl Campbell rushed for 123 yards on twenty-seven carries and had three touchdowns. It was one of the most exciting football games I'd ever seen. Seeing it from the sidelines was a treat. After the game, in a practice long since abandoned, reporters made their way through the dressing rooms and interviewed the players as they showered and dressed. Men and women from television, radio, and print walked through talking to the players. Today, you go to a waiting room, and the coach and a handful of players will walk out for interviews. Then? You could spend all night talking to anyone you wanted as long as they would speak with you. Oliver Luck was one of my favorite to talk to because he was humble, good natured, and informative. Earl Campbell was the same, but when you saw the man walk through the locker room, you wondered how he could walk at all. Even while he was still playing, you could see the heavy toll the punishment he delivered and took while running the football had on his body. I never saw a running back run as hard or hit as hard as Campbell. You often hear tall tales about running backs who carried three or four people on their back into the end zone. Earl Campbell is the only person I ever saw who actually did it. There were high school football coaches across Texas who had game film of Campbell doing it in high school. They'd shudder as they showed the tape.

But that night, I wanted to talk to Bart Starr. One of the first books I'd ever bought from the Scholastic Book Club when I was in grade school was a biography on the former Packers great. He and John Lennon were the only two popular culture celebrities from my youth I ever looked up to. I respected Starr's dedication, determination, and ability to overcome obstacles. He was drafted in the fifteenth round—they don't even have that many drafting rounds today. He had to fight his way into the Packers starting lineup and excelled when others thought he was done.

He was putting on a shirt, calmly and quietly, as I approached him. I had conducted all my other interviews before I made my way to talk to him, and I found him alone.

"You know, growing up I didn't have many heroes," I told him. "But you were one of them. Mind if I ask you a few questions?"

Okay, strictly speaking, I didn't approach him as I would any other interview subject. I wasn't the most objective, but I wanted to do a profile piece, and I thought I'd be honest. He smiled, thanked me, and then spent about an hour talking to me. I followed him out to the team bus, where eager fans were shouting out things like, "I was Boyd Dowler's love child," "I went to school with Ray Nitschke," or something similar. We parted, and I headed back to write up my story. It was a Sunday, and I had the luxury of not using the cutting-edge Tandy 100. I had the whole day to craft my story.

When I finished and laid it out, I saw Maxine had taken her "photo blue" pen and marked up several mistakes on the page. Now, Maxine was a Dallas Cowboy fan and apparently never forgave the Packers for defeating "America's team" to go to the first and second World Championship games (the game was not yet called the Super Bowl). But she also didn't know how to spell Bart Starr's last name—out of either spite or neglect. It was the one time I won an argument with her. "Two r's," I told her. After that, when we got into an argument, I would just flash her the peace sign—two "r's."

I learned a lot at the *Conroe Courier*, and the most important thing I learned is that I didn't want to sit at a desk managing others. I wanted to cover the news. I didn't like dealing with budgets or reporters who had bad spelling or work habits. The first person I ever had to fire was a young sports reporter I hired who slept at his desk and routinely missed assignments. I liked him, but he was completely unproductive. Our managing editor was a man who claimed to be a relative of the actor Kevin Bacon. The editor was known to hit the bottle a bit hard. He and I had several run-ins. While I liked him and even respected his journalistic abilities, he could be abusive with others. One day, he came in and gave the forty-eight-year-old city editor a public dressing-down. She was one of the wisest people in the newsroom, and I thought the managing editor was a pig, and I told him so. He said I should watch out because my sports pages weren't all that great either. I resisted the urge to pop him one in the mouth, a remedy that had no professional accolades attached to it, and I decided to move on.

So, midway through the late spring, I quit, having secured a position in Laredo at the *Laredo News* as a county beat reporter. The presidential race was in full swing, border politics was hot, and I knew I would have a lot more fun covering that rather than covering local sports.

One of the few perks of covering sports in Conroe was getting to see the Houston Astros, the Houston Oilers, and the Houston Rockets. The

Oilers had Archie Manning, Warren Moon, and Oliver Luck on the team at quarterback. Manning got hurt, and Moon became the starting quarterback, but I thought Oliver Luck was better than both of them. It also seemed funny to me that Luck and Manning fathered all-star quarterbacks and were on the same team together.

But the lure of covering Houston sports wasn't strong enough to keep me working at a small daily in a sleepy little suburban town outside of Houston. I wanted something raw. I wanted the romance of a free press whose destruction had already begun under Ronald Reagan. In thirty-seven years, I've never seen the ideal. I've seen the opposite. It culminated in Donald Trump.

Donald Trump didn't take a question in the James S. Brady Press Briefing Room of the White House until February 26, 2020. The last time he showed up there was Friday, November 6, 2020, following his reelection loss.

He had, in fact, conspicuously avoided the room. His favorite method of interaction with the press was responding to shouted questions from the South Lawn whenever he departed the White House aboard Marine One—the presidential helicopter. He also liked having a small pool of about fifteen reporters cram into the Diplomatic Room, Cabinet Room, or Oval Office to witness some interaction between him and a dignitary or his cabinet, after which he would allow a few questions before a wrangler would shout at the press, usually in a high-pitched squeal, that it was time to leave.

Trump also hadn't held a solo press conference at the White House since February 15, 2019. On that day, he told me to sit down after I asked him about cooking the books on illegal immigration in order to convince the American public about a crisis on the border most everyone else in government said didn't exist.

The February 2020 press conference in the Brady Briefing Room was also the first time a president held a briefing there since former president Barack Obama held his last one during the final week of his administration. Three long years had passed. An entire year had passed since the press secretary used the room to regularly brief the media.

Wednesday, February 26, began like any other day in the Trump White House—it was chaos.

Trump, completing a week of traveling to California, Nevada, Colorado, and then India, was expected to return early Wednesday morning for an easy day of rest and relaxation, several nasty tweets, a couple of comments on Fox, and maybe a White House gaggle on the Front Lawn's driveway with special adviser to the president Kellyanne Conway on the side.

But the latest news on the coronavirus broke, and Trump didn't want to be caught flat footed. After all, deaths he can handle, but when the stock market began a serious tumble heading for a record week of losses, something had to be done.

"I will be having a News Conference at the White House, on this subject, today at 6:00 P.M. CDC representatives, and others will be there. Thank you!" he tweeted at 8:03 a.m.—just an hour and a half after he returned to the country.

Of course, reporters who covered the White House had a lot of questions. The first one was, "What does he mean by a news conference?" Trump had called pool sprays and his "chopper talk" sessions "news conferences" in the past. There was also the matter of who was going to appear with him and where in the White House he planned to conduct this public display of information.

"His definition of a news conference is different than other people," I was dutifully informed by Judd Deere, then deputy press secretary. "And we don't know where he wants to have it. If it's in the Diplomatic Room, it'll just be press pool. But I think he wants to talk."

I was told this at noon, 2 p.m., and close to 4 p.m., just two hours before the event was to occur, and no one knew who, what, when, where, or how it would happen.

"I got nothing," a wrangler told me when I went back to ask for the tenth time.

"It really boils down to the venue," I was told.

"Well, if it's a real open-press news conference . . ." I began.

"I can set the Rose Garden up in fifteen minutes," I was told.

"But it'll be dark, and it's raining. That leaves only the East Room," I said. "Is anyone setting up the East Room right now?"

It was after 3 p.m. "No," I was told.

"Well, fine, just tell him to use the briefing room," I explained. "He can walk in and walk out, and it's already set up."

That got a laugh since Trump had avoided that room like the plague, but that's where we ended up doing his historical first briefing on the coronavirus.

For an hour, he took questions, including several not on the coronavirus, including one from me. That day, news also broke that Trump's reelection campaign sued the *New York Times* over an opinion piece. It was an opinion piece based on already published news. No new information—

just an opinion. The very essence of protected First Amendment speech—and Trump sued for libel.

So I asked him, "Your campaign today sued the *New York Times* for an opinion piece."

"Yeah," Trump said.

"Is it your opinion or is it your contention that if people have an opinion contrary to yours, that they should be sued?"

"Well," Trump said. "When they get the opinion totally wrong, as the *New York Times* did and, frankly, they've got a lot wrong over the last number of years. So we'll see how that—let that work its way through the courts."

I listened but had to follow up. "But that's an opinion, right?"

"No. No," Trump pushed back. "If you read it, you'll see it's beyond an opinion. That's not an opinion. That's something much more than an opinion. They did a bad thing. And there'll be more coming," he said, indicating he'd file additional suits. "There'll be more coming."

Trump's disgust with the press was well known. He called us "fake news" and the "enemy of the people" so often that his minions spit those words out without much thinking of the context in which they did it. When the head of the Centers for Disease Control coronavirus task force conducted a briefing for the press a couple of days later and told 50 reporters the dangers of the virus and then asked us to help get the word out on it, many of Trump's minions called us "fake news" for doing as the administration asked.

It didn't help that Trump, Mike Pence, Rush Limbaugh, and the whole propaganda apparatus from team Trump pushed the narrative that reporters were engaged in hyperbole in order to make Donald Trump look bad and, further, we were trying to drive down the markets, and the Democrats wanted millions to die from the virus.

As horrific as all that sounded, it was to be expected in the Donald Trump administration. It's always about him. When the market is fine, he's responsible. When the market is bad, he's a victim of circumstance—driven by the Democrats. That people are dying from a viral infection was secondary to Trump's stated concerns.

As frequent as this scenario played out in the Trump administration and as unique as that administration seemed, it was merely the cumulative effects of media policy that began with Ronald Reagan and has been endorsed and perfected by every president since. Trump is the symptom, Roger Ailes was the cause, and Ronald Reagan was the catalyst that led to media destruction.

4

DON'T WORRY ABOUT IT

In the mid-1980s, the nation was at a crossroads—though not everyone grasped that fact. Newspapers, already engaged in a buying frenzy in an effort to stay economically viable because of the influx of television and radio news, had to deal with two bigmouthed toddlers: the internet and cable news. In 1983, website addresses became easier to remember with the introduction of the Domain Name System, which created .edu, .gov, .com, .org, .net, and .int for naming websites. The internet as it existed then still catered to scientists and those in the defense industry. It wouldn't be until 1989 that commercial dial-up was introduced and the first commercial websites surfaced.[1]

Ted Turner launched CNN, the first twenty-four-hour cable news operation, in 1980, and Headline News followed in 1982. But in the mid-1980s, these venues had little impact on daily journalism. CNN wouldn't make its first big statement until the shuttle disaster in 1986 and wouldn't become a daily necessity until the first Gulf War. CNN struggled in the beginning to be included in the White House press corps. Today, it's a staple there.

But in 1984, during Reagan's reelection bid, network news had its last great hurrah dominating national politics and setting the agenda—mostly based on the reporting of newspapers that provided the fuel for television news. Roger Ailes as a political consultant was right in the thick of it. He acted as a consultant for both Reagan's second term and Mitch McConnell's first. His emphasis was always on the outlandish, the dramatic, and the attention-grabbing headline. It was outlined by his infamous quote, "If you have two guys on a stage and one guy says, 'I have a solution to the Middle East problem,' and the other guy falls in the orchestra pit, who do

47

you think is going to be on the evening news?" Ailes called it the "Orchestra Pit Theory."[2]

On the national newspaper front, some newspapers at the time, according to *Editor and Publisher*, had begun minor cuts in staff. Those cuts would accelerate as the decade wore on. The actions led to a "healthy financial year" headline in *Editor and Publisher* as it reported on the profits in the industry in 1985.[3] Of particular note, *Editor and Publisher* reported that while 1985 had been a year of modest economic growth, "most publicly-held companies reported healthy earnings gains." Consolidation of the newspaper industry was showing great results—for the bottom line—not necessarily in the newsroom or elsewhere in the newspaper industry. In the same issue of *Editor and Publisher*, George Garneau reported about a labor dispute at the *News-Tribune* in Woodbridge, New Jersey, after Macromedia Publishing bought the newspaper and changed and canceled employment contracts made by the newspaper's previous owners.[4]

The Newspaper Guild and other newspaper-related unions moved to try to stop the corporate takeovers that they said were destroying local journalism. The Guild tried to introduce to Congress legislation that would limit the size of newspaper chains to thirty newspapers or 3 million total circulation.[5] This effort—countered by lobbyists for corporate owners—failed.

"We think it's bad for America and bad for our membership to see so many newspapers fall into the hands of so few people," Charles Perlik, Guild president, told *Editor and Publisher* before he retired in 1987. In addition, concentrated ownership opened the potential for owners to abuse the press freedom by controlling the flow of information to further ideological agendas, the union leader said.

While newspapers consumed each other and Mark S. Fowler began actions to kill broadcast competition, President Ronald Reagan accused the American press and Congress of being influenced by communist disinformation. He was particularly upset with coverage of the Iran–Contra scandal. The Great Communicator also took other moves to get his side of the story out there. The General Accounting Office issued a report in 1987 that showed that the State Department created a unit that secretly paid for or ghostwrote articles designed to appear in major newspapers—but with the U.S. government's role hidden.[6]

Reagan's propaganda efforts were outlined in a memo written by Jonathan S. Miller to Pat Buchanan, the White House communications director. It led to op-ed pieces being submitted to the *Washington Post* and the *New York Times* regarding the Lieutenant Colonel Oliver North scandal. North came into the public spotlight as a result of his participation in the Iran–Contra affair, a political scandal during the Reagan administration in which he claimed partial responsibility for the sale of weapons through intermediaries to Iran, with the profits being channeled to the Contras in Nicaragua.

Robert Semple, the op-ed page editor at the *Times*, said he had no evidence op-eds were prepared by the State Department but admitted it "was entirely possible." He said the newspaper would never run the columns if it had been known the government was behind them.[7]

The Reagan administration's response? "Theirs is a disinformation campaign, we know, worldwide, and that disinformation campaign is very sophisticated and is very successful, including . . . a great many in the media and the press in America . . . and on Capitol Hill," Reagan said. Through his friends in the media, including *Washington Times* editor Arnaud deBorchgrave, Reagan flipped the script and disparaged members of Congress, claiming there were a number of "hard-left members of the House who are now acting as pro-Soviet agents of influence."[8]

Reagan set the table at which Trump would later feast. By trying to control the media and by submitting his own propaganda for publication, Reagan's harm and damage was real. There was little opportunity for local reporters to get involved in the national discussion at that time, in part because of Reagan's actions, though the issues local reporters uncovered were and remain the greatest source of many of the stories seen at a national level. It is well known among networks and national reporters that a lot of stories that become national news came to the public's attention when local reporters wrote about those stories first. In a rare case, a judge thanked a Miami reporter for uncovering the Jeffery Epstein scandal.

Sometimes, a national story surprises us—until we look back at the local stories across the nation and link them together. There had been a lot of reporting in a variety of local markets about Q-Anon and crazy conspiracy theories for months prior to the January 6, 2021, Capitol insurrection. Only afterward did prosecutors and reporters put the pieces together to show the breadth of craziness spreading across the country. In the future, piecing these stories together may become even more difficult, as there are fewer regional and local reporters in the country today than there were in the mid-1980s—though the population of the country has doubled in my lifetime. It is the combination of fewer regional and local reporters, coupled with the privilege of some of the national news reporters, that has led to a startling lack of awareness of the mood of the people. The American people, in turn, have become increasingly ignorant of what is going on in their own country and, more importantly, ignorant about how the news business works. They know something is wrong with news gathering, but they don't know what.

When I asked Mike Copps, former commissioner of the Federal Communications Commission, about the problem, he told me, "The American public needs to be better educated about the media. . . . The long-term solution is a K thru 12 program on media literacy. We need to have an understanding of how it works, how to find reliable sources and it has to be part of education." Copps, who fought against deregulation for years, also acknowledges that in some ways, national reporters are the most ignorant of the news they cover. Many White House reporters have never worked a city hall beat or covered law enforcement, a war, or a high school football game. Many have achieved a master's degree without any daily interaction with the people to whom they are then entrusted to report the news. This is where the "elitist" culture begins and why so many people distrust journalists.

It is not a new phenomenon; it is only one that has perpetuated itself during the past century and become increasingly ingrained in our culture. "For example, the problem of False News," H. L. Mencken wrote. "How does so much of it get into the American newspapers, even the good ones? Is it because journalists as a class are habitual liars, and prefer what is not true to what is true? I don't think it is. Rather it is because journalists are, in the main, extremely stupid, sentimental and incredulous fellows—because nothing is easier than to fool them—because the majority of them lack the sharp intelligence that the proper discharge of their duties demands."[9]

There is an underlying elitist trend to listen to anyone with a master's degree from Harvard or someone who sits on a network stage. I'm not disparaging those colleagues, but dismissing local voices is destroying our ability to track and report on local phenomena before they become national problems. Very often, the young reporter who covers local city hall has a much firmer grasp on issues that eventually bubble to the national surface than the White House reporter who sits in a booth in the West Wing for hours on end consuming machine cuisine from the small White House break room and sipping espresso from Tom Hanks's donated coffeemaker while diving in and out of briefings and luncheons with White House sources.

The problem now is that there are far fewer of the local reporters due to the constriction of the business and far too many local reporters covering multiple news beats. In some cases, one reporter at a local newspaper may cover two dozen different beats once covered by twenty-five or more reporters. Most major newspapers have withered, and many smaller newspapers, thousands of them in fact, have died in the past few decades—thanks to greed and, more importantly, the laws that changed enabling large "vulture" fund investors to buy them up and squeeze them out. Newspapers that used to hire hundreds now hire dozens. Some newspapers no longer have the buildings they once called home. The Pulitzer Prize–winning *Denver Post* is one of the largest to feel the squeeze—and push back with protests—only to be humiliated in the end with layoffs.

As the media landscape began to change in the 1980s, a local reporter covering specific issues had an opportunity to do so in newsrooms that still retained an amount of vigor not seen today. As a county beat reporter on a daily newspaper in South Texas, my day-to-day coverage required two or three stories a day based on what was currently going on. But if you wanted to dig (and what reporter didn't want to dig?), there were reporters who could cover you if you wanted to do so—or, more important, if you could convince an editor you had a need to do so. Copy editors, city editors, news editors, and a managing editor oversaw all the activity in the newsroom. Sports editors and feature editors had their own staff that answered to the managing editor. Today? Some staffs, even at larger newspapers, post directly to the internet and don't have copy editors to read copy prior to posting—only afterward.

The grand fight in those days was trying to get information made public: police reports, county agendas, planning board decisions, and so on. A reporter not only became well versed in the inner workings of the city or county clerk's office where public information was made available but also became adept at knowing what information was available and how to file a Freedom of Information Act request if for some reason a government entity decided not to provide the information you requested.

Shortly after I landed in Laredo, I requested a tour of the county from the local sheriff. Four police officers at night were responsible for patrolling the 3,700 square miles of Webb County. Since the entire county had a population of just under 100,000 and most of that was in Laredo, the overnight sheriff's deputies rarely had much to do. They often tried to *entertain* me with stories of officers finding dead undocumented workers in a field or on the side of a deserted road. Those deaths were often suspicious and rarely solved.

On my first night, the deputy who had been assigned to provide me a "ride along" for his shift smiled and asked me a question. "Do you know what happens when shit rolls down a hill?"

"Uh, where are we going with this?" I asked.

"Let me show you where the shit goes."

With that, he drove south down U.S. 83 to Espejo Molina Road to two subdivisions: Rio Bravo and El Cenizo.

There were no paved roads. There was no electricity. No water—but a water tank was in the process of being built. As explained to me by my sheriff's deputy guide, these two small subdivisions with maybe 1,000 residents were the source of most police action outside of the city of Laredo.

The subdivisions had been developed by a Standard Realty Investment, and behind that corporation was a gentleman by the name of Cecil McDonald, who had experience developing low-cost subdivisions. Cecil was an old Texas boy who perpetually wore a bolo tie. Gaunt, gray-haired, and crafty, he worked in the shadows, pulling the strings and developing land he didn't actually own—but was renting with the intent of purchasing. In Texas, that was illegal. My first stories, which would come after two weeks of investigating the two southern county development projects, would dub them "illegal subdivisions." They sprouted up all over South Texas from Laredo to Harlingen. They would later be known as "colonias."

Cecil always said he had the best intentions. He once mass-produced a handout in Spanish titled "Manzana Podrida," or "Rotten Apple," to tell those who purchased land from him how he was on their side in their struggles to be free and how he wanted to help budding immigrant capitalists who could own their own property—and how the government was a rotten apple intent on killing their dreams.

The details were different for each colonia he developed, but it was essentially the same story for Cecil, Standard Realty Investment, and any other Rio Grande Valley developer: Developers would sell land to undocumented workers or other extremely poor individuals who fervently believed in the American Dream: a plot of land to call their own and the hope of a better life for their children.

The colonias lacked in basic infrastructure. After a heavy rain left ruts in the middle of Cadena Street in El Cenizo waist deep, I saw two men trying to fish their trailer out of the Rio Grande with ropes and a grappling hook. On July 13, 1984, the *Laredo News* reported, "A fire that apparently broke out in an air conditioner of a trailer at El Cenizo Project might have been put out with a couple of buckets of water, according to witnesses at the scene. El Cenizo has no water supply and must depend on shipments from neighboring Rio Bravo for drinking water."[10]

Because of the lack of water, the trailer burned to the ground before a fire company in South Laredo (some seven to ten minutes away) could get there.

The contracts for sale for the El Cenizo project were in some cases open ended. You put what you could down ($50 to $100 was the going rate at the time), and then you paid $100 to $250 a month for life for mortgage and to maintain your deed.

Although the main street in Rio Bravo was named after a county commissioner and his daughter operated a grocery store there, the county government at first claimed not to be aware of the problem when the *Laredo News* started producing stories about the plight of the people living there.

Those who lived in trailers had it good. Those who had actual brick homes or freestanding homes of any kind were rare. Some people lived in homes of hammered-flat tin cans for walls and tree limbs and stumps used as load-bearing frames and support. Some camped out on the ground. At age twenty-three, I was given quite a thorough lesson in the extremes of poverty in the United States that my suburban upbringing in Louisville, Kentucky, had denied me. I was made acutely aware of those who had less than I.

I had seen poverty in Chicago, New York, Washington, D.C., and my hometown—but nothing like the complete despair and squalor I saw in southern Webb County in 1984. Still, some in the government wouldn't admit it existed. It was hard to believe that it could on this side of the Mexican border. I would see similar conditions in Third World countries, but until I saw the conditions firsthand in El Cenizo, you could never have convinced me such conditions existed in the United States. I was naive.

Without the work dozens of other reporters and I did throughout the Rio Grande Valley, this issue would never have made news. Boots on the ground in the affected areas made the news of exploited undocumented immigrants a national story. "I personally don't know anything about El Cenizo. I believe it is the county attorney's problem," County Commissioner R. C. Centeno, who had a street named after him in neighboring Rio Bravo and who was the commissioner for that area, told the *Laredo News*.[11]

The first stories on El Cenizo and Rio Bravo ran on May 19, 1984, outlining the "lack of water, sewage, drainage and road facilities in El Cenizo." Laredo City Manager Marvin Townsend urged county officials to "do something about this immediately. It is a disgrace to let this go on."

The investigation lasted for months with daily stories—that irritated Standard Realty Investment, which had developed the subdivision, and those who told me I was "too damn nosy for my own good."

It led to other stories as people in the Laredo area came to understand their local newspaper, locally owned, was interested in telling people what was going on in their community. We broke stories on illegal county meetings. We broke stories on questionable police activity, questionable dealings by the local district attorney, voter fraud, and much more.

On February 8, 1985, I walked into the local Laredo police chief's office. He had been a good source and wanted to clean up the problems of corruption and drug dealing on the border. As we spoke, I noticed an "Eyes Only" document sitting upside down on his desk. To this day, I do not know whether he wanted me to read it or whether it was accidentally left on his desk so I could. But, being a reporter dutifully trained in the art of reading things upside down, I read a brief description about a Drug Enforcement Administration (DEA) agent who had turned up missing in Guadalajara. I called my DEA sources to confirm.

"How did you get that information?" I remember one of my federal contacts asked me.

I didn't say, but that document led to one of the first stories about Kiki Camerena—the DEA agent who wound up being kidnapped, tortured, and killed by Mexican drug dealers. Other local reporters in the Rio Grande area published similar stories. Soon, despite initial efforts to downplay Camerena's disappearance—it became a national story. It began as a local one.

Covering the border was exceptionally dangerous the closer to the bone you wanted to get. Coyotes smuggled in the poor who had come thousands of miles searching for a better life in the United States. It is always hard to take those seriously who talk about building walls when you see drug tunnels being used as superhighways from Mexico to the United States to ship illegal drugs and illegal immigrants. It is even harder to see the struggle families go through when parents are trying to make sure their children have a better life than they had. Border Patrol agents routinely fished dead undocumented workers out of the Rio Grande—so often they weren't even included in official statistics. There was no secret to the amount of people trying to get over the border. After the collapse of the oil economy in Mexico during the 1970s, when the value of the peso crashed so hard that it took more than 100 pesos to buy what one used to purchase, the numbers of immigrants coming across the border had steadily increased.

Central and South American undocumented workers, even those from the Middle East and eastern Europe, swelled as those who suffered pushed hard to build a new life in the oasis of the United States.

In the case of those seeking a new home who came from outside the Western Hemisphere, internal political strife led to their search for America. In the case of every refugee from Central and South America, Brigadier General Smedley D. Butler, one of America's most decorated soldiers, told us the U.S. government, which waged numerous raids, police actions, and acts of war, was responsible for creating the political strife that led to the banana republics and the depressed living conditions in the Western Hemisphere. "I helped make Mexico, especially Tampico, safe for American oil interests in 1914. I helped make Haiti and Cuba a decent place for a National City Bank boys to collect revenues in. I helped in the raping of a half a dozen Central American republics for the benefits of Wall Street. The record of racketeering is long. I helped purify Nicaragua for the international banking house of Brown Brothers in 1909–1912. I brought light to the Dominican Republican for American sugar interests in 1916."[12]

If that isn't plain enough, there is this. "I spent 33 years in the Marines, most of my time being a high-class muscle man for big business, for Wall Street and the bankers. In short, I was a racketeer for Capitalism," Butler said in his book.[13]

Fifty years after Butler warned of the fallout from America's corporate wars in the Western Hemisphere, it was easy enough to see the result any day or night on the Rio Grande. Channel 13, KVTV, at the time the CBS affiliate in Laredo during the mid-1980s, was about 100 yards from the river. On any given day, dozens of undocumented workers could be seen trying to scale the fence of the television station in order to make a mad dash for the nearby train yard and hop on a northbound freight train. More than once a month, some unlucky bastard would make a running leap for the trains as they pulled out and be rewarded with dismemberment or death. I saw that often.

But one of the most humbling experiences came on me suddenly. One day, along with a few Border Patrol officers, I walked through the maze of the reeds near the Laredo water plant's main intake point on the river. The Rio Grande was a shallow creek at this location, and consequently rush-hour foot traffic from Mexico into Laredo and sometimes going back to Mexico wasn't uncommon.

The two cities at one point had been one—until the international borders changed and some of Laredo's families decided to build the city of Nuevo Laredo in the state of Tamaulipas, Mexico—directly across the river from Laredo. Until the 2001–2005 drug wars decimated Nuevo Laredo, turning a popular tourist town in northern Mexico into scorched earth, families, money, and jobs routinely crossed the border—and not always at the legal checkpoints. But in 2020, there are people living in both cities who haven't seen their own family members in a decade due to the drug gang violence that resulted from the demand for illegal drugs in the United States.

I still remember the day in mid-February, walking down to the Laredo water plant. There were three dead people, facedown in the mud, along the bank of the river. One of them, a young woman, still grasped at a small baby girl in a diaper who miraculously had survived whatever had taken the lives of her mother, father, and a family friend.

"The coyotes are always around," said a Border Patrol agent I knew—speaking of the human scavengers who preyed on the poor who risked it all and carried everything of value with them on their trek north. Illegal immigrants often had small wads of cash on them. Individually, it didn't add up to much, but a coyote could rob dozens or more and make an adequate living doing so—if one didn't mind beating or killing your fellow man.

On any other day, that story would probably have been page one news. But it was eclipsed by another story: Border Patrol officers found a U-Haul truck stuffed with illegal immigrants. They were stacked like cord wood in the truck, and those on the bottom had suffocated and died.

I never knew what happened to that young baby—still in diapers when I saw her in 1985. If she survived, she would be in her late thirties today. I hope she lived and has had a better life than her parents. They died trying to give it to her.

I was warned by members of the Border Patrol that to see what I saw—as often as I did or, more accurately, as often as they did—made you run the risk of becoming numb to the plight of the less fortunate, but I never saw that among the members of the Border Patrol I routinely knew as sources. I saw them feed, clothe, and even befriend some of those they captured—even as they routinely returned those people to Mexico. "We figure that eventually they're going to get through," I was often told. "We only catch one out of every three if we're lucky."

The city desk at the *Laredo News* gave me ample time to investigate these stories, as did KLDO-TV—the new network affiliate I joined after Randy Kent and Dot Peterson became the two main anchors there. I was offered an incredible raise that meant I could finally work above the poverty level as a reporter. My wife and I began to buy more than liver and onions for dinners. I bought my first suit from our sports anchor, who also ran a men's clothing store.

While I was still at the newspaper, I was able to track down some information on large U.S. corporations and local businesses that were paying cash to bring in undocumented workers. Until the Simpson-Mazzoli Bill passed in the mid-1980s, it had been illegal to work in the United States without proper immigration papers—but it wasn't illegal to hire them. American companies were making money hand over fist hiring illegal immigrants, paying them under the table while avoiding paying taxes and health care.

As I began to ask around, there were two or three members of the local government who apparently were involved or accused of possibly being involved in smuggling undocumented workers into the United States for money.

The sheriff and district attorney were often accused of many things, along with the judge for the 49th District. All of them were quite friendly when you met them, but they were not the most forthcoming to reporters.

After I took my inaugural ride through the county with a sheriff's deputy, I was told by my city editor—Peter Lee, one of my early mentors in the business—that I should meet the sheriff and ask him a few questions about a story our police reporter had been unable to ask questions about. This was standard on newspapers when there was more than one reporter covering an entire county. We had a city hall reporter, a courts reporter, a county beat reporter (me), a police reporter, two general assignments reporters, a state house reporter (he worked in Austin about five hours north on I-35—or four hours if I drove it), as well as features and sports reporters. If we could help each other out, then we did, especially if your city editor or news editor requested it.

So, I walked into the sheriff's office on a fine Tuesday morning and was told to wait outside his office by the sheriff's chief deputy. The chief deputy asked me why I was there, and I told him to meet the sheriff, to thank him for the ride along, and to ask a couple of questions on a story our police reporter was working on. He asked me what the story was about, and I told him. For ten minutes, I sat outside the slightly opened door and listened to the sheriff discuss the story I was there to ask him about—*in Spanish*.

Then he let me in. I thanked him for the ride along, and he smiled. "Quite an education," he said with a smile. "Yes," I agreed. "Pues, pero este . . . ," he said before explaining how strange the city could be to someone who wasn't from the Laredo area. I agreed, and then I began asking him questions. At first, I got perfunctory answers. Then his answers started varying from what he'd told his chief deputy. When I mentioned this to him, he asked how I knew what he told his deputy. I informed him I was sitting outside the door. It was open. I could hear everything he said. "But we were talking in Spanish," he said. "Well, yeah, I speak Spanish," I told him.

"You never told me that." He said grimly.

"You never asked," I replied.

He thought I was trying to trick him, and we never really got along after that. So, when I began hearing rumblings of possible corruption, I had to be extremely careful to make sure the information I got was legitimate, verifiable, and accurate. I knew the sheriff was not a fan and would kick up quite the fit if I had anything remotely wrong.

I had interviewed a convicted coyote who told me some information about the sheriff and some compatriots. Before I could even verify or attempt to verify the information, I got a visit in our newsroom from a member of the district attorney's office. I was marched downtown before an empaneled grand jury. It certainly hadn't been empaneled for anything I wrote since I hadn't written anything yet. And it wasn't empaneled for anything I'd written previously. When I asked why the grand jury had called me to testify, I was told to sit down and answer the questions. A deputy district attorney then began asking me about my sources—in particular, the convicted coyote I'd recently interviewed. As I had not published or even begun to write a story about something I had yet to confirm, I was curious as to why I was being asked and who was interested. No one would answer that—and I was told I could go to jail for obstruction of justice if I didn't answer their questions. I deflected their requests for the name of my source by saying, "I can neither confirm nor deny that I have such information. But under the rights granted to me under the First Amendment, I could not tell you the name of my source."

I got blank stares from the prosecutor and the members of the grand jury. I was asked one question: "Are you sure?" I answered, "Yes."

They let me go.

My editor just laughed. "They're a bunch of idiots," Peter Lee told me.

I agreed. "And don't worry," he said. "We have your back."

That means everything to a reporter. If you put your neck on the line to try to uncover the news, you want to know that your employer will pay for any legal representation you need. That legal representation can be needed if you're hauled before a grand jury and threatened with jail as I was—or if you defend a source and subsequently jailed. The State of Texas at that time had a "shield law," which on the surface protected reporters from having to divulge a confidential source but was often challenged by the government in court.

Most states have a shield law but not all—and all of them offer a varying degree of protection for reporters who wish to protect a confidential source. I testified in Virginia at the beginning of 2020 when House member Danica Roem introduced that state's first shield law—more than thirty-five years after I first encountered a problem in Texas. How many Virginia reporters in thirty-five years simply gave up or didn't pursue a story of vital interest to the public because they knew there was no protection for doing so? There's no way to answer that question, but there is no doubt the problem existed. The Virginia Press Association and several reporters testified along with me as to the need for such protection.

But a shield law cannot protect a reporter from possible violence. A week after I testified before a grand jury, my wife and I were victims of a drive-by shooting. In Laredo, drive-by shootings were not unheard of, but they were not a daily occurrence. My wife and I packed up our belongings and for a few nights stayed at the city clerk's house just to be safe. I also called the FBI, which sent two agents from San Antonio to talk to me. At first, they seemed more intent on getting my source, which I would not give, than investigating the allegations of corruption I was investigating. In the end, they came around, but neither one of us shared information with each other—despite my continued badgering of them and theirs of me. As it should be.

On November 4, 1984, Walter Mondale showed up in the Rio Grande Valley on his last campaign trip of the presidential race. Mondale scored well in his debate with President Ronald Reagan on October 8, 1984, in Louisville. Reagan had seemed out of sorts, indifferent, and lethargic. There was talk that Mondale might overcome the Great Communicator, but less than a month later, Mondale was significantly trailing Reagan. Appearing at Buccaneer Stadium in Corpus Christi, Texas, before some 20,000 supporters, Mondale told an enthusiastic crowd, "Forget the polls, we are going to the White House."[14]

Texas Governor Mark White and Senator Lloyd Bentsen appeared in solidarity with Mondale, who decried Reagan for his tax policies. "I told you he would raise taxes," Mondale said. "But he wants to raise taxes of lower- and middle-income people. He wants to tax your workman's compensation, unemployment benefits, and he even wants to tax your taxes. Mr. Bush's janitor pays more in taxes than Mr. Bush, and Reagan's solution to the national debt is to raise the taxes of Mr. Bush's janitor."[15]

Reagan won reelection. His tax policies led to the beginning of a deep division and increased distance between the "haves" and the "have-nots" that led to the decline of the middle class and the rise of demagogues like Donald Trump.

But his reelection also gave him the opportunity to kill attempts to offer criticism on local, state, and federal government that inevitably led to the cries of "fake news." In his second term, an unfettered Ronald Reagan, with the assistance of Roger Ailes and Mark S. Fowler, killed U.S. journalism by making efforts by reporters at smaller newspapers—like mine in Laredo—next to impossible.

It began as Reagan pushed to deregulate the media and downsize the federal government. Previously constrained from becoming too large because of federal regulation, the resulting media consolidation would help end independent newspaper, television, and radio ownership. An emphasis to pad the bottom line of media conglomerates would lead to fewer reporters, fewer investigation, and little or no legal backup from attorneys—and ultimately would reduce American journalism to the equivalent of a "shopper." Filled with ads, pablum, and short news articles that made *USA Today* seem like a novel, newspapers slowly declined. Television, already criticized for its shallowness, became more vapid.

The biggest change came in television news. "It became a venue for propaganda, nothing more," Newton Minow later told me.

The drive to enhance the boardroom would undercut journalism salaries—which were already low. This in turn drove out experienced reporters who would have the experience and knowledge to ask the tough questions and seek out the difficult stories.

Ben Bagdikian, whom I got to speak with twice before his death, warned of the impending doom brought about by the Reagan era. "Reagan wasn't about diversity of opinion," he told me. He later was famously quoted as saying, "The safest way to ensure diversity of opinion is diversity of ownership. But this ideal has been sacrificed by our government."

Reagan's moves, followed by those of George H. W. Bush, Bill Clinton, Barack Obama, and George W. Bush, led us to Donald Trump. Bagdikian saw all of it coming and warned me once that it would be increasingly difficult to do decent reporting. We spoke about my efforts in Laredo, and I had sought out his counsel knowing his role in the *Pentagon Papers*. He was a kind man on the phone and very forthcoming to a young reporter he never met. But his warnings were icy cold and deadly in their accuracy.

"Trying to be a first-rate reporter on the average American newspaper is like trying to play Bach's St. Matthew Passion on a ukulele: the instrument is too crude for the work, for the audience and for the performer," he famously said.

For me, he offered a bit of personal advice I've never forgotten. "If you want to be a reporter, be prepared to be anything but loved." He said it with a chuckle. But he wasn't kidding.

5

A WONDERFUL
BURSTER OF BALLOONS

For several decades of the late twentieth century, the *Courier-Journal* and the *Louisville Times* were two of the most respected newspapers in the country. Thick. Full of news. Full of ads. Full of information from around the world. They routinely made the list of top ten newspapers in the country as ranked by a variety of news organizations. Run by the famous Bingham family from Louisville, Kentucky, the papers won multiple Pulitzer Prizes and hundreds of other journalistic awards.

When Supreme Court Justice William O. Douglas appeared at the University of Louisville, he famously hailed the newspaper. "This community is blessed with the *Courier-Journal*, one of about 10 newspapers in the country in the days of Joe McCarthy that stood up for the rights of people."[1]

The *Courier-Journal* was Louisville's morning newspaper. The *Louisville Times* was the afternoon edition of the paper. Both are part of my earliest memories of life, from Kennedy's assassination to man landing on the moon and the daily news tossed on my parents' doorstep of the escalating and horrifying war in Vietnam. No one alive during that time can forget picking up a newspaper and reading about those deaths every day. The Louisville papers made those stories seem personal—even to a prepubescent child growing up in middle America. Those papers were my window through which I saw the world. Being a voracious reader, I absorbed quite a bit. In college, I was to learn they were considered the quintessential example of what journalism could aspire to be.

The story of these two newspapers is also the quintessential story of newspapers through U.S. history. In the early nineteenth century, there were several newspapers of varying success in Louisville. The first began in 1826, when the population of Louisville was around 7,000.[2]

In 1830, the *Louisville Daily Journal*, an organ of the Whig Party, was founded and by 1832 had absorbed the city's earlier publications. In 1844, the *Louisville Morning Courier* was founded by Walter Newman Haldeman. The two newspapers quickly became the city's fiercest news competitors. The Whig Party's *Journal* was vehemently antislavery. The *Courier* was pro-Confederacy and suppressed by the Union. It had to move to Nashville, Tennessee, but returned in 1868.

That year proved to be momentous in the history of the newspaper. George D. Prentice, who founded the *Journal*, persuaded a young Henry Watterson to come edit the paper that year, and the *Journal* and the *Courier* merged. The very first edition of the *Courier-Journal* was delivered on Sunday morning, November 8, 1868.[3]

Watterson was an influential editor who won a Pulitzer Prize in 1917 for editorials demanding the United States enter World War I.[4] The city's major transportation highway loop, I-264, is named the Watterson Expressway. Henry Watterson oversaw the founding of the companion afternoon edition of the paper, the *Louisville Times*, in May 1884. His disparaging editorials and reporting on William Jennings Bryan over his support for "Free Silver" upset readers and advertisers—many of whom pulled their support for the *Courier-Journal*. The *Louisville Times*, with no strong editorial stance, remained solvent, however, and saved the newspapers from bankruptcy. But Watterson's crusade led the Commonwealth of Kentucky to vote, for the first time in history, for the Republican Party in the 1896 election, which saw William McKinley defeat William Jennings Bryan. Back then, the Republicans were the progressive party. The newspaper literally changed minds with its coverage, and, in being an instrument of change, it also survived challenges by advertisers, power brokers, and those who couldn't accept what the paper said. It did so in no small part because those who bought and ran those newspapers knew exactly what they were doing. Robert Worth Bingham purchased two-thirds interest in the newspapers in 1918 and acquired the remaining stock in 1920. He was far more liberal than his editor, Henry Watterson, who was in the twilight of his career. After World War I, Watterson's editorials opposing the League of Nations appeared alongside Bingham's favorable editorial. Watterson retired on April 2, 1919.[5]

The story of the *Courier-Journal* until that point was quintessential nineteenth-century journalism. The Bingham family propelled it headlong into the twentieth century.

I walked into the downtown Louisville offices of the *Courier-Journal* and the *Louisville Times* for the first time when I was just five years old. My mom and dad signed me up to be on *T-Bar-V*—a local children's television show on WHAS-TV, owned by the Binghams—which featured country singer Randy Atcher and Tom "Cactus" Brooks, brother of well-known comedian Foster Brooks. There were skits, songs, and cartoons, the standard bill of fare of a mid-1960s television show. The kids, all of whom were celebrating birthdays that week, would get to go up to Randy and Cactus and tell them what they wanted for their birthday. Randy, the host, was very popular with the kids. He sang to us, encouraging us to brush our teeth each morning and get lots of sleep at night. He told us to "cross at the corner of the block, never in between. And when the light is red, you stop. Go when it turns green. And always remember each day and every night, before you start across the street, look both left and right."

I dutifully told Randy what I wanted for my birthday (it wasn't a BB gun) and then took my place with the other kids for the highlight of the show; Randy and Cactus would get together with all the kids and sing "Happy Birthday" in front of a huge birthday cake with candles. I couldn't wait. The appropriate time came, and I stood in disbelief. It was a "you'll shoot your eye out kid moment" with Santa Claus. The cake. That luscious, beautiful vanilla cake with multicolored icing, filled with candles and a large "Happy Birthday" written on the face of it was made of *plaster*.

For many years, WHAS operated on the top floors of the Courier Journal building at Sixth Street and Broadway until it moved to its own location on Chestnut Street in the late 1960s. The Binghams owned WHAS, a CBS affiliate at the time; both local newspapers; and Standard Gravure, a printing company. They also operated WHAS radio. In 1986, Barry Bingham Sr. broke up the family media empire and sold the newspapers to Gannett, WHAS television to Gannett, and the radio station to Clear Channel Communications—effectively ending a dominant local presence in Louisville media.

When Robert Worth Bingham bought and began running the newspapers that would eventually become a local media conglomerate, his progressive ideas helped modernize Louisville. He pushed education and equal rights and supported African Americans and the poor in Appalachia. His newspaper became the newspaper of record in the state. When his son, Barry Bingham Sr., took over in 1933, he pushed his father's dreams further. He expanded the newsroom, partnered with other newspapers, and opened several bureaus both in the state and outside the state. The newspaper coverage became nationwide and, by the time of the Vietnam War, global.

I remember reading "Pfc. Gibson Comes Home" by John Fetterman. It was 1968. I read it again in high school for a journalism class and again in college. It was a Pulitzer Prize–winning story that was a huge influence on the antiwar movement. In 1974, Carol Sutton became the managing editor of the *Courier-Journal*. She was the first woman appointed to such a post at a major U.S. daily.

The Binghams accomplished all of this by a unique management style—they pushed quality journalism over maximum profits. In effect, they chose long-term steady profits over short-term maximum profits by providing a public service people came to count on—and their personal wealth helped them through lean times as their vision remained focused on coverage.

What they had to sell was invaluable: trust. This enlightened approach helped the newspaper increase coverage and provided a base of profits by which the family could purchase and operate a large printing press company that also made money from commercial printing, a television station, and a radio station.

At its peak, there wasn't any place you could travel in Kentucky where the *Courier-Journal* and the *Louisville Times* weren't known and respected—even if there were people who didn't like the newspapers or the Binghams. The newspapers influenced politics, the economy, entertainment, and education. A reporter carrying a press pass from the *Courier-Journal* had access to just about anything on the public agenda in Kentucky or anywhere the newspaper was known outside the state.

The philosophy as espoused by Robert Worth Bingham was enshrined in raised print above the elevators in the newspaper lobby: *"I have always regarded the newspapers owned by me as a public trust and have endeavored so to conduct them as to render the greatest public service."*

Many luminaries on the world stage passed underneath that print as they entered the building at Sixth and Broadway: Eleanor Roosevelt, Jimmy Carter, Muhammad Ali, astronaut John Glenn, and Holocaust survivor Elie Weisel were among them.[6]

It is the only place I've ever worked that spelled out its ideals and publicly displayed them. It was the only place I ever worked that placed the work product ahead of profits—and since media consolidation began, it will probably be the last. The building that housed those ideals—and indeed the raised print above the elevators in the newspaper lobby—went up for sale in early 2021.

In 1985, I worked in the Neighborhoods section of the *Courier-Journal*. This was the weekly supplemental newspaper with several different editions for different neighborhoods. I was a "dedicated stringer"—meaning that I was used full-time but paid as an independent contractor. It was a creative way to hire young reporters without providing health coverage while still using their services. It was, perhaps, not the most enlightened method of doing business, but by 1985, pressures on the business side of newspapers led to increasingly creative ways to staff a paper. Of course, when those methods ultimately failed for the obvious reasons, layoffs would follow shortly. My beat at first was the Shively area, but I later became a general assignment reporter. I covered tornadoes, crime, features, and local sports. On occasion, I traveled to Frankfort and covered the state capital. Politics there were rowdy, but due to the influence of the *Courier-Journal*, there was a thin veneer of reality that curbed the most extreme actions of clay-headed politicians—at least publicly. Too much crazy got you nasty press in the *Courier*, and nasty press in the *Courier* made fund-raising and ultimately vote getting much too difficult. The *Courier* was often seen as liberal on its editorial pages, but no one doubted its news coverage. It was as solid as any ever was. And readers in Kentucky knew the difference between the paper's clearly labeled opinion pieces and its clearly labeled news pieces.

My desk was a cubicle in a vast newsroom that looked like something straight out of a Hollywood movie. I personalized my cubicle space with a printout of a saying from H. L. Mencken about American reporters: "He doesn't wear himself out trying to get the news, as romance has it; he slides supinely into the estate and dignity of a golf-player. American journalism suffers from too many golf-players."[7]

Perhaps Mencken is why I never took up golf seriously—or why I always eye golf-playing presidents rather suspiciously. But it served to drive my ambition and encouraged me to do better. It was hard to make a mark at that newspaper then. I was young, and there were so many experienced reporters ahead of me. It seemed, with few exceptions, everyone's goal in the Neighborhoods section was to join the city desk. Joining the staff of that newspaper had been my lifelong ambition. I had read it since I began reading. I enjoyed Barry Bingham's recurring column in the newspaper. It was for me a romantic trip through journalism. In a 1959 essay, Barry Sr. wrote, "Journalism . . . is the best of all jobs for those who have the temperament, the mental and physical toughness, and the sense of humor it requires."[8] I was a true believer, and I learned a lot about large newspapers and mid-1980s journalism working there.

Three different editors oversaw our section. A roundtable of six different copy editors chewed us apart and spit us out. "How do you know this?" was the sentence most often uttered by our section editor. Our deadlines, though not as intense as on the daily side of the paper, were still stiff. We were producing half a dozen different supplements, and the copy had to flow.

One day, I walked into the office, a little downcast after a tough day trying to get interviews on a story about a faltering West End business. Our section had one receptionist/office manager/secretary who answered the phone for about a dozen reporters. She rarely gave me a glance.

"Brian," she called me as I walked in. "I have a note for you. Senior wants to see you upstairs."

I think I may have gone pale. Barry Bingham Sr. never wanted to see anyone. He had stepped down from the day-to-day operation of the newspaper in 1971, but he was a legend—and he never wanted to talk to the lowest man on the totem pole. Me.

"It's been a pleasure working with you," I was told. The implication from our receptionist was that she would no longer be burdened with the pleasure of working with me. I sure got the message. I wasn't sure what it was I'd done to anger the old man. Maybe I'd questioned someone too rudely. Maybe I'd pushed a little too hard. Maybe my copy had to be re-written by the copy editors too much. I didn't know. But I was floored. I was getting fired.

I made my way upstairs to an office dominated by stained oak still trying to figure out what I'd done wrong. I'd broken a story, "Drive-In Drug Sales Are Common on Several Corners in the City," that had angered some on the police department. I had quoted a cop who told me that "there's a whole new breed of drug dealer who has no fear of the law."[9] Some in the police department were angry I'd included the quote, saying it made them look weak.

As I entered Bingham's office, I introduced myself to his private secretary, whom I'd never met and couldn't identify in a lineup, and she smiled. "I know who you are Mr. Karem. Go right in. Senior is waiting."

The office was beautifully paneled in what looked like stained oak and had a large window that overlooked the city and to the north the Ohio River. At least if I was going to get fired, it was in a nice office. Bingham was courteous. He offered me coffee and a bite to eat. I was too nervous for either. I sat in a nice leather chair and waited for the ax to fall.

"Are you related to Fred J. Karem?" he asked. That was my grandfather. An immigrant who became a circuit court judge and helped start the Catholic Theater Guild in Louisville. When I acknowledged I was his grandson, he was very complimentary of my grandfather and my grandmother. He remembered she was one of the first women in the United

States to plead a case before the U.S. Supreme Court. I remember my uncle telling me how she had been worried more about the hat she wore in the Supreme Court than about the case she was arguing. After the introductions and the acknowledgment that the "Karem family should be proud of its contributions in Louisville," I smiled and thanked him and was too afraid to ask him why I was there. My two uncles had followed in my grandfather's footsteps and were attorneys. Edmund Peter Karem later became the chief circuit judge of the Jefferson County Circuit Court. David Kevin Karem would become the Senate majority leader in the statehouse and, following that, the head of the Louisville Waterfront Development Corporation, dedicated to helping the city grow.

Bingham seemed to know everyone in my family, and after he mentioned most of them, as if I had never met them, he then asked me a question I'll never forget. "Are you the young man who posted that quote from Henry above your desk?" I blinked. Henry? I said to myself. Then I remembered. H. L. Mencken. Henry Mencken. I swallowed. "Yes. That was me," I said.

"Why that quote?" he asked me.

"Well, I've read a lot of Mencken, and I enjoy his irreverence and his writing. I loved his description of the life of a reporter. His command of the language. How he went after politicians . . ."

"Yes," Bingham interrupted me and at the same time seemed to drift into a state of reverie. "He was a wonderful burster of balloons when many balloons needed to be burst."

For what seemed like the next few hours but in reality was probably less than an hour, Barry Bingham Sr. recounted for me his personal friendship with H. L. Mencken—including his disagreements with the "Sage of Baltimore" over Germany and Russia. "Henry was a remarkably funny man," Bingham told me. "But he was at his best criticizing politicians and reporters. I particularly liked his criticism of our business."

Mencken died on January 26, 1956, and I wondered how close Barry Bingham Sr. could've been with him. Bingham would've been close to his fiftieth birthday when Mencken passed, so I had to ask him. "We were fellow travelers," he told me without expanding much on that statement. But he said that he'd spoken with Mencken many times.

It slowly dawned on me that I wasn't going to be fired. Even more slowly, I came to realize our receptionist had been yanking my chain. Barry Bingham Sr. just wanted to talk about an old friend of his who was no longer with us—and he'd found a "fellow traveler" in me. I was moved. I asked him at one point how he came to know what was hanging above my desk in an obscure corner of a vast metropolitan newsroom. "Nothing happens at *my* newspaper that I don't know about," he said as he smiled and his eyes seemed to dance. I believed him. He had turned over the day-to-day operation of the newspaper empire to his son Barry Bingham Jr. in 1971, but I learned that day that Senior was still the all-seeing eye.

"Do you remember what Henry said about 'chain-store' journalism?" Bingham asked me at one point. I nodded. Indeed I had. It was a warning sign I had seen from the time I'd read the passage. "As a result of the application of chain-store methods to journalism . . . the individual journalist is less important. . . . There is little room, on the papers of such chains, for the young man who aspires to shine." Further, Mencken described just chain-store newspapers as "dung-hills."[10] I couldn't give the entire quote, but I paraphrased it well enough that Senior nodded in recognition. I looked over, and he had the quote highlighted in an open book penned by Mencken.

Bingham smiled. "Do you think I own a dung hill?" He asked. I said the first thing that came to my mind. "I hope not. I'd hate to think my professional goal for my life was to work for a dung hill."

He smiled and told me of his concerns for our business. "Our president is intent on destroying the free press," he told me, referring to Reagan. "And I fear he has allies great and small who can make that happen. Remember what Henry said about journalists: the rewards of the trade used to come in freedom, opportunity, the incomparable delights of self-expression; now they come in money."

Bingham expressed a fear that renewed efforts at chain-store journalism in newspapers and television would lead to the "loss of freedom I've spent a lifetime fighting for." I brought my notepad with me into the meeting and began taking notes. He didn't seem to care. He was in a reflective mood that day. "I won't live to see where this goes," he said sternly before he looked me straight in the eyes. "But you will." At the end of the meeting, I reminded him what he said about Mencken being a great burster of balloons. "Who is doing that today?" I asked. "Who indeed will?" he said, smiling. I took that as a personal challenge and have often wondered if that was his intent.

A short time later, I left the *Courier-Journal* and the *Louisville Times* for a full-time job covering the state legislature in Frankfort and a remarkable increase of pay that allowed my wife and me to rent a two-bedroom apartment near Cherokee Park in Louisville. The handwriting was on the wall for both papers with a sale to Gannett and rumors of cutbacks with new corporate overlords. I had often dreamed of spending my entire professional career at the Bingham newspapers once I got there. It lasted less than a year.

And while I had a healthy distaste for television news—because in my small amount of time in the business, it was apparent newscasts were slaves to quick sound bites, spot news, and stealing stories from the newspapers— they also paid much better, and I had a desire to afford housing while also feeding and clothing myself. While at WKYT-TV in Lexington, I covered the closure of the *Louisville Times* and the breakup of the Bingham independent media empire. In 1986, the Bingham family, embroiled in a vicious family fight, sold off its independent media holdings. Gannett bought the papers for $300 million and closed the *Louisville Times* in February 1987.

The *Courier-Journal*, as run by Gannett, became indistinguishable from a shopper. In December 2008, the paper laid off fifty-one employees, including seventeen who voluntarily took buyouts as part of a larger cutback by Gannett. Seven months later, forty-four more employees got the ax. WHAS radio, once a regional radio behemoth, became a talk-radio network featuring Rush Limbaugh. WHAS television switched its affiliation to ABC and remains the last of the former Bingham holdings still semi-respected for its news coverage.

The fall of the Bingham family's influence in Kentucky came at the same time as the fall of progressive politics in Kentucky. It was no coincidence. While the Binghams had helped demand a certain degree of professionalism among politicians, with the loss of the independent voice and all of the eyes on government that the Bingham family had helped ensure, people like Mitch McConnell and Rand Paul rose virtually unchallenged from the information-stripped landscape. The fewer eyes cast on government, the more politicians could get away with and the more their paid media could paint the picture—whether or not the picture was accurate. "To get an endorsement from the *Courier-Journal* meant something," former Third District congressman Mike Ward remembers. "It helped you everywhere. You had to appear before the editorial board. One person did the interview. Six people on the editorial board discussed the interview. Their interviews where very thorough and held politicians accountable," he recalled.

David Karem, my uncle, who was a state representative and then state senator, had similar experiences with the *Courier-Journal* and the *Louisville Times* editorial boards. "One of my fond memories is in regard to editorial endorsements," David told me. "Many candidates would go on and on that they did not care about said endorsements but would be the first to rush to get the paper hoping they got it. No matter what anyone says about endorsements, they were very powerful and influential. The *Courier* went through a very deep and thoughtful process of interviews, which made a difference in many races. No such process exists any more in this community, and it is a sad loss for the elections. Without this, where does one go for thoughtful info on candidates? Politicians generally were proud to list an endorsement on their campaign material."

In 1984, Mitch McConnell won election to the Senate based on a single ad that was disingenuous and factless. This happened as the *Courier* was unraveling but still had some guardrails in place. Imagine what McConnell could do without meddling reporters asking worrisome questions. By 1987, while still in his first term, he no longer had to worry about progressive media like the *Courier-Journal*—it was now a corporate entity far less concerned with the quality of its journalism and far more worried about turning over the maximum return on its $300 million investment for its shareholders.

Some of the first cuts the *Courier-Journal* made that I remember came to the statehouse bureau in Frankfort. In 1985, I was one of three reporters covering the statehouse for WKYT-TV in Lexington. The *Courier-Journal* had the largest bureau there—easily six reporters. Sometimes, it seemed like dozens of reporters from that paper were going through the activities of the state government. Multiple bureaus across the state and occasional reporters from those venues visiting Frankfort (plus reporters visiting from Louisville for features or investigative pieces) enhanced that perception. The *Cincinnati Post* (which covered northern Kentucky), the *Lexington Herald Leader*, the Frankfort newspaper, and other assorted newspapers across the state had bureaus in Frankfort of varying size. Television stations from every market in Kentucky had occasional if not full-time staffs covering politics in Frankfort. Ferrell Wellman from WAVE-TV, Mark Hebert from WHAS-TV, and Tony Hyatt from WKYT were standouts in television.

During the middle of the 1985 general assembly, many of us covering the session gathered for a group photo. The picture shows twenty-seven reporters of a variety of ages, of both genders, and of a variety of ethnic backgrounds standing at the speaker's desk. As I recall, it was only about half of us who were actually covering the assembly on a daily basis. During that day and age, every decent-sized daily paper and television and radio station covered state politics. Today? According to some polls, just 30 percent of daily newspapers even send a reporter to the nation's statehouses. You want to know why reporting sucks and people aren't getting their news? There's no one around to do the job.

After I was hired to join Hyatt in Frankfort, they downsized the bureau—just prior to the legislative session, sending our third reporter back to Lexington to work as a general assignment reporter. Hyatt and I, as did most television crews of that era, shot video for each other. When I was reporting, Tony was my crew, hauling around a ¾-inch videotape recording deck that weighed about fifty pounds, several ¾-inch tapes, an Ikegami-84 camera with the worst filter system I've ever seen on a camera, and a five-pound umbilical cord that connected to the deck so that what was shot with the camera could be recorded on the massive recording deck. We also carried a "Batman utility belt" of batteries for a massive "sun gun" light that we often attached to the camera for nighttime video shots. Along with that, we also carried a telescoping metal tripod and a twenty-foot cable that attached to the camera at one end and a handheld microphone at the other for when we wanted to interview someone. On top of the camera sat a second mic—a "nat sound" mic shaped like a foam cigar. We shot each other's "stand-ups" and edited our own video packages at a small office the station rented near the statehouse. The workday began early and lasted until we had supplied video packages or live shots for the late-night news.

At the same time, my Uncle David served in the state Senate. Tony did the stories concerning David, so I didn't have a conflict of interest—but there was never a shortage of things to cover in state government. There were stories about illegal dumps, toxic waste, drugs, and a small city in southeastern Kentucky that was being poisoned by yellow-cake uranium production.

One day, concerned protesters drove to Frankfort from Litchfield and dumped yellow cake on the steps of the statehouse—a move that prompted coverage, especially after the protesters called every newspaper and television in the state and told them they were coming. The police were grateful for the heads-up as well—apparently from a reporter who asked if there was going to be security at the statehouse in case things got dangerous. Only two protesters showed up, and they were impressed by the police response they managed to muster. The story carried across the state.

In 1986, one of the reporters we called "Sparky" (because he accidentally started his office garbage can on fire with his pipe) ushered me and others into the governor's office. Martha Lane Collins was in her office to watch the first teacher travel into space aboard the space shuttle *Challenger*. Collins had a keen interest in education and a healthy respect for good public relations. On January 28, 1986, I spent the early part of the day covering a protest by parents opposed to pornography. The dozens of protesters across the state presented reporters a list of books and movies they believed should be banned from publication.

"How did you determine these things were pornographic?" I asked.

"The executive committee read the books and watched the movies," I was told without any sense of irony.

"What's the difference between me doing that and them doing it?" I returned.

"They did it in service to the Lord and made the sacrifice for all of us," I was told.

I nodded and then asked them the only thing I could think of at that moment.

"Who asked them?" I said. "I sure didn't. I can watch and decide for myself."

I was called a variety of things, none of them nice, but I was told the protesters were there and believed strongly in the righteousness of their cause. Otherwise, the protest went off without a hitch—that is to say, nothing more than the modern-day equivalent of a high-tech book burning. I shot video and a stand-up and recorded the interviews by myself. Tony had another assignment that day as I remember, so when it came time to shoot my stand-up, I placed a light stand in front of the camera, marked its position, focused on the stand, turned on the camera remotely, kicked the light stand out of the way, stood where it had been, and looked at the camera as I described what went on at the protest. These were cost-cutting measures many television stations employed in order to produce the news. But managers at the time were at least dominated by people who felt there should be more people in the field gathering news, and they would do what they could to accomplish that goal. There are many a reporter and photographer from that era with bad shoulders, knees, and other body parts from lugging around the heavy camera gear. But we thought we were far better off than the generation immediately before us, who carried around heavier film cameras, film canisters, and wooden tripods and worried about film chains and syncing up sound. There was an often-told story of Monica Kaufman, the first African American anchor in Louisville, who once called for her first block of stories on the newscast—none of them were there because of a film chain problem. She apparently looked at the camera, told the audience they'd go to a commercial break, figure out the problem, and be right back. As the camera dipped to black, the mic was apparently still hot, and Monica could be heard asking, "Okay, what the —— is going on here?" The rumor was the receptionists at the other two network affiliates in town had their fair share of calls of complaint because they couldn't get through to the switchboard at Monica's station. So, no one missed film, which was far bulkier and more expensive than videotape.

After I shot the protest, I decided to check into our statehouse office space, little more than a desk in a cubbyhole on the third floor, and make a few phone calls about the story before I drove to the bureau and began editing. That's when Sparky grabbed me. I didn't feel like following him because there wasn't anything more in a shuttle launch than getting thirty seconds of video of the governor watching it. But I grabbed the camera and went down to the governor's office. The rest, of course, was a horrifying day in history. And because we were there, we had tape. We had the story. Amazingly, today, I could do all the work I did on that day with a cell phone, a portable mixer, a small microphone, and a laptop—all of which would weigh less than ten pounds and fit into a backpack or briefcase. Still, with the ease by which anyone can record anything today and how inexpensive it is to do so, for the most part, news staffs have not significantly increased—usually it's the exact opposite. It is not uncommon to see White House reporters shoot stand-ups and conduct live shots on the North Lawn of the West Wing with little more than a cell phone and a microphone. With companies having to spend so little for equipment today, there has been absolutely no commitment to hire additional staff to provide more expansive coverage in the past thirty-five years. The irony of course is that even a moderate increase in a commitment to personnel could eliminate a lot of complaints people have about today's media—and keep the companies from cutting staff because fewer people are watching or reading us.

By the end of the 1986 legislative session, I remember several of the reporters at the statehouse were talking about rumors that their organization was going to cut staff. This was the first of the great cullings to occur in the business. WKYT wasn't immune either. The company that owned the station had opened a new television station in Hazard. Some in management told us cuts would be coming. They did.

For spring sweeps week that year, our news director went out on a limb. David Lander, a tall redhead with an outgoing personality and fairly good news sense, had noticed an influx of what he assumed were undocumented workers in the Lexington metropolitan area. "What are they doing here?" he asked. The answer to me was simple—I'd seen people jump the freight trains at the border in Laredo. I wasn't wrong figuring a few might end up in Kentucky. Construction work was popular. Contractors loved using undocumented workers. They got paid under the table, were cheaper, worked their asses off, and never worried about health care—which small construction companies wouldn't pay. Until Kentucky Congressman Ron

Mazzoli sponsored the Simpson/Mazzoli Bill and it passed Congress, it wasn't even illegal for American companies to hire them—though it was illegal for them to be here.

In the spring of 1986, I put together a ten-part series for WKYT on the problem of illegal immigration, its impact on the commonwealth, and Louisville Congressman Mazzoli's efforts to enact immigration legislation. For that series, photographer Mark Renfro and I traveled to the border, where we recorded the drowning of some illegal immigrants, interviewed others, and traveled with the Border Patrol along the frontier—and of course I revisited El Cenizo and Rio Bravo. We also interviewed a wide variety of undocumented workers in Kentucky and discovered that many were there on a migratory route working on horse farms. They'd travel over the border, work for eight to nine months, and then return home. The oil economy in Mexico had crashed in the mid- to late 1970s, leading to the devaluation of the peso and subsequent poverty. Many of those who suffered in Mexico saw America as the land of opportunity and were willing to make a treacherous yearly trek just to feed their families. American business was more than eager then (and is still so now) to exploit the cheap labor.

To finish this series, I traveled to Washington, D.C., to interview Mazzoli and ask some questions of the Reagan White House. I walked in the James S. Brady Press Briefing Room that spring into a world that I had only seen on television and read about prior to my arrival. I tried to play it all off, but you cannot forget your first day walking into the White House. You never should. The history that has occurred inside those walls is momentous. The brain power that has visited the White House revolutionized culture and changed the world for better and worse.

I walked inside the briefing room and noticed the small number of seats, the small stage, and the lectern. Next to the door stood two racks that held numerous printouts of news made possible by the "pool" of reporters who followed the president everywhere they were allowed to be. There were large printers nearby that spit out the pool reports. I walked in, and the first person I met was Helen Thomas. I renewed my acquaintance with Sam Donaldson during my two-week stay, met Connie Lawn, and got to sit in on a few presidential briefings and even met President Reagan.

Helen Thomas was the easiest person I ever got to know. That may sound odd, but we shared a Lebanese ancestry, she was a wonderful Lebanese cook, and she knew members of my family. I've always been thankful for those who came before me, particularly family members who were held in esteem by those I respected. Helen gave me unbelievably sound advice.

She told me to never be afraid to ask a question and never worry about making friends among the press corps. "Get another job if you're looking for friendship," she told me. "So, if you have a question, then just ask the question. It doesn't matter if it's answered. It doesn't matter what the answer is. But once asked, they cannot deny the issue has been put before them."

She gave me a lot of other good advice, and, of course, there isn't a reporter who covered the White House during her time there that doesn't have a story about her. Many of those are fond memories. Those who worked for the White House who remember her always recall her rapier-like wit and her bluntness.

After pleasantries, Helen made a point to reintroduce me to Sam Donaldson. We'd met briefly on the 1984 campaign trail, and I was surprised he had remembered me. "You were the rude reporter who shouted out a question," he smiled. Helen shook her head and chuckled. Sam was, of course, Sam. He pointed at the front row of seats in the Brady Briefing Room and said, "Brian, there's probably 250 years of experience in this first row, so listen to what they have to say. Of course Helen probably has 200 years of it." He smiled, Helen said something smart that I cannot remember, and Sam replied, "It's okay to have an unexpressed thought Helen."

Helen smiled and said, "Sam, when it comes to you, I have a lot of unexpressed thoughts." They both laughed. It was a humbling experience for a young reporter to be in the company of two people I had grown to professionally respect as much as I respected them. But their kindness and their willingness to mentor young reporters—and young reporters willing to listen to what they had to say—made for a healthy, robust, and competitive press corps. Joe Lockhart, one of Bill Clinton's press secretaries, recalled how he came out of his first briefing very confident and expressed as much to Helen. She cut him down to size quickly, reminding him that all great feelings were fleeting. He routinely showed up in the morning with coffee and donuts for Helen on a daily basis. One day, he said he saw Helen sitting outside of his door and asked her why she always did that. "You really are stupid," he said Helen told him. He said he decided to bite. "Okay, how am I really stupid?" he asked. It was then that he learned how good a reporter Helen was. She could tell what was going on by sitting in the upper press area and watching how the staff reacted.

The White House press corps was a different animal then. It was more experienced and more professional. The White House staff showed a healthy respect for the reporters even if they wrote something the White House didn't like. Reporters were also more seasoned and far more professional. Most didn't overtly try to play the "access game" and suck up to the White House to get favored treatment. The access game was played then, as now, with pool reporters getting better access to the president, but there was still a wide variety of reporters and organizations at the White House. The president respected the press covering him well enough, and the press corps was far more bold than it is now.

When some of us began pushing back against the Trump administration, younger reporters were shocked, and some were offended that there were those who did so. We were accused of "making it all about yourself." Many of those reporters were happy to be stenographers who sat still while others risked access to hold truth to power. One of the NBC engineers set one of those reporters straight one morning after I had a run-in with one of Trump's press secretaries. "He's not doing anything Donaldson didn't do," the photographer told the young reporter. "Except Donaldson was better doing it," I smiled.

WKYT-TV's ten-part series *Across the Broken Border* aired in the fall sweeps of 1986—just weeks before the Simpson-Mazzoli Bill became law. It dealt with a variety of problems of illegal immigration and the horrible inaction by the United States on the matter.

The Immigration Reform and Control Act (Pub. L. 99-603, 100 Stat. 3445, enacted on November 6, 1986, also known as the Simpson–Mazzoli Act or the Reagan Amnesty, signed into law by Ronald Reagan on November 6, 1986) is an act of Congress that reformed U.S. immigration law. The act

- required employers to attest to their employees' immigration status,
- made it illegal to hire or recruit illegal immigrants knowingly,
- legalized certain seasonal agricultural undocumented immigrants, and
- legalized undocumented immigrants who entered the United States before January 1, 1982, and had resided there continuously with the penalty of a fine, back taxes due, and admission of guilt; candidates were required to prove that they were not guilty of crimes; that they were in the country before January 1, 1982; and that they possessed at least a minimal knowledge about U.S. history, government, and the English language.

At the time, the Immigration and Naturalization Service estimated that about 4 million illegal immigrants would apply for legal status through the act and that roughly half of them would be eligible.[11]

It was the first real step taken to deal with a growing problem of undocumented workers. Reporters had gathered information for years on the matter. The problem percolated up from the grassroots reporting, came before Congress, and Congress acted—together.

The act was not filtered through different information silos. There was no Fox News. No reports of caravans or anger or talk of building a wall. Republicans and Democrats worked together and forged a first-step solution to a real problem. It may have been one of the last times Congress did so. Fractured media and zero-sum politics that exploited media divisions would be the blame.

6

WHAT YOU GOT HERE
IS BRAIN BLOOD

By the end of the 1980s, newspapers, due mostly to the greed of news-paper owners, shareholders, and the influx of television and cable news, were in full decline. The *Courier-Journal* and *Louisville Times* weren't the only papers to falter. Moves by the federal government to deregulate television, such as allowing multiple ownership, did newspapers no favors either. Newspapers got indirectly caught in the mess created by it. The television networks, already getting a lion's share of advertising, amplified their message to garner more funds, and that put more pressure on newspapers. The irony, of course, was that television news always relied on newspapers to provide the primary reporting that led to their packaged news reports.

But talk to anyone who sold television advertising in the 1980s. There was pressure to increase their monthly contracts, and at the same time, by cutting some prices and providing commercial production, such as live shots from car dealerships instead of vendor-supplied images, the television stations undercut newspapers and destroyed the newspaper revenue base. It was a time for the robber barons. Why? One reason was the networks feared cable news and were out to make as much money as possible as quickly as possible.

In San Antonio, Texas, the media war claimed the *San Antonio Light*. The *Light* began in 1881 as the *Evening Light* and was renamed in 1883. It was a progressive newspaper and the only Republican daily newspaper in Texas—at a time when Teddy Roosevelt ran the Republican Party, not Donald Trump. The *Light* had an early reputation as a "fighting newspaper" for its progressive political stance. Although it was a local newspaper, it also included regional politics and, according to an assessment in the 1890s, was "energetic in promulgating its principles according to the Light that is in it." James Newcomb, founder and editor of the *Evening Light*, introduced journalistic innovations to San Antonio: editorializing digests of other local papers and providing weekend supplements, poetry, biographical sketches, and personal interest articles, among others. By the early 1900s, the *Light* contained an opinion page featuring an editorial cartoon; sports, society, and fashion pages; and household hints aimed at women. Classified advertisements ran daily, and comics, sheet music, fiction, poetry, and children's pages appeared in the Sunday editions. Although the *Light* abandoned its Republican political affiliation by the 1910s, it maintained its stated agenda to promote development in southwestern Texas.[1]

In 1924, William Randolph Hearst purchased the newspaper. Hearst was one of the earliest media barons and was lambasted by his contemporary H. L. Mencken for his "chain-store" methods of journalism. But, whatever you wanted to say about Hearst, he invested in the news product far more than the "vulture" capitalists of the early twenty-first century, and the *Light* remained a viable newspaper for almost seventy years afterward, finally closing its doors in 1993.

In the waning days of the 1980s, it was a proud newspaper with a strong staff that did battle with the *San Antonio Express-News*, the city's main daily newspaper. The *Light* broke a lot of stories. With few exceptions, the staffs of both papers were colorful and larger than life. Susan Yerkes for the *San Antonio Light* and Jeanne Jakel at the rival *Express* laid claim as latter-day Hedda Hoppers—digging out tidbits of interesting and sometimes salacious information on those of a higher community profile, local celebrities, and those in the music and movie business who often passed through the area. Bigger-than-life Texans dominated the news—both covering it and being covered by it. Master storytellers like Michael Pearson could describe a crime story with a special emphasis on telling you about a "big ole gun" that would actually have you sitting in your seat waiting for the next anecdote.

The place was as colorful as Sheriff Harlon Copeland, who campaigned in his own fire truck and who once asked Ann Richards, "Did you or did you not done drugs?" He once described a jail riot as a "butt kickin' contest and we won." Then there was Mayor Henry Cisneros, once considered a legitimate contender as the first Hispanic presidential candidate and who saw it all dissolve after admission of an extramarital affair. For two hours in two different languages, he did his Catholic boy best to confess to an affair everyone in town had known about for months—but no one had reported until someone dared to do so. After confessing to his crimes of the heart and lust elsewhere, he asked me how he did. I told him honestly, "Henry, if it had been me, I never would have done the press conference.

I would have stayed in the house and said no comment." There was no lack of locally colorful characters in the community. Did I mention Dennis Rodman, who came to fame dying his hair green and capturing rebounds with the San Antonio Spurs? He earned a lot of people's respect in the San Antonio community with his "If you don't like it, you can kiss my ass" attitude. Dating Madonna didn't hurt, nor did his Wesley Snipes–inspired "Demolition Man" hairdo and outfits.

San Antonio's news institutions in the 1980s were a part of that community. It was part of the corporate plan at most television stations and newspapers at the time: community involvement. Television stations had departments dedicated to community engagement. So did newspapers.

The city had a vibrant and competitive news community that typified the 1980s and early 1990s. It was a large metropolitan area but, true to Texas and most major television markets at the time, had a good cross section of rural, urban, and suburban residents of varying ethnicities and religions. The city itself was a melting pot but had its boundaries as well. Henry Cisneros grew up on the city's west side—the enclave for Hispanics and the site of the Alazan Apache Courts and other housing projects overrun by gangs, drugs, and violence. The east side was the residence of the poorer African American population. One night while loading up for a ride along with east-side police, my television crew for KMOL-TV heard a gang fight erupt in gunfire and a shotgun blast less than a hundred yards from the police substation as we were loading our equipment. "Hurry up. That's a shooting. We're gonna get the call," the officer I was riding with told me.

The south side of town was filled with poorer white people and littered with meth labs. On the occasion of once a month, you'd get a call as a crime reporter to cover a meth lab that accidentally blew up—with about a 50/50 chance of covering a gruesome fatality caused when the meth lab owner blew himself up, too. China Grove, that cute little town that became the inspiration for a Doobie Brothers hit song, was at one time exceptionally notorious for its meth labs.

The volume of news kept everyone busy, but the *Light* had it harder than the *Express*. The staff was smaller. It seemed to lose reporters by attrition at a daily rate, and, as others in the market noticed, if you worked at the *Light*, your salary was light but your workload was heavy. The news stations in San Antonio were doing fine. KENS, the CBS affiliate, dominated most of the local news. KSAT, the ABC affiliate, was a close second. KMOL, the NBC affiliate, was a distant third in the ratings for most of its shows. But all of these stations were vibrant, profitable, and well staffed for television stations. Roger Ailes was right. People abandoned newspapers for television to get their news all throughout the 1980s, but television reporters still relied on the newspapers for their news—which also helped explain the healthy bottom line for television stations around the country. The attitude in local television stations across the country was, "Why pay for reporters when we can get our news from the newspapers for free?" Okay, maybe for the price of subscribing and occasionally advertising in the local paper—but that was a far cry from paying for the size of a news staff needed to cover a major metropolitan area.

Television stations made more money and had far smaller news staffs than the local newspapers. At a newspaper like the *Light* or the *Express-News*, the state legislature, the crime beat, breaking news, general assignments, city hall—all of them could and often were separate beats, and there may be more than one person working on each beat, particularly on crime, the legislature, and city hall. At a television station, one person usually covered all of it. There were beats, but reporters rarely had time to break a story on their primary beat. Instead, they would be called on to cover a story on their primary beat, and, if on a particular day there wasn't a good story there, then you'd cover something else. Newspapers had the luxury of two or maybe three deadlines a day. Television had deadlines for the morning, noon, 5 or 6 p.m. newscast, and the 10 or 11 p.m. newscast. One person usually was saddled with doing stories for all of them in the course of an eight-hour workday. The exception was made for the "big" story of the day, when fresh faces would repackage an earlier effort for the nightside.

Today, with a constantly rotating news cycle, television, radio, and newspapers are bound to file stories more quickly on the internet and to follow them up during the course of the day. Everyone is an online newspaper—even the networks that publish written stories in addition to their video packages and television shows. There are fewer copy editors making sure the stories are free of mistakes and misspellings, and there are fewer reporters doing the work.

Morning news staff meetings at KMOL and other television stations during the 1980s routinely consisted of assignment editors cutting out newspaper articles and handing them to reporters to turn into that day's video news. I noticed then that many television reporters didn't have a lot of experience working as beat reporters. Television news was for the most part superficial and quickly done—that too was part of the deregulation of the media. With television stations trying to build profits by holding back on staff, there was a downward pressure on salaries for most people—

except for the anchors who smiled and brought in the ratings. A typical television package consisted of two sound bites, copy that was read by the reporter over the video the viewer watched, a "stand-up" when you saw the reporter on camera telling you something, and an intro by one or two anchors and maybe an outro read live at the anchor desk to close out the story—though more than likely not.

In the KMOL newsroom, the *San Antonio Light* and the *San Antonio Express-News* were equally used as sources of news. The *Light* seemed at times better written, better sourced, and more serious, but at other times, the *Express-News* prevailed. The crime beat, my main beat unless the legislature was in session or the president visited town, was populated by some of the most colorful reporters I ever knew. The *Express News* shined with crime reporter Tom "Kid Death" Edwards. He and David Elizondo (a straight-up John Belushi look-alike) from the *Light* were two of the hardest-baked crime reporters in San Antonio—a city known for its violent crimes and murders—including a huge controversy surrounding a serial-killing vigilante police officer Stephen Smith and his demise at the hands of fellow officer and partner Ferrell Tucker. Tucker later went on to infamy as the man who welcomed the public and police officers into the main police station in downtown San Antonio—the only post he was allowed to hold for years after a jury exonerated him for killing his murderous partner. The scandal cost two police chiefs their jobs and sparked an $8 million lawsuit by eleven families who claimed they were victims of Smith's vigilante attacks. In their final arguments, prosecutors said that Tucker, age thirty-six, probably killed Smith, age thirty-one, to save his own job. Tucker said that he shot Smith in self-defense and claimed that Smith, who was on suspension on brutality charges, planned to kill then–Assistant Police Chief Frank Hoyack, Deputy Chief Robert Heuck, and then–Bexar County District Attorney Sam Millsap.

One day when covering a triple murder, David and Tom found each other talking shop at a crime scene. The parking lot at an office complex was littered with blood, spent bullet casings, and a huge pile of gelatinous blood and sinew.

Elizondo, munching on a mountainous sandwich from the Pig Stand, a local eatery on Broadway, eyed the blood trails and entrails before musing on the gelatinous mound of blood he had taken a special interest in. Edwards eyed it as he munched on his own sandwich.

"What you got here is brain blood," Elizondo said. He took a big bite out of his sandwich and then sucked on the straw supplying him a Coke.

"Oh yeah," Edwards said with appreciation. "Nothing like brain blood. Like jelly."

In case you miss the point, reporters who covered crime and police who covered crime often adopted a dark sense of humor—as many cops do—because of the number of dead bodies we often saw in the course of doing our job—often found in the most horrifying states of decomposition or twisted states of torture. Crime beat reporters were required to stay close to the action in the city. There were a healthy number of us and a healthy number of crimes. We were at the end of an era, though, and we didn't know it. Today, most major cities do not have the number of people covering crime who covered San Antonio in 1989. Each television station had at least one overnight photographer. Ours was a part-time fireman named "Daffy," who carried a camera and got overnight video and the occasional interview for every car wreck, fire, plane wreck, shooting, stabbing, freak storm, or anything else that happened from 11 p.m. until the morning crew pulled in before the crack of dawn. Every television station, every newspaper, and most radio stations staffed this one beat with multiple people not only because of the volume of news but also because, in San Antonio, "If it bleeds, it leads" wasn't just a cliché. It drove ratings.

At that time in the 1980s and early 1990s, there was a huge move toward covering "harder" news—which in television was a euphemism for spot and breaking news. It was easier to cover a fire with "really neat flame video," as one KMOL producer always said, or a shooting than to spend hours or days trying to decipher the inner workings of city hall or public policy. It was cost effective (i.e., cheaper) and appealed to more viewers (i.e., lowest common denominator) and was usually noncontroversial (everyone watches sports, big weather, big crimes, and fires). There was a similar move in newspapers, but it led to different results. *Editor and Publisher* reported that Bill Kovach, the former *New York Times* Washington, D.C., bureau chief, took over the *Atlanta Constitution and Journal* and, wanting to make it a "world class" newspaper group, planned to stop concentrating on the sway of columnists each with "his constituency and viewpoints" and return to hard news reporting. "Reporters here feel like somebody opened the cage doors and said, Fly. Baby Bly," Wendell Rawls, a Pulitzer Prize–winning and one-time *New York Times* Atlanta bureau chief, said. Newspapers then were having the same problem cable networks have now. Of the columnists who left or were pushed out, only one of them signed on with CNN.[2]

For newspapers, the move was toward providing *substance*. In television, it was flash over substance—and the flash won. Although that same year newspaper industry officials cheered Judge Harold Greene's decision preventing regional Bell Operating Companies from providing their own information services for at least three years, the handwriting was on the wall for newspapers—despite whatever attempt they could or would make to provide in-depth coverage of news. The people using newspapers as their primary source for news would fall, while those using television stations and cable providers as a primary source for news would rise. Those broadcasters would continue to use newspapers for their source, but the newspapers—facing the increased competition—could not supply the information they once did, at least not as quickly. Today, anyone with a cell phone at a fire, shooting, natural disaster, or any other spot news event can instantly livestream the event. By the time a live truck, camera operator, producer, and reporter get to the site of a breaking news event, it may well be over. Live television cannot keep up with livestreaming—provided someone with a smartphone is on scene. That's approximately equivalent to what happened with newspapers once microwave technology took over and television stations made "extra" editions of newspapers obsolete. Microwave live shots used line of sight to the television tower to enable television stations to broadcast live—which kept most live shots within approximately a thirty-mile range of the station from which they originated. Once television stations and networks began using satellite technology to broadcast from anywhere on the planet—live—newspapers were never able to keep up on spot news.

That type of technology cost money, and until deregulation, only the largest stations and the networks invested heavily in the technology. Some stations had their own traffic helicopter. Most had at least one live truck, and many had multiple live trucks. The investment in the technology paid off and gave the stations something to sell. When stations began buying each other up, it became easier to afford the technology and was a convenient method by which the stations and networks convinced their audience they were on top of things. "We have the latest technology!"

There just wasn't room for newspapers anymore, and those on shoestring budgets became, like the *Light*, among the first to fall.

Still, there was a healthy competition among all of the reporters in San Antonio when I got into town in 1988 as the dayside police beat reporter for KMOL. My own opinion was, if you get an exclusive story off of my beat on Monday, watch your ass on Tuesday because I'll beat you on the beat. Reporters were not privy to the budgets. We didn't know about the ongoing constriction in the business. Sure, through our subscriptions to *Editor and Publisher*, we knew some of the problems in our business, but those seemed distant. Reporters in the field still operated as they always had—trying to get the best story, first and factual. The fact was it didn't matter. The television stations and the newspapers were being so horribly managed that journalism, like the kind that many dreamed of practicing, simply ceased to exist. In its place was "feel-good news" and live shots— lots and lots of live shots for no other reason than we had the capability to do them and by doing them we justified the expense, so more money was spent on the live trucks. Thus was a vicious cycle born.

Politicians in Texas and elsewhere across the country remained as they always had been: horrible. While covering a public school education bill that generated some controversy, Carl Parker, a state senator and the author of the bill, called me a jerk when he got irritated at a question I asked. "If you've been here and you've seen what's been going on and you can't tell whether or not I've worked for the interest of all of the children of this state, you don't deserve an answer and you're a jerk," he told me. I replied, "Thank you" as I continued to ask him my question. "I've talked to you all I'm going to," he responded and told me not to "push your luck." Later, when the controversial measure hit the Senate floor, my photographer found himself unable to get a shot because Dallas Republican Senator O. H. "Ike" Harris kept leaning into his camera. I quietly asked him to move, motioning him to do so. "Look buddy, I'm a state senator, and I can stand where I want to," he screamed. For this, I was asked to leave the Senate.[3]

Reporters have to be on the ground and in the thick of things. They should never be bullied by politicians and have to hold them accountable. Politicians are not leaders—though they can be. They are public servants, and I've never held any one of them up as virtuous or idolized or bowed to any of them.

As media constriction began, news organizations often found themselves paying for coverage in ways they hadn't thought about. News services and public relations firms sometimes produced and sold video packages that some local stations then ran as news pieces. But the stations paid in less direct ways. Two stories from Texas can illustrate the problems in local news during that time. Hurricane Gilbert is the first.

In the second week of September 1988, during the height of hurricane season, Hurricane Gilbert formed in the Gulf of Mexico and headed for the east coast of southern Texas and the northern coast of Mexico. Naturally, a weather system that large and potentially devastating was a major local story for newspapers, radio stations, and television stations. Moreover, it was an opportunity to make money. Television stations with satellite trucks could help pay for the behemoths by selling time to stations that did not possess or could not get their satellite trucks to the affected area. I, one other reporter, two photographers, and our assistant news director who executive produced our coverage headed to Corpus Christi, where the hurricane was scheduled to make landfall. The "Texas Ranger," KMOL-TV's satellite truck, was brand new. I had done the first live shot with the Ranger outside of Eagle Pass just a few weeks previously for a violence-on-the-border piece. You could still smell the paint on the truck as we pulled into Alice, Texas, some seventy miles from where we expected the worst of the hurricane. There was literally no weather there for the first two days. We drove from Alice to Corpus Christi and then back to Alice in the evening to perform our live shots and feed our packages. To make money, the station sold time in five-minute increments to stations all across the country that wanted to send reporters or their weather crew to cover the hurricane. This led to some unintended hilarity. One night, a weatherman from Alabama did his stand-up in the parking lot of a motel where we parked the Texas Ranger. A cricket walked across the man's shoulders during his five-minute live shot as horns from truckers and jake brakes operated in the background. There wasn't a cloud in the sky where we were, and some wondered out loud if the cricket got the American Federation of Television and Radio Artists minimum. The worst was an anchor crew from somewhere in the South who did part of their nightly show live from the Alice parking lot. They wore yellow rain slickers and had an intern splash them with water to complete the illusion that we were in harm's way.

On September 17, the storm finally made landfall in northern Mexico with winds of 135 miles per hour causing a tidal storm surge of up to five feet. The damage was minimal in the United States, but northern Mexico got pounded pretty good. I spent that day trying to do a stand-up on the top of a motel near Corpus Christi Bay. I got blown over by a gust of wind, and my photographer and I grabbed on to a standpipe. As we looked behind us, we saw that a tornado had formed nearly overhead and headed off into the distance to become a waterspout in the bay. Tornadoes turned out to be the worst part of Gilbert, and San Antonio got the worst of it. It turns out I didn't have to go anywhere to cover the story—it had come to us. But the station made money and promoted the coverage for weeks.

The silly part of covering news in Texas was a relief from the serious. As mentioned earlier, covering news in San Antonio could be costly. Satellite trucks, microwave live trucks, cameras, tape, edit facilities, and newsrooms were all fixed costs for television as printing presses, ink, paper, darkrooms, and chemicals were for newspapers. The newspapers had the larger staffs and consequently broke most of the stories—those that weren't breaking news. The television stations had the technology and often took the newspaper coverage and turned it into television. Television and radio often beat newspapers on spot news but rarely broke stories otherwise. Some of us were arrogant enough to think we could change that—and sometimes we did. I often refused to take newspaper clippings and turn them into video stories—even if assigned them. Once I was handed a newspaper story and told to cover it. I read the story, and it was one that I had broken earlier in the week. The newspaper had followed me! I rolled up the newspaper and chucked it into the garbage.

This insubordination didn't make me many friends on the assignment desk. I was supposed to book interviews and a time to shoot videotape and a stand-up, then schedule a time when I could use a photographer to get my job done in time to get back to the shop and edit a two-minute story. Well, two minutes total time. I was expected to have a fifteen- to thirty-second wraparound on the set so our anchors would have something to do when they introduced my story.

I usually just headed out in the morning and took Roy Pedroza, who, more or less, was my photographer partner on the crime beat, and I made stops at the sheriff's department, police department, Drug Enforcement Administration, and so on. I made calls from the car and napped (if I could) as we drove, and by noon, I'd usually have a story that I'd tell the desk about. After quizzing me, the producer would determine where in the newscast the story would play. Sometimes it all got scrapped if something big broke, but usually things worked out well.

About six months after the hurricane, early on Monday, March 27, 1989, on a dark, cool morning, Henry David Hernandez and his brother Julian, after having a minor disagreement exacerbated by alcohol, pulled over their white Mercury Marquis into a vacant parking lot near the San Antonio beltway on the city's north side. They argued for a bit and then drove some more, finally pulling into an old abandoned Burger Boy restaurant near Broadway and I-410 where they continued arguing.

Police officer Gary Williams on overnight duty saw the pair. They were young Hispanics and driving in and out of parking lots—enough to arouse suspicion in Williams's mind and thus give him probable cause to pull them over.

The last six months had been considerably violent in San Antonio—in a city known for it. I had left standing instructions for Daffy, the overnight photographer, to call me at home no matter what time should there be any more police officer–involved shootings. Shortly after 2 a.m. that day, I got the call, and my wife drove me to the crime scene. All I knew when I got there was that police officer Gary Williams had been shot with his own service revolver and police were looking for two Hispanic brothers. As I arrived to meet with our overnight photographer, I saw the officer being placed into an ambulance. He seemed alert. I felt a sense of relief. Then I went to work.

A few hours later, Williams died. A few hours after that, a local attorney who claimed he represented the brothers said they would soon turn themselves in. I started to put together the story.

By noon that day, I'd already put in a ten-hour workday. I would stay working through past midnight that night—working nearly twenty-four hours straight. It yielded results. Through three different sources, I was able to secure a phone interview with Henry David Hernandez from jail. It was a difficult endeavor that involved confidential sources, some duct tape, and a microphone that sometimes worked and sometimes did not. In the interview, Hernandez admitted he shot the police officer. According to him, Williams approached the brothers with an attitude and pulled his gun on them, and they struggled for it before it fired and skirted the officer's Kevlar vest, ultimately killing him. The police surmised Henry, smaller and admittedly inebriated, had taken the gun from the officer with his brother's assistance and stuck the gun under Williams's vest, killing him in cold blood. The brothers said the officer had "some kind of attitude or something" and began fighting with them for no decent reason.

This local story soon became a national story, as both the prosecutors and attorneys from the American Civil Liberties Union who represented the Hernandez brothers wanted my raw tape and notes from the interview—as well as my confidential sources. NBC News declared the case could redefine reporters' rights for all reporters. I wrote extensively about this in *Shield the Source*, my first book.[4] But some of the specifics, in retrospect, speak to the end of a reporting era that I and others couldn't see at the time.

I was jailed four times fighting the subpoenas to give up my notes. The prosecutor often said they couldn't have a case without them. They did. The defense attorneys from the American Civil Liberties Union (ACLU) kept saying they had to know what was in them and how I got my interview. I kept asking them—sometimes in court from the witness stand as I was hauled before a judge—why didn't they just ask their own client how it went down. They had better access to him than I did, and he knew far better than I whom he talked to and how he was able to call me from jail. The judges always liked that point, and I got kudos from the attorneys (especially the ACLU attorneys) and the judges for bringing it up—but I got no sympathy.

My sources became much more important when toxicology reports came back and showed that Williams had been speedballing (taking cocaine and heroin) the night of his death and perhaps really was acting overly aggressive to the two brothers. The racism of the police department and the city came out into the light in the case as some questioned out loud why two poor Hispanic brothers were out late at night on the city's upper east side if they weren't up to no good.

But more than anything else, the story highlighted the need for decent local reporting, the need to stay with a story, and the commitment that it takes to defend the stories. A wise man once said good journalism is always about bringing up information people want buried—otherwise, it's nothing more than propaganda. But doing real journalism costs real money. KMOL and its owner, United Television, had to pay hundreds of thousands of dollars to defend me in court as my case made its way up the judiciary ladder. Finally, it landed before the U.S. Supreme Court. In one of Justice William Brennan's final moves at the Court, he asked the Court to decide whether in the case of *Karem v. Priest* (named for Pat Priest, the local judge who first threw me in jail) I could be released from jail while I pursued my case in the Supreme Court. By a 5–4 decision, the Court decided I should stay in jail.

A few days later, my last source in the case came forward—after Sheriff Harlon Copeland named her (it had been one of his deputies who also helped me set up the telephone call with Hernandez that produced the confession). And after four times going to jail, the last time for a week and a half, I was finally freed.

In the years since then, reporters have asked me how I handled being in jail. I have said point blank that it was the support from the station, my news director, his executive producer, and our attorney Larry Macon that made it possible for me to survive. I've been asked this dozens of times in the past thirty years, and as I tell these reporters what it took to support me and how much money it costs, increasingly I've been told that today they are sure their station wouldn't support them. Investigative reporting has almost ceased to exist at most television stations. One former investigative reporter told me that stations won't back hard-core reporting for the fear they'll end up in court paying extensive legal fees like United Television did. One reporter lamented that he was reduced to doing investigative stories about the amount of soap in automatic car wash machines and comparing the amount of cheese on pizzas from local pizzerias. "No one wants you to investigate city hall. No one wants you to investigate the cops, and no one knows how to investigate the government," I've been told on numerous occasions. All of this occurred after Ronald Reagan began to allow news broadcasters to buy each other up.

Following my court case of *Karem v. Priest*, which ended up being considered by the Supreme Court, the National Press Club flew me to Washington to accept the Freedom of the Press Award on March 14, 1991.

I had been back from the Gulf War for two days.

I attended a couple of briefings in the White House on Wednesday and then went to New York. There at a lunch, I met Walter Cronkite. It was, quite simply, one of the greatest honors for me as a young reporter. He was polite and engaging, and I enjoyed our conversation. I asked him about his famous incident on set about the Vietnam War. I will never forget what he said to me. "It was the right thing to do. I've been asked about it many times. And I wouldn't do it differently. You owe your audience the truth." It wasn't much different than what Ben Bagdikian had said: the obligation is to the people, not to who pays you, your editor, or your sources.

But as Cronkite acknowledged to me that day, it was becoming increasingly difficult for reporters to do what they need to do without the financial backing of the corporations that give them their voice. "American journalism is in trouble," he told me. A September 1991 headline in *TV Guide* asked, "Is network news crumbling?" If it wasn't crumbling, we certainly knew by then where television news and news in general were going. "The American people, I am convinced, really detest free speech and at the slightest alarm they are ready and eager to put it down," H. L. Mencken said in *The Diary of H. L. Mencken*, published posthumously in 1991.[5]

The events of the 1990s would bring that idea into sharp focus.

7

YOU'RE A LITTLE DOG

One of the lessons the American military learned from the Vietnam War was that pictures of soldiers or civilians getting killed tend to motivate the citizens of this country to stand up and protest an active war. It is hard to forget the image of "Uncle Walter" Cronkite uncharacteristically denouncing U.S. involvement in Vietnam on national television after he covered the aftermath of the Tet Offensive. On February 27, 1968, at the end of a CBS Special Report, "Report from Vietnam: Who, What, When, Where, Why?," Cronkite offered a rare editorial that stunned the nation. What Cronkite saw in Vietnam so moved him that it forced him to step outside his role as a balanced, unbiased newsman and to be blunt with the American people. In his editorial, he said that to believe we are winning the war is to trust in the optimists who have been wrong in the past. "To say that we are mired in stalemate seems the only realistic if unsatisfactory conclusion." He then made it plain. "It seems to this reporter that the only rational way out then will be to negotiate."[1]

On seeing the editorial, President Lyndon Johnson reportedly said, "If I've lost Cronkite, I've lost middle America." A few weeks later, he announced he was not going to run for reelection in 1968.

Johnson and the military learned a lesson from Cronkite that night, but the military's reaction was not that of the president's. More than twenty years after Tet, what the military learned was to try to micromanage coverage—and to some extent they were successful in doing so. Since the time of the Vietnam War, the U.S. military had seen some limited military action in places like Grenada and some catastrophes like the destruction and death at a barracks in Beirut, Lebanon. But there had not been a massive movement of troops in more than fifteen years. By the time of Operation Desert Shield and then Operation Desert Storm, it was obvious the American war machine had sufficiently recovered from the Vietnam debacle to reassert itself in an appropriately oversized fashion.

After Saddam Hussein's Iraqi regime overplayed its hand and invaded Kuwait, a move he mistakenly thought the United States would support, President George H. W. Bush had an opening. He gathered a coalition of countries for a nice, neat little war with allies signed on, an isolated opponent, and little chance of pushback from either Russia or China in the offing. The Gulf War posed one public relations problem: how do you show a war without bloodshed? The answer: arcade-style videos showing smart bombs plunging into buildings in flashes of white. The military also pioneered another idea during the Gulf War: military-chaperoned visits to the front for reporters. Those chaperoned visits would later become "embedded" reporters during the next Gulf War and during other military ventures.

The idea was that chaperones could act as censors and control the access, video, and information they were providing to the reporters whom they brought to the front and at the same time give the appearance of unfettered access to the major networks, newspapers, and wire services. Covering the Gulf War was not unlike covering the White House. There were dozens if not hundreds of reporters mulling around the Dhahran International Hotel who attended briefings, ate from a smorgasbord in the lobby, and worked hours away from the front while covering the Gulf War. The Joint Information Bureau (JIB), headquartered in the hotel, was fond of telling reporters how many checkpoints existed between Dhahran and the front and how they were heavily manned by no-nonsense U.S. troops. The JIB officers told plenty of horror stories of reporters being held at gunpoint by angry Military Police (MPs) who apparently were as eager to shoot reporters as any Iraqi.

Then they'd tell the story about CBS reporter Bob Simon. Simon was captured by Iraqi forces when he crossed the border between Saudi Arabia and Iraq without a military chaperone and spent forty days held captive—mostly in solitary confinement—until he was freed. He later said it was a stupid mistake that he regretted making. Simon was a luminary and a mentor to many young reporters who came to respect the man who had covered every major world conflict since 1969. After Simon died in 2015 in a car accident, Dan Rather told CNN that Simon was the rarest of reporters. "He didn't just witness history, he strived to understand it. Yes, he was fearless when bullets were flying, but he also never blinked when staring down a despot or thug in an interview. . . . He knew when he was being lied to or toyed with, and rather than shirk from the challenge, he would embrace it and become more determined to expose the truth. . . . There was no issue he couldn't cover, no story he couldn't tell."[2]

The military used Simon's capture in the opening of the Gulf War as a cautionary tale of what could happen to reporters who ventured out on their own. Meanwhile, when it came to another reporter and crew, they chose to completely discredit them outright. Peter Arnett, Bernard Shaw, and John Holliman at CNN found themselves in Baghdad and with an open phone line as a means to broadcast when the bombs began falling on January 17, 1991. Our military spokesmen, including Pete Williams, who later went on to work for NBC, told us of the precision bombing by "smart bombs," which sounded like they'd knock on a door and ask for identification before blowing up in the enemy's face. Arnett's reporting included accounts of civilian casualties and was not well received by the U.S. coalition attacking Saddam Hussein's regime. White House sources would go on to attack Arnett and claim he was being used as a propaganda tool by the Iraqi government. Two weeks into the war, Arnett got an exclusive, uncensored interview with Saddam Hussein, and the Gulf War thus went on to become the first war to be broadcast live on television. It boosted CNN's audience numbers across the world, diminished the efforts of traditional broadcast companies that didn't televise the war 24/7, and devalued the impact of newspapers and wire services that could not keep up with the speed of the war and the news coming out of the Middle East.[3] The news cycle went into hyperdrive.

In an appearance at the National Press Club immediately on his return to the United States on March 19, 1991, Arnett spoke about his coverage of the war. He spoke about Iraqi military censors and how some of them knew little about what Arnett did or how to censor it. But he also spoke about the accusations of the U.S. government against him and how he believed the American people. "I don't think, as I suggested in my prepared remarks, I don't think the U.S. public really has a real concept of what the press does. Part of it, we are to blame."[4]

That ignorance, combined with the military's desire to obfuscate the facts, led to a wide variety of problems covering the Gulf War and a lot of confusion. It also led to accusations against Arnett and accusations of anti-Americanism leveled at the press in general.

The stain of Vietnam was apparent throughout the Pentagon's moves and filtered down to individual combat and support units that still had, in many cases, personnel who were Vietnam War veterans. Sergeant Robert Blocker of the 41st Combat Support Hospital (CSH) said before the first shots were fired that his biggest struggle was "keeping morale up" among the younger soldiers in his charge. Ken Jonson was among those who said that "one of the biggest fears is that people will quit supporting us and it will turn around on us like it did in Vietnam."[5]

The 41st CSH was stationed at "Bamcee" (Brooks Army Medical Center) in San Antonio, Texas. When it was active and training locally, the hospital might see stray shootings or car accidents, and, as it turned out, that was perfect training for Saudi Arabia. I traveled with the hospital unit to Saudi Arabia during Thanksgiving week in 1990, interviewing Colonel Bob Abodeely, the unit's commanding officer; his executive officer, Major Tom Wittman; and as many of the 300 members of the unit as I could in order to tell the story of a modern MASH-like hospital deploying into a hot war zone.

On my return, I produced a half-hour documentary called *Good to Go* about the 41st CSH before Christmas. San Antonio was and is a military town. At the time, there were five bases in town: Kelly, Lackland, and Randolph air force bases as well as Fort Sam Houston and Camp Bullis. The 41st CSH, stationed at Fort Sam Houston, was to be in the thick of it if and when the shooting started—reportedly, it would be the forward-most deployed hospital in the theater of battle, in other words the closest to the front. The documentary I produced showed the hospital in training, packing and leaving for the Gulf. It featured interviews with the doctors, nurses, support staff, as well as friends, family, and loved ones of the hospital. The documentary I produced would be bestowed several awards, including a Texas AP award. It was a story that could not be told on a national level. It was an intimate and very personal tale including the birth of a child while the father was overseas serving his country, a taped marriage proposal from a deployed soldier to his very accepting fiancée in San Antonio, and a tale of a young married couple who traveled to war together. By Christmas, it was clear I would return to Saudi Arabia, and after the bombing began, I found myself along with fellow KMOL reporter Gabe Caggiano back in the Middle East by the end of January. The first time I traveled to Saudi Arabia was as a guest of the military to cover the hospital's deployment. I came back after working out a deal with NBC to help supplement the network coverage and after the station I worked for, KMOL, agreed to pay more than $15,000 in expenses for the monthlong stay.

Colonel Larry Icenogle, a pit bull in uniform, lashed out at me in the JIB at the Dhahran International Hotel.

"What are you doing here?" he asked me. "I mean, why are you here? The networks are here. The big dogs are all here. I don't have time for you. You're a little dog."

I had the audacity to believe I was in Saudi Arabia to talk to Texans involved in Operation Desert Storm and cover a war for millions of viewers in the Lone Star State. I had set up shop in the NBC bureau and worked with Steve Handelsman, Brad Willis, Mike Boetcher, and Arthur Kent—the "Scud Stud" who had been trying to cover a war from a well-lighted stage on the roof of the Algosabi Hotel in Dhahran for two weeks.

The trip into Dhahran had been dicey, and since our arrival, the JIB had shown no interest in helping me get to the front lines where I knew the 41st CSH had deployed.

The major newspapers and television networks had leveled plenty of criticism at the military's attempt to control coverage of the buildup and the consequent war—but they didn't have to fight to get noticed. Those of us who weren't with the major dailies, wire services, or networks had a hell of a time getting the military to acknowledge our existence. Although I was providing news for a city with five military bases and believed that would be of some importance—especially to those in the military—I was routinely told to "go away."

KMOL was an NBC affiliate, so the NBC bureau didn't mind using our resources to augment their own coverage. Cameras, tapes, and two reporters who could also shoot and edit video proved to be invaluable, and the NBC producer, Heather Allen, not only thanked me but also helped point out people I could talk to in order to try to get into the pool rotation to travel to a forward location. But most people in the military's JIB were not honest. Icenogle was combative and insulting, but he didn't lie to me. I bluntly explained to him one afternoon, about four days into my sojourn, that I was tired of being lied to. I requested on numerous occasions to visit the 41st CSH.

"We can't find them," one military press officer told me.

"What do you mean you can't find them? They're a hospital," I said.

"Well, we have no communication with them. They're just out there somewhere," I was told with a straight face. I was left with the impression that 300 people were mindlessly wandering through the desert searching for the meaning of life. Another communications officer told me that the JIB had spoken to the 41st CSH and that they "don't want to see you now." Part of my preparation for finding them was contacting the commanding officer's wife—as well as the wife of the executive officer. Both had spoken recently with their husbands. They supplied a map showing the approximate location of the mobile hospital as well as gifts they wanted me to give to their husbands. I knew the folks in the JIB were lying.

Icenogle said he felt sorry for me and arranged for me to show up at Dhahran International Airport with gear at 10 a.m. the next morning to visit the 114th Evacuation Hospital with a reluctant member of the JIB as my chaperone—I guess as some sort of consolation prize. Still, it never worked out. The trip was canceled at the last minute, and I got furious. "Why was the trip canceled?" I asked. "Well, they've taken some casualties and can't have visitors," my JIB escort told me. The ground war was still more than ten days away at that point, so naturally I was curious as to what casualties the hospital was handling. A very nice major told me not to ask those questions. The military didn't want us there. They didn't want to assist us in any way possible, and they intended to make sure that no one else could do what Arnett, Shaw, and Holliman had done for CNN. "No unilateral trips without escort," I was told repeatedly. Icenogle told me bluntly why I was not getting help. "We know you don't care about what's best for the military," Icenogle said.

Some of the older technicians and photographers who had covered the Vietnam War were pressed into service for the Gulf War and thought the military was attempting to brand it and sterilize the war experience as much as possible. "They don't want us covering the war because they don't want public opinion to get away from them," I was told by more than one old hand.

The military was quite good about keeping you away from the action. There were roadblocks set up throughout Saudi Arabia, and they routinely turned back reporters who tried to get past them without an escort.

I was determined to resort to subterfuge. I got all the gear I could from the NBC bureau, some load-bearing equipment that had been given to me on my trip when the 41st CSH deployed, some camouflage gear, flak jackets, ponchos, gas masks, and everything else I needed to convince someone at first glance I was a soldier. I wouldn't lie if asked, but if no one asked, I wasn't going to volunteer anything. Caggiano and I rented a Nissan 4 by 4 and I took some gray gaffer's tape and installed the gel panel on the roof I'd seen the military vehicles post—apparently something that identified to airborne members of the military who liked to fire missiles at strange-moving trucks that you were Americans so that the airborne troops wouldn't shoot your ass. The other thing I installed was the giant upside-down "V" with tape that also visually identified you as an allied vehicle.

Furious, I gathered my helmet, flak jacket, and poncho and walked over to the NBC bureau and told Heather Allen, the NBC producer who oversaw all the activities of the NBC correspondents. Handelsman, who did most of the coverage for the NBC affiliates, asked what I had in mind. I told him I was planning to run the checkpoints and get to the front. He wished me luck and told me it would be a good idea to see if I could get the countersign to the password I would be challenged with should I go. Honestly, until he told me this, I hadn't thought of it. The MP I had wrangled that day reluctantly fessed up that the sign was "kitchen sink" and that the countersign was "footstool." I thanked him and asked him if he wanted to go with me. He just laughed.

I next consulted with my old friend Sam Donaldson, who told me the French reporters were supposedly experts at checkpoint running and could give me good advice on how to get to the front. My goal was to get to visit the 41st CSH since I'd deployed with them when they first traveled to Saudi Arabia. To get to them was the equivalent of a trip from Houston to Dallas via San Antonio—about 700 miles. And I wasn't exactly sure where they were but figured a hospital wouldn't be hiding. Loaded up with water and Meals Ready-to-Eat (MREs) as well as a bunch of chocolate bars, Caggiano and I made our way north.

It took me twelve hours of driving through dozens of checkpoints to get to the border of Saudi Arabia and Iraq. Most the time, I just got waved through the checkpoints without a care. My costume worked. I even had a beautiful Kevlar helmet, and to sell it, I chewed up a cigar and clinched it in my teeth and gave a little growl.

Only twice in my first trip north did I get stopped. The first time was about three hours into our journey—just outside of Hafir al Batin. A military gas tank had overturned, and traffic was rerouted through the sand. Tapline Road, the main supply route to the northwest of the country, was little more than a single-lane highway. It was called Tapline Road because it was actually a maintenance road that ran the length of a huge oil pipeline that crossed the northern part of Saudi Arabia. A young soldier approached us as we stopped at the makeshift checkpoint.

"See you guys got everything in that truck but a footstool," he said.

"Yeah. We even have a kitchen sink," I said, giving the countersign.

"I said, you guys—footstool," he frowned.

"I know. Kitchen sink," I said.

He looked at our equipment. He looked at us. He looked at Caggiano. He looked at me.

"Say, who you guys with?"

I smiled.

"You ain't military," he declared. I sheepishly smiled. He looked down at the ground, then looked right at me. "Have a nice day," he said and waved me through.

Apparently, the JIB's admonition about angry and petulant MPs ready to shoot stray reporters was a bit oversold.

The next time I ran into trouble driving was on Tapline Road (also called MSR Dodge by the military—or Main Supply Route "D") just outside of Rhafa. There, a young MP caught me in the full light of the early morning sun and told me right away he didn't care if I knew the password, he knew "damn well you ain't no military." His southern drawl was almost cartoonish, but I wasn't going to argue. So, I struck up a conversation and told him why we were in the country and why we were risking our necks without a military escort to get to a hospital that might soon be treating casualties. He said he understood. He was young and feared getting killed. He wished he could say something to his mother and father. I told him, "Actually you can." I picked up the camera, stuck it in his face, and handed him a microphone. "What would you like to tell them?" I asked. He told me where he lived—outside of Houston—and then spoke to his mom and dad. "I hope I get home, and I love you," he closed his brief greeting. It was the first of dozens of such greetings we would videotape during the next few weeks. I had done that for many members of the 41st CSH when I deployed with them, and I knew it was one thing the rank and file really appreciated—a chance, before the time of livestreaming, to send a video message to a loved one. After that, any time we had trouble at a checkpoint, we found that the common soldier had more in common with us than the brass and was encouraged and enjoyed having us around. Not only did our videotaped messages from the troops to family members play well on KMOL, but we gave many of those greetings from soldiers outside of Texas to NBC, which also used dozens of them.

By the time we got to Rhafa, it was very early the next morning, and the outskirts of the city looked like something out of a Mad Max movie. I'm still not sure what the different monuments were, but there was no denying the dystopian-like vibe. I had no idea where the 41st CSH was in the area, but I figured some of the soldiers around might. We happened on a group of them at a public pay-phone bank (remember those?) near the center of town. I approached one young man leaving a phone and asked him if he knew where the 41st CSH had set up. He said he didn't but there was a guy he knew who recently went there after a car accident, and that guy was in the restaurant across the street. So, Caggiano and I walked across the street and sat down. The restaurant was named Yomammah, and it served fried chicken, Syrian bread, and Coca-Colas. The menu said southern Kentucky. The decor felt like southern Nuevo Laredo, Mexico. We took a seat at a booth after ordering and looked around. There were probably twenty or so soldiers milling around inside—including a table of mercenaries in the back who looked for all the world like the French Foreign Legion. Turns out they were.

I found a guy whose arm was in a sling, and he told me approximately where the 41st CSH was located—not too far from where we sat. "What happened?" I asked about his injury. "Car wreck. I was driving a truck and swerved to avoid a local," he explained. I nodded. Tough luck. Travel to a war and get hurt in a car accident. Caggiano and I ate our food, drank our Coca-Colas, and then headed back to our Nissan before leaving. "Wait up," our tour guide said. "I'll go with you. I need to see a doctor again anyway." With that, he hopped in, and five minutes later, we found ourselves at the outer gate of the 41st CSH—in the middle of a war, in northern Saudi Arabia, not four days after we landed in Riyadh. A short time later, we found ourselves in the tent of Colonel Bob Abodeely, the commanding officer, and we were mutually happy to see one another.

I handed a box filled with smoked oysters to the colonel and a box wrapped in a plain brown wrapper to Tom Wittman, his executive officer, who diligently unwrapped the package to expose a box of *Playboy* magazines. "Boy, I love my wife," the man said. I shuddered. I had no idea what was in the box. I didn't open it. His wife didn't tell me. But I traveled to a repressive country that gave me a full-body search when I entered. I wondered what would've happened if they'd opened that box.

The biggest news we learned that day was that the ground war, long suspected, would begin within the week. We also learned about one of the most untold stories of the Gulf War. We had witnessed several traffic accidents on our drive to the front, and as it turns out, there was a very good reason for that—and one of the reasons our handlers in Dhahran didn't want us to travel to the hospital. As explained to us by some of the doctors at the hospital, the Saudi government was partially to blame.

About a decade before the beginning of the Gulf War, the Saudis made a deal with Toyota for the purchase of thousands of pickup trucks. These white pickups with flame decals on the side were ubiquitous in the hinterlands of Saudi Arabia, and there was a good reason for that. The government had given them out to the native Bedouin as a means of transportation to replace the equally ubiquitous camels in the desert. The plan was widely praised and wildly accepted. There was just one problem, as a doctor explained it to me. "They didn't teach the Bedouin how to drive or anything else about the rules of the road." This led to thousands of deaths as the Bedouin would throw up their hands and say, "In Shallah," or "Whatever God Wills," in some very dicey situations. So, just prior to the Gulf War, the Saudi government determined that God willed that people who owned the trucks should know how to drive and be vaguely aware of the rules of the road. Still, many of them had never encountered any traffic out in the desert. Sand dunes are not fun, but if you run into one while driving, your chances of survival remain high. Unfortunately, when the American military showed up and tried to run two-way traffic down single-lane Tapline Road to deliver tanks and other military equipment, it led to a lot of serious traffic accidents. The doctors of the 41st CSH remained convinced there would be more Americans injured in traffic accidents during the Gulf War than would become casualties of war due to being injured in battle. The situation was so serious that when the ground war began, we saw MPs set up along the side of the road with radar guns trying to keep traffic speeds down. I always wondered how you would defend that ticket in traffic court. "I was on my way to kill Saddam Hussein, but I got caught doing seventy in a forty-five-mile-per-hour zone, your honor."

We spent about two hours at the front shooting a variety of stories. One of the last shots I took was of a pensive young soldier on his knees overlooking an empty desert while observing the setting sun. When Heather Allen saw the video when we got back to Dharan, she used it as the closing piece of video on the NBC Nightly News. But that was twelve hours down the road as we left that morning. We hoped to be back in the NBC bureau on the east coast of Saudi Arabia by dawn, making it basically a one-day turnaround. But the cost was taxing—no sleep, no food (except MREs), and limited places to refuel. Once, as I decided to switch off driving duties, Caggiano ran out of gas. We were both extremely tired. I had to leave him with all of our equipment on the side of the road while I hitched a ride ten miles behind us to get to a gas station. My limited ability to speak Arabic served me well that day. We also had car trouble. The Nissan sputtered to a stop once, bogged down as if it were out of gas when it wasn't. I removed a gas filter and blew out sludge and accumulated sand while a large American tank came riding over a berm and then headed off into the distance. "I drive them, I don't fix them," Caggiano said as I tried to get the Nissan running. Finally, that night as we left Hafir Al Batin on the road to Dhahran, both of us fell asleep. I was still driving. I don't know how long I was asleep, but I woke up driving through sand dunes and at first couldn't find the road. It was several hundred feet to my left, and in the inky darkness, with no lights, no traffic, and a new moon, the road was difficult to find. I was shivering as I drove. No matter how tired I was, I knew I wouldn't go back to sleep for a while. Caggiano woke up and looked over at me. "What was that?" he asked groggily. "Jackals," I said. "Big blue ones." He just rolled over and went back to sleep. We were in an editing bay in Dhahran after sunrise when he finally realized what I had said.

"Jackals?" he said with a wry smile.

"Yeah. I don't know. I fell asleep," I admitted.

Our intrepid network producer Heather Allen was happy with what we had obtained for KMOL and NBC after she debriefed us on our return. We had been able to get independent confirmation on when the ground war would begin—something the Pentagon was keeping under wraps—and we also came back with some unique video, interviews, and stories. After editing, eating, and showering and maybe with an hour of sleep under our belts, Caggiano and I went back to the JIB. This time, I had a letter written and signed by the commanding officer of the 41st CSH asking for us to be given an escort to their location just south of the Iraqi border.

"How did you get this?" a JIB officer asked me.

"What do you care? Just process it," I said flatly.

"Well, it'll take at least three to four weeks. We don't do unilaterals here," he said.[6]

At that point, we simply decided to be "pool busters," as Donaldson and others affectionately used the term. We ran checkpoints. We ignored the military, and we went after the story even as the military tried to keep us from it. We weren't the only ones who did it. I remember vividly listening to Heather Allen recommend that the networks and large newspapers quit sending their Pentagon or White House reporters and instead send "crime beat reporters who know how to cover news the cops don't want you to get." Heather was simply my favorite network producer I ever worked with—and that goes for my entire career. She had a wickedly sarcastic mind and was funny, hardworking, and very, very bright. She went on to become a senior producer for the Nightly News, but during the Gulf War, she was, in a very real sense, NBC News. Arthur Kent, known as the "Scud Stud" or "007" by some for his James Bond–like appearance and for his work standing on a rock-and-roll type of soundstage speaking to the country every night, was the face. But Heather was the soul. I remember once as Kent walked into the newsroom, he complained his soup was cold. "Why don't you blow on it 007? You're full of hot air," she said, smiling,

She encouraged independence and was not happy with the shackles the military tried to slap on the coverage. She told me once that the "video arcade footage is banal" and was not always happy with how the press—or some reporters in particular—seemed to cozy up to the military in hopes of greater access.

This was echoed by Tom Brokaw, who arrived in the country as the ground war began. He praised the efforts of "independent reporters such as yourself who got to combat hospitals and told the stories" and was not happy with how the military had tried to control access to the war. Caggiano and I visited the 41st CSH two more times before the ground war began and traveled with them as it began, spending a couple of days in a nine-mile-long convoy headed into Iraq. I was thankful the Iraqis had no air force, as that convoy was an undeniably large target, and the truck next to the one I was traveling in was filled with explosives. After staring at this for two days and getting no closer to the battle, I flagged down a National Guard helicopter and talked a pilot into returning me and Caggiano to our Nissan, which we left at the forward staging area near Rhafa. From there, I drove like a bat out of hell back to Dhahran. Caggiano and I changed clothes and loaded three twenty-gallon drums with gasoline along with our camera gear, MREs, and two cases of bottled water. Shortly before midnight on February 27, 1991, twenty-three years to the day after Cronkite made his announcement about the Vietnam War, I prepared to drive across the Saudi border into Kuwait to cover that nation's liberation during the Gulf War. On February 28, shortly after 2 a.m., I crossed the border at the very same point where Bob Simon was kidnapped several weeks earlier. At the border was a makeshift fortification of rusted-out cars the Iraqis had evidently tried to use to prevent American tanks from entering Kuwait. By the fires, general disarray, bomb craters, blood, and isolated body parts, it was obvious the efforts had been unsuccessful. Nearby was an Iraqi troop transport that had been hit. I don't know how many were killed or had been inside, but the skin of the soldiers was blackened like overdone barbecue, and the bones I saw looked bleached white. A U.S. MP I ran into didn't try to stop me but gave me directions to Kuwait City and urged caution. "There are land mines everywhere," he told me. Numerous bomb craters littered the highway and turned a three-hour trip into a six-hour trip. At one point in the middle of the night, we stopped to interview Saudi troops firing their guns into the air because they'd successfully turned back the Iraqis.

"We are so happy for our Kuwaiti brothers," one of the few who could speak English told us. We simply couldn't get much in the way of interviews. The soldiers were giddy and looked at our camera, surrounded us, and cheered uncontrollably. At another point in time, an Iraqi soldier with an AK-47 waved us to the side of the road. We'd heard they were giving themselves up to Americans, but I didn't stop to find out. He was armed with an AK-47, and I was armed with a Sony Betacam. We drove through the remains of a battle—or perhaps the heart of one. We saw tracer fire, heard tanks firing, and saw multiple explosions. As the sun started to rise, we could see multiple fires that threatened to turn the sky dark with soot from the oil fields the fleeing Iraqi troops had ignited.

We found our way to the U.S. embassy in Kuwait City. Across the street was a mobile hospital, but not the 41st CSH. They'd set up in Iraq and were handling casualties from the ground war, including some Iraqis who'd fled. Across the street from the U.S. embassy in Kuwait City was a luxurious hotel, and most of the American media settled there once the city was cleared. By the time we got there, that had only been, literally, hours previously.

Kuwait City was a nightmare. Fortifications littered the city, and it looked like a pack of ravaging teens had gone through the city and looted it. Clothing stores and handbag stores, grocery stores, and the local Walmart (or its equivalent) were all looted. The population, dazed from the occupation, came out to tell us stories of cruelty and fear during the months the Iraqis had occupied their city. Ali Azzaga, a chemical engineer, had been living in fear since the Iraqi occupation began the previous August. "Thanks, Mr. Bush," he told our camera. "You said you were going to kick his ass. And you really kicked his ass."

Today, there might be few in the Middle East who'd praise American military might, but Azzaga did. "You know what's hell? This is more than hell. I saw one person, twenty-five to thirty, left in the middle of the street. Did you see a man without a head, a woman with an ax in her head? I've seen these things."[7]

Some of the locals talked about secret police and pointed us in the direction of a burned-out building the Iraqi secret police had used to torture and kill the Kuwaiti citizens—and how American troops had neutralized it. There was an overall sense of joy among those who survived. They offered to cook us food. They cheered the arrival of the American troops, and everywhere we saw pro-American graffiti. I'd never seen anything like it before. The military had struggled so hard to keep us from covering the war up close and personal that in my opinion they screwed themselves. The small stories of survival and the genuine relief at seeing American troops was a story that had to be told on the small scale. Shots of smart bombs hitting roofs shown on the national news told one story. People cooking meals for American soldiers told another, deeper story. Once again, it showed me that governments, even our own, that contrive situations and try to control the media do so not only at their own peril from those who become angry at what a government does but also to its own detriment when it actually does something good.

Inside the NBC bureau that day, Tom Brokaw and I shared a little corner desk to write our scripts. He was writing for his news show. I was writing for the NBC affiliates—assisting Steve Handelsman, who did most of that work—and for KMOL-TV back home. There was blood on the bed in the suite—apparently there after an Italian photographer accidentally got some of his fingers blown up while handling a blasting cap. "This is a very dicey situation," I remember Brokaw saying. He wasn't wrong. Even as we settled into the hotel, the battle was still ongoing on the outskirts of town. Smoke, fire, and the sound of firearms, large and small, could be heard and seen from the hotel balcony overlooking the city that NBC was using to shoot the Nightly News.

Most of the crew traveled with the "flyaway"—the satellite dish used to broadcast the news. They traveled from Dhahran and through the thickest part of the fighting. All of the crew were tired, and some of them still suffered from the tension of being in battle. When a hot plate someone brought with them to boil water and make coffee burst into flames, a balding young producer popped up off a nearby couch, seemingly from a sound slumber, and put the fire out as we discussed ways to extinguish it before it became larger. "I hate fire," he said as he turned and looked at me. Then he turned back and returned to a supine position on the nearby couch as if he'd never been awake.

Part of preparing for the broadcast and live shot I was scheduled to do from Kuwait City that day included talking with our producers back in San Antonio. We had a satellite phone that was constantly turned on, and it led directly to NBC's New York studios. Through the magic of engineering, someone there made it possible for me to talk to our producer prior to going live so that I could walk them through the cues and other details. "So, describe Kuwait City to me," my producer said. "Look, I'm a little busy . . . ," I started. "Let me give you . . ."

"Hey, we sent you there. The least you could do is cooperate," I was told.

I sighed. I was in the middle of a war zone, and a producer in San Antonio wanted me to describe the wallpaper. I got through everything as quickly as I could, and after I heard the producer hang up after thanking me, there was a pause, and then I heard the NBC engineer from New

York. "Who was that asshole?" he asked. "One of our new producers," I replied.

"They get younger and dumber every year," the engineer said quietly.

Following our live shots that day, Caggiano and I drove away from Kuwait City, hoping to reconnect with the 41st CSH. On our way out of town, we ran into what looked like blobs of melted wax. Turns out American warplanes found some fleeing Iraqis and turned their convoy into the sea of death I feared might be the fate of the convoy I'd spent two days in. Again, we ran into more pro-American graffiti and finally found my favorite combat support hospital again. The hospital was handling casualties—Americans and Iraqis—as well as prisoners of war. As I approached a holding pen filled with these prisoners, I was told I was looking at the elite Republican Guard. I saw men in ragged clothing, suffering from sun exposure and the beginnings of malnutrition. They didn't look that elite and certainly didn't look like any Republican I'd ever met. Many of these prisoners had been in the desert as the United States carpet bombed their position for a couple of weeks. One of the more memorable events in my time in an empty desert was staring up at a beautiful sky absent of light pollution. It was humbling. But along with the beautifully dark skies came the occasional flash and the "boom, boom, boom" in the distance as the bombers delivered their payloads.

While standing outside of the pen of prisoners who'd been on the receiving end of that bombing, I watched personnel from the 41st CSH throw ChapStick and Vaseline to the prisoners to apply to their lips and sunburned faces. They ate them. I watched a guy unscrew an entire tube of ChapStick and eat it like an orange push up. Then, in the middle of this pile of sweating, smelly humanity, I saw a guy in blue jeans, wearing a Walter Payton Chicago Bears jersey. Sweetness.

So, I yelled out to him after I caught his attention. "Hey, do you speak English?" I asked.

"Of course." He eyed me as if I was mentally incapacitated. His English was impeccable. Not a hint of an accent—unless he was from the Midwest instead of the Middle East.

"Where are you from?" I asked.

"Chicago," he said as he grabbed his jersey. "See."

"Well what the hell are you doing in with the prisoners of war?" I inquired.

"I flew into Iraq to visit my grandparents, and they drafted me. Put me in a trench out in the desert. I got bombed every day for the last month. Now I'm here."

We shot several hours at the 41st CSH and spent time with a variety of soldiers, doctors, and nurses. It was a real-life version of MASH, but it had a Texas flavor and a cast of characters who told incredible stories and lived through a historic moment. The U.S. military had perhaps one of its brightest moments of nobility in my life. It's easy to be cynical about it, but for those who made the journey, it was all about liberating a friend and ensuring that a foe didn't bully them. You might say this was the American military at its absolute finest. Altruists among us may not agree, but I was there, and I know how much goodwill the United States built with that war—and in the way it struggled to limit casualties and damage and also dedicated itself to helping the area rebuild afterward.

Two factors led to this being underreported and many years later underappreciated. The first factor was the military striving and contriving to limit the coverage of the war. The fear left over by the Vietnam War did the American military absolutely no favors—and it did reporters a great detriment, as did our need to cover the war like a football game. Peter Arnett and others who struggled to tell a more detailed story were the exception. The other factor was the speed with which the ground war was waged. Saddam Hussein swore we'd swim in rivers of our own blood, but months of carpet bombing had decimated his forces, and it took only four days to finish up the ground war.

We could've done much more. Bush drew short of unseating Saddam. It had not been the mandate of the coalition. But on that day with the 41st CSH in the heart of Iraq, there was never any doubt that U.S. coalition forces could've easily taken Iraq's capital. I could see the city from where I stood. But our president, George H. W. Bush, had different plans and didn't want to go there. Kuwait was liberated in a brief ground war after months of buildup and weeks of incessant bombing. CNN led the coverage, and the networks and newspapers just couldn't keep up.

One night following the Battle of Khafji, I took the cell phone, a big brick ensemble that was mounted in our rented Nissan 4 by 4, and decided to see with all the communication nodes if, by chance, I could call home and talk to my wife. It had been weeks since we'd seen each other. Somehow my call got through. We spoke for about fifteen minutes, and I tried to catch her up on everything that had happened. As it turned out, she had watched it all on CNN. The channel had rarely changed since I'd left, except to tune in to the NBC Nightly News and local KMOL news because she wanted to see if I was on either newscast. I marveled at the advances in technology.

The Gulf War was the first real-time made-for-television news war. Information was instantaneously transferred from the theater of war to everyone's living room. The Vietnam War was a war delayed by film processing and a lack of satellite phones, satellite transmissions, and cell phones. Its dominant coverage came via the newspaper—every day on your front doorstep.

It lingered. It stayed with you. It seared into our nation's collective soul until the most trusted man in America called it out for the fiction it was.

Twenty-three years later, the Pentagon knew enough to keep its wars quick, clean, and as free of death as possible. They packaged and sold it to news organizations, which in turn broadcast it to the world—without having, in many cases, the access that allowed us to put the war into the proper context. And since it was over with so quickly, it was just as easily forgotten by the American public, and never was it properly dissected or discussed. America had come to save the day. We blew in and blew out of Iraq and Kuwait with hundreds of questions left unanswered and hundreds more unknown. The corporate media had a new way to cover the news. The newspapers had little time to catch up. And there were fewer reporters covering the war.

One of the questions I got often on my return home to Texas was "why?" Why did KMOL go to cover a war? We were a local news station. Sure, I worked hard for NBC while I was there, and I was thanked for it. The network even picked up the tab for a lot of our larger expenses. That was a relief to our accountants at KMOL—one of whom questioned my purchase of the Hershey chocolate bars that had been Caggiano's and my only source of food for two days while in the desert.

There was no doubt our efforts were appreciated. But why did I want to cover the war in the first place? It hadn't been assigned to me. I volunteered. Some of the more cynical among us thought I did it for myself because I thought it was "cool." Those people have never had a gun leveled at them as I did. Those people don't understand what news is—and, like Peter Arnett said when he got back to the United States and spoke to the National Press Club, I truly do not think the American public knows what reporters do and why we do it. And I'll take it a step further—many reporters don't know either.

The Gulf War was a local story—at least in San Antonio. It was then and is now a huge military town. Everyone living there knows someone in the military or has a family member in the military. My neighbors were going to go to the Middle East to free a country few knew of, had visited, or cared about and for reasons that they didn't understand. Some said, "Why not leave it to the networks or the newspapers?" But more often than not, no matter whom I talked to, they just wanted to know why it was the American military that had to shoulder the responsibility. It was a hard story to tell, and many newspapers and television stations across the country didn't bother to try to tell it. Corporate management couldn't see or justify the spending of the money to do the job their communities demanded they do.

The networks handled the big picture, but the stories I told of fear and violence were not told by major newspapers or the networks. Tip O'Neill famously said that all politics is local. So is all news. The Gulf War was the biggest local story I ever covered—and what I found is the military didn't understand that, many of the reporters didn't either, and the only thing the large corporations that sent their reporters understood was generating money by feeding people's concerns and interest with the junk food of convenience all the time. Peter Arnett's pronouncement before the National Press Club simply didn't go far enough. Not only does the American audience not understand what journalism is and does, but some of its largest practitioners, corporations, and members of government have no idea either.

8

THE WAR ON DRUGS IS A JOKE

Ronald Reagan and his wife Nancy boldly told us to "Just say no to drugs."

The American people, in reality, have always thumbed its collective nose at this, even though millions supposedly support the effort. In 1987, the Partnership for a Drug-Free America launched public service announcements showing eggs frying in a frying pan with the accompanying voice-over saying, "This is your brain on drugs."

The thirty-second version of the first public service announcement shows a man in a starkly furnished apartment who asks if there is anyone out there who still does not understand the dangers of drug abuse. He holds up an egg and says, "This is your brain," before motioning to the pan and adding, "This is drugs." He then cracks open the egg, fries the contents, and says, "This is your brain on drugs." Finally, he looks up at the camera and asks, "Any questions?"

It was stark and blunt. And it made no impression on the millions of Americans who continued to do drugs. Reagan and, later, George H. W. Bush pushed the narrative that the country must wage a war on drugs, which prompted comedians like George Carlin to say, "The drugs are winning."

The "banana republics" south of the border were blamed for making drugs cheap and plentiful. Huge fortunes and cocaine empires rose and fell in Central and South America. I had covered some of those stories. Our government dumped paraquat on marijuana grown south of the border, stepped up enforcement against cocaine distribution networks, and promoted its efforts in the "war on drugs" with local and national media. The media rarely looked beyond the sexy busts and the pot and cocaine seizures to explore the root cause of the problem—American demand for the drugs.

According to the Rand Corporation, spending on pot, cocaine, heroin, and methamphetamines fluctuated between $120 billion and $145 billion each year from 2006 to 2016—roughly the same as we spent on alcohol consumption.[1] The Obama administration stated that drug use should be treated as a health issue instead of a criminal justice issue, yet every president since Reagan has spent billions on enforcement. The federal drug war budget was roughly $26 billion in 2015. Almost none of that was spent on lifesaving harm reduction services.[2]

Reporting about the failed war on drugs has been scant—and we've failed to look at this complex issue for a variety of competing reasons. Reporters have also failed in another complex issue: illegal immigration, which is often tied to narco-terrorism and the drug merchants making millions of the country's multi-billion-dollar demand for illegal drugs.

The problem of illegal drugs and illegal immigration rose at the time the independent press began to shrink. Reagan's media deregulation and the George Bush administration's continuation of Reagan's policies helped fuel the minimization of the press, and thus reporting on real issues like the drug problem and illegal immigration never got any deeper than breaking news. We began to follow these complex issues like football games and spot news—simply because we could do nothing else.

Fueling this inability to cover complex issues—especially at the local level—was another factor that came into play in the past two decades. One of the little-known battles in the war against the press was over public notice ads. Public notice ads in newspapers have been around as long as newspapers. Governments are mandated to notify the public about city council meetings, tax sales, foreclosures, and other actions taken on behalf of the public. It's the very essence of transparency in government. Ever been to a police auction? Ever been to an estate sale? Public notice ads let you know about these events. Local business owners routinely peruse them, as do other interested parties. As television news and, later, cable news began to dominate and advertising fled the newspapers, public notice ads served a dual purpose: they were verifiable proof of certain activities of local governments, and they became a guaranteed base of income for newspapers of record—and for smaller newspapers an *essential* source of revenue. During the first decade of the twenty-first century the *Sentinel* newspapers in Montgomery and Prince George's County, Maryland, would not have survived without them. I know, as I was the executive editor of those papers trying to keep them alive.

"From the U.S. Supreme Court to small school districts, calls frequently are heard to do away with these legally mandated ads that critics argue are too expensive, too difficult to read; ineffective as notices," *Editor and Publisher* reported in 1987.[3] Newspapers, already buying themselves up and facing a future of diminishing ads due to television competition, faced additional pressure on this vital source of revenue—and this was directly because state and local governments around the country didn't want to spend the money to be held accountable for their actions. The federal government never said a word about it. "Transparency" was never so opaque. The pressure by governments on this source of revenue gained momentum as the internet gained popularity and local and state governments decided the best way to notify the public was to publish vital information on their own websites without bothering to pay independent publishers to spread the word.

Meanwhile, the popularization of cable news was causing revenue problems at the major television networks. As a result, CBS News executive Don Hewitt proposed that a single television news service be formed to provide overseas coverage for the three commercial broadcast news companies. Such a service would help "avoid those awful bloodlettings" in the network news division by reducing costs and would put television news executives "out of the money business and back into the news business," said Hewitt—the producer of *60 Minutes*.[4]

As newspapers made less and become unstable, they consolidated. Television networks, facing competition from cable news, saw a similar possibility, and Hewitt tried to do something about it. His plan never caught on, but the idea of having fewer reporters do more work has definitely caught on during the past four decades.

We've seen it the most in newspapers as the chains continued to grow and independent newspapers ceased to exist. In late 1987, Dallas-based Media News Group announced within a five-day span that it had acquired the *Houston Post* and the *Denver Post* in separate transactions. The two dailies, it was announced, would "combine forces" for improving state news coverage. The acquisition of both newspapers gave Media News twenty-eight dailies and cost some $250 million. Despite the strategy to race to become the largest, Media News earned a controversial reputation as a cost-cutter in the newspaper publishing business. Many former employees say the company cut costs to the "detriment of good journalism."[5]

It got worse when Alden Global Capital acquired Media News Group in 2010. Margaret Sullivan of the *Washington Post* in 2018 called Alden "one of the most ruthless of the corporate strip-miners seemingly intent on destroying local journalism."[6] The term "vulture capitalist" was coined because of the actions of Alden Global, a huge hedge fund company that now owns hundreds of newspapers. "For years, Alden's unofficial nickname has been 'the destroyer of newspapers,'" the *Orlando Sentinel* reported in February 2021.[7]

That may not have been the intent in the late 1980s when Media News Group acquired the *Houston Post* and the *Denver Post*, but four decades later, there's little question as to what multiple acquisitions, first from large newspaper chains and then from hedge fund investors, did to journalism. The *Houston Post* closed in 1995. And it is easy to see in hindsight how the acquisitions made possible and encouraged by the deregulation Ronald Reagan and other presidents promoted catalyzed the demise of journalism. Instead of making media properties more profitable, it made them less profitable. Instead of making them stronger, it made them weaker in two very vital ways: economically and politically. The large companies that invested in media properties sold off assets and limited reporting in order to make more short-term profit. That led to a long-term collapse in the value of the property.

Independent reporting was the engine that drove journalism. Without it, why buy a newspaper? It was like buying a new car without an engine. These acquisitions and consolidations weakened the surviving newspapers and television news providers because they lessened the leverage journalists could apply on government to provide access. There were fewer reporters and fewer resources to fight for access, and when governments denied access to documents, meetings, and other necessities, newspapers and television stations didn't want to spend the money to litigate—if they made an effort to get the information at all. Many times, they simply never did. The handwriting was on the wall by 1990: in the future, there would be fewer reporters, fewer news outlets, smaller salaries, and fewer fights left in the free press. The government could effectively control the message and the messenger.

A September 1991 headline in *TV Guide* asked bluntly, "Is network news crumbling?"[8]

This was a discussion being held in newsrooms throughout the country. At the same time, Dan Rather said there was another problem to address: the familiarity between reporters and sources. As the number of reporters diminished across the country, those left in the field—particularly those covering government—out of necessity and survival were erasing the lines between government and journalists. The fewer the number of reporters, the more government could control them. Ronald Reagan's actions nearly a decade earlier were beginning to have tangible results in the 1990s. American viewers could see something was wrong, but without an adequate knowledge of how the media operate, they could not get a handle on the cause of the problem. Many never have. The media were to blame too because we didn't cover the problem well—if we covered it at all. There were stories in the trade publications to be sure but almost nothing out of the largest broadcasters and newspapers. While the dissolution of the precepts of a robust media were ongoing, few reported on it. But let's not limit the criticism to covering only our own demise. By the 1990s, we weren't pushing back hard on anything.

"We're gutless. We're spineless," CBS's Dan Rather told the *Boston Herald* in September 1991. "There no joy in saying this, but beginning in the 1980s, the American press by and large somehow began to operate on the theory that the first order of business was to be popular with the person, organization or institution that you cover."

ABC's Sam Donaldson had similar concerns and voiced them in his 1987 book *Hold On, Mr. President!* "I'm not advocating rudeness . . . but I'm far more concerned about the reporters who are either too afraid or too disinclined to ask a question," he said.[9]

I've never been disinclined to ask a question. But in 1992, it did lead to me getting fired—reporting on drugs was part of the reason.

During the early months of that year, President George H. W. Bush came to San Antonio for a "drug summit" with seven other leaders from the Western Hemisphere. They planned to take action and stage a news conference to address the ongoing war on drugs. I was put on the bus to the McNay Art Museum by my executive producer Forrest Carr, the same guy who had defended me so very well during my confidential source fight a year earlier. When the time came for the press conference, perhaps a dozen reporters in the president's travel pool took up the first row of seats for the outdoor event, which, more than anything, resembled a news conference in the White House Rose Garden. I got a second-row seat. We were told that each leader at the head table would entertain two questions. Naturally, the travel pool got the first few questions, and President Bush was asked about Pat Buchannan catching up with him in the polls in the ongoing primaries—it was reelection season. By the time Bush opened the floor for questions to anyone other than the travel pool, he'd already answered all of his questions. I smiled at him. He called on me—because, like most presidents, he just couldn't avoid my wonderful smile.

So, on February 27, 1992, just twenty-four years to the day after Walter Cronkite broadcast an editorial that sunk Lyndon Johnson, I got into this exchange with President Bush at the McNay Art Museum. Bush called on me and asked who I had a question for:

"Actually, it's to you, President Bush. The question I have to ask is, over the last . . ."

"Well thank you," Bush said as he interrupted me. "I'm not going to take any more questions. I just told you. You didn't understand it."

Of course, I did understand him, but I reasoned since we were gathered in San Antonio to talk about the drug summit that had just occurred and since our president had not taken one question about the drug summit, he could entertain at least one question on the subject. But Bush ignored me and tried to push past me as I continued to ask the question. "I'm very sorry. You're dealing with somebody who has made up his mind. And we're trying to be courteous to everybody here. Now, if you have a question for one of the other three, ask it. Otherwise, sit down."

It was the first time I'd been told to sit down by a president. It wouldn't be the last. And, as usual, I did not sit down. Instead, I told President Bush I would be happy to ask the question to the president of Mexico since it also involved Mexico, but I would like Bush to answer the question as well.

"He's already had a question. Sorry," Bush said.

"Well, he's only had one," I replied.

"Okay, you go ahead. We're not used to this, but anyway, go ahead," Bush said.

Then I asked what I thought every Drug Enforcement Administration (DEA) agent I'd ever spoken with would want answered: "I spent some time with narcotics agents over the last few days who made busts who tell us that they're tired. They don't believe the war on drugs can be won. They consider this summit a joke, and they consider the presidents cooperating in this summit to be a joke as well. What do you tell your people in the trenches, the people that are fighting it every day, what do you give them as a morale booster to tell them it's not a joke?"

I thought it was actually a bit of a softball question. But it had real ramifications. I'd seen so much violence in four years covering crime in San Antonio, and I knew I'd seen only a glimpse of it. I heard DEA, Customs, state police, sheriff's deputies, and local cops lament the constant pressure on them from dangerous narco-terrorists and how pointless the war on drugs was when the demand for drugs was so high. I knew dozens of those in law enforcement who supported decriminalizing drugs and legalizing most of them.

The president of Mexico, Carlos Salinas, gave an answer that included an acknowledgment of the risks facing law enforcement and how much all nations appreciated their efforts but added, "This is a true war in times of peace that we have decided to win against drug traffickers."

Bush? He never answered me at all and pushed past me to the next question. Bush hadn't called me a "little dog" like Icenogle had, but his intent was clear—he didn't want to answer the question. But the issue was solid. I knew because I'd spent so much time with DEA agents and local cops who were overwhelmingly tired of waging a never-ending battle they thought they couldn't win and wasn't worth fighting.

In my time in San Antonio, I'd gone on numerous drug busts with police, sheriff's deputies, state police, and the DEA. Once when the local police busted the "Cooler Gang"—a group of heavy drug users who targeted restaurants at closing time and locked the workers up in the refrigerated coolers while they robbed them (hence the name of the gang)—I got to ride in my own Pontiac Firebird with a photographer in the passenger seat. As we cruised up I-35, I was the middle car with three police cars in front of me, one on each side of me, and three behind me—all with sirens and lights blazing. I was going over 110 miles per hour with a police escort. That was the best of it.

Otherwise, the drug violence and the drug busts were overwhelmingly depressing and dangerous. One drug dealer, trying to escape from the cops, drew his gun on the cop while I and my photographer Roy Pedroza followed not five steps behind. Another time, a violent drug gang had turned a house into a turnstile walk-up drugstore. You walked up to the front door, put your money in a spindle, and turned the handle, and the drugs you wanted came out when the spindle came back around. It was as convenient as drive-through fast food. The house was reinforced, and the only way it could be effectively raided was to attach a chain to the door and yank it off its hinges with a tow truck. But the door was so well reinforced that when the narcotics officers did so, they yanked the whole front of the house off—nearly killing us all as we stood by. On a different occasion, while the Bexar County Sheriff's Department was serving a drug warrant, I ended up in the back of a car with a deputy and in the middle of a high-speed chase that ended when the man being pursued flipped his car and nearly killed himself and those of us in the car who were in close pursuit. On still another occasion, I covered a police-involved shooting on the city's north side when a drug dealer with a multitude of arrests and convictions—and who always went peacefully—decided to fire a shotgun with a one-ounce slug at a city police officer. The cop, who had a Kevlar vest and a metal insert, survived with several bruised ribs and a bruised heart. The felon ended up as Swiss cheese as every officer through the door unloaded a fuselage of bullets in the felon's direction. On another occasion, two local police officers pulled over a car full of teens and young twenty-somethings suspected of being involved in selling drugs. One officer got out of the car and unknowingly had to face off with five kids who had about seventy-five rounds of ammunition at their disposal while the officer had only a .357 magnum service revolver. The first shot grazed the cop's pants legs, forever earning him the nickname of "Iron Balls," while the hail of bullets the kids laid down hit nothing else. With five shots from his service revolver, the cop in question quietly dropped every kid. Two of them, as I remember, survived. I covered countless stories of criminals accidentally blowing themselves up while manufacturing methamphetamines. One night, after covering my third drug-related shooting of the night, one in which two rival drug gangs killed three people with semiautomatic pistols, I just sat on the curb and sighed. Sitting next to me was a homicide detective. It was his third case that night too. I will never forget the look on his face—the weariness and the exhaustion. It wasn't isolated to that day. It was common.

I had covered so many drug busts under so many circumstances I knew firsthand how the police in the area felt about the war on drugs. They were tired of risking their lives in a dangerous game that never seemed to end. Reagan told us to just say no to drugs, and Bush never pushed back against that. Few in government did. And few in the press did either. It was a fantasy we all bought into. But when you'd covered the death of Kiki Camerana and the numerous deaths of coyotes and undocumented workers and spent time with the burned-out members of law enforcement who didn't want to risk their life over the use of drugs, it seemed an issue that you couldn't give up. It remains one of the greatest hypocrisies I've ever had to report on. I saw people get shot and killed over a bag of marijuana. I know of teens who spent a year in jail for one joint. They went into jail naive and often poor and came out hardened criminals.

The idea of a drug summit was one of the biggest jokes ever and deserved to be questioned. As Sam Donaldson said in his book, "Our job is to challenge the president, challenge him to explain policy, justify decisions, defend mistakes, reveal intentions for the future, and comment on a host of matters about which his views are of a general concern."[10]

And I remembered well what Helen Thomas told me. You don't always get a chance, but when you do, make sure you ask a question of the president that matters. She had drilled that into my brain. So, I asked Bush the only question I thought mattered about the drug summit news conference. The question deserved an answer. It didn't get one.

I left the news conference thinking that at least Bush would now have to consider the issue a little more. I left thinking I had asked a decent question, and when I got back to the station, I was told I had indeed done very well. "You know these are dog and pony shows," my news director explained. I sighed, went home, and didn't think any more about it.

The next morning, I got a phone call from the office and was told not to come in that day. Had I earned a day off? No. I was being fired. My wife and I had just made the first payment on the first house we ever bought. She was five months' pregnant with our second child, and I was told I had embarrassed myself and the station. I was told I was just a bad guy. An embarrassment. Needless to say, I was a bit stunned since I'd been told the day before I'd done a good job. Jeanne Jakle, the local gossip columnist at the *Express-News*, turned up the volume on the story (this was a few years before anything could go viral). Later that day, I was doing a phone interview with CNN while sitting in my shorts on my couch. I got calls from all over the country from reporters. It was much like when I'd gone to jail for the First Amendment, only this time, I was on my own. I had no corporate support—only corporate derision.

Sam Donaldson came to town to do a story that week for *Prime Time*. In his story, he highlighted my dilemma. "Some people think Bush got snippy for no good reason. But others think Karem should've shut up when he was told to," Donaldson said in a voice-over. Then the story cut to a question-and-answer session between myself and Donaldson.

"He asked you to sit down but you persisted . . . and then the president made it very clear he was annoyed, to say the least, at you," Donaldson said.

"Yeah, he was annoyed," I replied.

"So then weren't you deliberately picking a fight with him?"

"No," I answered. "I just wanted the question answered. I didn't stand up to pick a fight with the man; I stood up to ask him a question. And he should've answered the question. And just because the president of the United States tells me to sit down doesn't necessarily mean I have to obey him. This isn't first-grade class. I respect the man, but he's President George Bush, not King George."

Sam came back with, "Well he's responsible to the people of the United States, but is he really responsible to you Brian Karem? I mean, who are you that he has to be responsible to you."

"Well I'm a reporter, and I'm the public's representative at that meeting. And I'm sorry, I'm not in a popularity contest."

Now, some may say it was the height of chutzpah for Donaldson to ask me those questions based on his well-known combative nature with presidents. But he was voicing the very concerns that many have about pushy reporters. He'd had those questions thrown at him most of his life. At the end of his piece, as he sat on the set at ABC, he told us where he fell in the argument as he assessed the arguments against me: "pushy he certainly is, if you can't stand the heat, then stay out of the kitchen. Normally you don't fire the cook."

A short time after this piece ran on *Prime Time*, I got a telephone call at home from Lance Heflin, the executive producer at *America's Most Wanted*. "I have a real need for an arrogant, obnoxious investigative reporter. Are you free?" he asked as an introduction.

"Mom? Is that you?" I replied.

I met Lance for the first time when he flew me to Washington, D.C., for an interview. It was my first time working for a network television show. *America's Most Wanted*, hosted by John Walsh, was, strictly speaking, not a news show. But I was hired to do investigations and the hard news portion of the program.

Everything was about the budget. The show had a set production budget, and while it technically was an independent production, the Fox network controlled the purse strings. Lance was interested in what I could bring to the show, especially since I could produce and report. "Two. Two. Two mints in one," he explained as he decided to hire me. I was already used to producing my own pieces and producing documentaries and had been doing so for more than five years by the time I ended up moving to Washington as an on-air correspondent and producer for *America's Most Wanted*. I was also aware of tight budgets, and Lance explained that was something I had to get used to in "an era of downsizing that won't go away soon." While I used producers for some of my major pieces, like covering the hunt for Pablo Escobar or pieces I did on the North American Man/Boy Love Association or when I did a piece on serial killer Kenneth McDuff that led to his capture, I was often covering stories with merely a photographer and myself—and occasionally a soundman. This was in contrast to how networks had routinely staffed magazine shows previously. But it was more in line with the constriction going on in the marketplace. It also led to another way for Fox to use me. On occasion, I would go downstairs and assist Fox-5 local news by covering crime—and later would assist the brand new Fox News national coverage. In short, I was a utility infielder—able to be plugged into whatever assignment fit. Although my starting position might be shortstop for *America's Most Wanted*, I could find myself at second or first base for anyone else in the corporate family who needed me.

In my first meeting with Lance, I found we had a lot in common—including the fact that we had actually rented and lived in the same house in college. Less than a year after he moved out, I moved in. But the substantive discussion we had in our first interview was about the problems in journalism. It came down to "making a difference," he explained.

He called me after watching me on *Prime Time* to work for *America's Most Wanted* because he thought I "could make a difference even as our business is scaling back." I remember those words because it was chilling to me.

I had been taught in school that I had to have three to five years of experience in a small market or at a small newspaper in order to be eligible to work for larger media organizations. By the time I had amassed that much experience, Lance told me I didn't need it. "We're hiring people straight out of school or with very little experience," he said. He named some very young producers whose first jobs were with *America's Most Wanted*.

The change in the business, he explained, was also leading to a more "Hollywood" aspect to news. I fought that as much as possible, being raised in the old-school news environment of the University of Missouri. Lance said he fancied that aspect of my personality and wanted me to rattle the cages to get to the bottom of some of the stories *America's Most Wanted* had covered. "I know people in government are lying to us. I want you to do the stories about it." As it seemed in my wheelhouse, I had no problem doing it. In fact, for the next few years while with *America's Most Wanted*, I would visit almost every state in the country and a few foreign countries. I exposed malfeasance and misfeasance, caught a few nasty criminals, and exposed lies in government and among the criminals—I mean the ones who weren't in government. All of it was done on a shoe-string budget.

I once showed up in Arizona for a story and was scheduled to meet my freelance shooting crew for the day as I got off the plane. A local photographer, carrying his station's camera gear with him, met me with his pregnant girlfriend, who was supposed to be my soundman for the day. I cut them loose, paying them for the day because I felt bad for them—though I'm sure the photographer's "on the side" activities, as he called his freelancing, were unknown to the station he worked for. On another occasion while shooting in Orlando, Florida, rather than board a flight and fly to southern Alabama for the next leg of my story, our production department had me drive to save money. After many hours of driving through the panhandle of Florida, I nearly fell asleep. I woke up as I approached an overpass—my terrified photographer screaming in my ear.

The glamour of working for a national show was overshadowed by the long hours and frequent cost-cutting measures. But overshadowing all of that was the subject matter. I was either dealing with politicians who'd screwed up the criminal justice system—as they had in the case of Kenneth McDuff—or dealing with a lot of parents of dead children—and that was the toughest to handle.

In the case of Kenneth McDuff, the Texas criminal justice system screwed the pooch badly. McDuff had entered prison in 1968 after enjoying a night of mass murder with an accomplice, killing a girl, her boyfriend, and her brother. His accomplice said McDuff made the brother watch while he killed the other two. For his efforts, McDuff was sentenced to die, but before the state could turn him off, the federal government got rid of the death penalty, and McDuff's sentence was commuted to life in prison. In 1989, as the state faced a problem with prison overcrowding, someone rubber-stamped his release without doing any fact-finding, and Texas set him and dozens of others free. During the next year and a half, police said he graduated from a mass murderer to a serial killer and was responsible for the deaths of as many as fifteen women. That's when he came to the attention of *America's Most Wanted*.

I produced a short story on McDuff's crimes. I even interviewed his mother, who couldn't believe her boy would do anything bad. She had covered the windows of her small, dusty central Texas home with tinfoil to "keep out the government rays." And she did the interview with me while rocking in a rocking chair—under which she kept a loaded .357 magnum "just in case." She said her hometown used to be a "regular walking around town" until crime overwhelmed it, but her boy, she said, wasn't a criminal.

After we aired our story, an *America's Most Wanted* viewer recognized McDuff as a guy working for a garbage hauling company in Kansas City, and three days later, I found myself in Waco to produce the capture piece as the U.S. Marshal Service brought McDuff back to Texas to stand trial. As a group of very nervous U.S. marshals walked McDuff into the courtroom to be arraigned, I heard several people who had assembled outside of the courthouse yell, "Get a rope!" Naturally, we did a follow-up to that story, which included an interview with Texas Governor Ann Richards. I knew Richards from my time at KMOL, covering the legislature, and we got along fairly well. She had an acid tongue and a quick wit. If you ever watch the documentary that aired on her, you can see me strolling next to her after her first legislative session asking her how the session went.

Richards was not happy with the questions I asked that day, and thought I was part of a "hit squad" from Fox to go after her. Fox News was an infant, but in the minds of politicians, anyone from the networks sent to ask them tough questions was out to do a hit job. "I always thought more of you. This is a disappointment," she explained.

Richards's concern was that we were going to blame her for what McDuff did—kind of a Willy Horton type of smear. The fact is that McDuff got kicked out of the system before Richards was governor, and I had no intention of blaming her for it—I just wanted to know what she intended to do about it. "Brine," she said pronouncing my name with that distinctive southern drawl, "I know exactly what you all want to do." She was wrong, of course, but it made no difference.

One time, I confess I got a prison warden to quit. I was at Taycheedah Correctional Institution in Fond du Lac, Wisconsin. A convicted murderer had escaped, and the circumstances surrounding the escape simply floored me. The convict got permission from a guard to walk back from a work detail to her barracks. She was placed on the honor system to do so. She honorably walked to the back of the prison yard in the woods and scaled a ten-foot fence—the only thing separating the prison from the nearby neighborhood. There was no guard tower in sight. When I asked the warden, on camera, why she would place any convicted murderer on the honor system (after all, by being a convicted murderer, they had already proven they couldn't be honorable), the warden said hopefully the thought of being prosecuted for another crime would keep them on the honor system. When I explained to the warden in my best Lieutenant Columbo imitation if she knew why I had to ask these questions, she said she did. She didn't like it, and she took off the microphone, walked away, and said she quit. I had never had anyone quit an interview like that before, on tape and live, to be played before a national audience. So, I contacted her supervisor with the state and let them know what had happened—and, by the way, could they supply someone else to answer the questions? They agreed to supply a state official to answer the questions, but they informed me I was mistaken. The warden didn't just quit the interview. She had quit her job—on camera—because I asked her a question she didn't want to answer.

One time in Texas, I interviewed parents whose daughters had been killed in a yogurt shop. One woman lost both of her daughters. Another woman lost her only daughter. The first woman, when I showed up to interview her, had the bedroom decorated as it had been the day her daughters died. In each bedroom were life-sized posters of her children. In the second home, I interviewed a mother who said she could still smell her daughter walking through the house. She clutched at a pillow and occasionally cried as I interviewed her. Both parents tore hard at my soul.

And then there was the father I interviewed in Texas. His son went missing after the father and his twelve-year-old son paid a day laborer to help them move to a new apartment. The father had left the day laborer with his son for ten minutes to pack up the last of their belongings while he drove to the new apartment and unlocked it. When he returned, his son and the day laborer were gone. I interviewed this single father, who said his whole life revolved around his son, and he told me how guilty he felt for making the mistake of leaving the child alone for even the short time that he did with a day laborer. He was overcome with guilt, and his reddened eyes betrayed the amount of crying he'd done. After we left the interview, I got a call from the police, who informed me the boy's body had just been found. It was no longer a missing persons case but a murder. I was told the father had been informed, so we turned around. We had to talk to him again before we left town. I usually began those types of interviews by informing the parents that I understood as a parent myself how difficult this interview could be. But I also said we were not like other media. We weren't there to just tell a story—but, with their help, to catch a killer. Any detail could help; even the smallest, oddest thing that may not seem like anything could lead to something that could help us catch the killer.

As I set up for the second interview with the father that day, I repeated why we had to interview him one more time, and I apologized ahead of time and told him I didn't want to intrude on his grief. But he'd been very forthcoming in the previous interview, and we were grateful he'd agreed to let us interview him again. It was then I found out that the police had not informed the father of his son's death. I had mistakenly done so, assuming that when the cops told me they'd informed the father of his son's death, they'd actually told the truth. The screams I heard from the tortured father that day forever changed my life.

But, ultimately, it was another parental response that made me glad to leave *America's Most Wanted* after five years of interviewing crime victims and politicians. I traveled to Mississippi to interview a woman who lived in a double-wide trailer. Her nine-year-old daughter had been kidnapped and raped before being released in another town on the side of the road two days later—as I remember. We showed up, and I was scheduled to interview the mother and hopefully the daughter. The double-wide trailer was in disarray. It looked like it had been ransacked but hadn't been. The most cherished possession of the mother was two Elvis dolls sitting in a curio cabinet inside the front door. As I went through my typical pitch for interviewing her daughter and assuring her I would be very careful in doing so, she responded, "Oh honey, she's a little girl. She'll bounce back. Kids are like rubber balls; they all bounce back. Don't worry. Now, do you have those *America's Most Wanted* T-shirts and hats like your secretary promised? I love your show."

I often said I got uneasy when people recognized me from being on *America's Most Wanted*. I feared they either were one of America's most wanted (we were a very popular show in prison and among the criminal crowd), relatives of someone we were searching for, or—and this turned out to be the case more than once—soon to become one of America's most wanted. Do not mistake me: that show had the most direct results I've ever experienced as a reporter. We were directly responsible for catching major felons. So, when I spoke to the Department of Justice, I got results—not the "We can neither confirm nor deny" standard response I usually got as a reporter. The White House responded to us. The Marshal Service loved us. I got to know them so well that when I saw Tommy Lee Jones in *The Fugitive*, his portrayal reminded me of at least six marshals I knew.

That point in the movie where Harrison Ford screams that he didn't kill his wife and the marshal responds, "I don't care," may have been the most accurate portrayal I'd ever seen. The marshals are merely bounty hunters. Guilty or innocent? That's for the courts to decide.

As good as *America's Most Wanted* was and as big a difference you could make working there, the budget pressures and the existential pressures of grinding out the stories week after week while dealing with the worst things human beings can do to each other made me extremely happy that after five years I moved on.

9

A TALE OF TWO CULT LEADERS

As the 1990s got under way, Roger Ailes left the world of political consulting and entered the world of broadcasting. He longed to create his own conservative network, but at first, he made his moves elsewhere. In 1988, he wrote a book, *You Are the Message: Secrets of the Master Communicators*. By 1993, he became president of CNBC and then went on to create the America's Talking channel, which became MSNBC. On America's Talking, he hosted his own interview program, but by 1995, Ailes was in trouble after allegedly calling David Zaslav—at the time an executive at NBC Universal—a "little fucking Jew prick."[1] He subsequently left the NBC family to work with someone whose political ideals more closely matched his own. In 1996, Rupert Murdoch hired Ailes to become the chief executive officer of the fledgling Fox News.

By then, as previously noted, the deregulation initiated by Ronald Reagan was firmly taking hold. Fowler, who left after five years at the top of the Federal Communications Commission (FCC), referred to himself as "Mr. Deregulation." He removed FCC regulations that "set off a wave of media mergers that sent the price of radio and television stations soaring when he raised the limit on the number of broadcasting stations one firm can own and eased restrictions on buying and selling radio and television stations," the *Washington Post* noted.[2]

Fowler pushed for elimination of rules-restriction cable television and, again, had begun dismantling the fairness doctrine. Ironically, he said that ending equal-time restrictions mandated by the fairness doctrine would mean "treating all members of the press, print or electronic, the same."[3] Of course, it meant just the opposite, and Roger Ailes and Rupert Murdoch would prove that point all too well as Fox News became popular.

As a final thumbing of his nose, when Fowler left the FCC, he claimed that he wished he could close it for good. "Free-market forces and competitive forces are better able to serve the public and police companies" than the government, Fowler claimed.[4] Former FCC chairman Newton Minow, on the other hand, said Fowler was a key architect of the one-sided media we have today.

"We need some form of the fairness doctrine and its loss was a loss for everyone," Minow told me for this book. The controversy was far from settled in the mid-1990s, though it was becoming clearer that Fowler's move was spelling trouble for television. Corporate greed, combined with a need to survive due to the consolidation of television properties into large behemoths, was forcing the sale and acquisition of radio stations and newspapers. There was little doubt this added to the press's inability to cover the news fairly and objectively. If you work for a large corporation covering the news, does anyone think the board of directors would want or allow inquisitive reporters poking their noses into the corporate business? No sir. In addition, newsrooms began shrinking—even at the larger newspapers supposedly protected by large corporate owners.

True independence in the press was dead just after the Gulf War. By early 1993, as Bill Clinton arrived in the White House, the business of journalism would even get worse. The news veterans told us of the coming doom. "The electronic era of instant communications is upon us, but unfortunately that doesn't mean the journalistic product is any better," Helen Thomas warned.[5]

Helen Thomas, Sam Donaldson, Dan Rather, Peter Jennings, Walter Cronkite, and Tom Brokaw are among the media luminaries who have, from time to time, spoke out against the shrinking of the journalistic world. By the mid-1990s, members of Congress sounded the alarm and tried to get the fairness doctrine reintroduced.

In a study conducted by the Media Access Project, it was shown that the repeal of the fairness doctrine led to one-quarter of all broadcast entities denying the public any local news or public affairs programming.[6] The results of such a loss are now writ large across the country—no democracy can function without an informed citizenry. Today, we are in the middle of an acrimonious and divisive national debate in a good part because of the destruction of local news both on television and in newspapers. "It is hard to visualize a situation where a few companies would own all of the media outlets," Thomas wrote. "But its impact would be devastating to the marketplace of ideas and viewpoints."[7] Today, we don't have to visualize it. We are living it.

In July 1992, Pablo Escobar "escaped" from his palatial prison overlooking the city of Medellín, Colombia. His prison in Envigado was as problematic as everything else about Escobar. He was the world's most infamous drug dealer. He was imprisoned in a compound he helped build. The gun turrets faced out—not in. The place looked more like a private estate for Bill Gates or Jeff Bezos than a prison. Escobar had a picture of his son and himself standing in front of the White House hanging on the wall in his office in his prison. Yes. He had an office. He had more than that. His prison was equipped with mountain bikes, a chapel, a soccer field, and all the amenities. It had everything a man could want—he had more than he could ask for and much more. There was even a bombproof bunker and a bungalow where he could entertain women—and did. So why did he escape? The Colombian government threatened to move him to a more traditional facility, and "Don Pablo" would have none of that. Robert Bonner, director of the Drug Enforcement Administration (DEA), said at the time of Escobar's escape, "The man is a gangster, a monster, a murderous thug. He's the worst we've ever seen—bar none."[8]

Escobar was credited with selling more cocaine to the United States than any single person. There were many a decadent party, brawl, and violent death the source of which was Don Pablo. He was a violent man who made Tony Montana in *Scarface* look like a monk. When things got bad, he lashed out—blowing up an airliner that killed more than 100 people—including two Americans. That led to an indictment in New York, and after Escobar escaped, his biggest fear was being kidnapped by the DEA and taken to the United States for prosecution. In August 1989, Escobar was found to be responsible for killing antidrug presidential candidate Luis Galan at a campaign rally—having him gunned down in front of thousands of supporters. "He's the world's premier example of a narco-terrorist," Bonner told me at the time for a segment on *America's Most Wanted*.

Escobar threatened innocent citizens and politicians and loved to threaten reporters. After Escobar's escape, the newspaper *El Tiempo* was surrounded by well-armed security for months. Enrique Santos, the deputy editor of *El Tiempo*, said Escobar directly threatened the free press, once kidnapping and holding the paper's city editor for eight months. "Can you imagine this in the United States?" Santos asked me. "How would your country react to someone threatening violence on your reporters? You would never stand for it. We cannot."

To be a journalist in Bogotá in 1992 turned out to be very similar to being a journalist in the United States in 2021. It was hard to see at the time. Few of us covering the drug wars could envision a professional landscape where reporters had to have body guards, where the public was divided on the need for or decency of reporters, and where walking into certain public events included an implied death threat. But everywhere Santos went, he told me he had to have his head on a swivel. Escobar's supporters—and there were many in and around Bogotá—would eagerly do a reporter harm to curry favor with Don Pablo.

I remember talking with the producer and camera crew of *America's Most Wanted* about the extra steps we had to take to be safe and all of us being thankful that we didn't have to face such harsh realities in the United States. A quarter of a century later, we did.

Santos summed up Escobar's personality as the ultimate narcissist. "He creates a collective panic, and he gets people in the government to negotiate with him so the terrorism will stop." When I arrived in Bogotá to cover the hunt for Pablo Escobar, the capital was in full lockdown. While life tried to go on normally, armed private security was everywhere—as were armed patrols of national police officers. Escobar was responsible for killing 350 police officers in the Medellín area of Colombia in one six-month period, and the police force had enough. They were going to hunt for Escobar, with the DEA's assistance, until they found him.

"Everyone was so thankful when he gave himself up," Santos explained. He was off the street. The national nightmare was done. They didn't seem to mind a posh country-club prison. The Don was gone. But when word got out that Escobar was going to be transferred to a more secure prison, he bribed a guard and escaped through a bunker he had built in the countryside of the prison grounds to protect him in case the United States decided to bomb him.

"The fact is that he is out and intimidating and it's very depressing to us. It is a blow for Colombian prestige," Santos explained. After he wrote an editorial criticizing Escobar, Santos got a handwritten letter from the drug kingpin—complete with a thumbprint to show authenticity. "It's a psychological intimidation," Santos said. General Miguel Gomez Padilla of the Colombian national police force told me part of Escobar's psychology was to convince those in the country that it was really the police, the press, and others who were the enemy. Escobar threw money at the poor and bought loyalty that way. When we stayed in Doradal, one of the small cities that was part of Escobar's stronghold and where he had a huge estate (complete with a zoo), we had to stay in a police compound guarded by national police officers. Our guide, Captain Omar Gonzalez, told us the city wasn't safe. "Escobar, he has people who love him. They will do anything for him, and you are not safe there." By day, we had escorts through the city and going to Escobar's estate. By night, we holed up in the police compound and passed our time playing poker. The police told tales of Escobar rallying the locals to violence in order to support him.

Six months after returning from Colombia on February 28, 1993, just twenty-five years after Cronkite told us about the dangers of the Vietnam War and just a year after I got into an argument with President George H. W. Bush, the federal government began a fifty-two-day siege of the Branch Davidians in Waco, Texas, after a botched Bureau of Alcohol, Tobacco and Firearms (ATF) raid.

The raid occurred as talks had progressed in Congress about the possibility of folding the ATF into the FBI—as both a budget-cutting measure and a way to streamline federal law enforcement. The good old boys at the ATF didn't like that idea, and sources inside the ATF told me at the time they were looking for ways to prove their vitality. They chose the Branch Davidians. The Davidians were a mixed bag of cultists whose leadership had fought among themselves for control of the small Christian-like sect for years. They lived and worked at a compound/church/school called Mount Carmel situated just outside of Waco.

Vernon Howell and George Roden, the two who fought the most vicious battles for control of the group, got into a gun battle over the exhumation of a corpse in 1987. Apparently, Roden thought he could raise the dead and challenged Howell to do the same. By the time sheriff's deputies arrived, Roden was pinned down behind a tree on the compound with a minor gunshot wound. As a result, Howell and his faction of followers were charged with attempted murder. One sheriff's deputy approached the heavily fortified compound and served the warrant. The deputies later told me that they approached Howell and said, "Look Vernon, I know you got a lot of guns in there, but come on out, and if you win in court, you'll get your guns back."

Howell did both. Then he changed his name to David Koresh, took control of the Branch Davidians, and announced he was the second coming of Jesus Christ. However, he was, as the *Waco Tribune-Herald* called him, a "Sinful Messiah" and didn't mind having sex with some fifteen women at Mount Carmel, all of whom he considered his wives, so he could spread his earthly seed. As he took control of the cult and approached his thirty-third birthday, he became more apocalyptic in his visions and began preaching about a coming doom. He saw the federal government coming to storm his citadel outside of Waco and convinced his followers to stock up on more ammunition.

Without the *Tribune-Herald*, few would have known about the Branch Davidians, and sources inside law enforcement at the time credited the paper with providing information they didn't have, even though they had undercover operatives in and around the Davidians. As it turned out, Koresh wasn't just dreaming of an apocalypse. He was trying to make one happen.

On that last day of February, both Tommy Witherspoon from the local newspaper and reporters from the local television station KWTX got tips that the ATF was going to serve warrants for the possession of illegal automatic weapons to Koresh and his Branch Davidians. It was a rainy morning on Double EE Ranch Road, twelve miles east of Waco, and shortly before 10 a.m. that morning, the reporters got more than they bargained for.

They watched trucks pulling cattle trailers, covered in tarps, speeding down Double EE Ranch Road from Elk Road, followed by a KWTX crew and another *Tribune-Herald* car. The trailers and the TV truck pulled into the Branch Davidian compound driveway while the reporters stood less than a football field away and witnessed the event. Dozens of ATF agents in helmets and bulletproof vests sprang from the trailers. Five reporters stood and stared at a military-style raid like none they'd ever witnessed before with agents scaling ladders and breaking windows. Then there was a fusillade of gunfire, and an agent on the roof fell on his side. Moments later, the five newspaper reporters were lying in a ditch, facedown in the wet grass, where they would remain until a cease-fire more than two hours later.[9]

"We're going to get blamed for this," one of the reporters who witnessed the event predicted.

The television crew, putting their own lives at risk, captured videotape that played in almost every newsroom around the world for weeks afterward. The photographs taken by the newspaper crew did the same. The local reporters had documented a part of history few of us alive at the time will ever forget. Today, it's doubtful, with the downsizing of newsrooms, that such an event would be as well covered. Doug Burgess, a longtime friend and news photographer who got his start in Midland, Texas, and went on to work in San Antonio, Dallas, Houston, and Seattle, once told me how he saw the news business irrevocably changed. "When I was in Seattle, every time we had a retirement, that job wasn't filled. Over the last thirty years, every newsroom I've ever worked in has downsized."

Four ATF agents and six Branch Davidians died in the shoot-out that day. David Koresh was apparently seriously wounded. But for the next fifty-one days, a Texas-sized standoff ensued.

I was among the first reporters from outside Waco to arrive and cover the siege. I was called by AMW and Fox since at the time I still lived in San Antonio and hadn't moved to Washington, D.C., yet. Within an hour of the news breaking, I drove five hours and got to Mount Carmel late in the afternoon on February 28. Within hours, there were dozens of reporters. Within days, there were hundreds of us. We set up a makeshift "Satellite City" outside of the police lines, which were set up far enough away from Mount Carmel that we could see the buildings there but not so close that we could become targets. Koresh and his followers, who apparently had generators and television sets, saw us and began hanging banners from the windows to try to get our attention. Since a federal officer died in the raid, the FBI took over the standoff and began briefing us daily.

In retrospect, it was a stupid raid. Those who lived in town knew it was coming—it wasn't just the news crews. The ATF agents had assembled and been seen by locals, some of them sympathetic to Koresh, and apparently warned him of the coming raid. A photographer, tipped to the event, got lost and accidentally let a Koresh sympathizer know some kind of police action was coming when he asked the man for directions to "Rodenville," the former name of Mount Carmel. Koresh wanted a showdown with the government and got it. And everyone acted as if it were a movie—which, of course, it later became. I remember asking the ATF agent who initially briefed us why he risked sending so many men into a heavily armed compound and why he didn't send just one man in like the sheriff had in 1987. He told me it would be an unwarranted risk that could've gotten one man killed. I reminded him that there were ten dead people, four of them ATF agents. He didn't want to call on me to ask questions after that in subsequent briefings.

There were other problems with the Waco tragedy, and there were questions that will probably never be answered about it. Day in and day out, the FBI tried psychological tactics on Koresh that apparently only hardened his heart and those of his followers. You could hear the sound of a telephone line off the hook blaring at all hours of the night from large speakers the FBI brought in. Other sounds were blared at the compound made to make the Davidians uncomfortable and give up. None of it worked. "WACO, We Ain't Comin' Out!" became a popular acronym for Waco and an accurate description of the Davidians' actions once the FBI set up a perimeter. Rather than trying to get them to leave, one local police officer who worked the perimeter suggested the FBI just declare the place a federal prison and start sending people in. Law enforcement became frustrated. The Davidians and Koresh, with a recording studio, a guitar, plenty of food, and multiple women he considered his wives, were hunkered down for the long haul and saw themselves as victims of oppression.

No one outside of Waco would ever have known what was really going on without the work done by the local media. Koresh was a smooth grifter with narcissistic tendencies and a messiah complex who victimized some of his followers. The ATF and FBI vilified everyone in the Davidian compound because no one gave up. In the end, when it all went sour and the place erupted in flames as the FBI finally tried to overrun the Davidians, the first thing the government did was blame the media as the local reporters said would be done. They were accused of tipping off the Davidians and causing the conflagration that led to the standoff.

That wasn't the only fiction. One of the other greatest fictions was that Bill Clinton's attorney general, Janet Reno, was responsible for the tragedy. She made the call on April 19 to advance on Mount Carmel, but it was based on recommendations from the FBI, who had their own playbook they went by. They didn't listen much to the ATF—at least as ATF agents told me at the time—and the ATF agents didn't do a decent job of preparing for an assault that should not have happened in the first place. As reporters on the scene noted, the ATF pulled up to the raid being towed to the scene in cattle trailers. And the commanders of the raid knew they'd been compromised before the raid ever started.

"There's a 'what the fuck' moment if there ever was," I remember being told at the time. In addition, blaming Reno was the height of absurdity. Janet Reno was the third choice to head the Justice Department. Bill Clinton took office a little more than a month before the raid. His administration had absolutely nothing to do with planning it. Reno grasped the reins of the Justice Department three weeks after the raid began. The ATF had made its plans and executed them.

The *Tribune-Herald* became part of the story because it ran its seven-part series, *The Sinful Messiah*, just prior to the raid. They concluded publishing it after the raid occurred. It was required reading for all of us covering the tragedy. KWTX provided the only video of the raid and later helped to escort wounded ATF agents out of the area. Imagine how poorly planned a raid was that a chance encounter with a television news crew helped provide transportation for wounded agents. Then imagine blaming those journalists for *your* failure. The failure in planning and executing the raid fell squarely on the arrogant shoulders of the ATF agents in charge, and unable to face the consequences of their own actions, they blamed the press.

"To this day we are sort of considered to be responsible," KWTX managing editor Rick Bradfield said in 2018.[10] "I've always resented the way we were portrayed." If KWTX resented how they were portrayed for shooting the video of the raid, the *Tribune-Herald* had an even larger reason to be angry. The newspaper investigated the Branch Davidians for eight months prior to the raid and got into it in the way most local newspapers developed stories—a reporter working a beat heard a story in the community that he, in turn, decided to investigate. In the case of the Davidians, reporter Mark England heard the local group was planning a mass suicide on Passover in 1992. When an editor asked if he had any Sunday feature ideas, England decided to pursue the Branch Davidian story.

The Davidians didn't kill themselves for Passover, but England started digging into their cult, and what he found was disturbing. Those he interviewed spoke about underage wives, child abuse, and the stockpiling of weapons. Darlene McCormick, a few years out of college and in her first job as the central Texas beat reporter, jumped in to help England, and together over the next few months, they documented disturbing stories that led to the *Sinful Messiah* series. The series was a finalist for the Pulitzer Prize in 1994 and was lauded for its efforts as a "high-water mark for investigative reporting at the *Tribune-Herald* and beyond, showing what a few dedicated reporters in a third-tier market could do."[11]

The focus of the series was on children who were abused and sexually assaulted, including a story of Koresh jumping in bed with a twelve-year-old girl and getting her pregnant. The two reporters worked on the project for months with few, other than their immediate supervisors at the paper, knowing what they were up to. They would work a regular eight-hour day covering their beats and spend after hours working the investigation. On more than one occasion, they'd be in the newsroom at 3 a.m. just so they could reach sources in Australia who had connections to the Branch Davidians. The pair spoke with members, former members, friends, and family members of the Davidians. They documented Koresh's proclaiming a "New Light" doctrine to the Davidians that gave him the right to have his way with the wives of cult members and prepubescent girls. One girl would later testify in court that Koresh raped her when she was ten years old.

When the ATF raided the compound, the reason for the series and the concerns it addressed were overwhelmed by the shoot-out and subsequent standoff. Many of the children the newspaper was concerned with and who had been an integral part of the reporting ended up dying with Koresh in the fire that consumed the compound after Reno okayed the final raid, which she did based on the concern for children trapped in the compound.

A few days into the standoff, T-shirt vendors showed up selling shirts and hats. Some featured "WACO, We Ain't Coming Out" printed on them. A circus atmosphere pervaded. One night, as I did a live shot for *Sky News* in England, an anchor said he had heard there were many cults in the United States. "Are they all as heavily armed as this one?" he asked me. I didn't know what to say. "Well, I certainly hope not," was all I could reply. He laughed. "Oh that wonderful yank humor."

Barbara Elmore, the former managing editor at the *Tribune-Herald*, said she became bothered when the focus shifted from the child abuse angle. "The ATF wanted it to get lost. ATF knew about this mess . . . and they didn't do a thing until they got wind of our reporting."[12] The ATF found out the local newspaper was investigating the case as they began to make inroads into the Davidians—though at first they wouldn't confirm for the paper that an investigation was ongoing. That's standard bill of fare for all federal law enforcement, and most reporters can quote chapter and verse what a federal investigator will say when asked. "We can neither confirm nor deny we have an ongoing investigation," followed by a quick request for any information the reporter has about the investigation that federal law enforcement agents won't confirm they are working on.

Throughout the fall of 1992, the ATF and the newspapers worked parallel investigations, and even though the ATF told potential witnesses not to talk to the newspaper, they did. McCormick had even reached out to interview Koresh, whom she described as "very charismatic." By January, the two reporters had enough to file a story—or so they thought. And then the wrangling began. Editors debated whether it was a story, how much of the story they had, and whether they should publish. Bob Lott, the paper's editor, decided to run with the story and explained why he did so when it was published. "We knew the situation at Mount Carmel had been going on for quite a while. It was a dangerous and sinister thing the public should know about. We're not talking just of stockpiling weapons, but such things as sexual exploitation of young girls and other abuses of children in the name of religion. Local authorities knew about the situation and, as best we could tell, had done next to nothing. We had been seriously looking into it for about eight months."[13]

The ATF attempted to get the newspaper to hold off, but there was no indication what, if anything, the ATF planned to do. The newspaper decided it was in the public interest to let people know about the sexual abuse and potential danger to residents. The story, as it originally ran, began thusly:

If you are a Branch Davidian, Christ lives on a threadbare piece of land 10 miles east of Waco called Mount Carmel.

He has dimples, claims a ninth-grade education, married his legal wife when she was 14, enjoys a beer now and then, plays a mean guitar, reportedly packs a 9mm Glock and keeps an arsenal of military assault rifles, and willingly admits that he is a sinner without equal.

In a September 1993 review of the media's role in the Mount Carmel tragedy, the Society of Professional Journalists praised the *Tribune-Herald* for its series as a "good example of thorough, contextual reporting" and concluded that neither the *Tribune-Herald* nor KWTX violated ethical norms in covering the event on February 28, 1993.

The same could not be said for the ATF. After the dust settled, documents showed that the ATF knew their cover was blown prior to the raid and they should've called it off. Instead, the government said reporters were at fault for tipping off the Davidians about the raid, even as some government investigators questioned the need for the raid in the first place. But the bitter taste of a government trying to shoot the messenger lingered and still haunts the reporters who uncovered the dirty secrets of the "Sinful Messiah," as does the arrogance of an ATF that bungled a raid trying to prove its relevance to a cost-cutting Congress. Investigations after the fact exonerated the newspaper and proved a majority of what it reported—including the fact that thirteen children found dead at Mount Carmel were David Koresh's. Investigations also proved that the ATF knew they had been compromised and should never have conducted the raid in the first place. Most of the world never would've known about the decadence and depravity conducted in the name of Christianity outside of Waco without the *Tribune-Herald*. I, along with every other television reporter there, found out what we found out initially from the "Sinful Messiah." We all quoted it and referred to it on air.

The government committed two sins in Waco that it has repeated over and over in my lifetime and that have become easier to commit as fewer reporters are available to report what our government does:

1. It lied to us.
2. Then it blamed the media instead of accepting the responsibility of its actions.

The newspaper paid a hefty price for its enterprise reporting. The *Tribune-Herald* was a family-owned newspaper until the 1970s when it was bought by the Cox Newspaper chain, which spent more than $1 million defending its actions in uncovering the Branch Davidians. Today, the paper is owned by Berkshire Hathaway, an American multinational conglomerate holding company headquartered in Omaha, Nebraska. It owns GEICO, Duracell, Dairy Queen, Long and Foster realtors, with minority interests in American Express, the Coca-Cola Company, Bank of America, and Apple. Warren Buffett in 2016 owned more than 30 percent of the voting shares of the company. The multinational originally began as a textile company, and according to the Human Rights Campaign Corporate Quality Index, in 2021 the conglomerate rated a 20—among the lowest of Fortune 500 companies.[14]

And, as a result of being owned by a conglomerate, the paper has fewer reporters today than the day of the Waco raid.

The denouement to the Waco standoff came in Texas but not at Waco. It came on the last Sunday in April 1997 when Rick McLaren and his hearty band of Texas separatists went ballistic. McLaren, a local rogue who'd pissed off most of the residents of the area by proclaiming that Texas wasn't really a state but its own country, had issued writs and battled his neighbors in court for years. For ten years, McLaren, who once was a member of a militia, had also been a thorn in the side of landowners, judges, governors, and anyone else he believed was part of the "de facto" government.

On that last day of April, McClaren and his followers kidnapped Joe and Margaret Ann Rowe and held them hostage in the Davis Mountain Resort, demanding the release of one of McClaren's friends and followers being held in jail in exchange for the release of the Rowes. For seven days, the "Republic of Texas" standoff rekindled memories of the Waco tragedy. I flew in from Washington to cover this standoff, and by the time I got there, another "Satellite City" of reporters had sprung up outside the standoff. Again, there were hundreds of reporters, and at one point in time, "Satellite City" became the second-largest city in the nearly vacant county. Mike Boettcher from NBC held court, and we talked about covering the Gulf War. Barry Schlachter, a venerable reporter from the *Fort Worth Star-Telegram*, talked about the difference between Waco and the Fort Davis standoff.

Boettcher would later produce an award-winning documentary with his son Carlos after being embedded with American troops in Afghanistan. He was the first to present a live satellite report on CNN. Schlachter, a longtime reporter in Fort Worth, worked for a newspaper rich in journalistic history.

The newspaper bears a rich and colorful legacy tied to the Old West. Its founding publisher, Amon G. Carter Sr., was a renowned booster of Fort Worth and West Texas. In fact, the newspaper was known by a phrase that still resides on its masthead: "Where the West Begins." Under Carter's leadership, the paper served eighty-four counties in Texas, some by stagecoach. In 1922, the paper began the first Fort Worth radio station, WBAP, "We Bring a Program." The *Star-Telegram* also established the first television station in the southern half of the United States in 1948. The paper was sold in 1974 to Capital Cities Communications, Inc. Under Capital Cities, which later became Capital Cities/ABC, Inc., in 1986, the *Star-Telegram* won two Pulitzer Prizes. It was later sold to Knight Ridder in 1997 and became a McClatchy newspaper in 2006.

The McClatchy Company, the second-largest local newspaper business in the nation, filed for Chapter 11 bankruptcy protection in 2020. The *Miami Herald*, *Kansas City Star*, *Sacramento Bee*, and twenty-four other publications in fourteen states were owned by McClatchy. The company's biggest acquisition was another newspaper chain, Knight Ridder. Craig Forman, president and chief executive officer of McClatchy, said online, "When local media suffers in the face of industry challenges, communications suffer, polarization grows, civic connections fray and borrowing costs rise for local government."[15] *New York Times* executive editor Dean Baquet made the ominous prediction that "I think most local newspapers in America are going to die in the next five years, except for the ones that have been bought by a local billionaire."[16]

I spent my time covering the Republic of Texas standoff similarly to covering the Waco standoff, and I ended up doing a live shot with, I swear, the same *Sky News* anchor I spoke with during the Waco tragedy. He asked me the same question about heavily armed American cults.

The Fort Davis standoff, as the Republic of Texas standoff was also called, was a comedy of errors by everyone involved. But Governor George W. Bush had insisted that the state would handle this standoff and that it would not end as the Waco standoff had—"with burning buildings on national television," as Texas Department of Public Service (DPS) spokesman Mike Cox told me at the time. It didn't. The DPS, the Texas state police (or the Texas Rangers), made sure nothing like that happened at all. The media were kept nearly nine miles away from the standoff "for our own safety," and only on one or two occasions was a pool of reporters allowed to travel with the Rangers within eyesight of the compound. The reporters and photographers who did so returned to the rest of us with tales of barbed wire and a grove of grape vines but very little useful video or information.

We stood nine miles away on park ground. There was a no-man's-land of 100 feet between the media and the police who had barricaded off the road leading to the Republic of Texas compound. The police didn't want us anywhere near the scene and didn't want us to talk to them either. I took to tap dancing across the imaginary no-man's-land line and was treated with grunts and threats.

On the first Saturday in May, as the horses got ready to run at Churchill Downs, DPS spokesman Mike Cox emerged to declare the situation over—without a shot and no fatalities.

"We learned our lesson from Waco," I was told by Cox.

I replied that we hadn't seen anything but a blank road for seven days, and we didn't really know what happened. "Exactly," he said.

The lesson of Waco—control the media and control the story.

10

OPEN THE FLOODGATES

Following Ronald Reagan, the president who had the single greatest effect on destroying the independent press, had to be President Bill Clinton when he signed the Telecommunications Act into law. He wasn't the architect of the act. You can assign blame there to some in his administration, communication lobbyists, and every member of Congress, but Clinton signed the act into law on February 8, 1996. Fairness and Accuracy in Reporting described it as a measure "essentially bought and paid for by corporate media lobbies" and noted that the law radically "opened the floodgates on mergers."[1]

The Telecommunications Act of 1996 was the first significant overhaul of the country's telecommunications law since the Communications Act of 1934. The act's stated objective was to open up markets to competition by removing regulations and barriers to entry, the idea being that with the emerging internet and cable television markets, anybody in the world should be able to jump in and compete. It was sold as a way to lower the barriers to entry into the market, making for greater competition and democratization of the telecommunications world. The reality was established communication companies had a huge head start; what the act actually accomplished was giving those giant corporations the ability to cannibalize the industry, allowing already large corporations to become larger by removing obstacles that stood in the way of corporations' plans to acquire multiple properties across multiple media platforms.

In other words, it only encouraged the monopolies that the act stated it would help prevent. Instead of allowing more competition, it only made it easier for the monopolies to gobble up smaller companies, becoming larger and more dominant along the way.

From 1980 on, Ronald Reagan, Roger Ailes, Rupert Murdoch, Bill Clinton, and Congress each decided that the best model for communicating with the masses was through raw, unregulated capitalism. The problem with that should have been seen ahead of time and, according to some lobbyists, members of Congress, reporters, and the written record, actually was. It didn't matter. The corporations got what they wanted, and the government delivered. The results are plain enough to see. Prior to 1980, the government acted as if communications were a public trust. People, no matter how rich, poor, ignorant, or educated, had the same rights, and government tried to make sure everyone had access to news and information. Free speech was not something we placed *entirely* in the marketplace. There were protections. We understood that a monopoly on communications would be to the detriment of free speech and the republic. Part of the checks and balances that allowed us to function as a democracy included a diversity of ownership of media companies. It also included the compulsory printing of public notices in community newspapers so that citizens knew what the government was doing. It included a respectful nod to the freedom of information. All of that has changed.

Today, governments block requests for information on actions that local and state governments and the federal government take on our behalf. There is a huge push to eliminate printing public notices altogether. There are fewer reporters covering anything government does. And with the advent of cable television and later the internet, we collectively lost our minds and pretended there was no way to regulate either—so why offer any regulation at all? Mark Fowler certainly favored little to no regulation on the airwaves. George Bush did nothing to stop the move Reagan began, and neither did Bill Clinton.

Clinton signed the Telecommunication Act legislation with much fanfare. He talked about how he encouraged Congress to pass the law and nodded at the speed with which Congress did so. "This historic legislation . . . embodies what we should be about in this country and in this city," Clinton said. "It clearly enables the age of possibility in America to expand and include more Americans . . . it will provide more information and more entertainment."[2]

"Before the ink was even dry on the 1996 Act," wrote S. Derek Turner, research director of Free Press, "the powerful media and telecommunication giants and their army of overpaid lobbyists went straight to work obstructing and undermining the competition the new law was intended to create."[3]

Perhaps it is no coincidence Roger Ailes took over Fox News that year from former CBS news chief Van Gordon Sauter. Sauter had his problems and his controversies. He was often accused of turning the CBS Evening News into infotainment. But he was no Roger Ailes. With Fox, Ailes had the perfect venue for putting together what he always wanted—a conservative network that, while stating it was fair and balanced, was anything but. The timing of the Telecommunications Act may have been serendipitous, but then again, since communication corporations had lobbied for the act, it may all have been one continuous move toward monopolization and commercial profit. At least the critics saw it that way. For sure, Clinton's signature on the Telecommunications Act had a profound impact on television, radio, and newspaper ownership. Ben Bagdikian warned us in 1983 in *The Media Monopoly* that just fifty corporations owned 90 percent of the media. Today, Viacom, News Corporation, Comcast, CBS, Time Warner, and Disney together own about the same percentage of the market.[4]

"In 1983, the largest 50 corporations controlled 90 percent of the media. Today, as a result of massive mergers and takeovers, six corporations control 90 percent of what we see, hear, and read. . . . These powerful corporations also have an agenda, and it would be naive not to believe that their views and needs impact coverage of issues important to them," Bernie Sanders said in 2017.[5]

This is rarely reported. Which board of directors of any of those companies would want the world to be aware of their acquisitions? Instead, we're told there's a "liberal" bias to the media when the fact is the bias is toward profit—whether it is preaching to the left, the right, or whatever group will increase ratings and advertising revenue. Each media company is merely out to make profits. Public service is not a priority unless it can turn a profit.

Prior to the passage of the Telecommunications Act, companies were not allowed to own more than forty radio stations. Today, iHeartMedia owns more than 850 of the 15,000 licensed commercial radio stations in the country. iHeartMedia began in San Antonio in 1972 as Clear Channel Communications and purchased its first radio station, WOAI (the sister to WOAI-TV, which became KMOL, where I worked before it again became WOAI-TV after it was sold and ended up in the hands of Sinclair). Sinclair has become the local television equivalent of iHeartMedia and owns or operates 294 of the 1,700 commercial television stations across the United States. Sinclair is in eighty-nine markets as large as Washington, D.C., and as small as Ottumwa, Iowa, and Kirksville, Missouri.[6] It owns or operates three stations in the San Antonio–Kerrville, Texas, market alone.

Many of the stations, in Sinclair's case, are owned outright, while others are operated by Sinclair through local marketing agreements that Sinclair pioneered in 1991 when it entered the Pittsburgh, Pennsylvania, market and wanted to avoid a Federal Communications Commission regulation that forbade duopolies.

Sinclair is well known as a conservative company. In March 2018, CNN chief media analyst Brian Stelter obtained an internal memorandum sent by Sinclair, which dictated that its stations must produce and broadcast an "anchor-delivered journalistic responsibility message" using a mandated script. The promos contain language decrying "biased and false news" and accusing unnamed mainstream media figures of bias.[7]

In the case of iHeartMedia, it owns eight stations in my hometown of Louisville that used to be independently owned—including former news and information giant WHAS radio, which iHeartMedia turned into a talk radio station. In many cases, both companies have cut staff, have changed formats, or, to paraphrase H. L. Mencken, have been turned into a chain store that offers generic product in a variety of cities. In every case where the giant changes entered, news coverage has suffered, and staffs have been cut. Some of the cuts at Gannett, which owns 100 daily newspapers and close to 1,000 weeklies, were once described as a "total bloodbath" in the *American Journalism Review*.[8]

The combination of acquisitions, mergers, and layoffs has reduced local news coverage to the point that many markets are now news and information deserts—and as a result, with only the large networks, cable, and internet websites getting the viewers and readers, the news has become more divisive, and local coverage is nearly nonexistent. Due in part to the combination of the moves under Reagan and Clinton, five of the largest media mergers occurred in the history of the United States following the 1996 Telecommunications Act. The largest media merger occurred on January 10, 2000, just shy of four years after Clinton signed the act. That year, America Online bought control of Time Warner for a total of $112 billion. AT&T and Charter Communications scored the second- and third-largest merger of all time in 2015 and 2016, respectively, when they bought control over Time Warner. Walt Disney scored the fourth-largest media merger, buying control over Twenty-First Century Fox on December 14, 2017 for a total of $84.8 billion.[9]

That buyout sparked controversy in the press. Jason Bailey, the editor of *Flavorwire*, noted that on November 3, 2017, Disney banned the *Los Angeles Times* from attending press screenings of its films in retaliation for the paper's coverage of their political influence in Anaheim.

"The idea of a major, multinational conglomerate being that petty and vindictive and really engaging in an act of retribution against an outlet, and against reporters who had nothing to do with the thing that they were angry about, gave some insight into the length they were willing to go against anyone who didn't toe the Disney company line. It's very worrisome and is more worrisome if they remain in control of this much more of the entertainment industry," Bailey wrote.[10]

Each merger and media acquisition caused some controversy, but ultimately, the companies that controlled the media that would potentially do the reporting that would reach the most people failed to cover their own corporate buyouts to any lasting extent. Certainly, most people today cannot tell you who owns which company or that if you're a fan of *Rick and Morty* or *Adult Swim*, you're also supporting CNN—even if you think it's "fake media." Want to go watch a movie at your nearby Showcase Cinemas? Well, then, you're supporting National Amusement, and then you're also supporting Simon and Schuster publishers and CBS News.

It's all one big, fat, happy corporate family, and the news is rolled right into the thick of it. Far from being an outside observer of what goes on in the marketplace, today's news is just another widget being sold *in* the marketplace. As such, cost-cutting measures are often employed that, while taking down the overhead of producing the news, also destroy the ability to gather news. Once again, the shortsighted idea of short-term profit kills any long-term profit by corrupting the inherent value of the product. What good is a newsroom that doesn't produce news—only the "appearance" of news? That is where we are today, and the Telecommunications Act of 1996 went a long way toward putting us here. After the act became law, it wasn't hard to figure that unfettered growth would lead to mergers and acquisitions. What is amazing is that the politicians sold this to an unsuspecting public. They were able to do it after the lobbyists for large media companies encouraged it to happen. They used the buzzwords of "free market" and "free speech" to purchase the opposite of those two thoughts. And they did so with the help of a president embroiled in scandal who wanted favorable coverage as he ran for reelection.

Ronald Reagan's administration put us on the path. Bill Clinton accelerated the efforts of media destruction. And the results are obvious.

By the time Roger Ailes took over Fox News, I was working for an O&O in Kansas City, Missouri. The term "O&O" is applied to "owned and operated" stations actually owned by the network that the local station is affiliated with. In the case of WDAF-TV in Kansas City, it is Fox. I went there after spending five years in Washington working for the network, and I left Washington needing a fundamental change in life.

My father died of lung cancer on October 17, 1995, just two weeks after the birth of our third son, Wyatt. At one point in time, two days before he was born, my wife was in false labor on one floor of the local hospital while my dad was apparently dying on the floor below. I spent that day running back and forth between floors. My father, seeing how worn out I was, asked me what was wrong, and I told him. He said, "I ain't going anywhere until I see my grandson. Don't worry." He didn't. One of my last photographs of my dad is him holding our youngest son in his arms outside the hospital where Wyatt was born. Dad got to spend two weeks with him.

One of the last things my dad said to me struck hard. He said, "I'm not sitting here dying wishing I'd spent more time at the office. I wish I'd spent it with you all," meaning his children. I told him it was okay because he was with me now, and that meant everything to me. But after he passed, I began thinking hard about that. Being a correspondent for a network show meant a lot of travel. I had visited almost every state in the United States and several foreign countries in the past five years covering a wide variety of crime. Interviewing the parents of dead kids was grating. Interviewing criminals was depressing, and traveling from the White House to Congress and to statehouses and local city halls talking to politicians about the continuing problems of gang violence, drug violence, abuse, and other preventable crimes made me bone weary. Politicians never listen. They have only their interests at heart. I began thinking that when Mencken said the only way to look at a politician "is down," he was on to something. Although I confess that I also enjoyed the saying that I look at politicians the way a dog looks at a fire hydrant.

Fox had an opening to begin an investigative unit in Kansas City. The job meant running the unit, anchoring the reporting, and creating a "virtual set" in front of a green screen—pioneering stuff at the time. The move would also allow us to live within a couple of hours of my wife's parents, who had a farm between Fulton and Columbia, Missouri. Pam's parents were aging, and we thought it would be best to try to spend some time with them. My own father passed at age fifty-five, and I didn't want to have a regret that we didn't allow the boys to see their grandparents in Missouri while they were still living. So, we moved. While Fox had a reputation then (and even more so now) of being a conservative network, I rarely ran into ideological constraints when investigating news stories. I was never told to lay off someone or put the pressure on someone else. I was given only vague guidelines. Sometimes I was asked, "Do we really want to do this?" or "Do we have all the information we really need to do this?" Since these are all legitimate news questions, it was hard to accuse management of any bias. Sure, these questions came when we investigated "sacred cows," but I was never told not to investigate anything—I was told only to be careful. I was surprised because at *America's Most Wanted*, there had been some pressure from Fox corporate suits to go after Ann Richards for the Kenneth McDuff killing spree and to make Bill Clinton look bad by highlighting an Arkansas criminal who had skipped bail while Clinton was governor. But in Kansas City, there was absolutely no overt pressure. Some of the key investigations we undertook in Kansas City concerned infrastructure, bail bonds, and the chemical Dursban. The last story would have national consequences, and it would lead to my departure after two years there.

Our story, titled "Risky Bridges," concerned aging infrastructure in and around the Kansas City area. It was troubling on a number of levels. We documented bridges that received failing grades from government inspectors and had never been repaired or replaced. One busy bridge in the downtown area had a gaping hole in the pavement, and I shot a stand-up as the camera pushed through the hole to the water below. I did that more than twenty years before Transportation Secretary Pete Buttigieg would make an impassioned plea for infrastructure reform in June 2021 from a similar bridge with a cracked support beam.

Another bridge we investigated was approved to allow for only four tons of weight, but school buses weighing at least twice that crossed the bridge daily with unaware bus drivers and schoolchildren making the haul. We had video of kids bouncing in their seats and singing songs as the bus traversed a bridge that could have easily collapsed. We stumbled across that piece of video while we inspected the bridge and warned the school system immediately. One bridge was so badly damaged that you could see support struts vibrating loose anytime a car crossed over it. We documented it all and because of those reports got local and state governments to dedicate time and money to repairing the bridges. We also did stories on the trucking industry and showed how many long-haul trucks had insufficient brakes and were a menace on the highway. I-70, which cut through the heart of the state, was and is a major trucking route. Our series on bail bonds showed how easy it was for anyone to "get out of jail free" and how the courts had little sway over the ability for dangerous criminals to get out of jail; we also showed the disparity of the system. A man or a woman charged with multiple murders might get out of jail before a man or a woman caught with a single marijuana cigarette in his or her possession. It was always worse if you were a minority—no matter what the charge.

While all of these stories made an impact on the community and proved the need for good, solid community journalism, one story we did proved not only the need for such stories but also the lengths to which large corporations would go to keep those stories from being produced or published.

I got a tip late in 1997 that almost two dozen workers in a rural Missouri courthouse had come down with chemical lupus after exposure to a pesticide called Dursban—a common ingredient at the time in wasp spray, among other things. Its application was, at the time, almost universal. I confess the stuff was most effective. Zap a wasp or a hornet with a stream of pesticide containing Dursban, and the knockdown ability was incredible, almost instant death. I'd used it many times outdoors, at my own home, and at my in-laws' farm. But never had I used it indoors. Apparently, at the Missouri courthouse, where it was used to go after a wasp nest, the pesticide got into the ventilation, and people got sick. We traced this tip and spoke with doctors, lawyers, scientists, and alleged victims—tracking the problem across the country. For months, we investigated Dursban, which was the Dow Chemical name for a compound called chlorpyrifos. It is an organophosphate, and according to the World Health Organization, it is "moderately" hazardous to humans based on its acute toxicity.[11] No amount of the chemical is deemed safe for human consumption, and most of us alive on the planet may have traces of the compound in our bodies due to the use of the pesticide in agricultural production.

When I started to tackle the problem in 1997, Dursban was one of the most common pesticides available. But as our research and investigation showed, it was dangerous to be exposed to it for any length of time. Exposure during pregnancy may harm the mental development of children, and it was found to cause autoimmune disorders in severe cases of exposure. We also uncovered the mostly unreported fact that Dow had to pay $732,000 as an Environmental Protection Agency (EPA) penalty for not forwarding reports it had received on 249 chlorpyrifos poisoning incidents—including several we were investigating.[12]

We put together a story based on our findings and prepared to air it. And while Dow Chemical wouldn't provide anyone to speak with me on camera about the piece, representatives from Dow insisted on viewing it before we aired it—and they wanted to produce a five-minute counterpiece that they demanded to be broadcast following our piece. It was an unheard-of demand, but Fox attorneys allowed Dow to do it. The only stipulation from our news director was that Dow had to cut out a portion of its videotape that attacked me personally.

So, Dow refused to answer questions from the public about the pesticide and produced its own video propaganda to counter the news we presented. And the network allowed them to tack that video on to our coverage, effectively trying to neuter our exposé. Later, in depositions taken for a challenge on the renewal of the license of WTVT-TV in Tampa, Florida, before the Federal Communications Commission, I was deposed to show that Fox, which owned the Tampa station as well, acted in bad faith and didn't serve the public's interest. I told them in the deposition that the news managers at WDAF allowed Dow to view our story ahead of time because in their minds it was the "best way to be fair, to be expedient, and to *avoid litigation*." In other words, our management thought that bending over for Dow, doing something we wouldn't normally do for anyone else, was the best way to be fair—because Dow had a lot of money and Fox didn't want to spend money defending the story in court.

Because of the row stirred by Dow, few elsewhere wanted to touch the Dursban story. This is the chilling effect on journalism that large companies working with media monopolies can employ. Friends of mine at two networks who worked on magazine shows decided the story was too tough to handle because of the "stink of litigation." Mind you, no one could deny the facts we presented at WDAF or the facts dozens if not hundreds of local reporters across the country had done on the problems of Dursban. Just a little more than two years after our series aired in 1998, the federal government banned the product for most residential uses—based on the reporting I and others like me had done across the country. One member of Congress from Missouri at the time told me he'd never even heard of Dursban until he saw the story we did on it.

There was speculation and questions about why Fox caved to the pressures from Dow. Was it simply because of litigation, or did the higher-ups at Fox and Dow have friendships and business entanglements that precluded any story from ever being produced without Dow doing as it pleased?

The *Village Voice* raised that question in a story it did at the end of November 2000. In a story that questioned Rupert Murdoch's claims of "fair and balanced" coverage at his network, the publication interviewed me and asked a very similar question: "This raises a larger question: If bias is inevitable, what's to stop the reporters and businesses who control the airwaves from slanting the news to serve their mutual self-interest? 'The election coverage is a microcosm of everything wrong with American journalists,' says Brian Karem, a former investigative reporter for Fox TV affiliate WDAF in Kansas City and, more recently, author of *Spin Control*. 'Instead of being disinterested observers, we're right there in the thick of it with those in power. It's all one big, happy club.'"

It was the end of my time at WDAF and with Fox.[13] I refused to be part of the club. Truth to power can't exist when you're part of the club.

By June 1999, I decided to move back to the Washington area, where we still owned a home and where my wife and I could raise our kids—we hoped—in an environment more conducive to science and free speech.

Chlorpyrifos remained legal for agricultural use and is still used to this day. Under the Trump administration, EPA administrator Scott Pruitt denied a petition to ban the pesticide outright.[14] On August 9, 2018, the U.S. Ninth Circuit Court of Appeals ordered the EPA to ban the sale of chlorpyrifos in the United States within sixty days. The ruling was immediately appealed by the Trump administration.

And Dow has been very successful in keeping Dursban in use despite the unquestioned danger to human beings. In 2011, the EPA estimated that, in the general U.S. population, people consume 0.009 micrograms of chlorpyrifos per kilogram of their body weight per day directly from food residue. And by 2016, the EPA could find no amount of chlorpyrifos that was safe in the human body.[15]

There are very few pesticides as effective as Dursban. But its use on fields and in agriculture make it a necessary evil, according to some. Dow paid $2 million to the State of New York in 2003 as part of a settlement in response to a lawsuit to end Dow's advertising of Dursban as "safe."[16] Actions have been taken at the state level in Oregon, California, and Hawaii.

Dursban today is used in a lot of countries, though some have made it illegal. In 2020, it was banned in Thailand, and after a deadline to dispose of or destroy the chemical, any person found to possess it illegally could face up to ten years in jail and a hefty fine.

But in this country, it still finds its way into our food chain, and with big media and big business working together, it is increasingly hard to hold the large companies accountable. After the initial series of reports, the EPA banned Dursban for personal use. But it was still allowed to be used on farm crops. Twenty-four years after I did stories on Dursban, on August 18, 2021, the EPA, under the Joe Biden administration, finally banned its use on crops. "Today EPA is taking an overdue step to protect public health. Ending the use of chlorpyrifos on food will help to ensure children, farmworkers, and all people are protected from the potentially dangerous consequences of this pesticide," said Administrator Michael Regan said in a statement.[17]

11

GIVE THE DEVIL THE
BENEFIT OF THE LAW?

The next blow to the free press occurred less than two months after terrorists crashed two passenger jets into the twin towers of the World Trade Center and one into the Pentagon on Tuesday morning, September 11, 2001. It was the deadliest terrorist attack in human history and the single deadliest incident for firefighters and law enforcement officers in the history of the United States.

The U.S. Congress responded with an act of Congress signed into law on October 26, 2001, by President George W. Bush, the same George W. Bush who, as governor of Texas, made sure he took care of the "patriots" from the Republic of Texas who wanted to start their own country. The U.S. Patriot Act was a quick and dirty act by Congress—never let it be said they can't work together quickly when they find the need—that expanded the abilities of law enforcement to conduct surveillance by tapping domestic and international phones. It eased interagency communication—a problem still lingering following the Waco tragedy. It also led to increased penalties for those convicted of terroristic crimes. It was quickly cobbled together from preexisting bills—all of which had previously failed to pass through Congress. Some were considered bad legislation, some unneeded. All of them were flawed in some form or fashion but gained quick favor following the attacks in New York and on the Pentagon.

Unseen and underreported was the Patriot Act's effect on the free press. The Reporters Committee for Freedom of the Press sounded the alarm, but few listened. According to the committee, the Patriot Act, once signed into law, allowed the government to require journalists to turn over their notes on demand, potentially forcing reporters to reveal the identities of confidential sources. This is the same issue that sent me to jail on four separate occasions and meant a giant step back for press freedom. But the committee also said journalists' communications could come under FBI surveillance without their knowledge. But the big concern was about the secret courts enabled by the act that could allow a government agent to gain access to a reporter or a news organization without their knowledge. In a written response on July 26, 2002, Assistant Attorney General Daniel J. Bryant conceded that newspapers were not exempt from the secret court orders. "Such an order could conceivably be served on a public library, bookstore, or newspaper, although it is unlikely that such entities maintain those types of records," Bryant wrote.[1] He declined to state the number of times the government has requested an order or the number of times the FISA (Foreign Intelligence Surveillance Act) court has granted an order. That information is classified, his letter said.

Over the years, the Patriot Act has had a debilitating effect on journalism, and there is absolutely no way of knowing how much. The government simply won't tell you who it has put under the microscope or why. One of the latest problems came to light in 2019. On February 13, 2020, the *New York Post* reported that the New York Police Department (NYPD) had issued a subpoena to Twitter for data from the account of the *Post*'s police bureau chief, Tina Moore. The subpoena, dated December 9, 2019, asked Twitter not to reveal its existence for ninety days and told the company to comply by January 10. Twitter did not comply, and when *Post* lawyers contacted the NYPD, it withdrew the demand. So, what did the police want? The department wanted to know who leaked the crime scene photos of a triple murder in Brooklyn the previous October and were later tweeted by the reporter from the *Post*.

It was an odd subpoena made more bizarre for one reason: the legal authority cited by the NYPD in the subpoena included both city law and an obscure provision of the Patriot Act. It also brings to light what that act was and what it actually did. While sold as an antiterrorism piece of legislation in the wake of 9/11, it specifically consisted of expanded law enforcement authority that the Justice Department had previously sought but had been denied by Congress. How else do you think such a comprehensive bill could pass within six weeks of the September bombing? It was already sitting around, and Congress needed to make a statement—any statement—even if ultimately a problematic one. The ability to participate in a knee-jerk reaction is, after all, a hallmark of Congress, be the party red with embarrassment or blue by holding its breath.

Section 213 of the Patriot Act, for example, expanded "sneak and peek" search warrants without prior notice to the target in *all* criminal cases—not just terrorism investigations.[2] Similar types of warrants had, in

Sam Donaldson and I discuss questioning presidents at the McNay Art Museum in San Antonio, 1991. *Photo courtesy of the author*

Some of the many reporters who covered the Kentucky general assembly in 1985. I'm the guy in the very back. This was less than half the press corps covering the Kentucky legislature. Today, this is more than the total number who cover the legislature on a daily basis. *Photo courtesy of the author*

Walking out of the district court in San Antonio handcuffed after refusing to reveal my sources. *Photo courtesy of the author*

Kuwait City, the day of that city's liberation during the first Gulf War, leaning against an abandoned Iraqi tank with a Betacam on my shoulder. *Photo courtesy of the author*

Posing with an unidentified member of the Colombian team searching for Pablo Escobar in the countryside outside of Bogota. *Photo courtesy of the author*

A still from a stand-up with the 41st Combat Support Hospital on Tapline Road in northern Saudi Arabia. From the documentary "Texans at War." *Photo courtesy of the author*

John Walsh, the anchor of *America's Most Wanted* (on the left), and me at a reception in the mid-1990s. *Photo courtesy of the author*

Standing room only for the last press briefing given in the Brady Briefing Room by President Barack Obama. It wouldn't be until the coronavirus pandemic that a president would brief in that room again. *Photo courtesy of the author*

Facing down President Donald Trump— asking him to defend the numbers he gave the country regarding illegal immigration— as he told me to sit down. *Photo courtesy of William Moon*

Prior to the pandemic, anywhere from 50 to 75 reporters would cram themselves into a small space on the South Lawn walkway outside of the Oval Office to catch a Donald Trump "Chopper Talk" session where he'd answer questions he liked and pretended he couldn't hear those he didn't. *Photo courtesy of the author*

The press conference in the East Room after the 2018 midterm elections. Trump got angry as I asked him about putting the country first—even if the Democrats tried to impeach him (which they did). *Photo courtesy of William Moon*

the past, been decried in the South. Jimmy Carter once criticized warrants where one police officer would go to the back door of a home and wait until another officer approached the front door and knocked. At that time, the officer in the back of the house would say to the officer at the front of the house to "come on in," and the raid was on. The Patriot Act removed the need for such inept and overbearing playacting by simply making sure that a police officer could more easily get a secret warrant, thereby making even the pretense of an invitation unnecessary.

The Patriot Act also gave additional powers to the FBI, immigration, and the Secret Service. All told, the Patriot Act changed or created dozens of federal statutes that could be used for terrorism but could also be used for some far shadier things. Senator Russell Feingold, a Democrat from Wisconsin, was the only senator to vote against the act, and he warned of its expansive nature. "We must grant law enforcement the tools that it needs to stop this terrible threat. But we must give them only those extraordinary tools that they need and that relate specifically to the task at hand."[3]

Feingold outlined extensive problems with the act, including deportation, jailing, and the stifling of free speech. He railed against the broad expansion of government power that would come under the Foreign Intelligence Surveillance Act or the FISA courts. The bill allowed law enforcement to monitor computers without a warrant. The bill, Feingold said, would deny detained persons a trial or hearing where the government would be required to prove that the person is, in fact, engaged in terrorist activity. He decried what the bill would do to the reporters and their First Amendment rights. "Of course, there is no doubt that if we lived in a police state, it would be easier to catch terrorists. If we lived in a country that allowed the police to search your home at any time for any reason; if we lived in a country that allowed the government to open your mail, eavesdrop on your phone conversations, or intercept your email communications; if we lived in a country that allowed the government to hold people in jail indefinitely based on what they write or think, or based on mere suspicion that they are up to no good, then the government would no doubt discover and arrest more terrorists."[4]

Feingold saw the Patriot Act as an existential threat to the United States, and quoting from *A Man for All Seasons*, Feingold said, "Yes I'd give the Devil benefit of law, for my own safety's sake."[5]

Using the Patriot Act to get a subpoena in order to erase a tweet of a photograph of a double homicide in Brooklyn, as it turned out, had absolutely nothing to do with terrorism. But it had a chilling effect on journalism. Once you make the world of journalism all about profits, take away its ability to investigate and report legitimate news, and remove sources of revenue at the state and local levels by eliminating, as previously noted, public notice ads and other sources of revenue, you have achieved a death by a thousand cuts. No single move killed journalism. All of them together did. Under the Reagan administration, as already noted, the federal government had secretly sent investigators out into crowds pretending to be reporters, and now the federal government apparently could do even more—it could passively acquire information gathered by newspapers or television stations with the flip of a switch. Edward Snowden brought the seriousness of this breach of privacy to the world's attention in 2013 with a series of articles that ran in the *Washington Post* and *The Guardian*. Snowden has been called everything from a traitor to a patriot. He fled, ultimately, to Russia, where he remains to this day. In early 2016, he became the president of the Freedom of the Press Foundation, a San Francisco–based nonprofit that aims to protect journalists from hacking and government surveillance. On September 2, 2020, the U.S. Court of Appeals for the Ninth Circuit ruled that the surveillance program exposed by Snowden was illegal and possibly unconstitutional.[6] Snowden still faces espionage charges in the United States. "I never imagined that I would live to see our courts condemn the NSA's [National Security Agency's] activities as unlawful and in the same ruling credit me for exposing them," Snowden said in a message posted to Twitter.[7]

The combination of surveillance, known, unknown, and suspected, on reporters essentially killed confidentially sourced enterprise reporting. "You can put a fork in reporting, because it's done," several national reporters opined. Others spoke of the stifling effect of the Patriot Act, including members of Congress who passed the act. Some tried to amend the act with no success.

By the beginning of the second year of the twenty-first century, the pressures brought about by greed and government interference made it crystal clear how desperate things had become for providing clear and up-to-date information to the American public. One case in particular highlights another problem brought about by media consolidation.

Just four months after the terrorist attack in New York and Washington, D.C., a lesser-known disaster occurred in Minot, North Dakota. Just after 1:37 a.m., a train derailed four miles west of the city. Five tanker cars ruptured and released anhydrous ammonia into the air and threatened the lives of the approximately 40,000 residents there. Emergency response to the disaster was, in itself, a disaster. Police had trouble getting the word out, and so did the local radio stations. Most of them were owned, at the time, by Clear Channel Communications, the forerunner to iHeartMedia.

According to reports at the time, either one person was on duty at the automated stations or no one was on duty. The fact is, for several hours, officials had trouble announcing the life-threatening event. There was confusion among first responders. There were few if any members of the press readily available—particularly at radio stations that were not locally owned. The incident is often cited as an example of the dangers of media consolidation. It certainly says something about the cost-cutting measures of not keeping overnight staff at stations.

Even if the police had trouble activating the Emergency Alert System, an overnight reporter listening to a police radio could've announced on a local radio station what had happened and given some notice to the community. As it was a dangerous spill of a caustic compound that could've easily killed thousands and went unreported for several hours, perhaps it would've been nice to be able to announce that more quickly. Today, first responders would need only tweet out the news and tweet it at a member of the media. But that option did not exist then. Either way, even today, an emergency or breaking news needs to "break" on several platforms to resonate. It isn't enough for news to go viral—it has to reach as many people as possible as quickly as possible. Radio, television, newspapers, and the internet are all equal partners in spreading the word.

Making a living as a television reporter by this time was an exercise in boredom and futility. Reduced to fires, murders, ambulance chasing, sound-bite grabbing, and very little enterprise reporting, most local television was infotainment, followed by sports and weather. Most national television news was reduced to headlines and sound bites from across the country. Newspapers continued to downsize. A typical reporter at your average small to midsize paper might cover two beats—if they were lucky. Copyediting started to become shoddy—if it was done at all. Sometimes, copy would be seen by only a single section editor before being published. Soon, reporters would publish directly to a web page and then be copyedited after the fact.

Magazines still had their standards, and in my case, my sensibilities were more in tune with Arthur Kretchmer and Hugh Hefner. Hefner made *Playboy* a worldwide sensation and one of the most sought-after brands on the planet. Anywhere I have ever traveled, a *Playboy* press pass gave me access beyond anything that a pass with *America's Most Wanted*, Fox, or NBC ever gave me. I considered it an honor to be published in a publication that presented the works of Kurt Vonnegut, Joseph Heller, Gore Vidal, Norman Mailer, Ray Bradbury, Alex Haley, Hunter S. Thompson, Malcom X,

Martin Luther King Jr., Jack Kerouac, Arthur C. Clarke, Margaret Atwood, Haruki Murakami, John Steinbeck, Ian Fleming, Roald Dahl, and others.

Hefner printed "more serious journalism and fiction than just about any other magazine publisher," as Pete Vernon of the *Columbia Journalism Review* noted. "*Playboy* has published extensive interviews, compelling profiles, deep-dive investigations, short stories, and essays, in between its NSFW photo spreads. The *Playboy* archives are a trove of journalistic might, and fascinating fodder for anyone interested in writing, culture, politics, or any combination of those."[8]

Playboy was interested in my political connections and sent me to cover the Supreme Court and conduct interviews with G. Gordon Liddy, Mary Matalin, James Carville, Anthony Scaramucci, and others. I began occasionally visiting the James S. Brady Press Briefing Room again, catching briefings by Mike McCurry after he invented the daily televised briefing— for which he tells me he now fully regrets—as well as briefings with Joe Lockhart and others.

Carville was one of the most interesting people I ever spent extended time with. He agreed to do the interview over a lunch at The Palm in Washington. "You want me in *Playboy*?" I remember him asking as he screwed up his face in that infamous grouchy-bulldog look. "What do you want my old ass for?" James was fascinating from the first second, explaining that in his experience, the men in his family were short lived, so "why the hell not," do the *Playboy* interview. He was headed to Memphis, Tennessee, to shoot his part in a movie, *The People vs. Larry Flynt*. We agreed to fly to Memphis together, where we could begin the process. The *Playboy* interview was, in its heyday, the quintessential long-form interview and was famous for exposing bias, giving insight and context. Jimmy Carter told the world that he "lusted in his heart" in the pages of *Playboy*. John Wayne exposed his inherent racism in his *Playboy* interview. I learned of the civil rights struggle by reading the interview that Alex Haley conducted with Martin Luther King Jr. I picked it up from my dad's collection and read it after King was assassinated in 1968 and a week after Bobby Kennedy suffered a similar fate. I didn't understand the nuance, but I was moved then and am moved more so now. To get such an in-depth interview takes a great deal of time, research, and care. Most of all, it takes money. The resources a publication must invest in an interview of this type could cost more than $100,000 a quarter of a century ago—once you consider the cost of printing, the salaries of everyone involved, the time, the travel, and other sundries. It was not a frivolous expense, but *Playboy*'s editor, Arthur Kretchmer, and Hefner himself took a great pride in "getting the journalism right," as Kretchmer explained to me the first time I met him. "We are serious," Kretchmer told me, looking as solemn as a monk. I never forgot that look.

James Carville was the ideal candidate for the *Playboy* interview. He was brash, bright, and bold—a rugged individual of self-deprecating humor and a steel-trap mind. He was a progressive who didn't shy away from the divisive politics of the Republicans. He took them on. I knew he'd be a challenge to interview with his energy and never-ending ability to spin a subject. As I said in the pages of *Playboy*, trying to gain insight into Carville's life is like trying to decipher the plot of a movie using a single frame of film. To wit, we began this interview as a casual chat on a commercial flight from Washington to Memphis; we continued our talk in fits and starts on the set of *The People vs. Larry Flynt* (where I had to share James's time not only with Miloš Forman—the director—but also with costars Woody Harrelson, Courtney Love, and James Cromwell). One night James called me in my hotel room and invited me to dinner with the rest of the cast. "Brian, I got to eat with some of these Hollywood types, why don't you join me." It wasn't a question.

At dinner, I met most of the cast and Forman, the director. "Dear boy," Forman told me, "I read there are 12 billion galaxies in the universe, who counted them all?" He wanted to talk astronomy. Then there was Larry Flynt. He explained to me how he was a Kentucky boy like I was and explained how he lost his virginity to a farm fowl. Flynt was entertaining, as was Harrelson and his younger brother, who talked about how their father was in federal prison for killing judge John H. Wood in San Antonio in 1979. "Yeah, I covered stories at the John H. Wood Federal Courthouse," I remember telling them.

The next day, James and I conducted a little more of the interview during breaks in filming the movie—in which James played a very conservative prosecutor. At one point in time, I sat in the hall of the Memphis courthouse waiting for a break when a production assistant came by and told me I was lucky to be there, asked what was I doing there and when I would leave, and said what an idiot I was to think I could be in the courthouse. "It's a public courthouse," I responded. "You're lucky to be filming here." Before she could respond, the door opened to the courtroom, and Forman emerged, ranting at Courtney Love about a scene and screaming that someone was "ruining his movie." The production assistant seemed to be in shock and told me to shut up. Forman continued to complain about something, causing most of the production staff to enter a state of apoplexy. As he walked by me, he caught my eye and smiled. "Dear boy. Twelve billion galaxies in the universe. Who counted them all?" With that, he left, and the production took a break. It was then the young production assistant approached me, pale and apologetic. "I had no idea you were a friend of Mr. Forman. Can I get you a coffee, sir?"

James and I spent a few more sessions in Memphis and then wrapped up the interview with an intense session on Larry Flynt's private jet flying from Memphis to Portland, Oregon, where Carville and Mary Matalin had a speaking engagement for Valentine's Day that year.

After spending the better part of a week with me, James saw his wife for the first time as we disembarked Flynt's private jet and walked into the airport. Matalin wore a flowing red chiffon gown and smiled at James—obviously glad to see her husband. "My. My. My honey, but you have a fine ass," he drawled as he smiled and looked right into her eyes. Then he looked at me. "Brian, you better say 'fine figure' for that magazine of yours. I don't want my young daughter growing up knowing I'm the hound that I am." He smiled again and then said, "Hey, you ever see a woman look so fine so soon after giving birth?"

James informed me that he was one of the few people in the United States who didn't think Bill Clinton had an affair with Gennifer Flowers, which was the recent topic of controversy in the *Oregonian* newspaper we picked up that morning. I told James I was probably one of the few people who didn't give a shit about Gennifer Flowers. We got along very well after that. I wanted to talk politics and the press; I didn't want to waste time talking about the soap opera shit.

Watching Matalin and Carville prep for their speaking engagement was enlightening. Matalin showed up with a binder full of notes and an assistant who prepped her and took notes as people spoke with her. Seeing all of that preparation, James turned to me and asked to borrow my reporter's notebook and a pen. He then introduced me to Phil Knight of Nike fame, who had come to visit James and Mary, and Knight asked me about the shoes I was wearing that weren't Nikes. James scribbled a couple of notes, made a few doodles, tore the page out of my notebook, handed the notebook and pen back to me, and pronounced himself ready to rumble.

For the next hour, Carville and Matalin held court and gave lessons in spin, deflection, and politics. Every moment I spent with Carville went into the *Playboy* interview, and we even did a sidebar with Matalin after spending time with her. Today, there are few places in journalism for extended interviews conducted in multiple cities or states at multiple venues over the course of several days. But those long-form interviews are extremely valuable to get to know news makers and to put things in a deeper context. During the interview, Carville admitted that he was masterful at spinning the facts and took pride in it. "Did I ever try to drive a story a certain way? Sure. Have I ever been manipulative? The answer is yes," he explained. But Carville also said while he wasn't a philosopher, he believed in his cause—and his cause was bigger than himself. His wife, longtime Republican consultant Mary Matalin, had a similar opinion. How could two people from completely different ends of the political spectrum be attracted to one another, get married, and raise a family? Today, the country is so divisive it would seem impossible to imagine.

So, I asked James if part of his job was to "spin" the truth.

"Certainly," he said. "I'm going to put the most faithful light I possibly can on the president. I can't think of anybody who has been better to me, nicer to me, or has given me more of a chance to be at the top of the world than President Clinton. And I hope I don't let him down. Does that mean I agree with everything he does? No I don't."

I pressed him to explain that point. "Do we, as Americans, lose something important if we can't count on people like you to tell us the plain truth?"

"No," he said. "Because people know. If somebody reading this magazine is too stupid to understand that I have the president's interests at heart, then he's probably too stupid to get this far in the interview. I mean if you're looking to me for objectivity, then put the magazine down. OK? I am not an objective guy. I am a guy with a point of view. I represent the interests of those I work for. People understand that. I don't pretend to be an impartial observer. I'm not. There's an adage in politics: if your guy is in trouble, throw water. If the other is in trouble, throw kerosene."[9]

A quarter of a century after I conducted that interview with Carville, we are still dealing with the same issues we discussed then: divisiveness; the state of the national political debate, Republicans, Democrats, and the press; and truth—who tells it and how? "There is no liberal bias in the press," Carville said. "There's sort of a 'bad news' bias. Like my friend Sam Donaldson once said, 'No one ever reports that a thousand airplanes landed safely today.' My point is, if you're going to report a crash, there actually ought to have been a crash. Don't make one up."[10]

The Democrats, Carville said, have better ideas than Republicans but are often outworked by them. He didn't want to whine about it. He wanted to "fight for the better ideas." And while both he and his wife decried the acrimony in politics, they both agreed that passion in politics brought heat to politics. "Look, politics isn't for the fainthearted," Matalin said.

Gordon Liddy, when I interviewed him for *Playboy*, said nearly the same thing, making me wonder if the GOP had outreach classes for indoctrination or if the Democrats needed them. Liddy, vilified by mainstream media for his role in Watergate, was sanguine about the press, telling me privately, "It doesn't matter what others say about you, but it matters that you know the truth yourself—and occasionally you can get it out so others can see it."

Long interviews were not the only thing *Playboy* did well. In the wake of the 9/11 fiasco, I investigated the Federal Aviation Administration (FAA) for six months and, in June 2002, wrote a story for *Playboy*, "The FAA—More Frightening Than Terrorists."[11] That's how *Playboy* promoted the story titled "Air Sick."

We took a look at the safety of nuclear power plants from terrorists, inadequate inspections, broken airplanes, substandard maintenance, and much more. Former FAA security chief Billie Vincent told us that long before there were problems with 737s, the FAA had many other problems—because of poor management. "The mediocre survive. They go along to get along. Leadership is weak," he told *Playboy*. In the course of our investigation, we found that the FAA had put an estimate on the price of a human being who could die in an air crash. It was a cool $2.7 million in 2002. That's because Congress mandated that all changes to FAA regulations be cost effective. The agency appointed a task force to produce a risk assessment study. The group determined that rather than improving gas tanks and lowering the risk of fire in an air crash, it was cheaper to let people die.

The investigation showed how the FAA caved to the major airlines on security breaches, failing to collect fines or failing to issue them at all. It showed how the FAA was torn between trying to provide safety while also trying to "keep the planes flying," said one insider. We also showed in the investigation that some in the industry, according to Vincent, accurately predicted a terroristic scenario like 9/11 but that airlines had successfully fought every regulation or safety change so they could streamline service and maximize profits. In a study of FAA documents, it was even shown that in the ten years prior to 9/11, unruly passengers managed to break through or damage flimsy cockpit doors on a dozen occasions.[12] The FAA nixed plans to provide a more secure cockpit door—until after 9/11.

Finally, the piece outlined how Congress "continues to do the airlines' bidding" even after the terrorist attacks.

Again, *Playboy* was an independent publication—not owned by corporations—and could devote the time, energy, and money to investigations that outlined what the public desperately needed and still needs to know. There are fewer and fewer of these publications each year still in business. In January 2021, *Playboy*, now publicly traded, announced it would cease publishing most of its original content by the end of March. National independent publications and their failure to survive threatens us all—as one story I covered in 2003 clearly showed.

12

IN A ROOM WITH MADNESS— POST-9/11

Talk to any local reporter, and they'll tell you they can cover a story in their community better than any national reporter. Usually, they're right.

They have the contacts. They know the community and all the players. Talk to any national reporter, and they'll tell you they can bring the light to more people on an important story than a local reporter. They'll stress that they can make a change. Usually, they're right. They'll also admit they use most of the local reporting as a beginning point for their own investigations and stories. Rare is it that a story begins at the top of the journalistic food chain. Today, the national reporters are becoming increasingly insignificant in uncovering news. The real power lies with the community reporters who are left to do the legwork—and members of the general public who can beat anyone to a breaking news scene and publish a video to the internet within moments of a news event happening.

As a case in point, police officer Derek Chauvin was convicted of murdering George Floyd mostly by a videotape shot on a cell phone by a member of the general public. Darnella Frazier, who received a special citation from the Pulitzer Prize Board in 2021, was a teenager. The video she shot resulted in a conviction of a police officer for kneeling on a man's neck for nine minutes until he died. As the prosecutor said, you didn't have to take anyone's word for it. Just believe the undoctored video you saw. The power of the people has never been stronger.

This is bad news—or it can be for the large mainstream media companies that have had a stranglehold on reporting news to the public. But this dearth of trained professional reporting is not to be cheered. While an untrained citizen can shoot video and provide expert testimony, it remains important for disinterested, third-party observers—as reporters are trained to be—to help frame arguments and report on the issues. The large companies can and should remain viable, but without some fundamental changes, it will be hard for them to do so.

People tend to live in their own professionally provided information silos and rarely see into those of their neighbors, if they bother to even try. Everyone complains about the media, but it's laughable how few actually sample the media. Reading headlines and reacting to the reaction of others on social media is how we get misinformed today. It turns out that members of Congress don't have a monopoly on knee-jerk reactions. But as much as the methods of distributing news have changed, the reactions by the audience have not. Viewers and readers still complain about the lack of "good" news. But, again, no one ever reported on the calm spring day, the millions of cars that didn't crash, the buildings that didn't catch fire, or the thousands of planes that landed safely. There are good news stories, of course, but news is often reported because something occurred outside of our normal, shared experience. We expect people to be kind to one another and airplanes to land safely, and we have a reasonable expectation that the weather or an earthquake, volcanic eruption, or asteroid won't kill us every day.

When those things do happen, we have to be aware of them. Sometimes, our very survival depends on knowing about some pretty scary stuff—including gas spills, fires, wrecks, crashes, eruptions, earthquakes, tornadoes, hurricanes, political missteps, war, and much more. Many of us hold accountable the people who tell us of this mostly unwanted news. If it is told wrong or if there is a mistake, then people have a tendency to accuse those bringing us the news of having a particular bias. Those who promote that idea may indeed have a point, but those who promote that idea also take advantage of mistakes that are naturally made by human beings doing their job trying to report the news in order to promote *their* own bias. From there, it's a short stretch to saying "fake media" and "enemy of the people."

As the Reagan-era deregulation, combined with the repercussions of the Telecommunications Act, really took hold, it became easier and easier to blame the media for all problems, real and imagined. News shows at each Gannett television station looked as if they were cut from a cookie cutter. The same could be said for Sinclair stations and other large chains. It's hard to convince the American viewer, as lazy as he or she may be, that the fix wasn't in when every news station and network covered the same stories, with the same sound bites, the same video, and reporters saying nearly or exactly the same thing. Anyone who ever read *A Wrinkle in Time* remembers the scene of ultimate monotony and repression where all the kids in a neighborhood played the exact same way for the exact same amount of time. Anyone who ever saw *Freaks* or *The Player* remembers Whoopie Goldberg and Lyle Lovett saying "One of Us. One of Us."

That's why Fox stood out when Roger Ailes took over the news division. Fox looked different from anyone else because Fox news broadcasted a different view of the same news. They weren't any better at delivering the news. Their talking heads just gave a different reason for what you saw. After eating nothing but peanut butter for years, it was as if the American news-viewing public was being treated to jelly for the first time. Lots of folks wanted jelly and didn't check the jar to see if it was real or not. They just wanted something different.

The truth, as they said in *The X-Files*, is out there—but increasingly the networks and newspapers had a hard time selling and telling it to the American public. The election of George W. Bush, with its hanging chads, calls for recounts, accusations of a "Bush coup," and the screaming of voter fraud and voter suppression, was a preview to the 2020 election, and it ended with the amiable dunce, George W. Bush, in office. Bush had the good grace to surround himself with a variety of people who—while obviously partisan—did not share the conspiracy leanings of some of today's right-wing radicals, and things more or less appeared to be running, if not smoothly, at least within accepted norms. After the initial controversy about the election process quickly subsided—made smoother and easier by Al Gore's conceding—the press got on board for the Bush agenda. And the truth of the 2000 election? Story is done. Move on.

Bush came into power wanting to invade Iraq. He said so in his 2002 State of the Union Address, calling Iraq a member of the "Axis of Evil," and declared, "The United States of America will not permit the world's most dangerous regimes to threaten us with the world's most destructive weapons."[1] He began to sell the idea in press briefings and through his surrogates. We were told Saddam Hussein had weapons of mass destruction and was harboring members of Al-Qaeda. I attended briefings in the White House during that time, and most questions seemed to be aimed at supporting the claims of the administration. Rare, it seemed, was it that White House Press Secretary Ari Fleischer ever called on anyone who questioned the authenticity of the president's claims. White House reporters' following similar narratives in their reporting as the administration has become the norm. It's not out of any conscious conspiracy but a matter of convenience and an example of group thinking. If the supposedly wisest among the reporters and the most experienced are traveling one path, it must be the right one. Right?

Why does this happen? Because there is very little diversity in the White House press corps. I'm not talking about diversity of ethnicity, religion, color, sex, or sexual preference. I'm talking about diversity of thought. Remember, these fifteen billionaires essentially own today's media: Jeff Bezos, Michael Bloomberg, Rupert Murdoch, Donald and Samuel Newhouse, the Cox Family, John Henry, Sheldon Adelson, Joe Mansueto, Mortimer Zuckerman, the Barbey Family, Stanley Hubbard, Patrick Soon-Shiong, Carlos Slim Helu, Warren Buffett, and Viktor Vekselberg.[2]

That means slightly more than a dozen people control hundreds of reporters who cover the White House. Hiring practices are thus standardized in a way that isn't easy to define but is very easy to recognize. Ever wonder why the question that comes to your mind is not asked during a briefing? It isn't that the question is silly, though honestly that too may be the case, but the simple fact is that corporate media stay within certain boundaries. The media owners are part of the club, and by virtue of being associated with the larger corporations, most reporters understand they share some of that prestige and access their bosses and their companies enjoy. In truth, they're waiters at the party and nothing more. They serve a purpose, but the owners of the media corporations know reporters are ultimately interchangeable. I've seen more care for favorite pets than managers provide the average reporter or producer at a news network.

There are independent voices, but few of them are left in today's news community. Any members of the club who decide to "go rogue" and produce news others do not produce are often looked at with scrutiny and a frown. "What's the story about? Where'd they get it? Nobody else has it. It must be crap." Those sentiments often surround independent reporting—along with the fear that someone else might have a better story.

The reporters at Knight Ridder's D.C. bureau fell into that hole in 2002 when they began to question the validity of the government's claims that Saddam Hussein had weapons of mass destruction. That, of course, was the overwhelming reason we were given to justify the need to invade Iraq. The president told us Saddam might get the bomb and use it. Many in the White House press corps ignored the Knight Ridder team's reporting and continued to take the president at face value. Truth to power? Those in power tried to create their own truth.

The Bush administration pushed its narrative for months in 2002 about Saddam Hussein. The president worked hard along with Colin Powell and Condoleezza Rice to build a coalition to topple Hussein. While Bush claimed it was for weapons of mass destruction that we invaded Iraq, those close to the president claimed the president wanted to finish what his father had started in the Gulf War. In October 2002, after months of consistent claims from the White House—including many that have since been shown to have been lies—Congress authorized Bush to launch a military attack against Iraq. The war began on March 20, 2003, when the United States, joined by the United Kingdom and coalition allies, launched a "shock and awe" bombing campaign. Iraq was quickly overrun—after all, the country had yet to rebuild from the devastation delivered to it following the previous Gulf War nearly a decade earlier. The delay from the October declaration until the beginning of the war in March is also a part of the story that highlights the problems of the press.

Knight Ridder reporters Jonathan Landay and Warren Strobel, as well as John Walcott and Joe Galloway, wrote a series of articles for Knight Ridder that criticized intelligence suggesting links between Saddam Hussein, his supposed possession of weapons of mass destruction, and Al-Qaeda. Those stories, which ran during the run-up to the 2003 war, were counter to reports in the *New York Times*, the *Washington Post*, and other national publications—and resulted in some newspapers within the Knight Ridder chain refusing to run the stories simply because the larger publications weren't writing anything remotely similar.

At the time, Knight Ridder was one of the nation's largest newspaper chains. It was later purchased by McClatchy in 2006, and that group subsequently filed for bankruptcy in large part because of the cost of absorbing Knight Ridder. Prior to the sale, Knight Ridder had a higher profit margin than many Fortune 500 companies and was often lauded for its technological innovations. For a brief time after the company went public, Knight Ridder was the largest newspaper publisher in the country. For most of its existence, the company was based in Miami, Florida, and headquartered on the top floor of the *Miami Herald* building. In 1998, it relocated to San Jose, California, where Silicon Valley was booming. It rented several floors in a downtown high-rise as its new corporate base. The *San Jose Mercury News*, a Knight Ridder paper, was the first daily newspaper to regularly publish its full content online. The internet division had been established there three years earlier. When it was bought by McClatchy, Knight Ridder was the second-largest newspaper publisher in the United States with thirty-two daily newspaper brands.[3] Still, the group was not held in the same regard as the *Washington Post* or the *New York Times*. But the work the group did on the Iraq War was, eventually, seen as the quintessential example of speaking truth to power, fighting against the voices of corporate media, and trying to tell the truth.[4]

The *Washington Post* and the *New York Times* paid for their lack of challenge to Bush's selling of the war. Judith Miller from the *Times* as well as Jayson Blair from the *Post* received a healthy amount of criticism. Miller got criticized after the fact for following the Bush narrative without question. She was a member of the team that won the Pulitzer Prize for Explanatory Reporting for the *Times*'s coverage of global terrorism before and after the September 11 attacks. On September 8, 2002, Miller and *Times* colleague Michael R. Gordon reported the interception of "aluminum tubes" bound for Iraq. The front-page story quoted unnamed "American officials" and intelligence experts who said the tubes were intended to be used to enrich nuclear material. Miller reported that Bush officials claimed that Iraq had gone on a worldwide hunt for materials to build an atomic bomb—a move that she wrote has "brought Iraq and the United States to the brink of war."[5]

No less than Secretary of Defense Donald Rumsfeld, Colin Powell, and Condoleezza Rice cited the article as justification for a buildup against Iraq. It became a key component in legitimizing the Bush administration's rush to war. The government thus duped a reporter and then used information planted in the public at one of the nation's most respected news institutions to start a war. The Bush administration replaced "you furnish the pictures and I'll furnish the War," said by William Randolph Hearst to beat the drum on the Spanish-American War, with "show me the tube and we'll go to war."

The brazen move by the Bush administration is another indication of the lengths the government would go to undermine the free press—like Reagan's planting government operatives within the media and years of lies shoveled onto the American public by a government that gives lip service to a free press but has no intention of respecting a free press. Was the *New York Times* at fault? Who could argue otherwise? But always forgotten, underreported, and often unseen is the hand of government guiding the greatest screwups and compromises of a free press. Did big media work hand in hand with government? It doesn't matter what you think. The facts show what the outcome was regardless of motive, and whatever it takes to make sure the outcome is different in the future is the issue at hand. What Judith Miller did was not so different than what other reporters did. If she hadn't used her sources in government to report the stories that she was later criticized for publishing, someone else would've been used by the government sources who wanted to get the story out in front of the American people. The sin of Judith Miller and the management at the *Times* was a sin of lack of vigilance.

The case of Jayson Blair is a bit more complicated. Blair was fired after it was proved that he had plagiarized reporting from the *San Antonio Express News* on a few stories he wrote for the *New York Times*. Some of those stories had to do with his coverage of wounded soldiers in a naval hospital he had never visited. He wrote about a pastor in Cleveland whom he never traveled to Cleveland to meet and copied portions of an article from an earlier *Washington Post* article.

And he was also called into question for the coverage of stories regarding the D.C. sniper—the news event that directly led to a delay in George W. Bush's headlong thrust into bombing and invading Iraq.

Some members of the press debated whether Blair was an indictment of affirmative action since he is African American. He later said he was suffering from bipolar disorder and went on to become a life coach. What the Blair story actually highlighted was the problem the press has hiring experienced reporters. Blair got hired at the *New York Times* after an extended internship there. His only other experience was as a college journalist at the University of Maryland, College Park. You can't blame him for wanting to work at the *Times* or being hired to report there. Blame the editors who should've known better. Previous generations of reporters spent years honing their craft at smaller news outlets before being seasoned enough to handle the pressure of working at the *Times*. Not now. The Blair story is a cautionary tale that has been ignored in the press by the media managers and consequently is nearly unknown by the rest of the world. Was Blair used by the *Times* to fulfill an equal opportunity slot—to show that the *Times* could and would hire black reporters? While there was some argument about it at the time, it completely misses the point and belittles diversity hiring.

The point was that the *New York Times* hired a reporter without experience and then assigned that reporter to cover incredibly complex and important stories he had neither the experience nor the sources to handle. It's obvious by the way Blair handled his reporting he was in over his head, and it is an indictment of the *Times*'s management more than the actions of a junior reporter who lacked the experience to handle his workload. It is also indicative of the growing pressure on journalism due to corporate greed, government pressure, and a lack of concern in management for the necessary experience to handle the nuances of major stories.

The D.C. sniper story was exemplary in showing the need for solid, experienced reporting on the ground and why it is so damn valuable in the pursuit of the truth. It was also, ultimately, one of the finest examples of reporting I've ever seen.

WTOP news radio broke the news to D.C. denizens on October 2, 2002, about James Martin, a fifty-five-year-old program analyst at the National Oceanic and Atmospheric Administration who was killed in the parking lot of a Wheaton grocery store. It happened toward the end of rush hour—and after school had ended—in Montgomery County, Maryland, that day. High schoolers were home for the day. Middle schoolers and grade schoolers were mostly home as well, though some were outdoors at football practice. I was coaching youth football that day, and at the middle school field, I first heard the news from one of my parents who lived near the shooting location. It was an odd occurrence though not necessarily unheard of in that part of the county, and there was some worry among parents as practice ended that day.

The D.C. area had gone through a year of chilling news: the attack on the Pentagon a year earlier, anthrax threats in the mail, unseen terrorists with homemade dirty bombs, and the possibility of war with Iraq—those were the headlines. The suburban shooting death of Martin, it was assumed, was a "drive-by" committed by a teenage gang. "They're out of control, coach," I remember one parent telling me.

The next morning in a little more than two hours, four people were gunned down in Montgomery County—all within a couple of miles of home and, in one case, literally across the street from where one of the youth football coaches I worked with at St. Francis in Derwood lived. My phone blew up immediately. One homicide investigator I coached football with gave me some very specific information. I spoke with my editor Chris Napolitano at *Playboy*, and we begin an investigation that would lead to a March 2003 feature that outlined the successes and failures of an investigation that was put under intense international scrutiny. There were dozens of reporters within hours at the Montgomery County Police Department's headquarters in Rockville, Maryland.

The police began printing laminated press passes as the reporters poured in from around the world. Mine was numbered 0039, if I remember correctly. In the end, there were hundreds if not thousands of them printed. Like Waco and the Republic of Texas standoff before, networks and newspapers set up operating bureaus outside of the police headquarters. The police set up a command post in a neighboring building, and reporters watched detectives stream between the two buildings like a line of ants. Police snipers set up on neighboring buildings to provide safety. D.C. Police Chief Charles Ramsey and Montgomery County Police Chief Charles Moose directed the Sniper Task Force along with Mike Bouchard, the chief of the Baltimore, Maryland, division of the Bureau of Alcohol,

Tobacco and Firearms. The task force would eventually include municipalities across Maryland and Virginia along with police volunteers who, during the next twenty-three days, would struggle to solve the case as the sniper continued to strike.

We all eventually learned that John Allen Muhammad, age forty-one, and Lee Boyd Malvo, a seventeen-year-old troubled teen whom Muhammad befriended and abused, were the two-person sniper team that operated in the D.C. metropolitan area that fall. Their crime spree actually began in February 2002, and it allegedly included murders and robberies in six states and the District of Columbia. The D.C. sniper threat lasted more than three weeks, from October 2, 2002, until the pair's capture after ten people died. They were caught at 3:19 a.m. on October 24 as they slept in their car at a rest stop off I-70 near Myersville, Maryland. It was an anticlimactic arrest following more than three weeks of horror.

I was president of a middle school PTA at that time. At our monthly meeting, held during the twenty-three-day sniper episode, a parent proposed erecting 100 feet of 5-by-8 plywood walls in front of the school to protect students coming and going through the school's front loading dock. The pair of snipers by that time had not shown any concern whether they were shooting people in a dark parking lot outside of a big-box store or from a sniper's position in the woods behind Bowie Middle School in Prince Georges County at 8 a.m. on October 7—a few days before our PTA meeting. The PTA board took the suggestion under advisement and took no formal action before the end of the snipers' grip on the area following their arrest a short time later.

The D.C. sniper case put everyone on edge. People would run zigzag style into stores—not everyone, but I know some who did on occasion. One of the high school kids I coached started using the pickup line "Can I pump gas for you?" to a varying degree of success. No one had seen anything like this before. It was insanity consistent with what I saw on the streets of Dhahran in Saudi Arabia during the Gulf War when the siren went off and people fled to avoid Scud missiles they had no idea where or when they would land.

The confusion and fear in the greater community brought about by the sniper incident echoed in the law enforcement community. The police had to appear to be in control. Mass panic would not help anyone. But the truth was Chief Charles Moose, who got the majority of cases in Montgomery County by sheer chance and who headed the task force, was in over his head from the beginning. Everyone was.

Local criticism of Chief Moose's participation grew with time and even following the release of his book about the details of the sniper attack. Moose had Lieutenant Nancy Demme follow him throughout the twenty-three-day ordeal. She carried a notebook and took extensive notes for which she was often questioned by curious reporters who constantly took notes. Apparently, those notes later came to be a source for Moose's book, and that cost him goodwill from many in county government who publicly and privately said Moose used investigative notes to further his private gains. But it was his decisions as the Sniper Task Force leader that caused him the most grief.

Many of the out-of-town officers who showed up on a voluntary basis were treated well and worked and played well with other investigators. FBI investigators who often big-footed or otherwise looked down on local police eagerly jumped in to help with no egos on the table. Despite whatever mistakes anyone made, especially those at the top whose mistakes reverberated throughout the investigation and did the greatest harm, none were done out of malice. While there was a sense of fear and at times terror, especially in the first week following the initial attacks, most people were also extremely tolerant of one another—to the point that an optimist might think the world could be a better place.

In 1980, John Lennon was gunned down outside of his residence by a deranged fan. I never forgot that a man who sang about peace got gunned down by a disturbed young man who should never have had a firearm in his possession. On Lennon's birthday, October 9, 2002, violence and a lack of peace were firmly on every citizen's mind in the D.C. metropolitan area. On that Wednesday, October 9, 2002, I had in my responsibility the lives of 150 children and their parents for a time. We had hired armed security to watch over our practice area. We had parents actively searching in the woods behind the field. We still called practice early as I remember, but people desperately wanted life to go on as normally as possible, and we struggled to make it so.

Early in the investigation of the first day's shootings, a lead developed about a white paneled truck. It was suspected of being the vehicle used by the snipers. One witness apparently thought enough about the possibility that it prompted police to search for what was the most common truck seen in a four-state area. After the first D.C. shooting, witnesses described a car that turned out to be Muhammad's, but that clue was overlooked by the task force headed up by Moose. The sniper shootings actually occurred from the trunk of the blue Chevy Caprice. The pair drilled a hole in the back of the trunk and had modified the trunk to be a sniper's lair.

Moose's first mistake was to overlook the description from D.C. witnesses (a move not popular with the D.C. police on the task force) and decide to search the world for white vans. Nobody was looking for a Caprice, though D.C. Police Chief Charles Ramsey reportedly fought for that to be the case for a longer time than anyone involved with the investigation cared to freely admit. Understandably, the focus on the white van *did not* lead to the end of the shooting spree.

Outside of the Benjamin Tasker Middle School in Bowie, Maryland, where a middle schooler had been critically injured but not killed, police found their first real clues—expended shells, matted grass, and a note written on a Death card from a tarot deck: "For you mr. police. Code: Call me God. Do not release to the press." That piece of evidence shook a lot of the investigators. This was real Hannibal Lecter stuff, and the police were afraid. That fear, some said, led them to some pretty bad mistakes and a rocky relationship with the press. At first, the police locked down all information—following the revelation that they might have found something substantive in Bowie. WUSA, Channel 9, broke the news of the tarot card's existence. Their local connections in the law enforcement community got vital information to the public—information that those who were running the investigation wanted to withhold from the public for fear of emboldening the killers.

It was simply logically flawed to think that a man who wrote that you had to call him God would react rationally, so some asked, why bother to humor him? Maybe, just maybe, telling the public through the press was the right thing to do—at least we would know exactly what we were dealing with. Time and again, I've seen government representatives fail to place faith in the people who place their faith in government representatives. In cases like this, the press is vital. The people deserved to know what they were dealing with—and, as it turned out, it was one of the most important news reports during the siege. WUSA told the world what the killers thought of themselves—and the shock at the depth of the killers' depravity helped to bring everyone together, even if for just twenty-three days. It brought 500 reporters, 500 investigators, and countless others to D.C. to find the snipers. When the police had to put up roadblocks and inconvenience residents, they understood—all because one news show did it right.

Congress okayed the attack on Saddam Hussein in October, but who was that? The nation was looking elsewhere. Michael Brooks of the Bureau of Alcohol, Tobacco and Firearms told me in *Playboy*, "I came to town from Toledo on Wednesday the 9th. There was a shortage of cars and the cops needed every car they could put on the road. Guys were working 17-hour, 18-hour days. You could see the tiredness in their eyes. Sometimes they would just go home, take a short nap and a shower, get a change of shirt and come right back. In the beginning they only took agents who could drive into town, because we needed our own cars. I drove in the day the tarot card thing was on the news [when Muhammad told people he was God]. . . . I was listening to that on the radio as I drove into town. Then I looked over at this white van that had pulled up next to me and it was this "Guaranteed Overnight Delivery" van. Big word, GOD on the side. I said to myself, 'well, here I go.'"[6]

WTOP radio became the go-to station during the sniper situation. When a shooting attributed to the snipers occurred near Fredericksburg, Virginia, prompting a multiple-jurisdiction search, some in law enforcement got upset that WTOP provided traffic news. Police thought that would help the snipers escape. The truth is the police badly fumbled their response to the snipers. Chief Moose encouraged the snipers to call police, and at first, the police missed the calls when the snipers did as Moose asked. Then, for days, the snipers played the police by having them read cryptic messages on television. Muhammad left long handwritten notes in sealed plastic bags, including a very lengthy missive that demanded $10 million and threatened the lives of children in the D.C. area.

Schools went into lockdown. No recess. No outside activities. Sports activities were canceled or heavily modified. Once, a telephone call was traced to a telephone at a gas station in Henrico County, Virginia. Police missed the suspects and mistakenly arrested two other people in a white van. By October 21, police were still mistakenly chasing a white van. Vans that routinely drove through the D.C. area could occasionally be seen with "Not Me" signs posted in their windows or on the side of the van. Later, police learned that they had stopped Muhammad's 1990 Chevy Caprice, or it had at least been checked by police near several shooting locations, but it was never stopped because everyone was concentrating on the white van. Ironically, Muhammad's Caprice was later discovered to have been used as an undercover police car in Bordentown, New Jersey.[7]

The federal government had better luck identifying the shooters, but it would be two weeks and nearly ten deaths later that—through the evidence, a fingerprint found in Bowie and a mention by the sniper in a telephone call about how smart he was and how the cops couldn't solve a crime he committed in Montgomery—the cops put together enough evidence to know they were looking for John Allen Muhammad. He'd acted as most criminals do: involuntarily or perhaps with subconscious intent, he gave up the information that led to his capture. He acted like nearly every criminal I'd ever covered for *America's Most Wanted*. He got himself caught.

The local police continued getting angry with local and national media for getting in the way of their investigation. It wasn't just the media's questions. It wasn't that we showed up at stakeouts or that we said things that police didn't want known. It was all of it. Michael Brooks said, "It was weird working the case and then seeing what was going on the television. I kept wondering if they knew more than us, or if they were working the same case." The number of leaks to the press angered some investigators and encouraged others. While some cops got mad at the press for reporting things that the cops thought were secret, others got angry because they believed the leaks were coming from the White House. The president's staff was briefed on more than one occasion, and some of those involved in the process surmised the White House staff couldn't keep its collective mouth shut. Still, others were upset that not more information was given to the press. Many of the members of law enforcement I'd worked closely with during my time with *America's Most Wanted* had come to believe that when you're trying to catch a fugitive, giving the press more information helps. Just ask those who captured Kenneth McDuff.

Barry Maddox from the FBI explained his consternation with too much information. "The leaks were worrisome. We didn't know where they were coming from. Hey, we can go to jail if we leak information. It's a different environment elsewhere, but we take those leaks very seriously."[8] It often seems law enforcement and government are more concerned about news leaks rather than the importance of the news itself.

By the third week in October, the area was tweaked, though most people were still trying to go about their daily lives with as few disruptions as possible. "I went out for a round of golf and was on the back nine when I thought to myself that I wasn't so bright," Chip Berman, the owner of the Outta the Way Café in Derwood recalled. His Derwood restaurant, open to this day and still owned by Berman, is near the location of the first shootings. The golf course he played at that day was also in the area. "I was a big target for any sniper. I look over my shoulder and I see these golf carts racing across the fairway with SWAT team members in them, all dressed in black and all business. I look over my other shoulder and see a helicopter up in the air over a hill. I just froze. It turns out there were a couple of kids in the woods deer hunting," he said.[9]

By then, Moose, whose task force conducted daily briefings with the press, was getting noticeably upset. His temper was exacerbated by the throngs of reporters from all over the world, many new to the scene, who often asked previously asked and answered questions. Moose amused those of us who'd been there from the first day as he erupted on newcomers who asked those questions. The one time I saw him rendered speechless was when a French reporter in one of the briefings asked if the sniper was a distressed former member of the French Foreign Legion. The look on Moose's face was priceless. You couldn't tell if he looked like a deer caught in headlights because he hadn't previously considered such an improbability, and now that he had, "Shit why didn't we think of that?" was pasted all over his face. Or he may have just been blindsided by what he considered the strangest question anyone ever asked him.

To add to the theater-of-the-absurd production, at one point during a dry spell between shootings and the ultimate arrest, Geraldo Rivera showed up to add his weight to the cause. Arriving in a limo to shouts from the crowd of people who'd gathered near police headquarters to see the international press camping out, he was later seen at a Hooters restaurant with his brother Craig. They apparently decided the best way to cover the story was to sign girls' bottoms, which they were seen doing with delight.[10]

On October 18, the public information officer, Lucille Baur, threatened to expel NBC's David Bloom. While making the rounds of the press gathered outside the task force headquarters, Baur told us that reporters were to ask no more than one question so everyone would get a chance. Bloom politely thanked her but said, "We'll ask questions the way we want. You can refuse to call on us. But we'll ask the questions." Baur got so upset she threatened to pull Bloom's press credentials. She later backed down. I laughed. Bloom was a man after my own heart. We knew each other peripherally, and since we held similar opinions about elected officials and government spokespeople, we naturally got along quite well. He was an outgoing guy who, like me, craved covering the "big story" and would do anything to be in the thick of it. He was an absolute joy to be around.

A month after my investigative piece ran in *Playboy*, Bloom died on April 6, 2003, as a result of covering the war in Iraq that the D.C. sniper incident had helped to postpone. Riding in a cramped tank for days, David developed a blood clot in his leg that caused a fatal pulmonary embolism.

As the investigation continued, tip-line operators fielded more than 100,000 calls that helped to develop 16,000 leads. One of those leads included a call from the killer that was overlooked because there was so much to wade through. It turns out the killers, while they kept considerable resources tied up from federal, state, and local law enforcement officials, weren't criminal masterminds. They just got lost in the shuffle—as it turns out, that was also part of Muhammad's backstory and that of his young murderous sidekick.

Apparently, being snubbed by police or effectively being ignored led the snipers to more bizarre behavior, and suddenly, Chief Moose was standing in front of the press quoting a curious line from a folktale about a duck in a noose. At one of the last briefings, Moose and the task force finally announced the names of their suspects—Muhammad and an un-named juvenile. The cops also didn't tell the public the two were traveling in a blue Chevy Caprice, nor did they give out the license plate number. WTOP radio and other reporters, using confidential sources, broadcast the make and model of the car as well as its New Jersey license plate number.

"The irony is the chief kept giving us so much grief. So, how did the two guys get captured?" Steve Eldridge, a WTOP traffic and news reporter asked rhetorically. "He got caught from the license plate number. A num-ber that the chief wouldn't give us. We got it from other sources. We put it out there. They vilified the press. We did our job."[11]

A truck driver from Kentucky, apparently listening to his radio, heard the license number and saw and recognized the car at a truck stop outside of Frederick, Maryland, and the rest ended not with a bang but with a whimper.

"Basically the snipers weren't caught," Steve Handelsman, my col-league from the first Gulf War, later recalled for *Playboy*. "They turned themselves in. They gave up. God knows how long it could've gone on if they wanted to continue. They tried to talk to a priest and that didn't work. All along the chief encourages them to call in and the killers appear to be trying to do everything the chief asks them to do. But the people on the other end of the line either didn't know what they were doing or were overwhelmed. You can't expect the snipers to be as polished as Tom Brokaw. You have to listen to them. If they call in and say, 'I'm the guy,' you have to listen to that. The way things went, with everyone looking for a white guy in a white van, these two guys could have driven up to police headquarters, gotten out of their car and announced to everyone that they were the killers and no one would've arrest them—except maybe Geraldo, who would have them taken to Hooters."[12]

In the end, the D.C. sniper story took a quick backseat to the "shock and awe" show that would follow a few months later as Bush unleashed hell on Iraq. Both of these international stories showed the press at its best and its worst.

The D.C. area had survived two years of continuous stress. A smaller and smaller number of media companies were dedicating fewer and fewer resources to covering the news. The government could and did begin to operate with near impunity except for the resourceful reporting of Knight

Ridder's D.C. bureau, which exposed the truth of the rush to war. Had there been more reporters on duty doing their duty at the White House, things might have been different. The electorate might have been better informed, and better choices might have prevailed. That is purely conjecture, but what isn't conjecture is how a well-informed community does react in a crisis. In the case of the D.C. sniper, reporters stubbornly risked their own lives trying to get vital information to the public about the nature of the enemy the community faced, who the snipers were, and what they looked like. Management in a multijurisdictional task force established to solve the crime got angry with the media for "butting in." But as Eldridge, Bloom, and Handelsman all pointed out, the media did their job and did it so well that local and national reporters worked together more effectively than I'd ever seen reporters work together. Maybe I don't get around much.

But the media collectively did a hell of a job reporting on the D.C. sniper. Today, it's doubtful there are enough local reporters with sources who can provide the information the press got to the public in 2002. The *Washington Post* used to have an extensive bureau in Rockville, but today, the reporter with all the institutional knowledge of the area is gone. The *Montgomery Journal*, a local daily newspaper, has closed, as have the two community newspapers, the *Montgomery County Sentinel* (one of the two newspapers I ran for twelve years and which was the last independent newspaper to close in Montgomery County just three years ago) and the Gazette newspapers, which Jeff Bezos closed when he bought the *Washington Post*. The community newspapers that initially developed sources that television, radio, and larger newspapers rely on are dying all over the country at the cost of real and vital information.

Handelsman's concern about the ability to catch the snipers is compounded by the fact that police departments and state and local governments are even more secretive today than at the time of the D.C. sniper incident because they no longer have as many reporters pestering them for information. What vital news and information are we missing?

13

WHAT THE HELL IS
THE ESPIONAGE ACT?

Until Barack Obama became president, it was almost unheard of for a
president to use the Espionage Act to plug information leaks to the
press. Since 1917, when the act was first passed, it had been used only four
times. Obama used it eight times in an attempt to stifle the free flow of
information to reporters.[1]

The Fourth Estate did almost nothing to push back.

CNN's Jake Tapper, as noted in the Poynter Institute's PolitiFact, was
one of the few reporters to mention the Obama administration's use of the
Espionage Act. "The Obama administration has used the Espionage Act to
go after whistleblowers who leak to journalists . . . more than all previous
administrations combined," Tapper said on CNN's *The Lead*.[2] President
Obama defended his prosecution of leakers and whistle-blowers in a press
conference in 2013. "Leaks related to national security can put people at
risk," the president said. "They can put men and women in uniform that
I've sent into the battlefield at risk. I don't think the American people
would expect me, as commander in chief, not to be concerned about information that might compromise their missions or might get them killed."[3]

Obama said this during a news conference in May 2013 with visiting Turkish Prime Minister Recep Tayyip Erdoğan. Obama specifically
defended the Justice Department's investigation that secretly gathered
private phone records of Associated Press (AP) journalists, suggesting that
protecting U.S. personnel overseas outweighs press privacy concerns. Earlier that week, AP president and chief executive Gary B. Pruitt disclosed
that federal authorities had secretly obtained cellular, office, and home
telephone records of journalists working in Washington, New York, and
Hartford, Connecticut. Some of the records included the main number
for AP reporters covering Congress and came after the Justice Department

investigated leaks that helped the AP produce a story that included details of a CIA operation in Yemen that prevented a bomb attack on a commercial airplane in the United States.[4]

In essence, the government got upset because the AP reported a story that made the CIA look good. Pruitt called the investigation a "massive and unprecedented intrusion" into news gathering.[5] It was, of course, made far easier to do so following the adoption of the Patriot Act.

Obama campaigned on a pledge to increase government transparency and many times said he respected a free press that could hold him and other officeholders accountable for their actions. "The whole reason I got involved in politics is because I believe so deeply in that democracy and that process," he said.

Attorney General Eric Holder Jr. got a lot of criticism for the prosecution of leakers and whistle-blowers and the use of the Patriot Act to investigate journalists, but it was Obama who expressed confidence in him. If the "buck stops here," as Harry Truman claimed, then you cannot dismiss what amounted to duplicity by the president, who claimed to support transparency while refusing to speak out about the Justice Department going after reporters. Obama's administration wasn't the first to hobble the press, and it won't be the last. But each blow from every administration since Reagan continues to make a mockery of the idea that the press is free, unfettered, willing, and able to speak truth to power. We're barely able to question royalty, aging athletes, or Grammy nominations.

Until the names Edward Snowden and Julian Assange became common knowledge, arguably the most famous person prosecuted under the Espionage Act who had anything to do with journalism was Daniel Ellsberg, whose release of the *Pentagon Papers* helped turn the tide against the war in Vietnam. Ellsberg was vilified and hounded by the White House at the time, but history has been kind to his whistle-blowing efforts.

The fact is most people know little about the Espionage Act of 1917—passed in June of that year shortly after the U.S. entry into World War I. The act has been amended several times and was originally intended to prohibit interference with military operations and recruitment and to prevent insubordination in the military or the support of U.S. enemies during times of war. The Supreme Court ruled in 1919 that the act did not violate free speech. The case in question, *Schenck v. United States*, came about when Charles Schenck and Elizabeth Baer, members of the Executive Committee of the Socialist Party in Philadelphia, helped produce a flier that was printed and mailed to 15,000 men who were slated to be drafted to serve in the war. The fliers urged men not to submit, saying, "Do not submit to intimidation" and "assert your rights . . . ; if you do not assert and support your rights, you are helping to deny or disparage rights which it is the solemn duty of all citizens and residents of the United States to retain." The leaflet Schenck produced compared military conscription to involuntary servitude (slavery), prohibited by the Thirteenth Amendment.[6]

The United States, then as now, was a divided nation, but both the far right and the far left opposed the draft and the U.S. involvement in the war for different reasons. Supreme Court Justice Oliver Wendell Holmes had opposed earlier restraints on the First Amendment, saying, "It is better for those who have unquestioned and almost unlimited power in their hands to err on the side of freedom."[7] In his dissenting opinion in *Abrams v. United States* (1919), a court case that upheld the conviction of several people who distributed leaflets advocating their political views, Holmes said, "We should be eternally vigilant against attempts to check the expression of opinions that we loath and believe to be fraught with death."[8] Holmes was known as the "Great Dissenter" in part for what he wrote in *Abrams*, but he wrote the unanimous opinion in the 1917 case *Schenck v. United States*. It was that opinion that gave us the term "clear and present danger." It also included this gem: "The most stringent protection of free speech would not protect a man in falsely shouting fire in a theatre and causing a panic. . . . The question in every case is whether the words used are used in such circumstances and are of such a nature as to create a clear and present danger that they will bring about the substantive evils that Congress has a right to prevent. It is a question of proximity and degree."[9]

Holmes seemed to back away from that opinion in 1919 as the Supreme Court embraced the idea of censoring thoughts and speech, but the use of the Espionage Act to stifle differing speech, particularly in wartime, was well established. A government during peacetime, it would seem, would be more tolerant of dissent than during a war. Curiously, that is the very same mind-set the Biden administration would use more than 100 years later. Press freedom was curtailed because of the "war against the pandemic."

The constitutionality of the Espionage Act has been contested in the courts since the beginning, particularly for its efforts to stifle free speech. The Julius and Ethel Rosenberg case remains the most infamous espionage case in history, but when Obama took office, his detractors accused him of weaponizing the act to punish journalists. He defended the need for security in a dangerous world. Some, such as *The Guardian*, pointed out that there appeared to be a double standard in who was targeted by the Obama administration—wealthy friends got off easy and leaked with impunity, while others faced more dire consequences.[10] That really misses the point. Talking about Obama's motives is also irrelevant. The results were easy enough to see. The issue is what Obama's use of the Espionage Act did to journalism. It was another cut in a death caused by a thousand such cuts. Perhaps journalism could survive the loss of the fairness doctrine, the Telecommunications Act, the Patriot Act or corporate greed, the use of the Espionage Act or a loss of some revenue, the internet, or any single challenge during the past forty years, but the constant bombardment of all of these issues has effectively brought the free press to its knees and produced an environment where journalism is increasingly caustic and irrelevant. People are free to scream about the problems of the free press being biased, a joke, or how reporters "don't know what the hell they're doing," and they're essentially right. We now have federal judges decrying the free press in Washington, D.C., as being the tools of the liberal elite. No one ever really talks about the real problem. That gives people like Donald Trump and others the ability to offer a nefarious reason for the problem that people swallow wholesale—because on the surface it makes some sense. Must be liberals. Right?

I defy you to name a "liberal" media owner—or board of directors. The bias is toward money, and it always has been, as we've seen.

The facts are ever harder to comprehend than that and are far more complicated. More on that in a bit.

By the time of the Obama administration, journalism wasn't just being threatened by everything we've already mentioned. As already mentioned, there is a growing and virtually unseen and unreported threat to every local paper in the country: the elimination of public notice and service ads. Those ads and notices are a key component in local, state, and federal government transparency. But, increasingly, a growing number of jurisdictions want to publish these ads on government websites rather in newspapers or on newspaper websites. As previously mentioned, the ads have been around since the beginning of newspapers, and since the first U.S. Congress, the government has used newspapers to publish public notice ads. These ads, along with open meetings laws and freedom of information requests, are the backbone of providing the public with government transparency.

During the Obama administration, state and local governments really ramped up their efforts to get rid of them. There are a variety of reasons why. Sometimes, governments think it's too expensive to publish the ads. Sometimes, legislators—uncaring of their responsibility to the public— think it's a great idea to publish the ads on a government website. Richard Karpel of the Public Notice Resource Center says, "It is the eternal battle between government and the press on providing information." Sometimes, there are more notorious reasons for cutting out the public notice ads. Some local politicians, particularly those who don't like what's been written about them, have purposely tried to curtail newspaper revenue and punish publications that do not report news the way the politicians want. "Around the turn of the century, we saw this rear its head. When the internet became widely used, and that trend has progressed, more internet connectivity, newspaper readership down and partisanship. In many cases, most of the places we have problems are in Republican states because republican officials hate newspapers. This is just revenge," Karpel explained.

Critics argue that Karpel has overgeneralized the reasons public notice ads have been so brazenly attacked by government, but you cannot argue with the simple fact that they are under attack.

The irony, as Karpel explains, is that the small newspapers that exist in the rural areas where many legislators live who propose this legislation are those hurt the most. "The legislator may have a beef about the big newspaper owned by a hedge fund, and they aren't hurting them. They're hurting the little community newspaper in their own backyard," Karpel told me for this book.

As the president of the Maryland, Delaware, District of Columbia Press Association and as the executive editor for two newspapers in suburban Maryland, I, our executive director Rebecca Snyder, and others testified before a Maryland legislative committee in 2017 to defend the continued publication of these ads. Maryland, which fancied itself a progressive state, at the time was home to Jamie Raskin before he would win election to the U.S. House from Montgomery County, Maryland, and preside as the chief case manager in the second impeachment of Donald Trump. In short, Maryland was one of the states thought to be safe from this type of press manipulation because of people like Raskin.

Unfortunately, it was not. Some in our press association thought we should approach the legislature calmly and with a mind to calmly talk it out. I preferred another method. First, I ran a story with the headline "Killing the Press" with a photo of the legislator who *did* propose the legislation. I took it with me and made sure everyone on the committee had a copy of that issue of our paper. I wanted to be blunt and let them know how wrongheaded their proposed legislation was, and I didn't mind if I got them angry. I wanted them to wake up and think.

Public notices are essential because they're accessible, independent of government, verifiable, and archivable. Governments are pushing to publish public notices on government websites and position the argument against paying for these notices as a "newspaper versus the internet" argument. That's not the case. It's a battle between newspapers and newspaper websites versus government websites. Independence must win.

I showed up in Annapolis, Maryland, at the statehouse and told the legislators they were killing newspapers by a thousand cuts. I accused them of being as anti-press as Donald Trump. Then I held up a newspaper—the very first newspaper ever printed by the Montgomery County Sentinel. "Here it is," I told them. "The internet is infinite and ephemeral. I can go in and change it at will. I can hack it. I can delete the message. But this," I stressed as I held up a copy of a newspaper from 1855, "is not. This is finite. What was published in 1855 can be read today. It can't be hacked. It can't be changed. In the court of law, this is more valuable, and this is why we need to continue to publish public notice ads and why the government should not. We are independent. We verify what we publish, and that has sway."

I angered the legislators when I accused them of being as problematic to me as Donald Trump, and I really got the local legislator who proposed the bill upset. But, in the end, thankfully, they dropped their attempt to destroy public notice ads. Over the years, I've spoken with local shop owners, lawyers, and politicians who picked up key information from reading public service ads. Who didn't pay their taxes? Whose estate is going up for sale? Who got promoted and was thanked at a local city council meeting? What's closing? When is the school board meeting? I know lawyers who have picked up customers, and I know salesmen who have picked up vital information for their job—whether it was knowing who to congratulate for getting a raise or why a certain piece of property is being condemned.

Newspapers remain inherently superior to the internet for public notices as well. "We find things in newspapers we weren't expecting to see. On the Internet, we search for specific information and ignore everything else," Richard Karpel said to me for this book.

In all fifty states, newspapers are the primary way of notifying people. In all fifty states, local newspapers are dying. I took over the *Montgomery County Sentinel* and ultimately the *Prince George's Sentinel* in suburban Maryland as a way to stay at home and coach football and spend time with my kids as they grew up. When I joined the staff as the editor in 2004, the *Montgomery County Journal*—a daily newspaper for the million people living in the shadow of the nation's capital, closed. Within the decade, the Gazette newspapers, a weekly newspaper conglomerate that was independently owned before being sold to the *Washington Post*, closed. That left the Sentinel newspapers, which I ran for twelve years as the only newspaper in a county of a million people. Today, only the *Washington Post* covers the area—though the *Frederick News Post* has eyed the northern part of Montgomery County as a customer base and supplies community news to Poolesville and other small communities in northern Montgomery County.

It's hard to overstate the importance of the local community newspaper. The *Montgomery County Sentinel* and its sister paper the *Prince George's Sentinel* won multiple editorial awards during the time I was there. That's a testament to the ownership that gave us the freedom to operate and the young reporters it was a privilege to mentor. We routinely put both newspaper staffs together once a year and took on an investigative project. These monthlong projects outlined problems in infrastructure. One year, we looked at the problems of clean water, spending money to have the water tested in dozens of locations across the two counties. We investigated local civic government, thoroughly pissing off some of the more questionable representatives. We covered the issue of Confederate statues, local sports, religion, and entertainment. The newspaper won the "Newspaper of the Year" award from the Maryland, Delaware, District of Columbia Press Association in its category four times while I was there. Some of our stories achieved "Best in Show" honors in annual competition, besting our better-resourced brothers and sisters at the *Washington Post*, the *Baltimore Sun*, and the *News Journal* in Wilmington, Delaware. Since we were in the D.C. metropolitan area and since many of those who worked in the Capitol actually lived in Montgomery County, we employed a columnist to write about the White House and related matters.

We covered the Supreme Court members who lived in our county. We covered the Department of Justice and the National Institute of Standards and Technology (NIST) and other government agencies that operated facilities and property in Montgomery County. One of the first people to pitch me a story when I took the job was a woman who claimed that she had worked at the NIST in Gaithersburg. She asked me, "Have you seen the show *Stargate*? The real *Stargate* is at NIST." I also had people claiming they'd seen Bigfoot at nearby Needwood Lake. I saw a bunch of cicadas there once but no Bigfoot.

Other story pitches were more mundane but led to actual news that was later picked up nationally. When the D.C. snipers went on trial, I remember watching two or three national and local television correspondents stand in front of one of our newspaper stands or hold up a front page of our newspaper that featured a photo and stories of the snipers while they did a stand-up. As the George W. Bush era ended and the Obama era began, the internet became a major player in local journalism. Websites sprouted up touting "citizen journalists" who often were actually just bloggers. But they began to proliferate, and it was hard for a local reporter to keep up. Our newspapers began producing video content, livestreaming, and producing podcasts. It was clear by the middle of the Obama era that being a newspaper or a radio or television station was not enough. To be valuable to the community, you had to be all of those and more. Our newspaper set a goal of becoming a one-stop shop for everything in the community. We featured a high school "game of the week" during football and basketball seasons that showed highlights and commentary from our sportswriters. It was obvious that the only chance for community journalism to succeed was to be a 24/7 news and information service that, coincidentally, published a weekly version of itself. The written word still had value, but there was no substitute for immediacy.

Ad revenue began drying up for the local newspapers, killing the ability to monetize these efforts adequately. No one, it seemed, could afford to do community journalism—the backbone of all journalism. The *Washington Post*, which owned the Gazette newspaper chain, cannibalized the reporting staff there and took the ad revenue from the weekly newspapers and folded it into the main newspaper. It was not too dissimilar to what the *Courier-Journal* did after Gannett took over operations and killed the weekly section where I used to work.

The Sentinel newspapers, while able to produce great copy, could not keep up with the *Washington Post* or local television—though on occasion we were the source of information for stories they did. We held political candidate forums. We interviewed candidates. We refused to endorse candidates, as our owner took a stance that he never wanted to be in the pocket of politicians. However, we covered politics extensively, and we asked questions on a wide variety of issues that helped inform local voters on issues that ultimately had national and international repercussions.

The first time Jamie Raskin got elected to Congress, he was not favored to win. Kathleen Matthews, a local news anchor and wife of Chris Matthews, was the heads-on favorite until months before the election. That's when David J. Trone entered the race. A billionaire liquor store owner, Trone and Matthews threw a record amount of money at the race. Raskin had a base, was heavily outspent, and was expected to finish third, according to some privately funded polls. There were nine people in that race.

The *Montgomery County Sentinel* sponsored a candidate debate, and I moderated it. Paul Schwartz, one of our local political columnists with extensive political experience, including the White House, gathered questions from the audience and, combining these with his own questions, acted as one of the questioners. At one point in time, David Trone, as noted by Bill Turque in the *Washington Post*, motioned that he was getting tired of the proceedings by pointing to his watch. I ignored him, and we went about our business. But the gesture was not ignored by the hundreds of people in the room, the thousands who viewed our livestream event, or the *Washington Post*. It did not bode well for Trone. He and Matthews split the votes that Matthews otherwise would've captured, and Raskin gained enough of the remaining votes, along with keeping his own votes, so he was able to win his race. It helped him out that of all the nine candidates we questioned that night, it was Raskin who never played games. People saw him as believable, honorable, and smart. In some small way, it was a community newspaper that no longer exists that enabled Jamie Raskin to get elected—and inevitably be the lead case manager in the second impeachment of Donald Trump.

Our small newspaper had a few run-ins with President Obama and his communications staff, too. They were a high-handed bunch who looked down on most reporters who weren't at the major networks or news services and, in fact, looked down at those media outlets as well, though they begrudgingly dealt with them. A small community newspaper? Bah! Humbug!

The quintessential example of the problems with Obama came when we were doing a series of stories on Pepco, the energy giant that had faltered badly. The joke in the county was that if your electricity went off, it must be a calm midsummer day. Pepco, which did not generate most of its power but transmitted across lines it owned after purchasing energy elsewhere, had not invested adequately in its transmission lines, and at the time, electric service became erratic—often without any intervention from big weather.

One day when this happened, I instructed a reporter to call the White House and find out if it had also lost electricity. Pepco supplies power to the D.C. area—so it was of interest as to whether the White House had been affected. Emergency generators and independent systems aside, all we wanted to know was if the White House had been affected. For half an hour, the White House communications staff kept my reporter dancing as more than one member of the junior press staff refused to answer the question—explaining that national security interests wouldn't allow them to do it.

Finally, frustrated listening to the conversation on my reporter's side of the line, I got on the phone with someone I knew and played bad cop.

I was told they didn't really like taking "this kind of questions—especially with a small newspaper."

Needless to say, that didn't wash too well with me, and after I informed my source that I wasn't out to do harm to the White House but trying to ascertain the problems with our electricity service provider, I simply said, "Look, did the lights flicker, even for a second? I want to know and want people to know how serious the electricity service problem is." When the staffer admitted to living in Silver Spring, Maryland, and was upset with Pepco as well, I finally got an answer—yes. The White House had some minor issues.

It was like pulling teeth.

During the Obama administration, the pressures on community newspapers and a loss of revenue for small independent newspapers and their larger corporate cousins contributed to the ongoing constriction of newspaper ownership. Larger companies were gobbling each other up, and smaller independent newspapers either were bought up and cannibalized like the *Post* did to the Gazette newspapers or the smaller companies just failed. According to figures supplied to Axios, the United States lost more than 50,000 newsroom jobs from 2008 through 2016.[11]

This made it harder and harder to provide important public information. There was one final move that occurred during Obama's tenure that also contributed to the decline of a free press. I have testified in the Texas, Kentucky, Maryland, and Virginia legislatures and conferenced with members of Congress about the need for a national shield law. Most states have a shield law that protects reporters to a varying degree, depending on the state, from having to cough up confidential sources. I've tried to strengthen them since I went to jail in Texas, a state that admittedly has a very weak shield law. During the Obama administration, a rare bipartisan effort grew to adopt such legislation at the national level. Future vice president Mike Pence, then senator from Indiana, was a sponsor of the bill, which cleared the House and died in the Senate. What killed it?

Julian Assange and Edward Snowden had something to do with it. So did Chelsea Manning. Those three cases helped to kill any pro-press legislation. Congress and members of the Obama administration wanted blood. Chelsea Manning is a former member of the army. She was convicted by court-martial in 2013 for violating the Espionage Act and disclosing to WikiLeaks nearly 750,000 classified or unclassified sensitive military and diplomatic documents.[12] President Obama commuted the bulk of her sentence, but the revelation of what she did turned Congress cold to the press.

Julian Assange still faced charges in March 2021 for what he did years earlier. He founded WikiLeaks in 2006 and published the leaks Manning supplied. The leaks included information on the Baghdad air strikes, Afghanistan and Iraq war logs, and Cablegate. According to WikiLeaks, the 251,287 cables consist of 261,276,536 words, making Cablegate the "largest set of confidential documents ever to be released into the public domain."[13]

Assange has remained outside of U.S. jurisdiction for years and was indicted in 2018. The AP reported the indictment raised concerns about media freedom, as Assange's solicitation and publication of classified information is a job that journalists have traditionally performed (maybe not so much anymore, as there are fewer of us). Assange is just another symptom of a fractured press. Large corporations that do business with the government are less likely to cross paths than is an independent publisher like Assange. While some politicians supported his indictment, civil rights groups did not. Senator Mark Warner said Assange was a "dedicated accomplice in efforts to undermine American security."[14] Government is always worried about its security, and from the local police department to the highest levels of the U.S. government, it is the number one reason given for jailing reporters.

Reporters Without Borders said Assange's arrest "set a dangerous precedent for journalists, whistle blowers and other journalistic sources that the U.S. may wish to pursue in the future."[15] It was just another indication of the power the government now has over the publication of information vital to the public. He remains imprisoned in London. In January 2021, a judge ruled Assange could not be extradited to the United States, citing concerns about his mental health and risk of suicide in a U.S. prison. A Justice Department spokesman confirmed in mid-February that the new Biden administration would continue the appeal to extradite Assange and force him to stand trial in the United States.

Around the same time, in 2013, Edward Snowden also jumped into the spotlight when he disclosed multiple global surveillance programs run by the National Security Agency (NSA). Snowden has been called a traitor, a hero, a whistle-blower, a patriot, and several words sailors fear to utter. Whatever you call him, you can call him gone. Rather than face espionage charges in the United States, Snowden fled the country and now has established residence in Russia.

Donald Trump, before he was elected president, tweeted in 2013 that Snowden was a traitor and "should be executed."[16] Attorney General Eric Holder told the Russian government that Snowden would not be subjected to torture or the death penalty, but Russia wouldn't turn him over. Daniel Ellsberg called Snowden's release of NSA material the most significant leak in U.S. history. Later, it was determined that the massive government surveillance program exposed by Snowden was illegal.

The U.S. Court of Appeals for the Ninth Circuit said the warrantless telephone searches that secretly collected millions of Americans' records were probably unconstitutional and violated the Foreign Intelligence Surveillance Act. "I never imagined that I would live to see our courts condemn the NSA's activities as unlawful and in the same ruling credit me for exposing them," Snowden tweeted.[17]

The American Civil Liberties Union viewed the ruling as a victory for privacy rights, but the man who exposed the surveillance, Edward Snowden, still can't come home without facing prosecution.

The Assange, Handler, and Snowden cases were a direct result of, at that time, more than three decades of media manipulation. When the *Pentagon Papers* were dumped on the public, several reporters at the *New York Times* and the *Washington Post* (and later others) went through the documents, putting them in context and developing stories that would tell the importance of the information. Handler and Assange did a huge media dump on the internet. Snowden thought so little of the mainstream American press that he took his story to *The Guardian*. The information made accessible to the world was unbelievably huge, and because reporters— or, more accurately, teams of investigative reporters with knowledge and experience—were not involved (or only peripherally so), the context was lost, and the real importance was underreported and largely not understood.

After the *Pentagon Papers*, most of the country understood our government had been lying to us for years and through multiple administrations about Vietnam. It angered us, and as a country, we did something about it. But the government learned from that mistake, and after Nixon, Ailes, Reagan, and all the other presidents who followed chipped away at our First Amendment freedoms and the ability of the press to function as a watchdog, few if any understand the significance of the Snowden, Handler, and Assange stories today.

The government is still lying to us, watching us, and doing so with apparent impunity.

History may well look on the Obama administration as one of the most dangerous threats ever against the First Amendment. There is no doubt the espionage charges against Manning, Assange, and Snowden poured ice water on the spirit of the First Amendment—no matter what else you think of the three people, personally, and no matter what other facts you wish to consider.

The collapse was nearly complete. Real information was becoming harder to get, and the consequences for getting that information were such that in the case of Snowden, the attorney general of the United States had to promise the Russian government we wouldn't torture or kill one of our own citizens. The weight of that statement alone belies the depths to which the American government has plunged and how seriously the threat is against free speech. We promised Russia we wouldn't kill one of our own citizens—and Russia didn't believe us.

The Obama administration took a high-handed approach dealing with the press, even as Obama's Justice Department took a jackhammer to free speech. But in at least one case, Obama acted a lot like Trump. Anita Dunn, then the White House director of communications, told the *New York Times* in 2009 that Fox was not a legitimate news organization and that "we're going to treat them the way we would treat an opponent."[18] The Obama White House also, according to spokesman Josh Earnest, had a history of freezing out Fox News. President Obama himself weighed in on Fox News, telling *Rolling Stone,* "We've got a tradition in this country of a press that oftentimes is opinionated. The golden age of an objective press was a pretty narrow span of time in our history. Before that, you had folks like Hearst who used their newspapers very intentionally to promote their viewpoints. I think Fox is part of that tradition—it is part of the tradition that has a very clear, undeniable point of view. It's a point of view that I disagree with. It's a point of view that I think is ultimately destructive for the long-term growth of a country that has a vibrant middle class and is competitive in the world. But as an economic enterprise, it's been wildly successful. And I suspect that if you ask Mr. Murdoch what his number-one concern is, it's that Fox is very successful."[19]

What Obama failed to say was that government intervention since Ronald Reagan made the journalism he claimed to love nearly impossible to do! What he, perhaps, failed to understand was that treating Fox News as he did was just fine with Fox. It drove people to them. It enhanced the size of their audience.

The Obama administration seemed at times to be at war with most everyone—except Democratic loyalists—and even they took a whack at him from time to time. Hillary Clinton even called him an elitist after he said people living in small towns in Pennsylvania were bitter. "And it's not surprising, then, they get bitter, they cling to guns or religion or antipathy to people who aren't like them or anti-immigrant sentiment or anti-trade sentiment as a way to explain their frustrations."[20]

A lot of the Obama criticism came from racists who were offended an African American man had been elected to the highest office in the land. This ugly, divisive criticism often stained any legitimate criticism of the president. Fox was so insipid in criticizing Obama the network tried to make a scandal out of the fact that he wore a tan suit to work one day.

Meanwhile, the "zero-sum game" of politics exercised by the GOP in Washington since the Clinton administration and the arrival of Newt Gingrich dictated there could be no cooperation with Obama. Senate Majority Leader Mitch McConnell proudly said just that. He was going to obstruct anything the president wanted to do if at all possible. Obstructionism took place instead of governing—though few ever accused McConnell of governing. Name-calling and extreme partisanship took over. The United States seemed to split in two—and into that gap came Donald Trump, who would show "how low can you go" wasn't just a trick in the limbo world.

But as we can now see, the rancor and divisiveness was a natural outgrowth of the actions the government took to kill effective media communication. While we preach that we have the First Amendment, there is no real meaning we can attach to it since we cannot publish certain material, only a few are allowed access to the people in power, fewer are allowed access to information, fewer reporters are covering government, and the federal, state, and local governments continue to do whatever they can to destroy the access to real information.

Under those conditions, I began to go more regularly to the White House while executive editor of the Sentinel newspapers to chronicle some of the problems. *Playboy* later expressed an interest in those columns, and we were off.

When I'd last attended briefings, we were still getting printouts by paper from dot-matrix printers located throughout the working press offices in the West Wing. I had been on the e-mail list since the White House first drew one up, but now I was getting notices and pool reports more quickly and far more often via e-mail than I ever did in previous administrations. I attended several briefings and asked a few questions during the Obama era, mostly to Josh Earnest during the last few months prior to the election and a few more after the election. Press attendance was quite low during the lame-duck portion of the Obama administration, and Earnest would often hold press briefings for so long that members of the press would beg him to stop. He often spoke about his favorite sports teams and bantered back and forth with some of the members of the press whom he knew and must've considered friends. I tried once to ask him about Russian interference in the 2016 election and whether it was an act of "cyber war" conducted by Russia. While the Obama administration abhorred Russia, it backed away from confronting Putin and Russia over the issues. Earnest never adequately answered my question, and that reverberates through politics as of today.

Then, during the last week of the administration, President Obama showed up to a packed James S. Brady Press Briefing Room for a victory lap and one last appearance. It would be nearly three years before a president would step foot in the briefing room again.

14

ENTER THE DRAGON

By the time Donald Trump walked down the escalator at Trump Tower and declared his candidacy for president, the stage was set. He walked into a perfect storm of diminished media expectations, political divisiveness, and a proliferation of conspiracy theories and ignorance made possible by forty years of the government's dismantling of the First Amendment—leaving most media corporations without the experienced staff to adequately take on Trump and his bombast.

Trump took advantage of it to the fullest. The media for the most part viewed him as a freak show that brought with it ratings gold. He was the combination of the dunking booth, bearded lady, and teacup ride at the county fair. Everybody wanted to interview him, quote him, or watch him rant. What was going on? What was behind the ranting? How would Trump govern? Who knew? Who cared. Just watch that guy make an ass out of himself, make fun of him, or defend him. Context? Meaning? Figure it out for yourself or invent your own.

Reporters I knew on the campaign trail with Trump said from the beginning he thoroughly enjoyed the media attention even as he griped about it. He routinely pointed to cameras at his rallies and claimed the "fake news" was turning off the cameras pointed at him as he criticized us. No one ever did—and he knew it. He told Leslie Stahl, in a now infamous interview, that he called us names and cast doubt on the media because he didn't want people to believe the truth when it was reported about him. In previous years, this would never have been possible. With a wider variety of voices covering a president, a handful of corporations couldn't monopolize the megaphone. More voices and more coverage from a wider variety of reporters allowed a greater flow of information without corporate constriction. But Trump successfully cast the small number of major broadcasters as enemies. He promoted those like Fox News and One America News, which would broadcast his propaganda virtually unchallenged. He agreed to go on those networks and supported people like Sean Hannity, who not only promoted but also magnified his point of view.

Trump's triumph over the media was his greatest victory as president. He survived two impeachments; untold and unheard-of scandals involving Russia, China, Ukraine, and his own businesses; and charges of violating the emolument clause, and he survived the devastating Mueller investigation (which pointed to ten possible incidents of obstruction of justice)[1] simply by screaming louder than anyone else and using the echo chamber of his supporters like Attorney General Bill Barr and favorable media to maintain power. By comparison, Richard Nixon, felled by an egregious scandal, was unable to get away with a tenth of what Trump managed to survive. It goes to show just how successful and at the same time how destructive Roger Ailes, Ronald Reagan, Bill Clinton, Barack Obama, George Bush, and Mark Fowler had been. Worse, because of the lack of institutional knowledge at the White House, many reporters were unaware of the previous independence of the press and look askance at those who practiced it.

Just prior to Trump's inauguration, veteran Associated Press radio reporter Mark Smith announced his retirement from the ranks of White House reporters. Smith, a former White House Correspondents' Association (WHCA) president, covered every administration since Jimmy Carter and everything from the war in the Falklands to President Clinton's impeachment. Smith was well respected and professional.

"I feel like I'm leaving you guys on the parapets at the Alamo," I remember him saying as coworkers toasted his retirement. Although I did not know Smith well at the time, his words stuck with me as I tried to keep the bigger picture in focus. I came to recognize that Smith's departure—which came in March 2017—was another example of a loss of needed institutional knowledge.

If we extend Smith's metaphor, what we lost at the parapet was a veteran who knew the tactics, the strategy, and strengths of the opposition—the federal government. Such invaluable knowledge can turn the tide in the battle. Without it, you end up like the folks at the Alamo. There is always a turnover of reporters at the White House when administrations change. But losing those with the most experience as Trump came to power also served to compromise an already weakened press corps. On one of the first days of the Trump administration, a young producer from a major network approached me and asked for directions and some guidance, which I happily provided. I then asked if this person was an intern.

I was informed I was talking to a senior producer for the network. I asked how old the senior producer was and was informed that I was speaking to a twenty-four-year-old senior producer. I wondered how young the junior producer was—twelve?

Some (but not all) of the younger reporters, producers, and assistants working at the White House enter slightly intimidated, even if they don't want to show it. Big eyes are soon replaced by closed eyes. The young reporter full of energy and ready to report on the stories of importance to the country soon becomes the cynical, jaded hack sucking up to minor bureaucrats in the White House and wondering if they'll be invited to the "right parties." It's an old story of course, and H. L. Mencken, back in the 1920s, addressed it with his usual aplomb. "Drenched with propaganda at home, he is quite content to take more propaganda from Washington. It is not that he is dishonest, but that he is stupid—and, being stupid, a coward. The resourcefulness, enterprise and bellicosity that his job demands are simply not in him. He doesn't wear himself out trying to get the news, as romance has it; he slides supinely into the estate and dignity of a golf-player. American journalism suffers from too many golf-players. They swarm in the Washington Press Gallery. They, and not their bosses are responsible for most of the imbecilities that now afflict their trade."[2]

The truth is most reporters, though not part of the club, definitely want to be and believe in the ways that matter they are. They are used by petty bureaucrats and gaslighting politicians to advance partisan causes or to get a good story told in the news. That's the job of the petty bureaucrat. Reporters used to be more immune to these obvious power plays, but today, many reporters are happy to follow along. They don't know how to do their jobs, or if they do, then they don't care. While this attitude is obviously not new, what is of concern is today there are far fewer chances an independent thought will be uttered in Washington, D.C., when the number of major employers hiring reporters is reduced to a number that can be counted on a single human hand. So, while the proximate man remains the greatest problem in covering the White House, a shrinking number of employers is the larger problem. As they hire cheaper labor (I recently had a friend of mine who's an editor at a large newspaper tell me his company was seriously considered hiring a reporter fresh out of college to cover the White House because such a reporter would be cheap), these companies ensure most of the reporters are unqualified to report on the president and are cheap and easily replaceable.

Those who still ask today, "How did we get here?" when assessing the loathsome and inadequate coverage of the Donald Trump administration lack an understanding of how the business works and how everything we've already talked about led us to "The Donald." Trump rode into town with Steve Bannon, Stephen Miller, a handful of GOP stalwarts, and a bag full of "true believers." His was a cult based on his personality and his bigger-than-life swagger. A look behind his circus tent showed he was and always has been a con artist. He invented his "border wall" strategy on the fly. He flew by the seat of his pants into the Oval Office, and he governed that way. In the beginning, he was just the guy screaming against the establishment.

Barack Obama had angered the far right, had muzzled the press, and had also failed to build his bench strength in the Democratic Party. All of these developments also helped give rise to Trump. The truth is while the Democrats are more like the old Republican Party—a central theme at the 2016 Democratic National Convention in Philadelphia—it was the Republican Party, stoked with racists, fascists, and more con men than the population of a midsize American city, that appealed to the working man. And it was Donald Trump, whom Anthony Scaramucci once referred to as the "blue-collar billionaire" when we spoke, that caught their attention.

Trump relied on Steve Bannon to guide him into the White House after the Trump campaign caught fire, and Bannon was masterful at manipulation. Bannon, a former naval officer and Goldman Sachs investment banker, was also a former executive producer in Hollywood who spent time at Cambridge Analytica and Breitbart before joining the Trump campaign as his chief strategist. He stayed with the Trump administration for its first several months. In August 2020, Bannon and three others were arrested and charged with conspiracy to commit mail fraud and money laundering in connection with the "We Build the Wall" campaign. Bannon pleaded guilty, and Trump, of course, pardoned him before his trial. In November 2020, Bannon got kicked off Twitter after he suggested that Dr. Anthony Fauci and Christopher Wray, the FBI director, should be beheaded.

A lot of Bannon's Hollywood work sounded a lot like the stories and narrative he would push as Trump's chief strategist. "In the Face of Evil: Reagan's War in Word and Deed"; "Border War: The Battle over Illegal Immigration"; "Fire from the Heartland: The Awakening of the Conservative Woman"; "District of Corruption"; and "Clinton Cash" were all titles Bannon worked on. Think what you will of him personally, but he brought to Trump an innate ability to manipulate, a track record for doing so, and a skill set that assisted Trump in playing the media.

Trump himself, an occasional walk-on cameo actor in famous movies, had the Hollywood swagger, and that too helped disarm the media on his rise to political prominence. Donald Trump had been in the public eye since the 1980s. "It was ultimately why I kept working for him," Michael Cohen later told me. "It was very alluring. That star quality. I sure didn't need the money. But he would call up with front row seats and backstage passes and that kind of celebrity is hard to deny."[3]

For the average reporter making less in a year than Trump would spend on a weekend trip and a private flight from New York to Los Angeles, those trappings were hard to ignore—no matter how hard-nosed you thought you were. For the anchors who had Trump on their shows or, later, his surrogates, like Kellyanne Conway, it was impossible to deny that rubbing elbows with Trump—even when castigating him—was ratings gold. And that is exactly why American journalism is in trouble and has to change.

For those of us who didn't cover Donald Trump on the campaign trail, it was obvious from the very first day how Donald Trump planned to manipulate the media, the truth, the American people, and his office for personal profit.

Sean Spicer, Trump's first press secretary, walked out into the James S. Brady Press Briefing Room for the first time on that day in January 2017 and told us that Trump had the largest inauguration crowd in history—period. Then he walked out and took no questions.

That was actually the high-water mark for the Donald Trump administration—a lie about the size of his inaugural crowd. I remember Spicer expressed some regret to me later about this event. He was, after all, a GOP stalwart and was not one of the true believers in Trump's vision. He told several people he left his office the night of the election convinced Trump had lost to Clinton and was totally surprised when Trump won. Some of the true believers told me that "God preordained" Trump's victory. Spicer was not *that* guy. So, when I asked him later why he went to work for Trump, he said squarely, "Brian, what would you do if the president of the United States asked you to serve your country?"

He had me there. If the president asked me to serve my country, I would do so. But I told Spicer it would end the moment he asked me to go out and lie to the American public about the size the inaugural crowd—or lie about anything else for that matter. That, as it turned out, was the difference between us. Spicer never looked comfortable trying to make the best of a bad situation, and he was also the only member of Donald Trump's administration to ever publicly apologize for anything. It happened within the first 100 days of the Trump administration. Syria was on everyone's mind. Trump had bombed the country. In his Monday briefing on April

10, I got the first question and asked bluntly, "How come it is okay to bomb Syria but not help out Syrian refugees?" Spicer stumbled with an answer by defending the bombing as helping out potential refugees and never addressed current refugees who need homes. But that was nothing compared to Tuesday, the next day.

The day after I asked him about bombing Syria, many of us in the press were still pressing the issue, and that led to the single biggest strikeout Spicer suffered within the first three months of the Trump administration. In trying to explain just how bad the leadership was in Syria, he said, "Even Hitler didn't gas his own people."[4] First silence, then groans. No one dared say a word. It was too much. Clocks stopped. Paint peeled. Mouths dropped. What could you say? No one could think of anything. Except me. I shot off my mouth. "He gassed the Jews," I shouted in the press room. Spicer sputtered. "Thank you. Yeah, yeah, I know."

Spicer later appeared on several networks apologizing for the misstatement and begging for forgiveness. Again, it cannot be said enough that Spicer was the *only* Trump official to ever apologize for anything. Spicer rebounded later in that same briefing when asked about North Korea threatening the United States. Trump hadn't yet established his "bromance" with the North Korean leadership, so Spicer's reply to the question was cast in a John Wayne light. When asked about potential threats from North Korea, Spicer replied, "It ain't a threat if you can't do it."[5]

As for the gaffe itself, some in Congress—particularly Nancy Pelosi—called for his head, pretty much guaranteeing Trump wouldn't fire him. And he didn't. But everyone covered the gaffe, the apology, and the Pelosi angle as well as comments and quotes from Jewish leaders and some of our foreign allies. The story extended for another news cycle. Once again, the press was diverted from what is real to chase the prurient and salacious. Did Spicer commit a gaffe and an incredibly stupid gaffe at that? Absolutely. Making it during Passover? Priceless. But the story of the moment is merely a momentary story. War in the Middle East, the budget, Russian interference in our election, North Korean and Chinese relations, another school shooting, Syrian air strikes, the Supreme Court, health care, tax cuts, and whether the Washington football team signed Kirk Cousins—those stories at the time were all more important than Spicer's gaffe as he tried to use hyperbole to sell how horrified everyone in the administration was about the Syrian gas attack.

My first problem with the administration came nearly six months into it. While I had kept my mouth shut for the most part and had merely made my appearances revolve around the questions, there is absolutely no way I could bypass what Sarah Huckabee Sanders did June 27, 2017. She was still the deputy press secretary at the time, and she was speaking from the podium on that day instead of Spicer. On June 27, 2017, the White House Press Office sent out its daily guidance telling us of significant events the next day. A press briefing was not among them, but we were promised notification by the following morning. The mood inside the White House press room had been on "simmer" since the president had returned from his first foreign trip and because rumors persisted about staffers coming and going—mostly going for good. On-camera briefings slowed to a trickle but not nearly as slow as they became later. That Tuesday morning, we were informed we would be on camera and Sean Spicer would show up with Rick Perry to discuss energy and other issues. Health care was sure to be addressed, as the Congressional Budget Office score had come out, and 22 million people, it was estimated, could lose their health care under the Senate's plan.

So, I went to the White House to ask about health care. The president told us in a briefing last week—in a question I posed—that he was happy with the bill and would veto legislation if he, theoretically, didn't like it. Meanwhile, Spicer traveled to Capitol Hill to apparently speak to someone who wasn't in the press corps, and we waited (again) for the briefing to begin. I usually waited until we were twenty to twenty-five minutes overdue and then poked my head into the press office and ask them to get a move on. The White House press people don't like this, but I think it's incredibly rude to keep 100 people waiting. Just make the time for the briefing later—I'm fine with that. But please, as my southern parents taught me, if you commit to be somewhere on time—then do it. The Trump administration never cared about such social niceties. To them, being polite was a sign of weakness.

Spicer, as it turns out, could not get back in time from Capitol Hill to do the briefing, so Sarah Huckabee Sanders showed up with Perry. I got to ask Perry the question I wanted and even followed up on a question Jeff Mason from Reuters asked regarding climate change. Although Perry told me he couldn't understand my question, I asked it again and got a response. Then Sarah Huckabee Sanders stepped up and joked about how long we had to wait and maybe we should just skip the questions. We had been waiting long enough, that's true, and Perry spent quite a bit of time in an animated and entertaining state. That's true, too. Sanders stepped up, and the first question came from a Breitbart reporter about Project Veritas founder James O'Keefe's release of a video that Tuesday morning of a

CNN producer saying the network's heavy coverage of possible collusion between Trump administration officials and Russia during the 2016 presidential election is "mostly bullshit."[6] Sanders was in her element, and we got to hear again how the media are at fault and that there is a lot of fake media out there, and Sanders urged us all to look at some video—that she admittedly had no idea of whether it was factual or true—but if it was, then, oh boy, we should see it. She then started browbeating reporters about using unnamed sources or no sources and how some reporters had to resign because they were just terrible people. It was the same thing that had been said every day for the first six months of the administration. It was always aimed at the "audience of one"—Donald Trump—and meant to disparage us for trying to report the truth.

No one had really ever pushed back strong on that narrative. And on that day, I had enough. As an independent reporter, I was not a member of the pool. I didn't have a seat in the briefing room and didn't get to go to the Oval Office or fly on Air Force One, and none of that mattered. What mattered was that every day for six months, the Trump administration felt comfortable shitting on the media, and we sat there and took it. I wasn't standing for it anymore and considered myself as having been patient far longer than was prudent. "Come on Sarah," I interrupted her. I stood along the left wall of the briefing room nearby the plaque that dedicated it to James Brady, the press secretary who was shot during the Reagan administration. "Any one of us are replaceable, and any one of us if we don't get it right, the audience has the opportunity to change the channel or not read us . . ."

At that point, Sarah tried to interrupt me, but I wasn't done. "You have been elected to serve four years. There's no option other than that . . ."

She tried to interrupt again. I still wasn't done. "We're here to ask you questions, and you're here to provide answers. And what you just did is inflammatory to people . . . people all over the country who will say 'see they're at again. The president is right and everyone else out here is fake media.' And everybody in this room is only trying to do their job."[7]

The confrontation never softened the administration or changed their tactics, and I didn't think it would. I merely watched my colleagues get hammered day after day for really only trying to do their job. I can criticize them on their abilities, I may even question whether they have them, but the bottom line is that we are all members of the voting public. We have a unique privilege of being able to ask the president and his administration questions about how they operate and, at the very least, deserve to be treated as fellow professionals, not get bullied by people who had no idea what *they* were doing let alone what *we* were doing. Some in the press corps got upset with me for that exchange, but I'd be lying if I said that meant anything to me. Members of the WHCA said I made their job more difficult, and one person accused me of preening for television. A very young reporter whom I later came to respect asked me if I wasn't afraid people would begin to think I was being antagonistic toward the White House.

"No. Because I am," I said. "That's the job. I'm not antagonistic because I have some burning personal animosity against Donald Trump. I barely know the man. My antagonism is against government in general, and it is our job to make the members of the government, whoever they are, responsible to the public by asking questions and probing for answers."

I actually received a thank-you from that reporter, who told me they'd never heard that before. I was not surprised. I was merely paraphrasing Helen Thomas—but she was long gone, and few in the briefing room today knew her personally. But in the spirit of full disclosure, I also pushed back against the White House because I don't like people trying to bully others. I don't like the entire institution of the press and free speech being castigated for no other reason than we either get stories wrong—which happens, and it should be then responsibly corrected—or report news the president doesn't like—which seems to happen even more often than getting stories wrong. The foundation of a free republic is a free press. You take the good with the bad, and you move on. Trump spent four years trying to beat us into submission, and when he couldn't silence us in one fashion, he tried other ways.

I quickly came to like Jim Acosta. He shared some of my same opinions about reporting and politics—and bullies. He, along with myself and others—namely, April Ryan and later scores of others—pushed hard against Trump. But in the beginning? It seemed like a lonely fight, as many reporters thought engaging in any pushback was as narcissistic as the president we were trying to keep in check. Let us be straight. No one I've ever known who covers the president believes they are "the story." Some do like to see themselves on camera, and some try to ask long questions so they can be seen. In fact, I know of one reporter who routinely asks questions that are much longer than the answers he gets—which looks funny when you read the transcripts. But I don't know of many who want to take on Trump or any president just for the sake of doing it.

God knows I didn't. I do remember one young reporter I saw sitting outside of the Brady Briefing Room one day. She was in tears. When I asked why, she told me that she was afraid of losing her job if she wasn't seen asking a question during the briefing and, by the way, she had been ignored that day. That type of behavior was rare too. Those who had experience knew what their job was and knew what it would take to honestly question Donald Trump. In the beginning, Jim Acosta was one of the loudest voices to stand his ground. He also paid for it.

The night after the midterm elections, November 7, 2018, Trump held court in the East Room for another press conference. The Democrats took back the house, and Trump was trying to explain how that was actually a victory for the Republican Party, so the stage was set. Trump of course told us all that the GOP had "beat expectations." He spoke about his taxes, immigration, and how much he liked Oprah. It sparked me to ask him why he was going on about his "Oprah love" so much, and he called me a comedian. "She didn't do the trick," Trump said in assessing how he felt that Oprah ultimately let him down. I didn't care. I really wanted to ask him. So, I settled down to ask him the real question I wanted answered. It was whether he could continue to work with the Democrats even if they began investigating him. "That if they start investigating you, you can investigate them," I started to ask. "Better than them," he said. "I think I know more than they know," he told me.

"Can you compartmentalize this and continue to work with them for the benefit of the rest of the country?" I was asking the question because that's exactly what President Bill Clinton did, even as the GOP impeached him. He continued to work with them for the benefit of the rest of the country. But Trump wasn't having any of it.

"No," he interrupted again.

"Or are all bets off?" I finished.

"No. If they do that, it's a warlike posture."

He wouldn't allow me to follow up, and he was obviously upset—though honestly to this day I don't know what angered him more: my question about how he'd deal with the Democrats or how he felt about Oprah Winfrey. But he chose his next questioner, and it was Jim Acosta. "Well, since it's Jim, I'll let it go," I said and passed the microphone to him. Trump looked pained. Jim smiled as he took the microphone from me, then turned to the president and said he wanted to challenge Trump on something he said on the campaign. "Here we go," Trump said before Acosta asked him about caravans of illegal immigrants invading the country. "I consider it an invasion," Trump said as he motioned Acosta to quickly wrap up. But, as he had done with me, Trump didn't really want Jim to finish his question and kept trying to interrupt him. Jim and Trump got into it, and Trump told Acosta he'd run the country and Acosta could run CNN. "That's enough," Trump shouted at him.

Then one of the press wranglers attempted to take the microphone out of Jim's hand as he continued to press the issue. "That's enough, put down the mic," Trump said as he walked away from the podium in a huff. Jim relinquished the microphone to Peter Alexander from NBC, who defended Acosta as a professional "diligent" reporter, but Trump would have none of it. "I tell you CNN should be ashamed of themselves having you work for them. You're a rude terrible person," Trump said.

It didn't end well. Most of us thought the president and his staff looked foolish, but the administration decided it was Acosta, who merely tried to ask a question, who was at fault. Trump yanked his press pass. Ted Boutrous, a First Amendment attorney from Los Angeles, took Acosta's case. The press world seemed ambivalent about supporting him. It was shocking to see people in the press missing the point of what the fight was about. When any member of the press is attacked, it is an attack on all of us. Jim did his job. That should've been the end of it, and we should all have jumped in the breach with him. There's no other way to say it. While some saw the issue for what it was, the WHCA was particularly slow to respond, coming in at the last moment and later trying to take credit for a courageous stance—which many reporters did not buy.

In the end, Acosta defeated Trump in court, and the administration gave up. Acosta kept his press pass, and Trump spun it as a win for his side, further inflaming his base. I watched Acosta endure a lot of criticism and more, including receiving threats at rallies, being required to have private security in place at some Trump rallies, and generally being treated as if he were caught by a lynch mob after robbing the only liquor store in a small town. I've never once seen Jim lose his temper. He has been far more patient than I know I would be in similar situations, and he often turns his detractors into fans.

At a Montoursville, Pennsylvania, rally, a woman who told me, "I hate Jim Acosta," then asked me if she could get a picture with him. A quick scan led me to believe she was unarmed, and I told her to ask Jim. "He's a friendly guy, he'll probably do it," I told her. The woman walked over to Acosta, who was speaking with other members of the public, and asked him for a picture. Jim smiled and obliged. The woman, who a minute earlier told me, "I hate Jim Acosta," looked giddy as she put her arm around him while a friend took the picture. As she left, she told me, "I love Jim Acosta." That's how flimsy the real antipathy is from the public to the press. Many just want to be recognized. They want to feel they are part of the system and not ignored by either our government or those in the press who cover the government. The audience wants to be recognized as being a part of the process. That means we have to listen, engage, and represent the public more thoroughly. It absolutely has to be done, yet the way the business is set up today, it often won't and/or can't be done. There aren't many like Jim who would wade into a crowd of haters and take selfies with them and smile. But it helps in ways we may never fully be able to assess.

But what we can do is make the networks more responsible to people. We can mandate that through legislation—and that would go a long way to solving the idea that we are "fake media" or the "enemy of the people." The government should require an hour a day of cable network airtime to be filled by local broadcasters. Local stations should participate in a pool to provide a variety of local programming to the national broadcasters. The problem is most people feel they are underrepresented. Most politicians have no idea why or how to deal with that, and local and network television cannot figure out a way to monetize the problem.

After forty years of government action that was meant to strengthen the press, the past decade has served to show that our government has utterly and completely failed. Even Dan Rather drew ire. In Iowa, after Rather got into a row with President Bush on national television, I saw staffers with "I'd *Rather* Be for Bush" buttons. People were upset. But Dan Rather didn't need private security to go to a presidential rally, and reporters weren't called "fake news" or "enemy of the people," nor were they routinely intimidated and threatened.

The demise of civility against the press occurred as Donald Trump lowered the bars on ethical, professional, and personal standards. Donald Trump gave the green light, as my comedian friend Kevin Lee said, for people to act as the worst version of themselves. The press, which had given him so much oxygen in the run-up to the election, began to seriously regret doing so. But Trump didn't care. Breitbart, the *Epoch Times*, One America News, the Daily Caller, and others were there to spread Trump's message. The rest of us really fumbled how we handled Donald Trump.

The press eventually did catch on to Trump, but the turning point didn't come until after a disastrous day in Maryland.

15

EVERYONE KNOWS IT'S WENDI

The best reporters I've ever known are beat reporters. Many were former war correspondents or police beat reporters, city hall reporters, community news editors, high school sports reporters, features reporters, business reporters, or reporters covering dozens of other beats. But everyone I've had the ultimate respect for knows how to develop sources, cover the news, be a part of his or her community, and pursue a standard of journalism that includes holding everyone—even themselves—accountable. If you think this is rare among journalists, you're either uninformed or mistaken or have never lived in a small town or read a community newspaper. The bulk of all reporting is done at this level and often by experienced, savvy reporters as well as eager and idealistic young women and men.

I managed two community newspapers for several years, and it was some of the most enjoyable time of my career. As a manager, one thing I will stand by, along with the many awards the staff won over the twelve years I was there: I was very fortunate to work with some very talented people. Putting a team together to produce a series on water quality or infrastructure problems or to investigate local political problems was as professionally satisfying as capturing a serial killer with a piece I produced for *America's Most Wanted*. In both cases, you could see firsthand how your work affected a community—the community in which you live. The joy with the community newspaper is in that everyday experience—the nearly instant reaction and the responsiveness from local residents and government officials—it is one of the purest experiences I ever had as a reporter. Chalk it up to the Kapiloff family, who owned the Sentinel newspapers in suburban Maryland from 1963 until they closed. I worked there from 2004 through 2017. Longtime chief executive officer Bernie Kapiloff had a great feel for what a community newspaper should be, and that made the difference—as did that I worked with some of the best young reporters, and it was a pleasure to mentor them and guide them. We introduced video production. We livestreamed. We covered live sports. There was never a chance to relax. We covered riots. We covered state football championships. We covered everything. When a local church official traveled to St. Louis, Missouri, I traveled there with a team consisting of two of my sons to cover the unrest in Ferguson. When my wife and I traveled to Europe the following year for our anniversary, we stopped at "The Jungle" in France—home to one of Europe's most infamous refugee camps.

We were not just a community newspaper—we tried to show how what happened in the world affected our community. I learned through this experience one universal truth in the newspaper industry that was taught to me from the time I became a high school reporter for my school newspaper: people don't like to see their name misspelled in print. All credibility begins there. If you can't spell their names right, then you can't hope to be taken seriously about anything else. To some, it's tedious, but there it is. By extension, you're taken less seriously the more misspellings and mistakes in grammar are seen in your pages. Large newspapers traditionally employed armies of copy editors to ensure these basics were maintained. It is no coincidence when newspapers began cutting copyediting staff, people began taking news less seriously. Again, Donald Trump resonated *because* there was a problem in journalism.

At community newspapers across the country, there is an entirely different attitude and method of working. Instead of being produced in a silo, news is produced more holistically. Budgets are smaller, and they have to be, and as a result reporters are often plugged into the community more directly, and that makes a big difference when doing something as basic as getting a person's name and title spelled correctly.

Since community journalists are notoriously underpaid, you often have semiretired reporters who aren't looking for a writing gig to pay full-time or even realistic wages and young hungry reporters who want to test the waters. Many will go on to law school or other master's programs. Some will stick with reporting as a career. Some will be out of journalism after this initial stop. All of them work where journalism begins and are often respected by members of their community while also being disparaged by those outside of it.

Inside those communities, it is a different story. The *Capital Gazette* in Annapolis, Maryland, is one of those different stories. *The Gazette*, like most newspapers, began as a family operation. William M. Abbott, who had worked for the *Baltimore Sun*, founded the newspaper with his daughter as its editor and his son as its business manager.[1] The newspaper turned over ownership, naturally, later and moved its headquarters seven times. It was acquired by the Baltimore Sun Media Group in 2014. That group became part of Tribune Publishing, which was acquired by Alden Global Capital in February 2021. Currently, a nonprofit is trying to purchase the *Baltimore Sun* and the *Capital Gazette* and exclude them from the merger of Alden and Tribune.

During the mid-twentieth century, the *Capital Gazette* was a well-respected newspaper. Elmer Jackson, a former sports editor and native of Hagerstown, Maryland, was appointed the editor in 1931. Jobs and pay were adequate to survive, and thus the newspaper thrived—with continuity and quality in coverage, which allowed it to enjoy a steady ad revenue.

That reputation continued through the twentieth century and into the first two decades of the twenty-first. The paper continued to thrive for the same reasons that brought it to prominence. Since it was geographically isolated from large television markets and larger newspapers couldn't realistically hope to compete with the well-established local brand, the *Capital Gazette* remained, in some way, a living relic of mid-twentieth-century newspapers that also advanced and adapted with the times to stay relevant in the age of the internet.

I had a friend who worked there. She wasn't a close friend, but we were colleagues, and she was active with the Maryland, Delaware, District of Columbia Press Association (MDDC) during my years of activity there. Wendi Winters was a force of nature. She had a great sense of humor and, according to her friends and colleagues at the *Capital Gazette*, was the heart of the newspaper. "She knew every human being in Anne Arundel County," editor Steve Gunn said. "The paper had such a strong vision about community news," he said, and Winters "encompasses what that newspaper was about." To put it bluntly, one of her close friends in the MDDC later said, "Everyone knows it's Wendi" when you see her.

I saw Wendi rarely, but at MDDC annual conferences over the years when I saw her, there was no doubt, by the way she spoke and the things she said, that she had retained over a career the verve, sense of fun, and curiosity that drove many of us into the business. She volunteered to help when she could, and I owe her a donut and coffee to this day.

Shortly after 2:30 p.m. on June 28, 2018, a year and a day after I challenged Sarah Huckabee Sanders about calling us "fake news" and the "enemy of the people," Jarrod Ramos walked up to the offices of the *Capital Gazette*. Ramos had a personal beef with the paper going back to 2011 when the paper published an article about Ramos being put on probation for harassing a high school acquaintance. Ramos brought a defamation suit against the paper, but Judge Maureen M. Lamasney dismissed the suit in 2015 after determining that the newspaper's reporting was based on publicly available records and Ramos could produce no evidence the reporting was in error. After that, Ramos adopted a different strategy and apparently began harassing the paper the way he'd harassed his friend—through threatening letters. The former editor of the paper, Thomas Marquardt, said the paper alerted police and consulted the newspaper's attorney about a restraining order against Ramos for his actions.

Ramos's rage against the newspaper culminated in his walking to the back door of the newspaper's offices on June 28, 2018; barricading the door; and then walking around to the front door carrying a Mossberg pump shotgun he had legally purchased within the past eighteen months, and opening fire.

Phil Davis, a courts and crime reporter, tweeted that Ramos "shot through the glass door to the office and opened fire on multiple employees." He described the newspaper offices as a "war zone" and said he remembered listening to Ramos reload. Although Ramos's name was known to newspaper management, no one who was there was aware of who he was when he walked up or why he was firing. Davis said it was the worst feeling in the world to be hiding in your newsroom and hearing a gunman reload.

Rachael Pacella tried to escape from the newsroom during the shooting but tripped and fell. She then hid behind a filing cabinet.[2] "I actually thought to myself during the shooting, 'Oh, this is news. This is a big deal.' Not in a victim-y way but in a newsy way. I was recognizing in real time that it was a news story, and I was surprised that news judgment occupied any brain space at all during that moment."

Ramos worked his way through the newspaper room that hours earlier had been the host for an MDDC executive board meeting that was attended by newspaper executives from all over the region. He fired, hitting and killing sixty-one-year-old Gerald Fischman, a columnist and editorial page editor. Rob Hiaasen, a fifty-nine-year-old assistant editor and weekend columnist, was killed too. John McNamara, a fifty-six-year-old sports reporter and editor and primary reporter for the *Bowie-Blade News*, also went down. Rebecca Smith, a thirty-four-year-old sales assistant who had just started her job, died. And so did my friend Wendi Winters. She was sixty-five. As Ramos made his way through the newsroom, Wendi stood up, confronted the man, and threw a trash can and a recycling bin at him. The move surprised no one who knew Wendi. She was always fearless.

Witnesses later said her action enabled others to escape and live. Wendi was not so lucky. She could prevent the loss of further lives but not her own.

The police response time to the shooting was within one minute of being notified, as timely as anyone could hope and quicker than many thought possible. It put the cops at the newspaper in time to stop further bloodshed. Police stormed the newspaper offices and found Ramos cowering underneath a desk.

The shooting became a national and an international story that night, but the community newspaper employees who survived the trauma knew exactly what would happen. Just hours after the shooting, *Capital Gazette* reporter Selene San Felice conveyed her disillusionment on live television. During an interview with CNN's Anderson Cooper, she said, "This is going to be a story for how many days? Less than a week. People will forget about us after a week . . . I'm going to need more than a couple days of news coverage and some thoughts and prayers because our whole lives have been shattered."[3]

One young reporter there that day had interned for my wife at a nonprofit before doing some freelancing work for me. I may have been the one to recommend her to look at the *Capital Gazette* for full-time employment. She was not happy with the "thoughts and prayers" idea either and said so on television. No one at the paper was looking for meaningless sympathy. The employees at the *Gazette* were traumatized, but they were not beaten. Chase Cook, one of the employees of the paper, tweeted out at 6:38 p.m. on June 28, 2018, just four hours after the shooting, what I believe—and know—is the ultimate expression of the spirit of journalism and was the greatest testimony to his fallen coworkers and friends: "I can tell you this: We are putting out a damn paper tomorrow."[4]

Damn straight.

The reaction nationwide at the time was sympathetic, but the country has been numbed over the years from gun violence. President Donald Trump was briefed on the shooting. I walked into the West Wing press offices after that early morning MDDC executive board meeting. I had been unable to attend in person and had called into Annapolis. Members who attended in person left the building a couple of hours before the shooting. When I realized the significance of the news, I walked upstairs in the lower and the upper press area trying to get someone to make a statement of support on the record for those journalists who had died. Trump declined to lower U.S. flags to half-staff as is custom despite requests from the Annapolis mayor and despite the fact that Maryland GOP governor Larry Hogan lowered the state flags. Finally, on July 3, Trump permitted the lowering of the U.S. flags on federal buildings and issued a proclamation that they remain there until sunset. Honestly, it was more than most hoped.

The day of the shooting, Trump departed the White House on Marine One and had one of his infamous "chopper talk" episodes outside the White House. Dozens of reporters, prior to the pandemic, would cram themselves behind a rope line and shout questions at the president—and, more often than not, he would answer a question or twenty, depending on his mood. That day, I and others shouted about the *Capital Gazette* shooting. He ignored us, though he did later tweet his condolences.

The loss was immediately felt at countless newsrooms and newspapers across the country that had been fighting for survival metaphorically and, now it seemed, literally. As I noted in an editorial for the MDDC, "In a very real way these people represent all of us in our extended journalistic community, from the smallest weekly newspaper to the largest daily; from the smallest radio station to the largest television network. We are all in this together. We are the people."[5]

The *New York Times* and other large media outlets again had to hire security. Watching video of security outside of CNN and the *New York Times* sent a shudder up my spine—reminding me once again of my time in Bogotá, Colombia, during the hunt for Pablo Escobar. The danger reporters faced in Third World nations had come home to settle in the citadel of democracy. In the United States, newspaper employees weren't safe. They were targets. Once again, there it was staring me in the face: in the United States, we are no safer than in a Third World country. We are not traumatized by narco-terrorists or invaders from foreign lands. Our government and our greed have done this. As the comic strip character Pogo said, "We have met the enemy and he is us."

There used to be fewer cries of "fake media" or calling reporters the "enemy of the people" because at the local level, it is all too observable that the reporters are people the same as everyone else. That has changed because there are so few of us left due to government action.

Still, there is but one person responsible for taking the lives of our colleagues and friends at the *Capital Gazette*—the man who pulled the trigger. But the vitriol leveled at reporters everywhere cannot be ignored. It is inherently more dangerous to be a reporter at every level today. We will not shy away from our job.

"Those who died in Annapolis deserve that much. They did their job. We will serve their memory best by continuing to do ours and remembering those we've lost," I also wrote in my editorial.

In 2019, at the MDDC annual meeting, as the MDDC president, I opened up the event with a speech acknowledging our industry's loss, "Last year, we lost friends, coworkers, and family in Annapolis. In our first annual meeting since this loss, let us not only acknowledge our loss but more—the endearing spirit of the entire staff in Annapolis." I spoke about the problems that journalism faces, many of which I've outlined in this book but far more briefly. Then about five minutes later, I closed with, "Thanks again for being here. We have a great program for you. For you younger reporters, you've chosen the right profession. Your challenge: stay despite the pay and make a difference. And for those who've been with us for a while—thank you for your service. And never for one moment should we ever forget the sacrifices our friends made in Annapolis or the spirit which binds all of us in this room together. Thank you."

In the more than two years since the shooting, the lives and deaths and the trauma have been forgotten behind a constant wave of mass shootings across the country. Reporters Without Borders remembered the Annapolis shooting when compiling its list of freest press nations. The United States came in forty-eighth, placing us in the "troubled democracy" category. Holden Wilen, a reporter who worked for me at one time and now works in Baltimore, said the shooting in Annapolis was a wake-up call for everyone in our business. Wilen said he prayed when he heard about the shooting, hoping that it was a random event and Ramos wasn't targeting a newspaper, but then he found out the shooter did, "and that's what scared the hell out of me. . . . What if I write something about somebody who doesn't like it? Am I now in jeopardy of getting shot?"

As Donald Trump prepared to leave the White House for the Fourth of July weekend a week after the Annapolis shooting, he finally came out and said he was upset about it. "My government will not rest until we have done everything in our power to reduce violent crime and to protect innocent life. . . . Journalists, like all Americans, should be free from the fear of being violently attacked while doing their job."[6] Of course, an hour later, when CNN's Jim Acosta asked in an East Room event if the president would stop calling the press the "enemy of the people," Trump ignored the question.

It was just one of the thousand cuts that presidents, legislators, and greedy media owners have made over the past forty years that have served to kill journalism. Donald Trump wasn't responsible for the deaths in Annapolis, but he certainly is responsible for the lowering of the bar of society that makes it easier for someone who would consider such a move to actually make the move. The ease by which those of a certain mind-set can manipulate public rancor to justify their own inhumane acts is why we all should be mindful of more decorous discourse. As the man elected to lead the nation, the highest standard—not the lowest—should be exemplified in the actions of the commander in chief of our country. But attackers are ultimately responsible for their own actions. To say otherwise allows fascists and despots to rise.

In my lifetime, we've graduated from hot Linotype to hot wax and from there to computer tapes to TRS-80s to apps on my phone that allow me to conduct interviews with the president's press secretary and broadcast them to millions of people instantaneously. We've gained a lot.

And I wouldn't go back, but I do look fondly on the newsrooms with production assistants, photographers, graphic design artists, reporters, editors, and salesmen all under one roof. It is far easier to build a team when you have the team together, and that's what we miss most today—that and the smell. As a young teen, I remember the draw of the newsroom. The smell of newsprint and ink and the sounds of phones ringing, typewriters clacking, and a hum of activity that aroused the senses. It was electric. Today's newsrooms are quiet, funereal, compared to the eclectic activity of my youth. They all smell like plastic if there is a smell at all. They're too sanitary. That is the nature of progress, but as our newspapers were made to serve a community, the community newspaper and the local paper also reflect the community.

The killings at the *Capital Gazette* were terrifying. They devastated families, friends, and colleagues across the nation. The president's first response was a spit in the face to everyone who ever worked as a reporter at a small newspaper. These people aren't pursuing "fake media," and they aren't the "enemy of the people." They live and work in the communities they serve, letting you know about local sports, library meetings, local infrastructure, housing problems, city hall, and so on. They cover the Shakespeare festival and the county fair. They are usually the first to hear or see the stories that later will become national stories. They are usually known by most first responders and whoever operates the local all-night diner closest to the newspaper office—as well as the nearest watering hole.

Community newspapers were the first on the scene in Waco, Texas. They're the first on the scene at hurricanes. They never leave because they live where the story is. Community journalism is the heart and soul of all journalism, and its demise is appalling. The deaths in Annapolis are a tragic reminder of the thankless nature of the craft. Headlines in 2021 show that, even more tragically, the loss of our colleagues reverberates; their deaths are symbolic for the death of community journalism.

"Corruption is flourishing in the rural corners of South Carolina as newspapers fold or shrink coverage amid a financially crippling pandemic," was the lead in the *Post and Courier* in February 13, 2021.[7] The story outlined "news deserts" and the accountability of government as corruption flourished around the state, with newspapers in Holly Hill and Santee, South Carolina, among those that had closed in rural areas. "When you lose a local newspaper, what you are losing is that person who shows up to cover the town council, the person who covers the school board and the local police beat," Penny Muse Abernathy, a visiting professor at Northwestern University's Medill School of Journalism told the *Post and Courier*. "At a minimum it provides transparency about what's going on in local government."

Today, those voices are being silenced by greed, a pandemic, government intrusion, and a public that little understands any more the vital role a community newspaper plays—and how without them we all will suffer.

16

FAKE NEWS

By the time Donald Trump became president, he was the beneficiary of more than thirty-five years of a successful governmental war to destroy the First Amendment. It began with Nixon and picked up speed with Ronald Reagan and Mark S. Fowler. George H. W. Bush continued the assault, while Bill Clinton killed us with the Telecommunications Act. George W. Bush gave us the Patriot Act, and then Barack Obama expanded the government's assault on free speech to go after whistle-blowers with the Espionage Act. Each president told us what they did was justified to protect state secrets or would be beneficial to the free press. Facts show all of those claims are false.

Naturally, Donald Trump would have no trouble lying, so his administration wouldn't have trouble doing what his predecessors did to reporters. Trump, as it turned out, was merely late to the table but fully capable of acting in the same manner.

Reality Winner found out the hard way what this meant. Winner, a former intelligence specialist employed by the military contractor Pluribus International Corporation, was convicted of removing classified material from a government facility and mailing it to a news outlet, the Intercept, in early June 2017.[1] The information she leaked was about Russia hacking the 2016 elections.

You might think Winner would be seen as a winner for letting the American public know such a devastating piece of news, but in August 2018, she was sentenced to five years and three months in prison as part of a plea deal—a typical prosecutorial tactic. Again, Winner was just the latest in the government's continuous attempt since the Reagan era to suppress information needed to be seen by the public—and was ultimately detrimental to poor government. She was released for her "good behavior" June 14, 2021.

Trump, of course, employed a sledgehammer from his bully pulpit at the White House to attack the press and the public, so Winner faded as other things happened. It wasn't just Donald Trump disparaging female reporters—which he did often. It wasn't that he insulted women and certain ethnicities. Any reporter of darker skin, Asian heritage, or the Muslim faith could tell you that. I once had a young staffer ask me about the origin of my last name.

"What kind of name is it?" I was asked.

"It's a last name," I said, refusing to explain myself. But some routinely mispronounced my name as "Ka-reem" even though a man with the same last name as mine served as Trump's body man for a time. "Is it Muslim?" I was asked. "It's a last name," I replied again. The person in question dropped that line of questioning.

Other than stray insults, Trump also threatened us on more than one occasion, and his hateful rhetoric was the cause for an increase in Maalox in a lot of diets. Donald Trump presented unique challenges to the Washington press corps. At times, I was reminded of NBC producer Heather Allen, who during the Gulf War recommended sending police-beat reporters to the war because they knew how to get information from people who routinely lie to them and obscure the truth. That was Trump's White House. And whether you like him or you can't stand him, as a majority of American voters showed in 2020, I don't know anyone who trusts him. In rare moments of candor, everyone I've spoken to who actually knows the guy well confesses he'd sell them down the river for an insider trading tip or much less.

The problem with Trump is he didn't attract the best people. You can argue there weren't any, but there were people who knew Washington, had a modicum of intelligence, and could communicate. Few of those people wanted to work for Trump. Those who were that smart worked Donald Trump for their own gain. Everyone else was a true believer or just anxious for a job and then became true believers. Often, the press was left unable to adequately deal with people too stupid to have their job but smart enough to lie and abuse their position. Some White House reporters struck Faustian deals to retain access. Some of them tuned out and turned off and put their reporting engine in neutral. Some fought back. Those who did paid a price.

Jim Acosta was the first to lose his press pass. Kaitlan Collins got kicked out of an event. Other reporters were denied access to interviews or the Oval Office or were routinely looked over by Trump's press team. White House Deputy Chief of Staff for Communications Bill Shine, who at one point in time was as professional as anyone got during the Trump administration, smiled when I asked him if there was a plan. "You've been around here long enough to know there's no plan," he told me. He was right. He saw his job as "cleaning up after the elephant in the circus." That was the plan. Trump was the defecating elephant who flew by the seat of his pants. I had, of course, been crossways with him from nearly the beginning. I didn't choose that path. I just wanted to ask decent questions. In the first week, I asked the administration if it would support reporters doing their jobs by backing a national shield law. By the second week, I asked in a briefing, "How is this president going to address the fact that people are looking to him to bring people together and yet, with his own words, seems to be driving us apart?"

At the beginning of the third week, I asked about Trump's statement about certain detractors in the press being public enemies. "I want to clarify a little bit of something that happened Thursday and Friday about the 'public enemy' statement. Are you saying that all of the press is the public enemy? People who didn't vote for the president? Just the people in this room, or—is it just Bill Maher and maybe Warren Beatty? Can you clarify what we're talking about?"

By the time of my birthday in March, I also asked about the emolument clause, military spending, immigration, NASA, and, again, immigration. Sean Spicer began his briefing on March 10 offering me a "Happy Birthday," and when he called on me, I asked about the president's ideas for replacing Obamacare and the perception from the public that congressmen and senators and other members of the government "get better health care than the rest of us." In April, I asked why it was okay to bomb Syria but not okay to assist the refugees from the oppression that caused us to bomb the country in the first place? I asked about the uselessness of a border wall since I spent time covering the drug trade for years and had shot stand-ups in drug tunnels that were far deeper than the wall would go and the fact that a ladder could easily defeat it. I asked about Michael Flynn, Russian hacking, poverty that leads to terrorism, and blue-collar versus white-collar workers. I asked about gang violence and climate change.

The questions were often followed by anything but an answer.

That became the way during the Trump administration. Spicer left, giving us Sarah Huckabee Sanders, who was never qualified to hold the post of press secretary. She was naive and inexperienced and didn't know the purpose of her office or how to deal with the press in a functional way.

She abandoned the traditional role of press secretary in favor of being the president's chief defender. On that task, she never faltered, come hell or high water, a lack of factual information, and, as the Mueller investigation would show, she casually lied to the press corps.

Inevitably, this led to a showdown. So, a little more than eight months after Acosta lost his press pass and had to sue to get it back, I lost mine. Specifically, I lost mine after Trump had another event in the heat sink of the Rose Garden. It was July. It was unbearably hot, and Trump had called for a meeting with some of his social media supporters. I was not inclined to go. I was thinking of leaving early that day—I had enough information for my column. But I was coerced by a few fellow reporters to stay and watch. Trump's new press secretary, Stephanie Grisham, was now running the communications for Trump, and I was told there were some interesting issues that would be undertaken at this "social media summit." So I went.

It was a rowdy event. The guests heckled some reporters; I remember one giving Jim Acosta grief about his book. Another yelled at an unidentified reporter about being part of the "lamestream" media. I was tired. I ignored the hecklers. The members of the summit had seats that day—as presidential guests usually do—and the press stood—as we usually did. The difference was many of the social media "influencers" were very antipathetic to the "mainstream media" and believed Trump was acknowledging their supremacy. I didn't care. I didn't know any of them. I didn't follow any of them.

I was interested in getting the president to stick around after he said some nice things about his guests and take some questions. I was standing about ten feet from him and asked him if he would do so. He looked right at me and sniffed before walking off without a sound. Someone then commented that the president had already talked to the "real press," while someone else said, "Poor baby." I shook my head and spoke to a colleague of mine standing next to me. "Wow, here's a crowd that looks eager for demonic possession." I gave a slight Rodney Dangerfield inflection on the delivery—my go-to impression. It became my favorite of the Trump era because visually on a couple of occasions, Trump reminded me of Rodney. One day, early in the administration, a large gaggle of reporters gathered outside on the South Lawn to watch the president board Marine One and leave the White House. As he walked out of the Oval Office, I saw him in his red tie, white shirt, dark suit, and graying blond hair caught in the breeze. For all the world, he looked like Rodney Dangerfield. This was before "chopper talk," so reporters tried pressing him with questions—to no avail. I shouted, "Hey, Mr. President, 'tough room,'" in my Rodney voice. He turned and approached us and took some questions. I guess in some ways I created "chopper talk."

On the hot July day in the Rose Garden, my impression drew some laughs and a guy named Sebastian Gorka.

I really had little clue as to who he was. I didn't care to. I knew he had worked briefly at the White House and was a source for some reporters who knew him and valued his input. I never got to know him. But he decided to ramble over and yell at me. He called me a punk, which a D.C. judge later acknowledged was not a call to a polite sit-down—especially among residents of the county jail. I invited Gorka to have a conversation or to go outside the Rose Garden and "have a long conversation."

The president had already left the Rose Garden. The ropes were down, we were waiting to leave, and I was still tired. Nothing happened. Some people yelled. Some people laughed. Somebody dressed like they were in a Fourth of July parade tried to lecture some reporters on how important the social media people are—and then we all walked out the same Palm Room doors together. It was all show. The truth is, on principle, I defend the right for these social media groups to exist. They are vital. Those who use the internet to voice opinions are important to the spirit of the First Amendment. But I have a problem when they pretend to be telling us facts or to defend "alternative facts" without vetting them. It was obvious that day most of those in attendance as the president's guests had little idea of what the basics of journalism are. And while I have my own beef with some of the tenets of modern journalism, as I told one of those social media influencers who asked me that day, to be a journalist, you must have at least one crotchety copy editor questioning every statement of fact you present—and correcting your typos. Without that minimum, you're just someone spouting your opinions. That's fine to do but should never be mistaken for journalism.

Unfortunately, because of the constriction in our business, there are fewer and fewer news organizations adhering to that standard either. So, the media influencers have a real issue that they can use as a wedge against corporate media. When the lines are blurred, are you a journalist just because you work for a network or a major corporation? Of course not—and on that point, the social media influencers are dead right. Still, you cannot criticize, for example, the Democrats and then side with the Republicans—or Trump, as his guests proudly professed. That doesn't make you a journalist. That makes you a propagandist. That, too, is a growing problem in this country, as we seemed to have forgotten the idea of critical thinking. Do not assume because I criticize Trump that I won't criticize the Democrats.

They may not merit the same level of criticism as Trump—but they'll merit some. Believe me. As I've often said, I look at most politicians the way a dog looks at a fire hydrant.

It is hard to believe many social media influencers because they do not adhere to those critical standards. Many of them do not know how to find public information. Some don't understand what it is and how it works. Mainstream media also have this problem. Some younger reporters simply don't have the acumen to handle the job. It is why social media influencers began cropping up. We aren't doing the job.

Watch as younger reporters think they have to "go after" Democrats or Republicans to show they're not biased. This leads to some of the dumbest and lamest criticism that further erodes the public trust in journalism—and all of this is because there are fewer reporters with experience and educational background available to do the job. Arrogant and ignorant may be no way to go through life, but it certainly is a way for social media influencers and modern reporters to get ahead. Media management cares little because they are looking at a short-term bottom line for their investors without considering the future landscape.

On the audience side of things, with a lack of critical thinking spreading like a virus through the population, the social media influencers are the revolutionaries. "They tell it like it is," I've been told by those who swear by the social media gurus. "They tell it like they want it to be," I've countered. "What's the difference?" is sometimes the response.

Again, all of this cacophony rises from the fact that something is wrong with the mainstream media. The audience has no idea what it is. We don't report on the problem very well, and millions are ready to listen to anything that sounds different.

In *The American President*, the character Lewis Rothschild, played by Michael J. Fox—channeling his inner George Stephanopoulos—argues with president Andrew Shepherd, played by Michael Douglas—channeling his inner Michael Douglas. Rothschild wants the president to defend himself against slanderous accusations made by an opponent and says "in the absence of genuine leadership," people will listen to anyone who steps up to the microphone. They are so thirsty for leadership "they'll crawl through the desert toward a mirage, and when they discover there's no water, they'll drink the sand."

Shepherd tells Rothschild, "People don't drink the sand because they're thirsty. They drink the sand because they don't know the difference."

That's exactly why social media influencers have caught on in the United States today.

For three weeks after the incident in the Rose Garden with the social media influencers, I heard nothing from the White House. I came and went as usual. Then one day, after Trump called on me twice for questions in a "chopper talk" session, I left the White House that afternoon to find my press pass had been suspended for thirty days. Although I had been at the White House all day, no one bothered to tell me. Stephanie Grisham, rarely seen and even more rarely heard from, was nowhere. Others had to know, but no one said anything to me.

My first call was to Jim Acosta to get the phone number for his lawyer, Ted Boutrous, who had defeated Trump after the president yanked Acosta's press pass. I'd met Ted at a Hefner Awards Banquet earlier that year when the Hefner Foundation and Hugh Hefner's daughter Christi Hefner presented Ted with an award for defending Acosta. I was impressed with his understanding of the spirit of the First Amendment and even more impressed with his ability to defend Acosta when it seemed to me some of our colleagues were not willing or able to do so. I could empathize. When I went to jail in San Antonio, Texas, there were some who supported me, some who attacked me, and some reporters who literally searched my garbage in my front yard for some kind of incriminating evidence. That last move really angered my dad, who was staying with my wife and our young son at the time. But you have to let that go.

Ted took over my case, and we sued the Trump administration. He and Anne Champion led a team of lawyers who not only successfully sued Trump but also defended the decision twice on appeals. Still, it wasn't until March 2021 that the Biden administration told us it would not pursue the case to the Supreme Court. The result was, much like the Acosta case, a solid win for every reporter. It made it much more difficult to throw reporters out of the White House on a mere presidential whim. The victory established clear guidelines for administrations that wanted to yank reporters' credentials and laid low Trump's claims that if I wasn't disciplined, then the president couldn't keep reporters from running through the White House grounds mooning people. The D.C. appeals court dismissed that contention as "absurd."

"The White House can rest assured that principles of due process do not limit its authority to maintain order and decorum at White House events by, for example, ordering the immediate removal of rogue, mooning journalists," Judge Tatel wrote.[2]

Boutrous and his team established themselves as key players in the First Amendment battle with the victories in Jim's case and mine. He reinforced in court that facts matter, and he was able, along with Champion, to apply those keen skills in a case after mine—Mary Trump's battle versus Donald Trump.

While reporters were given more solid ground to maneuver with the decisions in my and Jim's case, most White House reporters didn't push the point. The battering from the president, the constriction in the business, and the continued concern of getting access to the White House managed to cripple most reporting. As Dan Rather warned in the *Boston Herald* in a 1991 interview, most reporters still want to be popular or accepted by those they cover—never realizing that's not the right way to do your job.

In February 2019 at a press conference in the Rose Garden, formerly the most colorful area in the White House until Donald Trump turned it into a funeral arrangement, the president tried to push his idea that there was a "crisis" on the border. Jim Acosta asked him a question about the border problems, and Trump blew him off. He called on me next. I picked up the gauntlet and followed Acosta's question with my own—about Trump inventing numbers to sustain his contention there was a border crisis. He got upset with me, told me to sit down, and then again ranted about a crisis that didn't actually exist and that only he could solve.

Once out of office, he would try the same thing in March 2021, using the same words to decry the efforts of President Biden, who was actually trying to deal with the problem. To break it down, the United States has had a problem with illegal immigration on the border of Mexico since the oil economy in Mexico collapsed in the 1970s and the peso was heavily devalued. Overnight, the problem became a crisis. Ronald Reagan didn't handle it. Neither has any other president. For forty years, we've either played political football with the issue or used it as a wedge issue between conservative and progressive voters. The truth is we are responsible for many of the problems in South and Central America. And those problems are at least a century old. Marine Brigadier General Smedley Butler wrote in his book *War Is a Racket* that the problem was American foreign policy. "I spent 33 years in the Marines, most of my time being a high-class muscle man for big business, for Wall Street and the bankers. In short, I was a racketeer for Capitalism."[3]

We in the media have a very limited understanding of the problems—and yet we often pretend otherwise. Although the problems on the border have deep roots, beginning in earnest in the late 1970s and early 1980s, most of us jumped on the Trump train when he called it a "crisis" at the border. If by a crisis he meant an ongoing problem that until he came along was often ignored, then, yes, it was a crisis. But we still do not have a firm grasp on the causes of the problem, nor do we confront the president about the two overwhelming factors that drive people to leave their homes and walk hundreds if not thousands of miles to the United States:

1. U.S. companies entice and hire the cheap labor.
2. The U.S. demand for illegal drugs fuels the violence and unrest that forces families to relocate.

Trump never wanted to touch on those two subjects—and no president ever really does. We tried a "war on drugs" in the Reagan era, but the drugs won. So, what's left? Can you imagine any president supporting the legalization of most psychoactive drugs and treating drug abuse as a social problem rather than a criminal problem? Can you imagine strict enforcement of the Simpson-Mazzoli Act, passed in 1986, that finally made it illegal for companies to hire illegal immigrants? Can you imagine reporters savvy enough to handle this deep problem—or networks that would actually dedicate themselves to something other than the latest drama on the border? A political will doesn't exist for the former and can't exist without the latter. Yet, as Trump proved time and again, it's easier to scream about a nonexistent crisis than to solve an actual problem. The press—traditional, nontraditional, and that which exists in social media—usually falls right into the crevice of this wedge issue.

Back in February, Trump merely told me to sit down. I wouldn't sit. In fact, I refused to sit even as he screamed at me, "You get one question. Now sit down." Then he told me the facts I got—from the U.S. government—were wrong, but his facts from the U.S. government were right about illegal immigration. There's only one set of facts, but Trump was on a roll and angry.

He stayed angry but continued to call on me several times during his administration—even as he was trying to have me kicked out of the White House. But his ability to con the majority of Americans came screeching to a halt at the end of February 2020.

On February 28, 2020, Trump approached a South Lawn gaggle for another adventurous performance of "chopper talk." He waved off my question about COVID-19 and said there were no deaths and his policy was yielding results. He then blew off my follow-up question to announce his latest rally. Forty days later, 11,000 people were dead.

That's when COVID-19 took over the news, nationally and internationally. Trump's minions, including Kellyanne Conway and Larry Kudlow, defended the White House response to the growing pandemic and told us it was under control. I stood mutely in the background in early

April when Conway tried to chastise CBS's Paula Reid when Reid ask if the virus was spreading. "It's being contained," Conway said. I actually had to bite my lip as I stood in the James S. Brady Press Briefing Room next to Paula as she asked the question. She later shared the video with me, joking about my "poker face." She was right. I had struggled to keep my mouth shut as Conway lied to us. But I did so because Paula expertly dissected Conway.

On April 14, Trump called on me in a Rose Garden news conference, and I said, "Mr. President, I've interviewed hundreds of people who say they still cannot get tests and others who say they don't practice social distancing because they've watched you not practicing it while preaching it. What do you say to the millions who don't believe you?"

Trump told me to sit down and be quiet. Then he threatened to leave if I didn't. "I told them if they put this guy here, it's nothing but trouble. He's a showboat. If you keep talking I'll leave," Trump said. I didn't stop talking. He didn't leave, and he never answered my question.

On April 27, 2020, I again pressed Trump. He had urged people to ingest disinfectant to deal with the coronavirus. I told him that Maryland governor Larry Hogan said people were doing it and then were being shipped to the hospital after listening to the president. Trump said he couldn't imagine that was happening and took no responsibility for it.

But it wasn't just Trump. Vice President Mike Pence also had problems dealing with the press and the pandemic. On March 4, I asked Pence in the Brady Briefing Room, as he claimed the risk of getting the coronavirus for the average American remained low, if the uninsured could get tested. He walked away, and one of his assistants said, "Screaming for the camera isn't going to get you anywhere."

"It's a legitimate question," I countered.

"Yes. Yes it is," John Oliver said on his show that night as he replayed the clip from the briefing and comically and effectively eviscerated the Trump administration for their poor response to the pandemic.

Trump, who had made a point of not showing up in the White House briefing room, finally did so at the beginning of the global pandemic. I hit him with a question about COVID-19 he didn't answer, but in a rare case, he did answer *another* question that had been on my mind. Donald Trump's reelection campaign sued the *New York Times* for an *opinion* piece. "Is it your contention that if someone has an opinion different than yours they should be sued?" I asked. He answered, "Well if they get the opinion totally wrong . . . as the *New York Times* did . . ."

And how do you have a "wrong opinion" in the world of Trump? You just have to disagree with him. At the end of his first extended appearance in the briefing room, Trump said it hadn't been bad. I invited him back. Unfortunately, he took me up on my offer.

Donald Trump took advantage of every bad move Ronald Reagan made. He's the culmination of everything Reagan, Ailes, Murdoch, Mark S. Fowler, and Mitch McConnell fought for since the downfall of Richard Nixon—a buffoon who manipulates the media that the government controls by constantly staying in front of the camera.

Look at the big picture of Donald Trump's triumphant ride into Washington. He is a failed businessman who took a job on a reality show to make ends meet. He appealed to approximately the same demographic as professional wrestling—making him a good commercial investment. But Trump thought more of himself. He was always looking for the next big con. He got into the presidential race in 2016 with little realistic hope of winning—his closest supporters, including people like Michael Cohen, said Trump was just trying to increase the profile of the Trump brand. Many of his staffers later admitted they went home election night convinced they'd lost the race.

But the con man successfully conned America and himself. Trump, who sought only to raise the profile of his brand, suddenly found himself the most powerful politician in the land—and actually believed he could do the job. In the beginning, the old-guard GOP tried to help Trump, supplying him with as solid personnel as could stomach Trump and work with him. They later abandoned him as Trump co-opted the GOP and turned Republicans into Trumplicans.

Through it all, he battled the press as he vilified it and stood in front of live cameras, soaking up the attention as he did so. As the pandemic wore on and his reelection approached, it became clear that Trump had finally lost his ability to handle reality—though it's questionable whether he ever lost his ability to handle the press. And, as our numbers shrank, it became easier for him to do it.

17

IF YOU STOP COUNTING BALLOTS

During the four years of the Donald Trump administration, I was able to ask him a number of pointed questions. I did so only at "open press" events. These are events anyone who has a press pass can attend. The pool reporters get to travel on Air Force One. They get to visit the Oval Office or the diplomatic rooms or catch the president in more intimate settings. The White House loves to play the "access" game—dangling these as carrots in front of reporters, who then in turn become intimidated by the access to power. The best of us don't fall for it. But there are many who do.

I never cared for this nonsense, and don't think I ever will. All I've ever asked for is the ability to ask questions in the briefing room or at open press events. I have faith in my ability to be heard and to ask a rational question and believe both will serve me well enough without having to modify my behavior to be close to the commander in chief. It is also a fact that depending on which company you work for, the access to the president has already been predetermined. Independent reporters may struggle to get that access or play games to get it, but if you work for the *New York Times* or the *Washington Post*, the access comes with the job. There are some reporters who take full advantage of this access without kowtowing to it and make a hell of a difference.

David Nakamura from the *Washington Post* became the first Western reporter to ask a North Korean leader a question because Nakamura traveled with President Trump on a foreign trip in February 2019.[1] As he later tweeted, "I asked Kim Jong-un if he felt confident he could get a deal with Donald Trump. He replied, 'It's too early to say. I would not say I'm pessimistic.'"

The exchange came as Kim Jong-un and President Trump sat across from each other at a wooden table. Before reporters were rushed out of the room during a photo op, Nakamura made history when the leader of the world's most closed society answered a question from a foreign journalist. As Nakamura later told the story, pool reporters worked together to figure out what they might reasonably ask of the North Korean leader and get an answer. Nakamura took a chance as the reporter in the pool that day, and while the response may not have been extraordinary, it marked a first for North Korea engaging with the American press.

It is precisely why the press is indispensable and why we have to fight so hard to keep our independence. A good reporter should be able to ask anyone anything at any time. But you have to be in the right place at the right time and have the courage to speak truth to power—and it sometimes helps when colleagues forgo their own selfish desires for something greater. The American press made history that day. It was a small step, yes, but you have to take one before you can take another. As I later said, how this was done and how reporters worked together and what Nakamura did should be required reading for everyone in every journalism school across the country.

In the spring of 2020, Donald Trump hired his last press secretary. Kayleigh McEnany was a thirty-one-year-old highly educated public spokesperson with a background in the law who apparently "loves to argue." As I said at the time, "Big deal. In my family this sentence would be cause to argue."[2]

Yet I was also told by a senior White House adviser, "She is one of the more dangerous individuals out there. . . . Give her a case to argue, and she'll relish the argument." Her many critics said she doesn't get her facts straight and she could act sophomoric and come off as condescending and arrogant. Those traits made her an excellent hire in the Trump administration.[3]

McEnany revived the daily press briefing her predecessor had canceled. And it happened at a time that gave her a decided advantage. The growing coronavirus pandemic gave the Trump administration a way of dealing with hundreds of those who, like me, are not in the press pool. Because of the pandemic, we were just kicked out. Make no mistake, Trump loved the attention the press gave him. He didn't like scrutiny—neither did his minions. All of them wanted the Trump show to be invulnerable to bad reviews. But Trump got plenty of bad reviews with the arrival of COVID-19, and, oddly enough, it was the pandemic that helped ameliorate the criticism. The board of the White House Correspondents' Association (WHCA), after consulting with health officials, voluntarily limited press access to the president in the name of social distancing.

It was the healthy thing to do, but there's absolutely no doubt what else it did. Trump got exactly what he wanted—a small room, a few warm bodies—and he capitalized on it. Lights, camera, Donny action! For the last nine months of the Trump administration, only fourteen reporters, along with a few photographers, got to watch and ask questions of the national tragedy unfolding as the pandemic overcame the nation.

Through the first three months of the year, Trump was still holding court on the South Lawn with 100-plus reporters and technicians present. By the middle of April, the White House that I've covered off and on since Ronald Reagan's administration was gone.[4] The James S. Brady Press Briefing Room would not be the site of a press secretary briefing for 819 days until Jen Psaki reopened it to everyone in the press on June 7, 2021.

Jonathan Karl, as president of the WHCA, played a huge role in limiting the number of reporters covering the White House, as did the rest of the WHCA board. Karl has defended the move as the best way to help protect the health of some 500 reporters who cover the White House—and, friends, he ain't wrong. But Karl also invited criticism by voluntarily limiting briefing room access on a rotating basis to those organizations with assigned seats. The move created an "inner circle," as some critics said, of reporters on whose narrow shoulders all of the reporting about the president resided. All pigs were equal, but some were more equal than others.

For some, it smacked of favoritism or elitism, and the White House obviously agreed with that and countered by issuing a "guest" invitation to favored outlet One America News (OAN), a cable news network with a right-wing bent—even on days when OAN wasn't in the rotation. The WHCA stated that such a move constituted a breach of the agreement between the White House and the WHCA to ensure a healthy work environment. It also took punitive measures against OAN, stripping it of work space and pool access. It was a punishment with no teeth, though, because the White House continued to invite OAN to the party.

Attorney Ted Boutrous filed a complaint with the Department of Justice about the White House move. That led to two days without OAN, pending the Justice Department's response. Government lawyers admitted that the administration showed favoritism but blamed the WHCA for the problem. OAN started showing up again. Boutrous countered on April 8, saying, "The notion that the OAN correspondent was invited to the briefing as a 'guest' and not a reporter is flawed and misleading. Even if the press secretary on occasion invites 'guests' to the briefing room, the OAN reporter was not invited merely to observe as the press secretary's aides, family or friends might. Instead, that correspondent was welcomed to actively participate in the briefing as a reporter and was given the opportunity to ask questions of the president."[5]

Meanwhile, Trump added Karl to the list of reporters he publicly berated in his press briefings, calling him a "third-rate reporter." This was no doubt a response to Karl's actions against OAN and a slap at his recently published book, *Front Row at the Trump Show*.

Karl, who was also ABC's chief correspondent, courted his own controversy in his book when he publicly criticized CNN's Jim Acosta, accusing him of "playing into the explicit Trump strategy of portraying the press as the opposition party." Karl admonished Acosta for giving "speeches from the White House briefing room." He told the *Daily Beast* he would defend to death Acosta's right to report from the White House, "but I have some issue with the style in which he has done so."[6]

Trump, I was told by a senior administration official, loved watching the president of the WHCA criticize one of his colleagues. "You all always eat your own," I was told with a smile. So perhaps Karl was as guilty of playing into the president's strategy as he accused Acosta of being—if not more so. But he had second thoughts. I watched Karl, ever the arbiter of taste, decorum, and style, show up in the basement of the briefing room, walk to the CNN booth, and tell Acosta how much he respected him and enjoyed his work. He said something about being taken out of context and said how, as soon as this was over, Karl would get a drink with him.

Meanwhile, Trump had set the stage for future coverage of the president—whether or not he meant to do so. A smaller number of reporters, more limited access, and control of the press, aided by the pandemic, was simply a matter of fact by 2020. Fortunately, Trump couldn't control himself—even as he tightened the noose on the press, he still had enough rope left to hang himself. He often stuck his foot in his mouth, and we still sent reporters to cover it—even if the numbers were smaller.

As Boutrous noted in his letter to the Justice Department, "We remain committed to protecting the role of a vigilant press in our society—a role particularly needed in a crisis such as the ongoing pandemic."

It's not hyperbole to say lives are at risk.[7]

It also almost goes without saying that Donald Trump cared very little about the coronavirus pandemic. He told Bob Woodward how serious it was, but he also called it a Democratic hoax, claimed he had it under control, and ignored calls for social distancing and wearing masks while holding rallies and White House events that ended up being described as super-spreader events. There simply is no way of knowing how many people got sick or died because of Donald Trump. While for more than a year the White House press corps voluntarily practiced social distancing and masked up, the Trump White House personnel rarely wore masks and didn't respect social distancing, which led to many people on the staff getting sick—including Trump, who was rushed to the Walter Reed Army Medical Center after he experienced difficulty breathing due to the coronavirus.

Nothing surprised us about Trump by this time. He had survived a Mueller investigation that pointed to ten different possible cases of obstruction of justice. He survived trying to extort a foreign leader in a quid pro quo telephone call to the Ukrainian president. He survived impeachment—twice! His party suffered in the midterms, but Trump appeared to be an alley cat with nine lives. With fewer of us covering the daily dose of fetid corruption the president fed us every day, it appeared we would never be able to get ahead of him and frame an issue so people could understand exactly what was at stake.

With OAN in the room at the request of the White House (a move, in all honesty I had little problem with—I just wanted to be there, too) and with fewer reporters overall, it appeared Trump would skate through to a second term—even though he continued to screw up the response to the coronavirus pandemic. I got upset with the White House for using the small number of reporters to stack the deck in its favor, so I began showing up once a week at the White House—despite COVID restrictions. I socially distanced. I wore a mask, but the WHCA seemed to be incapable of dealing with the White House's attempts to stack the deck, so I figured I would. Two members of the WHCA board later thanked me for doing it. Others called me arrogant.

I would show up and stand at the back of the briefing room with the OAN reporter or on a few occasions with reporters from the *Gateway Pundit*, the *Epoch Times*, and OAN. Again, I had no problem with them being there. I had a problem with the White House taking advantage of COVID restrictions to limit others from being there. McEnany never called on me in the many months I did this, but she got upset—once telling me she didn't call on activists and on other occasions calling me delusional, deranged, and a misogynist. The *Washington Post* was compelled to write a story about it, and I told reporter Paul Farhi bluntly, "I'm there to ask questions—that's my job—whether they answer the question or not. I'm doing my damn job and whoever doesn't like it, tough."[8]

I also figured since I had struggled very hard to keep my hard pass, I had to go to court three times to keep it, I might as well use it. But I also infuriated the new WHCA president, Zeke Miller of the Associated Press, who told the *Washington Post*, "We're fortunate that the overwhelming majority of journalists who cover the White House have recognized their role maintaining the health of journalists and everyone else who utilizes the press workspace," Miller said. "It is deeply disappointing that some individuals have abandoned what is a collective responsibility to public safety. ... By exacerbating the risk of COVID-19 spread in the workspace, they have also potentially jeopardized the press corps' ability to maintain a protective pool that covers the president in close quarters, the most critical function of journalists assigned to the White House."[9]

Miller, of course, was under the impression that only the "protective pool" should have access to the president during the pandemic and that anyone else would put the entire press corps at risk. I didn't care what he thought, either. I was locked down at home, and the greatest risk I took was coming to the White House, where members of the administration didn't mask up and often didn't socially distance. The elitism of Miller's statement—to the point of thinking we had to somehow set up a "protective pool" around the president—was, honestly, laughable and naive and speaks to a lack of experience. To think that being in close quarters is the "most critical function of journalists assigned to the White House" simply shows how little some members of the press understand what our job is. It was Helen Thomas, the first female president of the WHCA, who often said the greatest role of a White House reporter is to speak truth to power—and never be afraid to do so. I agree with Helen, and I also agree with something else she said—if you think I'm antagonistic to government, then you're correct. That's my job—and I have a passion for it.

The idea that we're there to provide a "protective pool" without mentioning our true mission to speak truth to power by questioning authority is one of the single biggest problems brought about by the constriction of the press, the monopolization of it by large companies, and the resulting lack of institutional knowledge that is espoused by anyone who thinks the press is in any way responsible for providing protection to the president of the United States. The Secret Service provides the only "protective pool" the president needs. We're not part of government. We're there to question it. Snuggling up to the president in a "protective pool" begs the question, whom are we protecting? Millions of Americans think we're only protecting our own agenda and access.

As time wore on, even though I was supported privately by members of the WHCA board, few other than Miller spoke publicly about my sojourns into the White House. But I made it quite clear why I was there and who I had a beef with—the White House. Most independent reporters also said they were "privately" cheering for me. I thanked them, but I would've done the same thing whether or not I got any support. What the White House did was wrong. And the bigger picture was that they were trying to divide the press into at least two different groups—the haves and the have-nots—and wanted to provoke a confrontation between the two groups.

Nothing spoke to why I did what I did better than the events of September 23, 2020.

We were just six weeks away from the election, and Trump was already screaming about election fraud, and the election hadn't happened yet. The pandemic was costing Trump every day as the number of deaths and infections continued while the president talked about ingesting Clorox, claiming he had the pandemic under control or denying the severity of it. When he got angry, which was often, he disparaged Asian Americans and encouraged violence against them because the site of the first viral outbreak was in China. More and more, Trump sounded like he wasn't going to go gently into that good night—and might actually do the unthinkable—try to stay in office even if he lost.

On that day, I showed up for my weekly visit to the White House. Writing a weekly column about the White House necessitated my actually showing up at the White House—even if the White House and the WHCA didn't want me to do so. I was resigned to standing in the back with OAN again. But on that day, there ended up being an empty seat in the very back of the briefing room. Instead of fourteen reporters, there were only thirteen in the room. I had said if I was there and a seat was empty, I intended to take it—and on this, I had members of the WHCA board nod their head in the affirmative. I never thought it would happen, and they probably thought the same. I can tell you for a fact it only happened one other time when I was there—June 4, 2021—the last day the Biden White House limited access to the briefing room.

On September 23, 2020, Trump was scheduled to visit us in the briefing room, and as he walked out to make a statement, I took the empty seat. Trump made his usual speech blaming others for his misfortunes, attacking those he didn't like, and spouting gibberish more appropriate for a professional wrestler talking trash than a president of the most powerful nation on the planet. I sat in the back of the room in a black suit and yellow tie and wearing my "America needs journalists" mask I'd purchased online from the WHCA website.

As I sensed Trump winding down his diatribe, I raised my hand. I didn't think he'd even call on me since we often verbally sparred, he tried to have my press pass pulled, and he had on numerous occasions jabbed his stubby index finger at me while grimacing and calling me "fake news." But I was wrong. He did call on me that day and actually called on me first. I blinked, and said to myself, "Well okay, buckle up. Here we go."

I looked at Trump and asked him if "win lose or draw," he would commit to a peaceful transfer of power after the election. I pointed out there had already been violence in several American cities, but Trump didn't care. His essential answer was, "We're going to have to see what happens." He also said if we stopped counting ballots, there would be no transfer of power. He told me there were already problems with the ballots, a fact he claimed I knew—and, as I told him, I did not know that. "And the ballots are a disaster," he said. I will never forget that moment. It was one of the most frightening answers I have ever received from someone I've questioned. I interviewed murderers and serial killers and never felt a chill like I did when Trump answered that question. He went full despot with the answer. The world saw it, too.

No one followed up on the question that day, but the following day, Jon Karl did. After the election and Biden took over, I asked Karl why he had followed up on the question. "I thought it was a good question and deserved a follow," he explained. I ran into Fox's John Roberts a week after I asked the question, and he too acknowledged that the weight of the question was undeniable.

McEnany had a fit when Karl asked her about it the following day— accusing me of being deranged or delusional—but couldn't explain why the president wouldn't agree to one of the basic tenets of our democracy. The peaceful transfer of power is one of the things that separates us from the wannabe dictators and the second-rate banana republics of the world. No matter what, we have always engaged in a peaceful transfer of power. Trump changed all of that. As the news blew up, the WHCA got complaints from reporters because they saw me sitting in a briefing room seat and wondered how it happened. I told the truth to those who called me and asked: I got lucky. But you make your own luck by showing up. Some members of the WHCA board got mad because I did so. Never mind that I asked a salient question—and perhaps the most important question of the election season. I wasn't supposed to be there—according to those who wish they had been.

Joe Biden, when he heard about the question and response, asked rhetorically, "What country do we live in?" To some, I broke the rules, and they wanted consequences for it. When I spoke with one board member, I simply said, "It was your responsibility to fill the seat. You didn't do it, and we shouldn't leave the seat empty."

Others smacked Trump hard for his authoritarian leanings with his answer, and he continued to shed support. Did the question have anything to do with his ultimate loss? I don't know. I do know that it was an international story. I was able to frame the issue in very simple terms—best for Trump and many others to understand. I didn't allow him to change the subject, and he dug his own grave with his answer. I considered it a job well done for that day. I've asked better questions, I'm sure, and I've asked worse ones.

But I had just a few moments to come up with a question. I didn't expect to be seated. I didn't expect to be called on, and I had no reason to believe Trump would answer me. But, fortunately, my experience came into play. I can't pretend it was brilliant. But I approach each attempt to ask a president a question thinking, what should I ask that most people want to know? How should I frame the question and the issue? How can I keep it succinct and get a relatable answer? On September 23, 2020, the stars aligned, and I got lucky.

As the election approached, Trump and his administration spiraled more out of control each passing day, while his staff continued to get sick. At the beginning of October, Hope Hicks tested positive for the coronavirus. A short time later, Kayleigh McEnany did as well. Mark Meadows came out of hiding long enough to ignore questions about reunited children at the border and to blame Democrats for a lack of a new stimulus package. Larry Kudlow came out to the sticks on the driveway of the North Lawn one day to talk about economic stimuli. When I pointed out that he didn't have a mask on, he said he was far enough away, but then he acquiesced and put on one that matched his blue/gray suit, blue tie, and blue shirt.

Trump? I asked him on one occasion, "You admitted on tape that you misled the American people [referring to the taped interview with Bob Woodward]—so how can you claim any credibility on the coronavirus?" He made a face at me and walked out of the room without answering.

That compelled me to ask McEnany, "If he's a law-and-order president, why does he keep breaking the law?" She refused to answer that one too, as well as, "Why did he call it a hoax if he's not lying?" But those weren't the only questions I asked that went unanswered. Trump and McEnany also continued to avoid questions about creating a crisis on the southern border to suit their purposes.

The administration wasn't answering my questions, but they were getting frustrated with them. One day, a young press aide tried to grab me by my shoulders and forcibly move me during the briefing. I shook him off and told him not to lay hands on me. He backed off. One day, McEnany's husband showed up in the back of the briefing room and stood where I normally stand. I was told after the fact by an administration staffer I trusted that she had strategically placed him there to confront me. As it so happens, I had no idea at the time, and it wasn't my day of the week to be at the White House. Instead, I was told McEnany's husband got into a minor confrontation with another reporter. McEnany continued to go on Fox and complain about "that *Playboy* reporter"—which helped spike the number of physical threats I received. I got more death threats in the last six weeks of the Trump administration than I received in the previous nearly four-year span of time.

I can't say that I cared. I didn't. My only personal concern was for my wife and my children. The larger concern was Donald Trump's administration. It was off the rails and taking the country into an abyss. I wanted no part of it, and I wanted to hold them accountable for it. And if you thought it was bad before the election, after he lost, Trump showed everyone exactly what he meant when he told the world in September—after I asked him—what his idea of peaceful transfer of power meant. It meant "no transfer."

He still has never admitted he lost the election.

On November 13, 2020, at an event in the Rose Garden, I said, "You lost the election. When will you admit you lost the election? When will you admit you lost the election sir?" The video I shot on my cell phone went viral with more than 2.4 million views, and viewers got to watch Donald Trump walk off and ignore the question.

After that, I gave up any pretense of being polite. Trump was a lame duck and acting like a spoiled child. So, a week later when I was in the White House, I asked McEnany, "Do you understand what sedition is?" And then I asked her about Trump losing. She walked off without answering. Trump came out in the same briefing to talk about the "America First Healthcare Plan," and I asked him twice when would he admit that he lost. He frowned, snarled, and walked off. "What will it take for you to admit you lost the election sir?" became the only question worth answering, and very few of us covering the president from the White House were asking it. The rest of the journalistic world—and indeed the world at large—wanted that question answered, but Trump wasn't budging from spreading the "big lie" that he had actually won "by a landslide," an election he clearly lost.

Mark McKinnon from *The Circus* visited the White House the Friday after the election when Biden had been declared the winner and asked me what I thought. It was the last time I thought we'd see Trump in the briefing room and said as much. Trump predicted the stock market would crash and there would be violence in the streets if he lost. I reported on spontaneous partying at Lafayette Square—the place I had been mere months before when I and some of the Black Lives Matter protesters were introduced to the wonderful smell of tear gas. The stock market soared. Trump was wrong again. But nothing stopped him. He declared time and again he was "fighting the fake news," and time and again we were actually fighting a fake narrative from a corrupt and dangerous president. I came to believe early in the Trump administration he was the greatest living threat to our democracy. I reasoned that my greatest use to the country was to continuously challenge Donald Trump's con game.

On January 6, 2021, after weeks of denying he'd lost, after selling his "big lie" to his supporters, fomenting insurrection, and threatening those who questioned him, Donald Trump's attempt to stay in office culminated in a day of violence like none I'd ever seen at the U.S. Capitol. It began, as most days do when I go to the White House, with me driving and parking at a nearby parking lot and then walking for about a block to the entry of the White House campus at 17th Street and Pennsylvania Avenue. For months, this area had been fenced in. Lafayette Park was closed, and the entire White House compound, again, reminded me of a visit to Bogotá, Colombia, or Riyadh, Saudi Arabia, during the Gulf War.

As I crossed the street that morning, I saw a large, somewhat bulbous man carrying an even larger Confederate flag and waving it vigorously. He recognized me and said he hoped I died soon. Thus my morning began. Inside the White House, there was a heightened sense of concern for everyone's safety as rumors had been flying about armed protestors, rioters, and a bunch of "Proud Boys" storming the Capitol because Congress was meeting that day to certify the election and Trump was encouraging his vice president not to do it. He was still preaching his "big lie"—that widespread voter fraud had caused him to lose the election. None of it was true. He'd lost every major battle in court. Republicans and Democrats who counted the ballots at the local levels throughout the country vouched for how well the election had been run. Members of the GOP told Trump to stand down. The Supreme Court shot down every appeal Trump took to court. Nothing could get him to stop. His warning on September 23, when I asked him about a peaceful transfer of power, was coming to a violent conclusion.

In a speech to his followers outside of the White House that morning, Trump urged his supporters to continue fighting. One of his interchangeable sons showed up to urge on the followers, and Rudy Giuliani cheered on the faithful, urging them to "trial by combat." With that, those who gathered to hear the president speak marched toward the Capitol and tried to "take back our house." Others screamed they wanted to hang Vice President Mike Pence, and violence overwhelmed the march. Protest became riot, and that became an insurrection. I walked back to the White House and watched most of it from the television sets in the basement. I had never dreamed that I would see what I saw that day. Not in the United States of America. Not at the U.S. Capitol. Not in the land of the free and home of the brave. On that day, I shook my head. The United States could no longer hold itself up as being any better than a third-rate dictatorship.

When Trump gassed the Black Lives Matter protestors in Lafayette Park, I remarked how I felt I was back in a war zone. Washington, D.C., was every Third World country I'd ever visited—Humvees, men in uniform, helicopters buzzing low overhead. But January 6, 2021, was the absolute worst.

Trump continued to push the "big lie." His minions made excuses. Some of the very congressmen whose lives were in danger sided with the president, and everyone pushed their version of events on social media. It was the lowest point in my professional life. The United States of America, led by a deranged narcissist and aided and abetted by social media and a lack of belief in the mainstream media, came within a hair's breadth of being leveled by a coup.

I don't ever want to hear anyone tell me it wasn't that bad. I cannot listen to anyone who defends what happened that day. I know what happened. I was there. I witnessed it firsthand. Everyone in that crowd was driven to march and attack the Capitol because of Donald Trump. The marchers told me they were going to the Capitol because their president told them to do it. There were no Antifa members pretending to be Trump supporters. These were dyed-in-the-wool Trump fanatics who thought they were upholding the principles of democracy because the president told them they were. To argue otherwise is to argue insanity.

Because our media have been compromised by forty years of abuse and neglect, millions of people in the United States actually believe in insanity.

18

WE REALLY WANT MORE
REPORTERS COVERING US

With an hour remaining in the Donald Trump presidency, I found myself on my knees in the basement of the White House press offices. A cockroach had been spotted, and a fellow reporter asked me to deal with it; I was successful. I gave an appropriate eulogy for the cockroach and then flushed it.

Yes, the scene could be read as a metaphor for my four years covering the Trump White House. But there is no rest for the wicked. A new administration swept into the White House doors on January 20, 2021, bringing with it a fresh agenda and new protocols. I watched from the North Lawn as President Biden walked into the White House grounds for the first time holding his wife's hand and smiling. Naturally, I shouted a question at him. "Mr. President, what is your first priority as president?" He turned his head, looked at me, and seemed to grin. I know he heard me. He was just fifteen feet away, and there was no helicopter noise to interfere, but he didn't answer. He waved with one hand while holding on to Dr. Jill Biden's extended hand with the other and walked on.

With Biden's arrival, there was a lot of hope we'd get a president who could deal with the coronavirus pandemic realistically and would interact with the press without accusing reporters of being the "enemy of the state" or "fake news." You know, like it used to be, but in the words of the president, "Build Back Better." For the most part, Biden's first 100 days in office was a marked improvement over Donald Trump. But the bar was so incredibly low that any reasonably cogent person could easily clear it.

Biden did but also proved in those first days he was no real friend of the free press either. Or it could be that the atrocities against the media have become so engrained in our culture that we take them for granted and are unable to understand what a truly free press is and what it is not.

239

For the younger members of Biden's staff, one could definitely understand if they didn't know who Helen Thomas was or how things were supposed to work, but the president, on his election, was seventy-eight years old and has dealt with the press for more than fifty years. He knows exactly what he's doing, how to do it, and why.

A couple of early issues in the Biden administration showed we in the press still had a long way to go to gain respect and independence. The first issue came as the Biden administration walked into the Oval Office. New protocols were established for reporters. While the Trump administration had required the press pool of fourteen to be tested every day because of their proximity to the president, they had not tested the rest of us who came and went at the White House, and they didn't actually restrict our numbers. The White House Correspondents' Association (WHCA) and every reporter covering the White House voluntarily restricted ourselves. It was the WHCA that came up with the social distancing seating in the James S. Brady Press Briefing Room, and I was one of the volunteers, along with Tamara Keith from National Public Radio, who helped tape the seating assignments to the chairs in the room. The WHCA board asked everyone to be conscious of the problems brought about by the pandemic. As a result, in the year since the outbreak of the coronavirus pandemic, though a few of us had tested positive for COVID, not one reporter had infected anyone—not our colleagues or anyone at the White House. The same couldn't be said for the Trump administration. That staff was like a bunch of Typhoid Marys. But *we* had performed admirably.

It was one of the few practices from the Trump White House that actually worked when it came to dealing with the press. But members of the Biden administration made it clear when they got there that things would be far more restrictive. Everyone had to be tested, and we were going to be limited to just eighty members of the press who could be present on the White House campus on any given day. The Biden White House placed the WHCA in charge of a lottery to determine who could visit outside of the pool and forced those who weren't in the pool to pay for their own tests—at a cost of as much as $170 per test. The richest media companies who operated the pool would not have to pay. The foreign journalists and the independents were forced to pay to play. It amounted to a regressive tax and squelched the voices of a free press—unless you're one of the reporters from the largest corporate media companies. The White House also had board members of the WHCA act as policemen during the first few days of the new administration—urging those who had already been admitted to leave the campus.

The sad part was that by following strict protocols, the National Football League managed to have a relatively productive season and has been cheered for its efforts. The White House press corps arguably managed to do better than the NFL, but we weren't cheered for our efforts. In fact, we were sanctioned despite them.

In the beginning, the Biden administration wanted just forty people to be inside the West Wing, and the other forty had to work outside. That didn't go over well and was never enforced. "I'm trading my risk of getting COVID for the risk of getting pneumonia," one technician told me.

The Biden people said they had to demonstrate they were taking the pandemic seriously—where Trump had not. It ended up being two sides of the same coin. The Trump team underreacted to COVID but used it to reduce the number of reporters at the White House. Biden overreacted and did the same thing.

Reporters in the presidential pool, which includes WHCA board members, were guaranteed access to the briefing room and the president on a regular but reduced basis. Everyone else was shut out with no guaranteed direct access. The only slim hope—extremely slim hope—of getting into the briefing room was by winning the daily lottery *to do your job—and then having someone who had a seat not show up*. But since they'd left a seat open in September and I'd taken it, the WHCA board had not made that mistake again. Members of the pool and the WHCA board seemed happy with the arrangement—on the first Sunday of the Biden administration, WHCA president (and Associated Press correspondent) Zeke Miller said as much to Brian Stelter on CNN—while many other reporters and WHCA members found the Biden policy draconian and unnecessary.

As a result, some White House reporters haven't been able to ask a single question of the president or his representatives for nearly a year. Under the new rules, sitting in the Brady Briefing Room when no briefing is going on is also a no-no. "Why can't I?" one reporter asked no one in particular as she sat in the briefing room on Biden's first day. "We're social distancing and only using the same seats used during the briefings. What's the problem?"

Compounding the problem Biden brought to the table was the daily limit of eighty members of the press. What if I was there for only two hours? What if I came only to do a stand-up and left? Could someone else come in? How do you police it? And how did you arbitrarily arrive at eighty?

That limit was barely enough to get network television crews, members of the pool, and a handful of independents through the door. (In pre-COVID Trump days, it wasn't uncommon for about 350 press people to be on the grounds on a daily basis.) The Biden team created a huge mortal sin by putting the WHCA in charge of determining which of their professional comrades could enter—in effect making reporters who are granted the best access agents of the government to determine everyone else's access. No reporter should ever be saddled with the task of deciding who gets access to the president. The Secret Service does that job quite well. And the reporters all have their own job to do. Their job shouldn't be doing work for the White House—in any capacity.

But some members of the WHCA board warmed to the task. Miller angrily marched through the briefing room after the inauguration, seeming to act as the new administration's police force, reminding everyone—"and you know who you are"—that we should leave or go outside. People ignored him, including an older television technician. "I'm not going out in the cold to make him or the administration happy," said the same tech who quipped about COVID and pneumonia. The conflict of interest in utilizing reporters to police other reporters was unprecedented. It's one thing to determine who gets a seat in the briefing room—since in the past we all crammed into the briefing room and if we didn't have a seat, we were all just "aisle people," standing in the aisle trying to ask a question. It's quite another to have reporters doing what the Biden White House employed the WHCA to do for them. When reporters police other reporters, it gives the impression that those who are acting as cops have access others do not and made a Faustian deal to get it. And while you can get angry with the WHCA for agreeing to this, the blame has to be firmly placed on the White House for implementing the policy. It is a total disregard for the free press. We may live in desperate times, but those measures were more than desperate. They were wrong.

I was not happy with this plan, and I introduced myself to White House Press Secretary Jen Psaki less than three hours after she took office. While she told me, "We want as many reporters as possible" to cover the president, she also said her hands were tied. A scientist, which she wouldn't or couldn't name, had somehow analyzed the White House grounds, the West Wing, and the North Lawn of tents where television reporters conducted live shots and stand-ups and had somehow come up with the number of eighty reporters. She also said that was all the tests she could get for us on a daily basis. I questioned the veracity of both statements—asking her to produce the person who had determined that only eighty could attend and then reminding her that she worked for the president of the United States and that if he wanted 200 or 300 tests available at any place at any time, he could get it, and we both knew it. She had nothing to say to that. So, I wrote a follow-up letter to her and got several independent journalists to sign on to the letter. I pointed out everything we discussed and also said,

> For the last year the restricted pool and a select few others who the WHCA board approves, with no posted standards or method of determination, have been given various degrees of access to the briefing room and the president himself. Everyone else has been frozen out.
>
> As a result people in our business face the very real possibility of *losing their jobs* if they lose access to the White House.
>
> That's a fact. The best solution to this problem would be to limit the access in the fashion the Trump administration did—and give us quantifiable standards when the sanctions will be lifted. In addition, on occasion, (perhaps once or twice a week) the briefings (particularly when Dr. Fauci is talking about the very serious problem of the pandemic) should be moved to the theater in the Eisenhower Executive Office Building or to a similar venue in which larger numbers of reporters can attend and social distancing can be more easily maintained.
>
> Thanks for your time.

Psaki never adequately responded to the letter. Still, overall, as a reporter, there were other things to be thankful for in the first week of the Biden administration. Every member of the staff wore masks, and the new crew acted professionally and at times were charming. No one ever accused anyone in the Trump administration of being charming—with the possible exception of Judd Deere, who was the only senior person on Trump's staff who acted professionally in the four years Trump held office.

On the first Friday of the Biden administration, Psaki held a small gaggle (an informal briefing) outside her office, spending about ten minutes talking to me, Steven Portnoy of CBS, Peter Alexander and Kristen Welker of NBC, and a few other reporters. We were able to get explanations and clarifications on several issues that cropped up that day. It was the first impromptu gaggle I attended in two years. Part of it was the pandemic, and part of it was Stephanie Grisham and Kayleigh McEnany—both of whom assiduously avoided me and many other reporters whenever possible. During her Friday impromptu gaggle, Psaki said many of the senior staff had already been vaccinated at least once. So, if the staff was relatively well protected and if the correspondents had shown they can stay healthy even during the Trump days, why was a stricter attendance policy necessary? If it is not based on fear and paranoia, is it based on a desire to control the press? Whatever the reason, the results were as undeniable with Biden as they had been with Trump. The quality of coverage of President Biden suffered immensely because fewer people were involved. The briefings became frustrating for many reporters to watch—as well as the general public. We didn't follow up. We didn't ask questions that mattered. We asked about Biden's dogs pooping in the White House. We asked if Biden was violating Centers for Disease Control protocols by traveling on Air Force One (the most secure and exclusive airplane on the planet). We asked "housekeeping" questions that could easily have been answered in e-mails or face-to-face meetings with Psaki or any of her deputies during the course of a business day. And we asked about things that didn't matter at all.

I noticed that some of the younger reporters simply quit going back to the White House press offices at all—content to try to ask their questions in the televised briefings that fewer and fewer networks were carrying live. John Bennett, who covered the White House for *Roll Call* and the *Independent* and is now an editor at the *Washington Examiner*, recalled that the face-to-face contact on a daily basis was critical to doing the job. "I'd walk back there sometimes and figure out what I wanted to ask on my walk to the office. Sometimes it's just being there that matters," he explained. "You have to show up."

This was the exact advice Helen Thomas gave me years ago and what Joe Lockhart remembered about Helen—sitting in a chair in the upper press offices and watching what was going on. It had served me well over the years, too. After Biden had his first cabinet meeting, I was able to gauge how the meeting went and to get some offhand comments from cabinet members—simply because I was in the press office after Biden's first cabinet meeting broke up and the participants went their separate ways. The Biden administration saw a great influx of young reporters who hadn't covered the White House before but cut their eyeteeth on the campaign—maybe it was their first or second job, but there were few veterans. John Roberts was gone. Jim Acosta was gone. Hallie Jackson wasn't around. Most of the print reporters with experience were gone as well, and those who were left began writing the flimsiest of stories. Psaki told me on numerous occasions (I was winning the lottery on average of about once a week, so I could still visit the White House but could not ask questions in the briefing) that she wanted things to open up "as soon as possible" and stressed how the administration wanted more reporters around.

I've heard that from every press secretary since Larry Speakes of the Reagan administration. To echo T. S. Eliot—between the idea and the reality falls the shadow, bub.

The fact is, if the president—any president—wanted to open up briefings and news conferences to more people, then he or she easily could and still respect pandemic protocols. Across the street from the White House in the Eisenhower Executive Office Building—part of the White House campus—sits the South Court Auditorium. It's less than a minute's walk from the Brady Briefing Room and comfortably holds as many as 400 people. Even with social distancing, it could easily seat seven or eight times more people than the Brady Briefing Room does during COVID and three or four times more than the thirty people who attended Biden's first press conference in the East Room. The Biden administration has even used the auditorium for a presidential address in April—but limited the number of reporters to just eighteen.

No one in the Trump or the Biden administration ever gave an adequate reason why that room wasn't used more frequently. In fact, no one answered that question at all. But it is necessary, as many saw in the first 100 days of Biden, to have as many reporters as possible involved in covering the president. Everyone has different questions—the more people in the room, the easier it is to follow up on other questions, and the president needs to hear from as many voices as possible, especially from those who are supposedly trained to challenge his authority. You cannot be satisfied with "town hall" meetings—though they are necessary.

One of the most important questions I ever had the opportunity to ask a president would be impossible under the restrictions imposed in the early days of Biden. Remember, I was not part of the press pool on September 23, 2020, when I showed up for my weekly visit to the White House. But when a pool member did not show up, I took the empty seat. Under the Biden administration's rules, I wouldn't have been able to ask that question. Fewer voices are not better for the United States. We need more—now more than ever. Limiting the press is a recipe for disaster—just look at Donald Trump.

There was other fallout from Biden's first days in office. The WHCA and I parted ways. Although some of the board—behind the scenes—had supported my attempts to even the odds during the Trump era by showing up to counter the presence of "guests" given spots and able to ask questions in the briefing room, publicly they never did and used my appearance in the briefing room during the Trump era to deny renewing my membership.

The real reason why the WHCA got angry is because I criticized the board's petty bureaucratic maneuvers to keep themselves close to the president. It is the corporate media that need to be scrutinized—and the

WHCA—while saying it pushes for transparency by the government—affords very little transparency to its members. There's no discernible policy about who gets into the pools and who does not. The WHCA is simply a choke point that no longer needs to exist. Back in the day, the WHCA could make sure through the pool system that the largest number of people were afforded a view into the president's activities by stocking the press pool with reporters from the largest newspapers, then radio and television stations. Today, those numbers are meaningless. I can—and have—videotaped interactions with Trump and Biden officials on my cell phone and then, using a variety of apps, including TikTok, Twitter, Facebook, and Instagram, broadcast a video sound bite that garnered millions of views before the end of a press briefing or gaggle and before a television reporter, newspaper, or radio reporter can identify the bite he or she wants to use, include it in a story, and either publish or broadcast it. The old ways are meaningless. So, all the WHCA board does is limit competition by protecting the corporate media giants, who would have less relevance if they had to compete in the open market with the rest of us.

But, all of that aside, in bringing back the White House daily briefing, Psaki and Biden took a giant step back toward normalcy. Reporters were relieved to simply *have* a daily briefing—and to not be threatened, insulted, or called "fake news" or the "enemy of the people." Because of that, some of us in the press were criticized for appearing to give Psaki an easy time. She also benefited, as her predecessor Kayleigh McEnany did, from dealing with just fourteen reporters in the briefing room for more than four months thanks to COVID precautions—instead of the seventy-five or more that would be present in normal times. That gave Psaki an enormous home-field advantage. Joe Lockhart, former press secretary for President Bill Clinton, once explained to me how difficult it can be when several reporters "lock in on" the press secretary during a briefing. Following each other's line of questioning and drilling down, reporters can expose a topic that the press secretary is ill prepared to handle.

Psaki did not have to deal with that scenario in her first 100 days, and she's smarter than McEnany at playing to the crowd. But she also got herself into some early trouble. On an off-the-record call with WHCA members, Psaki encouraged reporters to give her a heads-up if they planned to ask something difficult, according to the *Daily Beast.*[1] "If you're a reporter with a tough question for the White House press secretary, Joe Biden's staff wouldn't mind knowing about it in advance," Maxwell Tani reported.

That seems innocuous on its face. Reporters often ask questions about complex issues ahead of time so they can get a well-informed answer.

There's nothing wrong with that. And if Psaki wants to know questions ahead of time in order to research the answer, that can be okay too. But if she will allow only questions that she has prepared answers to ahead of time or if she won't call on journalists because she doesn't want to address the question she knows is coming, then that's a problem. She never appeared to make that move, and the early criticism seemed invalid.

Besides the problems with the press, the WHCA, and access, the Biden administration blundered badly on one other press-related matter: Jamal Khashoggi.

Khashoggi was a columnist for the *Washington Post* who lived in Virginia and hailed from Saudi Arabia. He had been critical of the Saudi regime, something the crown prince of Saudi Arabia, Mohammed bin Salman, known as MBS, apparently took personally. On October 2, 2018, Khashoggi walked into the Saudi consulate in Istanbul to obtain documents related to his planned marriage while his fiancée waited outside. Once he walked in, he never walked out. Within minutes, Khashoggi was suffocated, killed, and dismembered. By November 16, 2018, the CIA concluded MBS ordered Khashoggi's assassination. On December 11, 2018, Khashoggi was named *Time* magazine's person of the year for his work in journalism, along with other journalists who faced persecution for their work. *Time* called Khashoggi a "Guardian of the Truth."[2]

Among the things that apparently angered the royal family in Saudi Arabia was an April 3, 2018, column Khashoggi wrote for the *Washington Post* that said, "Women today should have the same rights as men. And all citizens should have the right to speak their minds without fear of imprisonment." He also wrote about secularism and how the Saudi government must find a way to embrace it. In a posthumous article, on October 17, 2018, Khashoggi wrote, "What the Arab world needs most is free expression."[3]

Donald Trump Jr. called Khashoggi a "jihadist."[4] And his father, the president at the time, refused to believe American intelligence about the murder or to put the United States relationship with Saudi Arabia in question because of Khashoggi's murder.

It wasn't hard to figure out MBS was behind the assassination. In 2017, MBS said he would go after Khashoggi "with a bullet" because he thought the reporter had tarnished his image as a progressive.[5] According to Bob Woodward's book *Rage*, Trump protected MBS from Congress after Khashoggi's death. That figures: in 2016, MBS supposedly protected

Trump after Khashoggi wrote disparaging things about the president. The Saudi government banned Khashoggi's writings.[6]

The killing of Khashoggi brought with it a whirlwind of criticism against the Saudi government. It also highlighted something that is rarely stated. If a ruler is willing to kill a higher-profiled member of society, such as a reporter, what will that ruler be willing to do to someone who does not enjoy such a profile? Many reporters noted that worse atrocities were perpetuated by Saudi leaders in Yemen during that multiyear war (Khashoggi criticized the government for that war)—and the Saudi leaders survived that. In fact, few spoke about it. From the Saudi leadership's point of view, weathering the murder of Khashoggi was a doable matter.

But should it be? Further, if the U.S. government will tolerate the death of a reporter working and living in the United States by a foreign power, what else will *our* government tolerate?

A study published by the Radio Television Digital News Association at the end of April 2021 showed that one in five employers at local television stations had employees who were the victims of violent crimes in the past year—and the most dangerous places for reporters and camera operators were rallies and other outdoor events.[7]

In the United States during the Donald Trump era, we saw reporters castigated, beaten (sometimes by members of government), arrested and prosecuted for covering the news, threatened, and intimidated. How far of a stretch is it to believe our government would tolerate or even be a part of killing a reporter on our own soil? Police have gone on trial across the country for beating and killing members of the public. Derek Chauvin's well-documented choking of George Floyd in Minneapolis is a warning call to everyone. If someone working in the government wants you dead, it can happen—and possibly with few if any consequences.

Reporters Without Borders in 2021 again rated the United States as a troubled democracy, though it rated a little higher, at forty-fourth, rather than its forty-eighth ranking in 2019. "Press freedom in the United States continued to suffer during President Donald Trump's third year in office. Arrests, physical assaults, public denigration and the harassment of journalists continued in 2019, though the numbers of journalists arrested and assaulted were slightly lower than the year prior. Much of that ire has come from President Trump and his associates in the federal government, who have demonstrated the United States is no longer a champion of press freedom at home or abroad. This dangerous anti-press sentiment has trickled down to local governments, institutions and the American public,"[8]

Reporters Without Borders stated on its website after the United States rose to be ranked forty-fifth in 2020.

In the case of Jamal Khashoggi, Trump never seemed to care. He defended MBS and continued to do business with the Saudis, releasing a statement in November 2018 saying the United States was "standing with Saudi Arabia" for strategic reasons. "It could very well be that the Crown Prince had knowledge of this tragic event—maybe he did and maybe he didn't!"[9] After information tying MBS to Khashoggi's assassination became public, Trump went so far as to cast doubt on the evidence. "I've seen so many different reports," he said in June 2019 on *Meet the Press*, then telling host Chuck Todd about the Saudis, "Take their money. Take their money, Chuck."[10]

Some reporters, with information planted by Trump's friends, worked against their own self-interest and tried to paint Khashoggi as a radical. While a detailed report from the investigation into the reporter's death was due to be released by the government, Trump never released it during his tenure as president.

Joe Biden, on the other hand, while on the campaign trail trying to unseat Trump, promised to treat Saudi Arabia as a pariah state as punishment for killing Khashoggi. He also vowed to release the government investigation—which everyone already knew about. In his documentary *Dissident*, Academy Award–winning documentarian Bryan Fogel outlined every single step in Khashoggi's killing and showed how and why the Saudi government—led by MBS—executed him. The movie had a hard time finding a distributor because of its subject matter. But it spelled out everything anyone need know about the killing.

Still, with all the facts already known, Biden promised to give Congress the long-awaited declassified report and did so in February 2021. It named MBS as the architect in the murder, to no one's shock. Ahead of the release of the report, State Department spokesperson Ned Price told reporters, "I expect that we will be in a position before long to speak to steps to promote accountability going forward for this horrific crime."[11] The shock was that the accountability never came.

Although Biden released the report, his punishment of MBS, in effect, amounted to little more than literally revoking his phone privileges. During the previous year, Biden had condemned Khashoggi's death and Jared Kushner's cozy relationship with MBS as well as a lack of punishment. After he got into office, Press Secretary Psaki said "our administration is focused on recalibrating the relationship, as we've talked about in here previously, and certainly there are areas where we will express concerns and leave open the option of accountability. There are also areas where we will continue to work with Saudi Arabia, given the threats they face in the region."[12] After President Biden spoke with King Salman bin Abdulaziz al-Saud for the first time, the Biden administration released a five-sentence statement that made no mention of Khashoggi but noted that Biden and the king had talked about the American commitment to help Saudi Arabia defend its territory "as it faces attacks from Iranian-aligned groups." It also noted Biden affirmed the importance of respecting "universal human rights" and the rule of law.[13]

In short, the Biden administration did nothing. It promised to "leave open the option of accountability," which means MBS and the Saudi government weren't held accountable for Khashoggi's death. Biden gave the Saudi government one free pass on killing a journalist. The only thing Psaki said the Biden government would do was return to a peer-equal footing. In other words, Biden would talk only to the king, not the crown prince. Biden didn't want MBS on the phone when he spoke with his daddy. The sadder part of this is *not one American journalist* brought this up to Biden in his first press conference in the East Room in March. Thirty reporters asked some very insipid questions. Not one spoke up about Khashoggi, though it is an issue that burns at the heart of a democracy. Do we condemn or allow the death of a person who expresses his or her free speech? How do we deal with this?

This, again, is a by-product of a lack of experience in the press corps that has swept through the country. The closest anyone came to asking Biden the real question about Khashoggi was George Stephanopoulos, who scored an exclusive interview with Biden for ABC. Do not forget Stephanopoulos is not a trained reporter, either. And his questioning style definitely showed he let Biden off the hook:

> George Stephanopoulos: How about Mohammad—
>
> President Joe Biden: —it's not free.
>
> George Stephanopoulos: —bin Salman? You said during the campaign that you would personally punish the Saudi leaders if they were found to be responsible for this death of Khashoggi. They were found to be responsible. Mohammad bin Salman—Salman was found to be responsible. He was found to have acknol—authorized it. Yet, you didn't personally sanction him.
>
> President Joe Biden: Well—
>
> George Stephanopoulos: Why not?

President Joe Biden: Three things. One, I'm the guy that released the report. That report had been done for a while. It wasn't released. I insisted it be released, number one. Number two, when I spoke to the king, I made it clear to the king—the king, his father, that things were gonna change. And I insisted on several things. Number one, we held accountable all the people in that organization—

George Stephanopoulos: But not the crown prince?

President Joe Biden: Not the crown prince because we have never, that I'm aware of, when we have an alliance with a country, gone to the acting head of state and punished that person. And—and—ostracized him. But here's the deal. We said, number one, end the war in Yemen. End the starvation there. Number two—and I went down the list of the things we expected the Saudis to do. And they're in the process of doing those things. And if they don't, we're gonna—it's a changed relationship. It's a changed relationship we have with Saudi Arabia. There's no blank check.[14]

But apparently, there is a blank check, and Biden gave one to Saudi Arabia. "It's very disappointing," Arabic author and writer Wajahat Ali told me. "Biden has done a lot of good, but this was not his best effort."

The problem is the United States is (or was) looked at as an example for the rest of the world, and we're setting a horrible example. If we signal that there is no price to be paid for these sorts of crimes, then there will be more of them, and the strains on our democracy will only worsen. The Biden administration should officially condemn the assassination of Jamal Khashoggi and impose some consequence on the Kingdom of Saudi Arabia and its crown prince. Precedents matter. And geostrategic stability rests on establishing a firm understanding of what America will and will not tolerate. What happened to Khashoggi could happen to us all—if we do not stand up and make those responsible for the crime accountable for it.

Joe Biden could sell off the Lincoln Bedroom's furnishings or let his dogs Champ and Major take a dump in the Oval Office and most of the country would give him a pass, thanks to what Trump did as president. That's the problem. With the bar set so low, many are willing to accept a lot of bad behavior. There is every indication that because of the forty years of dismantling the media, we are no longer able to systemically speak truth to power. *Individuals* still rise to the occasion, but there is no effort by any of the *major news corporations*—whose parent companies do business with the government and whose board members are friends with those in power—to hold our government responsible to the people.

19

A STAPLE IN YOUR NAVEL

Today's headlines about the press can be overwhelming if you're a reporter. Large corporations are teetering on bankruptcy. Some are closing. "Vulture fund" investors are swooping in and buying newspapers for pennies on the dollar, laying off staff and trying to find ways to turn journalism into quick "clickbait" profit-driven enterprises.

I joked that when Jeff Bezos bought the *Washington Post*, if I had known how little he paid for it, I would've taken up a collection at church. Bezos became a savior for the *Post*, but after he bought it, the newspaper closed its weekly local paper the *Gazette*, a separate entity that published in multiple locations across the D.C. urban area. Bezos is actually now considered a beacon—a guiding spirit—a billionaire who saved a great newspaper. Several newspaper articles since then, in a variety of publications, have suggested other billionaires should be as philanthropically minded. Remember the line in the Orson Welles movie *Citizen Kane*? "You're right, I did lose a million dollars last year. I expect to lose a million dollars this year. I expect to lose a million dollars next year. You know, Mr. Thatcher, at the rate of a million dollars a year, I'll have to close this place in sixty years."[1]

If there were other independent-thinking people with means at their disposal, then perhaps American journalism might at least be more prolific—if not profitable. But today, many other publications, large and small, have not been as lucky as the *Washington Post*. Tribune publishing fell to a hedge fund in February 2021. The headline in the *Post* read, "Tribune Publishing, owner of major U.S. newspapers, to be acquired by hedge fund known for slashing newsroom jobs."[2] Alden Global Capital said it would take over as the owner of the *Chicago Tribune*, the *Orlando Sentinel*, and the *New York Daily News*. As part of the deal, Tribune would try to spin off the *Baltimore Sun* to a nonprofit organization headed by Stewart W. Bainum Jr., a Maryland businessman. Bainum's nonprofit would also acquire the *Capital Gazette* in Annapolis—the newspaper that suffered the loss of my friend Wendi and other staffers in a mass shooting.

In March 2021, the *Post and Courier*, a Pulitzer Prize–winning newspaper founded in 1803, noted that "accountability suffers as newspaper closures grow in SC, nation." A prominent picture of the boarded-up *Holly Hill Observer* and the *Santee Striper* accompanied the story of how government corruption began to flourish after several small newspapers folded.[3]

An Associated Press story in April 2021 reported on a recent survey conducted by the Media Insight Project, a collaboration between the American Press Institute and the Associated Press-NORC Center for Public Affairs Research. The study pointed out problems the American public has with the shrinking, convoluted, and, at times, confusing American media. "I do believe they should be a watchdog, but I don't think they should lean either way," said Annabell Hawkins, a forty-one-year-old stay-at-home mother from Oklahoma. "When I grew up watching the news it seemed pretty neutral. You'd get either side. But now it doesn't seem like that."[4]

Patrick Gideons, a sixty-four-year-old former petroleum industry supervisor who lives south of Houston, said he lacks faith in the news media because he believes we offer too much opinion.

This echoes an opinion offered by Victor Pickard, a professor at the University of Pennsylvania who's spent a great deal of his career in scholarly research on the problems of the Fourth Estate.

"It's all commentary today—it's not journalism. We don't know the difference. We seem to be living in a great golden age—but all of that information is commentary," he told me for this book. "Newspapers are the main feeder for the news ecosystem, and they are disappearing—and being replaced by talking heads."

According to Pickard, "The journalism story is particularly sad. We have to do better. When you think about the significant role that state government plays in our life—and there's nobody there covering them. What's really interesting—go see how many paid lobbyists there are—the number of state lobbyists has tripled in the last few years, and at the very moment you need the watchdog, he's been taken out to pasture."

When I reentered the White House briefing room on a regular basis, during the end of the Obama administration, I called my old friends at *Playboy* and offered my services as their White House correspondent. I already had a press pass through the Sentinel newspapers, and it seemed to me the *Playboy* audience would enjoy weekly updates, too.

Hugh Hefner was still alive, but the magazine had dramatically changed. His daughter was no longer running it. Arthur Kretchmer, one of my favorite editors I'd ever met or worked with, was long gone. Chris Napolitano and Steve Randall, who were a joy to work with and who had solid reputations as journalists, were also gone. The new crew was eager, feisty, and up for anything—including someone whom Trump would later call a "loudmouth" and "that Playboy reporter."

Within a year of my return, Hefner died, and the board that took over the operations of *Playboy* slowly closed up shop. It was the quintessential tale of journalism in the twenty-first century. I produced a weekly column for the online edition of the magazine and was scheduled to do some investigative pieces for the print version, too. During the four years of the Trump administration, *Playboy* shut down its monthly edition. It became a quarterly and then ceased publishing a printed copy altogether. I went through four editors. The content shifted dramatically and, other than my column, began to disappear. There were at least three rounds of layoffs. After the White House tried to take away my press pass, Ben Cohn, the chief executive officer, brought me out to Los Angeles to speak with the staff and encourage them to continue their efforts. It was a far cry from the heyday of *Playboy* I'd first experienced. There were no New York offices, no Chicago offices. By 2018, the mansion was gone. The clubs were closed. The editorial staff wasn't much larger than the staff I ran at two community newspapers in suburban Maryland, just outside of Washington, D.C.

Cohn seemed to be married to a business model that many corporate media companies have adopted—enslaved to clickbait and forever chasing readers with provocative headlines and making profit through "multiples." Multiples show how much investors are willing to pay per dollar of earnings as computed by the price-to-earnings ratio,[5] in short, how much are we paying to produce the product versus how much we're earning on the product. By conducting business this way, companies strive to create the greatest profit for the least amount of investment in the product. It's a great way to do business if you're selling cars I suppose, but how do you quantify investigative reporting? How much worth can you put on reading a great short story or an in-depth interview versus how much it costs to produce it? Those intangibles are almost impossible to quantify. It is what fundamentally makes journalism incompatible with capitalism.

Marketing merchandise and resting on the laurels of the past, *Playboy* ceased to exist as I had known it. Breaking a story meant little. Those things cannot be quantified. There was no direct turnaround—no sales of merchandise they could directly attribute to a decent story or through coverage.

Raising the profile of the brand by being vilified by the Trump White House was neither a good thing nor a bad thing. It was a sales-neutral thing. If I took a selfie from the White House wearing a *Playboy* mask and people bought masks from the website, that was more favorably looked on than a good news story or column.

Playboy always had a valuable reputation in the journalism and literary world. And despite how much the far right professed to hate the brand, when *Playboy* held an after-party in Washington following the White House Correspondents' Association dinner in 2017, those very people who screamed the loudest about *Playboy* debauchery lined up to get tickets to go to the party. I have never been to a bad *Playboy* party, and that night we had the hottest party in a very stuffy town. At one point, I went outside to see the lines of people trying to get in, and people I didn't know were claiming to be my friend. "Everybody's Brian's friend tonight," one of the ladies at the door said. I just laughed. It wasn't me. I was not deluded into thinking anybody cared about me—it was the *Playboy* mystique.

I experienced it once during a trip to the Middle East. I had a black *Playboy* tag on one of my bags. I was pulled aside, and I thought I was done for. A strip search might ensue, and maybe a large payoff would have to take place. Suddenly, I imagined being in a scene from *Midnight Express*. My worry was unfounded. The military guard who pulled me aside asked me in a very quiet voice why I had the *Playboy* tag. I told him I was a reporter doing and researching a story for the magazine. He looked furtively about and demanded a business card. I produced one and handed it to him. Then he drew me in close. "If I go to the United States, can you get me into a party?" he asked. I eagerly nodded yes, and he let me go.

There is no understating the importance *Playboy* had on American journalism and publishing. I met the late Larry Flynt in Memphis while Milos Forman was shooting *The People vs. Larry Flynt*. I was there to interview James Carville for *Playboy*, and Flynt was a die-hard fan of Hugh Hefner. "I would not have been possible without him," Flynt told me. And he delighted in telling stories about Hefner and his staunch independence. Flynt also told me about losing his virginity to poultry, but that's another story.

The truth is during the twentieth century, once you got beyond the staples in the navel of the monthly pinup, *Playboy* offered commentary and investigative stories on politics, sports, entertainment, and everything else that affects the human condition.

Gore Vidal, Hunter S. Thompson, Alex Haley (who interviewed Malcolm X and Martin Luther King Jr.), Norman Mailer, Haruki Murakami, Joseph Heller, Ray Bradbury, Ian Fleming, Roald Dahl, Kurt Vonnegut,

Margaret Atwood, and scores of other famous writers and journalists all published in *Playboy*.

In his interview, Martin Luther King Jr. famously said,

> I mean to say that a strong man must be militant as well as moderate. He must be a realist as well as an idealist. If I am to merit the trust invested in me by some of my race, I must be both of these things. This is why nonviolence is a powerful as well as a just weapon. If you confront a man who has long been cruelly misusing you, and say, "Punish me, if you will; I do not deserve it, but I will accept it, so that the world will know I am right and you are wrong," then you wield a powerful and a just weapon. This man, your oppressor, is automatically morally defeated, and if he has any conscience, he is ashamed. Wherever this weapon is used in a manner that stirs a community's, or a nation's, anguished conscience, then the pressure of public opinion becomes an ally in your just cause.[6]

David Sheff, in February 1985, interviewed Steve Jobs during the early years of Apple:

> A computer is the most incredible tool we've ever seen. It can be a writing tool, a communications center, a super calculator, a planner, a filer and an artistic instrument all in one, just by being given new instructions, or software, to work from. There are no other tools that have the power and versatility of a computer. We have no idea how far it's going to go. Right now, computers make our lives easier. They do work for us in fractions of a second that would take us hours. They increase the quality of life, some of that by simply automating drudgery and some of that by broadening our possibilities. As things progress, they'll be doing more and more for us.[7]

Miles Davis in 1962 talked about how the prejudice he saw as a young man drove him to be better on the trumpet than "anybody white. . . . I have thought that prejudice and curiosity have been responsible for what I have done in music."[8]

It was interviews such as these that set *Playboy* apart and made the *Playboy* interview the quintessential platform to discuss serious issues and to do it in such depth that anyone could read and take something from it. It was a unique communications app (to paraphrase Steve Jobs) that is no longer available to us today.

The fall of *Playboy* and its acquisition by a publicly traded company by early 2021 was not unique. It was typical. The Sentinel newspapers closed two years after I left them. There is no local news produced today in one of the largest counties in Maryland. The voices of the civil rights movement, the women's rights movement, and other progressive causes I read about in the pages of *Playboy* have all struggled to find a viable platform in the third decade of the twenty-first century. It is all part of the craze to chase short-term profits at the expense of a long-term future.

I have friends at *Politico*, the *Washington Examiner*, *Yahoo News*, the *Independent*, the *New York Times*, the *Washington Post*, and scores of other publications where management determines content by the number of clicks on a story. The quality of the story—the relevance of the reporting— is determined solely by how many people click on the story. It isn't news that people need; rather, it is news that people *want* to read. We don't endeavor to educate, only entertain. And we contribute to the division in our country by playing to it.

"We have young reporters who don't know how to cover beats. We have few people left who can teach them how," said an editor friend of mine at a large newspaper in the D.C. area.

This is the world bestowed on us by those first moves made by Richard Nixon fifty years ago.

Since the day I rolled into Laredo, Texas, in 1983, the population of the city has tripled. There used to be three English-speaking television stations and one Spanish station. There were two English newspapers and in Nuevo Laredo a Spanish paper. There were several radio stations that covered news. Thirty-five years later, there is one television station, one newspaper, and one radio station.

The government—beginning with Ronald Reagan, who turned Richard Nixon's dreams into reality with Mark S. Fowler and Roger Ailes and allowed the airwaves and newspapers to be treated like "toasters" through unfettered capitalism—has destroyed the media. Some are trying to fight back. In Virginia, Delegate Danica Roem got a shield law passed in 2020 to protect reporters from going to jail when they protect their sources. At the federal level, Maryland Congressman Jamie Raskin attempted to pass a shield law in 2018. If you want to look at the desiccated corps of the press, look in South Carolina. Forty years of evisceration plus the coronavirus pandemic finally killed newspapers there. The *Post and Courier*, in February 2021, outlined the death of the *Holly Hill Observer* and the *Santee Striper*. It noted that "seven of our state's newspapers closed their doors in the past year" and said the loss hit hardest in the "vast rural stretches of the Palmetto

State, in places such as Allendale County, which has struggled for years with soaring poverty, failing schools and government mismanagement."[9]

According to the article, corruption was up in parts of rural South Carolina.

"When you lose a local newspaper, what you are losing is that person who shows up to cover the town council, the person who covers the school board and the local police beat," said Penny Muse Abernathy, a visiting professor at Northwestern University's Medill School of Journalism in Evanston, Illinois. "At a minimum, it provides transparency about what's going on in local government."[10]

As I write these words, we still don't know the future of American journalism. We only know that it is far from secure. People operating independently without access, without the knowledge on how to get it or to obtain real information, are calling themselves journalists and crowdfunding on the internet to fuel their efforts. I do not wish them ill. I do not think we should quiet their voices. But they are also not journalists. They are people with opinions, and while everyone is entitled to an opinion, not all opinions have equal weight. A board-certified brain surgeon with years of education and experience has more credibility talking about his or her profession than someone you saw on a YouTube video who calls him- or herself a brain surgeon. In fact, you'd be crazy to consider the latter a brain surgeon at all. The same can be said for journalists.

It isn't just the education. It is experience and education combined. Many study journalism and never practice it. Many have years of experience and the education: those opinions have more merit than those of someone who hangs a shingle without ever once attending a city council meeting or a PTA meeting.

The first scene in the first episode of Aaron Sorkin's *The Newsroom* is about as close to the bone as a television drama ever got to describing the problems with American journalism today. Jeff Daniels, as an anchor, is attending a symposium and is asked what makes America the greatest country in the world. He offers a platitude, agrees with the other speakers, and hopes to move on, but the moderator holds him to a real answer. In an answer that could've been penned by hundreds of journalists, the character Will McAvoy gave a "human moment" that describes exactly why we need to fight for a free, open, and robust press, one that does not subjugate itself to those in power, one that is antagonistic, informative, passionate, honest, and, above all, tireless in its pursuit of providing facts to a nation and world that desperately needs the information and knows we're getting screwed even if they are mistaken or misunderstand how they are being screwed. In fact, it is precisely because people are mistaken as to why and don't understand how they are being screwed that we must redouble our efforts to keep the public informed.

It won't make us rich. It won't make us many friends, and it definitely won't make us as popular as many in the media want to be, but it is necessary and vital to our survival. We must communicate better.

"There's absolutely no evidence available to support the statement we are the greatest country in the world," Jeff Daniels's character tells us. "We're seventh in literacy, twenty-seventh in math, twenty-second in science, forty-ninth in life expectancy, one hundred and seventy-eighth in infant mortality, third in household median income, fourth in labor force, and fourth in exports." We lead the world in three categories, we are told: the number of incarcerated citizens per capita, the number of people who believe angels are real, and defense spending, where we outspend the other top twenty-six nations combined—twenty-five of which are our allies.[11]

Is that true? Look it up. Here's another sobering fact to remember. Although we live in a nation that codified free speech in the very first amendment ever written to our Constitution—and said amendment has been a driving force for free speech across the planet—as of today, remember, we are only the forty-fourth-freest country, according Reporters Without Borders, when it comes to the press. We are a troubled democracy.

Our government, lobbyists, and corporations have spent the past forty years or more trying to convince us they are helping us, but they are only helping themselves, and the greed displayed by all of them has effectively destroyed free speech and education and has made great strides in destroying self-governance. Our representatives have gone from serving their constituents to playing to them as if they are a fan base for a professional wrestler.

Think long and hard about Jamal Khashoggi. A reporter working and living in the United States for a U.S. newspaper was murdered overseas in Turkey at the behest of a foreign government, and two presidents have done nothing to hold the Saudi Arabian government accountable. If you can kill a journalist with a high profile for exercising his free speech, how free is the speech of those without that profile, without the supposed support of a large company with wide influence?

Donald Trump sued the *New York Times* for printing an opinion, not a factual error but a clearly labeled opinion, and when I asked him, he said he did so because "they get the opinion totally wrong." Hardly anyone bat-ted an eyebrow at that statement. Hardly anyone in the press covered it. It was mostly ignored. That's even more frightening than the statement itself.

Corporate media have us following the "news of the day" rather than long-term stories of impact. And there are too many reporters called "media" reporters who believe their job involves covering just celebrities.

We ceased framing the narrative.

We ceased covering things that are not clickbait.

We ignore the growing social media contributions instead of embracing and co-opting them.

We do not listen to our reporters.

We lost institutional knowledge.

We do not defend ourselves. We often fight among ourselves.

Trump was able to construct a fictional world by capitalizing on the eroded faith in the Fourth Estate. He didn't destroy the faith in the press, he merely took advantage of our loss of faith in it. The simple fact is we cannot make the land safe for democracy until we make the land safe for facts and safe for those of us presenting facts—whether we find those facts (or those who present them) pleasant or unpleasant.

President Joe Biden recognized this in the first policy speech of his administration, saying, "A free press is essential to the health of a democracy."[12] Two legislative proposals have been introduced on Capitol Hill: the Global Press Freedom Act and the Jamal Khashoggi Press Freedom Accountability Act. The latter bill, introduced in early 2021 in the House by Representative Adam Schiff and in the Senate in late 2020 by Senators Amy Klobuchar and Patrick Leahy, aims to strengthen U.S. resolve to protect journalists and hold accountable countries and foreign individuals found responsible for killing or harming them.

"The United States' commitment to the protection of journalists and the promotion of press freedom internationally is critical given its prominent role on the world stage," said Anna K. Nelson, executive director of Reporters Without Borders, of the bill. "Not only does this bill seek justice for the senseless murder of Jamal Khashoggi, it also increases protection for reporters who risk torture, imprisonment and even death as they report critical information."

The Global Press Freedom Act would institutionalize the U.S. commitment to advancing press freedom abroad by creating the role of an "ambassador at large" who would engage with governments and organizations to draw attention to violations of press freedom and reporter safety.

Both acts are needed. But we are still waiting for Biden to take a critical first step toward protecting freedom of the press.

The January 6 Capitol insurrection exposed some reporters, for the first time, to the kinds of physical dangers that journalists around the world routinely face. Still, we have been slow to insist that Biden clean up one of Trump's most grievous offenses—the threat against the truth.[13]

The question remains—how do we clean up this undeniable mess?

"We reached for the stars. We acted like men," Jeff Daniels said in *The Newsroom*. "We aspired to intelligence; we didn't belittle it. It didn't make us feel inferior. We didn't identify ourselves by who we voted for in the last election, and we didn't scare so easy. We were able to be all these things and do all these things because we were informed."

We are not as well informed today. Government and businesses have seen to that.

We must see that this changes.

To do that, we must hold government accountable. We must make sure that when President Biden says, "We believe a free press isn't an adversary; rather it's essential," these are not just empty words.[14]

20

FREE THE PRESS

L ike most people, I assume, I was born with a sense of wonder at the world around me. And like most people I've known, I've wanted to know more about this strange existence into which I was fortunate enough to have been born and have had the pleasure to experience.

I realized at a young age that to know more, I had to ask questions. I had to seek out the knowledge of others. I was born a clean slate, with some programs hardwired into this corporeal body but with so much more obtainable only if I sought knowledge. Inherently, we all trust our parents, but it was through them that I also learned that not everyone was as honest or free with the facts as my parents. Some, like my grandfather, liked to gently tease. Others just lie.

As I aged, I realized that I needed to apply the scientific method to gathering information if I wanted to obtain vetted facts with which to make cogent decisions regarding my existence: question, test, and give up on the ideas that were proved by facts to be false. This meant navigating between outright lies, implied lies, mistakenly told lies, subtle humor, brash humor, opinions, sarcasm, and every variety of communication employed by humans. A lift of an eyebrow can sometimes say more than an entire sentence. Learning the subtleties of human communication is a lifelong endeavor, and, of course, none of us ever master it. Some are more proficient than others, but anyone can be taken by a con. Anyone can lie. Anyone can misinterpret what someone else says or does. Anyone who ever played the "telephone game" knows how easily words can be misunderstood and changed. Anyone who has ever witnessed an event—like a ball game—knows how it differs from the event when seen on television—or how different the experience is inside the ballpark depending on the seat in which you sit.

Different perspectives begat different opinions, and some, in this day and age, want to *cancel* others for expressing their opinions based on their perspective—sometimes even though what was said may be a random inappropriate comment or a mistake or those who witnessed the communication misinterpreted it. Sometimes people just don't understand another's sense of humor. Sometimes people are truly obnoxious and mean spirited. Today's culture has created a minefield for communication that probably would leave someone like comedian Don Rickles unemployable today. We have become a brittle culture because of it.

This makes the science and art of journalism very difficult to do well and why it takes a lifetime to try to get it right—and ultimately why we all make mistakes doing it no matter how good or experienced we think we are. The first thing I realized as a young reporter, drilled into me by parents, teachers, copy editors, and one irascible old editor at the now–defunct *Jefferson Reporter* in Louisville, Kentucky, is that, like medical doctors, the first thing we must commit to as reporters is to do no harm to the truth or to the facts. We cannot make the waters muddier. We must struggle to be understood clearly and do so concisely. A journalist should never knowingly tell a lie. Always double-check and verify your facts. Always label opinions as opinions. Try your best to do no harm by spreading misinformation.

Still, as I advanced as a reporter, I found there were other problems. A lack of cultural understanding and critical thinking began to overtake the profession as large media corporations consolidated and faced shrinking bottom lines. It takes a well-rounded education to compete as a journalist—not necessarily a diploma. In fact, you can make an effective argument that most journalism degrees are nearly useless. On-the-job training and living a well-rounded life has served many of us quite well. And while you can be "crowdfunded" and call yourself a "citizen journalist," that doesn't necessarily make you a journalist either. You can't simply shoot your mouth off. You need a copy editor or fact-checker and a working knowledge of civics, sports, entertainment, conflicts, crime, politics, and a host of other issues to be effective in asking questions and understanding issues and answers. Unfortunately, if you have such knowledge, then you are also positioned to make more money elsewhere in the job market—hence the reason journalism doesn't always attract the best and the brightest. Don Henley spelled it out right in "Dirty Laundry," when he sang, "I could've been actor, but I wound up here."[1]

This was extremely evident to me from the beginning of my career, and one incident from the 1990s is more representational than others in illustrating this point. At a morning story meeting at KMOL-TV, the staff was going over possible story ideas when a young assignment editor who had been looking over the Associated Press wire mentioned that Jack Ruby's gun was going up for auction. "Wow," someone said. The assignment editor asked what the fuss was about. "Who is Jack Ruby?" she asked.

"The guy who killed Oswald," someone else answered.

"Who's Oswald?" she asked.

After the dust settled, the assignment editor defended her position, saying, "Well that happened before I was born."

"Beethoven happened before I was born," but I know who he is, our anchor Alan Hemberger answered. Alan, who is no longer with us, was one of the television anchors who seemed then and even more now a product of a bygone era. He was smart and inquisitive and always had a way of putting things in context that promoted understanding.

The story that sticks with me most about Hemberger was when KMOL covered the twentieth anniversary of man landing on the moon. Alan said, "I remember it well. I was slogging through a jungle in Vietnam when I got the word that Neil Armstrong and Buzz Aldrin had landed on the moon. As it happened it was a very clear night and as I carried my rifle, I looked up and saw the moon and thought to myself there's quite a distance between there and where I was."

How did Alan survive Vietnam to become a television anchor—and ultimately at a top ten market in Houston? He would laugh at that question. "I'm adaptable," he said.

My father once told me if you have a complaint, then you'd better have a solution. "People bitch about everything," he routinely told me. "They seem to like that more than solving problems." I've often thought about that as I've spent a career covering news. It is increasingly popular to merely ignore those things with which we don't agree and treat people the same way. That's hardly a solution. It only creates more problems.

My pop also preached to me about adaptability, as did Alan, and that is a lesson I've tried to apply in every part of life—adapt. By the time Alan was preaching the same thing, it was a lesson I'd already learned, though it was still much appreciated.

Today, the changing media landscape calls for adherence to some of our strictest tenets while at the same time adapting to how we deliver the news to the public. Our democracy demands it.

The local paper is perilously close to completely disappearing. Large swaths of this country live in news deserts. According to a study published by Axios in June 2021, the United States has lost some 37,000 newsroom jobs since 2016.[2] And, according to a study released on May 1, 2021, by the University of North Carolina's School of Media and Journalism, more than 1,300 communities across the country have lost all news coverage.[3]

Among other findings in the study:

- About 20 percent of all metro and community newspapers in the United States—about 1,800—have gone out of business or merged since 2004, when about 9,000 were being published.
- Hundreds more have scaled back coverage so much that they've become what the researchers call "ghost newspapers." Almost all other newspapers still publishing have also scaled back, just less drastically.
- Online news sites, as well as some TV newsrooms and cable access channels, are working hard to keep local reporting alive, but these are taking root far more slowly than newspapers are dying—hence the 1,300 communities that have lost all local coverage.[4]

To adapt to this undeniable fact, we have to make newspapers more viable and easier to sustain. We cannot afford to let newspapers disappear because they play a vital role in delivering information that the internet cannot reproduce. When you go to the internet, you are usually on a hard target search for information. When you pick up a newspaper, you're scanning for information and are open to read anything presented to you. You may not know what to search for, but you know what you want to read when you find it. Newspapers are smorgasbords of information. The internet isn't and cannot be set up that way.

So, how do we save newspapers? There are a variety of business models currently under consideration. Nonprofits hold promise but as of yet haven't gotten the traction needed. A big push was made to save the *Baltimore Sun* through a nonprofit, and this may indeed be the best way to save newspapers since the job they do for society is completely incompatible with capitalism.

"There's no question about it, I don't think any problem facing the country is any more severe than what is facing our news information infrastructure," Michael Copps, formerly of the Federal Communications Commission (FCC) told me. "I saw it. The first call I got from the chairman when I joined the FCC was about the merger of Fox and Chris Craft. That set the tone. I thought going to the FCC was the coolest job on earth. We'd be serving the public. And then I realized I spent a lot of time meeting CEOs who wanted to seek approval of their mergers. The FCC, more often than not, approved the mergers. Then a rival would come in and gripe and say in order to compete, they had to have a merger."

The free market obviously isn't the answer. It only allows politics and information today to be played and reported on as sport. Walter Cronkite, Dan Rather, and others saw it coming. This is a very steep mountain to climb, and there is no commercial solution to the problem. The corporatization consolidation, as Copps told me, "is too embedded in the system. How do you get beyond that?"

The government has to exercise its antitrust laws, and we need to think about public media. Put the brakes on corporate mergers. "Subsidies are key," Victor Picard, a University of Pennsylvania communications professor, explained to me. He works on the intersections of U.S. and global media activism and politics, the history and political economy of media institutions, and the normative foundations of media policy.[5]

"It's the commercialization, the dedication to clickbait, and profits above all else. That's what's driving this. There's no commercial incentive to do it right. Journalism often isn't sexy," he said.

While there isn't one perfect model, Pickard said he could see "subsidized subscribers," or a voucher plan. Everyone gets a $100 voucher, "and they can buy media of their choice. It guarantees a certain method of support. Subsidize the news outlets themselves. My preference is to radically expand and reform our public broadcast system—so they can actually be politically independent."

Pickard also supports public media centers "in every city across the country. Public libraries, schools, and j-schools [journalism schools]. That's in my radical plan. It is healthy to have a mixed system—independents, nonprofits, public benefit corporations, and standard for-profit companies."

The driving force today in journalism is capitalism, and it's driving our journalism into the ground. "The fact that we hook journalism so close to capitalism is the problem," Pickard explained.

But, for those who try to exist under the old business model, federal, state, and local governments should consider a variety of tax breaks on labor and capital to make local newspapers more viable.

But all of this pales in comparison to fixing the bigger problems in journalism.

The first thing we must do is make sure there are more reporters. The only way to do that is to make sure there are more media companies. The best way to do that is to break up the media monopolies. Use antitrust legislation. Force the old guardrails back into place. They have to be reintroduced. There have to be caps on the number of media properties you can own and how many you can own in a given market. Companies like Sinclair and the hedge fund group Alden Global Capital should be forced to divest themselves of most of their properties. There should be penalties to pay for dissolving media companies when you buy them.

Unfortunately, we are not moving in that direction. On May 17, 2021, the latest media merger was announced:

> On Monday morning AT&T (T) and Discovery, Inc. (DISCA) announced a deal under which AT&T's WarnerMedia will be spun off and combined with Discovery in a new standalone media company.
>
> The deal, subject to regulatory approval, will combine two treasure troves of content, including the HBO Max and Discovery+ streaming services. CNN will be included in the transaction.[6]

It cannot be said often enough: For newspapers and television news to survive, Congress must take advantage of existing antitrust legislation to break up the big media monopolies. This isn't going to be popular with any of those companies that own most of what we see, read, or hear, but it has to be done. Ben Bagdikian warned us. H. L. Mencken warned us. Sam Donaldson, Dan Rather, and scores of others across the years have warned us about the accumulation of too much power in too few hands in the media world. It is destroying free thought, in-depth reporting, and critical thinking. Today's national press is often nothing more than stenographers and drones following each other into blind alleys and avoiding real issues as editors dictate story ideas, sometimes ignoring facts, and other times only choosing the facts that fit their narrative. When your coverage is driven by what people want to see rather than what they need to see, then you've abandoned journalism for entertainment.

Think of the baton twirler in *Animal House* who led the band into a blind alley where they crashed into each other. That is today's journalism.

Breaking up the media monopolies is only a first step. We must reinstitute some semblance of the fairness doctrine. We have to break America out of the habit of one-sourced news gathering. Breaking down the silos of information is key to bringing everyone back together under one tent. We have to see what others think. We have to confront the misinformation with facts and truth. None of that is possible as long as journalism remains a slave to an audience that chooses which news it wants to hear without a desire to see what they need to know.

We also have to quit taking shots at each other. I may not like Fox, One America News, and Newsmax. The reporters there may not like

MSNBC, CNN, ABC, CBS, or NBC, but at the end of the day, insulting each other serves only to harden the hearts of the "true believers" on either side of the coin—and that does no one any good either. You can't change minds if people won't listen—and people almost always refuse to listen when you scream at them and tell them they suck. They merely get defensive.

This also goes for politicians—many of whom think they know what reporters do but in reality have only the vaguest notion. It's not just Trump calling us "fake news" or the "enemy of the people." It's members of Congress who think we get in the way or that we don't have a right to ask them a question or who have no idea how to communicate effectively and blame the reporters when they bungle. And it is also President Joe Biden. At the conclusion of his first overseas trip after a summit with President Vladimir Putin of Russia, Biden staged a news conference and took a question in Geneva, Switzerland, on June 16, 2021, from Kaitlin Collins of CNN. She asked him, in essence, if he was overly optimistic about his summit with Putin. Biden got upset. Later, as he was boarding Air Force One, he apologized and then said, "Look, to be a good reporter, you got to be negative. You got to have a negative view of life—okay?—it seems to me, the way you all—you never ask a positive question."

Even Biden doesn't understand what it is we do and why we do it. Is it that reporters are negative people? No. Not most of them. They're just trying to do a job, and those who do the job and those whom we cover need to be better aware of what's going on from the floor up. Life is in the nuance. So is reporting.

To solve all of these problems, any president calling the Oval Office his own must set up a presidential blue-ribbon commission and spend some time with reporters, professors, and others who understand why the press is under fire and then do something about it. That assumes that a president wants to save the Fourth Estate. No president in my professional lifetime has wanted to do anything more than control the press—no matter their platitudes—and if they all think like Biden, then we know why.

On World Press Freedom Day, May 5, 2021, Julian Assange still sat in jail, and there were people who sought to remind others that he was in prison because he took private corporate information and gave it to the public, while others, like Mark Zuckerberg, were free and making millions by taking private information culled from millions of individuals and selling it for a profit to large corporations.

But on World Press Freedom Day, I remember Jamal Khashoggi. No human being should be viciously murdered, dismembered, and cremated because they have an opinion contrary to those in charge of companies, countries, or the local PTA. The guiding principle across the planet has to be, "I disagree with what you say but defend to death your right to say it," or anarchy will ensue.

Editors complain today of an entire generation of reporters and young editors who are driven solely by clicks on the internet. Clickbait often isn't good journalism, though it can be. John Avlon at CNN is a proponent of another method of metrics that could help sustain journalism. In a new white paper from the School of Media and Public Affairs at the George Washington University School of Media and Public Affairs, the idea of "attention analytics" explores the idea of the financial benefits that could be derived from trading on user attention rather than impressions.[7]

In a webinar on April 20, 2021, called "Battling Deep Fakes and Misinformation—Media's Role and Responsibility," hosted by the consultant group Prophet, Avlon argued for a way to make journalism "sustainable without clickbait"—a central challenge for today's journalist.

But the fact also remains you cannot rely on what you want to know as your total news diet. You must be open to what you need to know, what you may not know, what you don't want to know, and what you are currently ignorant of. Reintroducing a fairness doctrine will force everyone to play on the same field and, if done correctly, could reintroduce readers and viewers from opposite sides of the spectrum to each other. The biggest argument against this is that it will be difficult to enforce on Facebook, Twitter, and other social media platforms. However, if you can produce an app that targets advertising, you could certainly find a way to enforce a new fairness doctrine. This is perfect stuff for a presidential blue-ribbon commission to consider.

Finally, we must have a national shield law for reporters. Most states have one to a varying degree. They all provide cover for reporters who deal with confidential sources and whistle-blowers. A shield law gives a reporter the ability to deal with these very delicate sources who often provide the most controversial and yet the most necessary information. Many legislators have grappled with a national shield law, and it has drawn an odd assemblage of legislative bedfellows. Both Congressman Jim Jordan from Ohio, a well-known Trump supporter and conservative, and liberal Jamie Raskin from Maryland, who was the Democratic case manager in Donald Trump's second impeachment trial, led to one of the most recent attempts to secure a national shield law for reporters. Former vice president Mike Pence also pushed for one when he was in Congress, but when the Edward Snowden case broke, it effectively killed any congressional attempt to help reporters shield their sources.

But without a reporter being able to effectively and safely work with confidential sources, much of the most interesting and consequential information simply cannot be had—and most definitely won't be reported. Jim Jordan wants to support a shield law because he thinks whistle-blowers might help curb the activities of people on the left side of the hall. Perhaps Raskin thinks the same of the right. It doesn't matter. What matters is that for the good of the country, a national shield law must be passed.

And while we're on the subject of change, there's one other thing we should change: the White House Correspondents' Association (WHCA). The WHCA is a slave to the large corporations that own most of the media, and while there are many decent people who serve the WHCA—and, in full disclosure, I once ran for its board—it has outlived its usefulness.

While some of what I say here will sting, ultimately it is the best thing to do to keep the organization vital and at the same time serve the nation. The WHCA is a chokepoint for presidential coverage and, as such, is easily and often manipulated by the White House and the large corporate entities that contribute the lion's share of people and officers to the WHCA.

The in-town pool system is completely antiquated. It limits the number of reporters with direct access to the president and acts as a government gatekeeper.

No reporter should ever be in a position to determine whether another reporter can cover the president. The Secret Service and the White House vet the holders of the coveted "hard pass" that gives reporters access. Every reporter with a hard pass should be given an opportunity to sign up and be part of the pool of reporters given access to the "local" or "in house" press pool visiting the Oval Office, the Diplomatic Reception Room when the president is there, and so on. The WHCA can continue to decide who sits in the seats of the James S. Brady Press Briefing Room, and it should continue to coordinate the travel pool because, without getting too far into the weeds, the problematic nature of traveling with the president dictates that someone has to manage access and the cost of travel. But anyone who has a hard pass should be allowed into the Oval Office or the Diplomatic or Cabinet room on a rotating basis.

The archaic means by which the WHCA decides who is in the pool is at issue, as are some of the choices made by individuals in the WHCA with grudges or friendships they wish to react to or against. Supposedly, the larger-circulation newspapers, television networks, or radio stations have the inside track because the idea is that more people are represented by those who represent the largest media outlets. Today, this is simply a comical error. I can—and have—tweeted out a video that I shot on my cell phone that rivals network video and audio. I have reached millions of viewers in a matter of an hour. I was able to do so before the end of a gaggle with Kellyanne Conway on the North Lawn driveway and easily an hour or more before the networks prepared their own edited version for broadcast. Some of those events I posted—whether on Instagram, Twitter, or TikTok—went viral, and some continue to this day to garner viewers. The video is easy to access, is well labeled, and by any measure would meet the criteria for a threshold of viewership.

The truth is anyone today with a hard pass and a reasonably sized social media following can reach millions of readers or viewers via TikTok, Twitter, Facebook, Instagram, or a variety of other apps available on your cell phone. It used to be only the largest media companies could reach the largest audiences, and it made sense to give those companies the greatest access. Today? No. The method of disseminating information is much more democratic—but the WHCA isn't. Today, it's the WHCA still acting as if the large media corporations have a monopoly on reaching an audience. They do not. They merely have control.

It isn't in the president's best interest to always tell us what he's thinking. Indeed, ultimately, it isn't even in the best interest of the people of the United States to know what he's thinking about everything. It's hard to run any office if you can't have a private thought. A wise reporter will know when and how to ask the right question about a president's thoughts. A wise press secretary will know how to answer those questions without giving voters the idea that the president has something to hide.

Trump never once had a press secretary who knew how to thread that needle. They were all incompetent and argumentative, reflecting the very worst characteristics of their boss.

New press secretary Jen Psaki, in her very first press briefing, showed she may indeed have the mettle of a professional. When asked whether President Biden favored a conviction in the Senate on Trump's latest impeachment—a question that goes to Biden's claims of wanting unity in the country—Psaki wisely demurred and said that was up to the Senate to decide. She was absolutely right, and she made her point without bombast, without a tirade, and without trying to humiliate the reporter, in this case one from Fox News, because someone dared to ask the question.

The truth is, in order to heal, this country is going to have to be both accepting of the opinions of others and, at the same time, intolerant of the crimes committed based on differing opinions.

You can hate me, but you cannot act on that hate. You cannot excuse a crime based on a political opinion any more than you can forget the crime based on personal passion.

But the briefing room on the first day of the Biden administration was not the place for such nuance, nor was it the place to trumpet Biden's personal opinion about Donald Trump. It was a place where the press secretary talked about the rule of law and sober, critical thinking.

It was a huge change from any briefing that occurred during the Trump administration.

"I know speaking of unity can sound to some like a foolish fantasy," Biden said in his inaugural address. "I know the forces that divide us are deep, and they are real," but Biden's moves during his first day in office put the train back on its tracks.

His first 100 days in office also exposed the soft underbelly of journalism created by four decades of greed and government interference. The press corps was lampooned and ridiculed for our questions before Psaki. She was criticized for being snarky and trite when we asked stupid questions— and, boy, did we ask some stupid questions. Without calling anyone out, it simply remains that the institutional knowledge we once had doesn't exist. The turnover in administrations brought even more young reporters into the briefing room. Because of COVID pandemic restrictions, only fourteen of them could be in the room at one time. Many of them are told which questions to ask by their editors. We didn't follow each other up. We didn't listen to the answers given, and when Psaki said something like, "You obviously didn't understand me," there was no pushback.

Whoever is in the White House or whoever covers a city hall or a state legislature can and must do their job better. We cannot be intimidated by the government. We must always challenge the government. Helen Thomas once said indeed she was critical of government, and, yes, she was antagonistic. Why? That's our job.

So, while it is critical that we clean up the business of journalism, it is also critical to clean up what it is that journalists do and how we do it. The problem with so many young or inexperienced reporters in the White House ("I just got thrown into this. I don't have a background in journalism," one White House reporter told me) is that fewer of us know what the hell we're doing. So, here is a twelve-step practical guide to reporting in the White House for some young reporters, anyone calling themselves a "citizen journalist," and anyone else who is just curious about how we do what we do from my nearly forty years in the business and from listening to my mentors—those wiser than me who came before me:

1. *Just ask the question.* Helen Thomas, one of my mentors, told me that you should always ask a question. Get the question out. The answer often isn't as important as the question, for once the question is asked, the administration cannot truthfully deny the issue exists. Of course, Sam Donaldson also taught me how to shout to get the question heard.

2. *Back each other up when you can.* This means listening to the person asking the question in a briefing and to the answer. Sometimes follow-up is better than the question you came to ask. Sometimes supporting each other by asking the person conducting the briefing to answer the previously asked question is in order. But sometimes it is not. It is the reporter's call based on issues, answers, timeliness, deadlines, and so on. Not immediately backing each other up does not mean you're not supportive, either. It may mean only—especially during the Trump administration—that briefings are few and far between and short in duration and there are many issues to cover.

3. *Do not walk out.* No matter how poorly we are treated, walking out of a press briefing only plays into the hands of the oppressor. We are not protesters. We are reporters. We must stay and tell the public—no matter what our personal feelings—what is going on.

4. *Do not make yourself the story but do not back down when bullied.* You cannot simply sit there as a spokesperson avoids you, belittles you, and calls you the "enemy of the people" or "fake news." However, pick your battles judiciously, realizing that when you do push back, politicians can and will accuse you of grandstanding or being rude. The day he called us "enemy of the people" was the day President Trump made us the story. We cannot play by the old rules when he changed them on us and continued to attack us.

5. *Asking a question is not "rude" or "inappropriate," even if it is shouted and the president or his surrogates find it inconvenient.* The answers may be both, but with few exceptions, merely asking a question isn't the problem. When the administration pushes back in such a manner, be assured you are on to something.

6. *Do your homework and observe.* Do not rely on briefings to be the sole source or the soul of your reporting. Work your sources. Take

notes about everything—what they wear, what the temperature is, where it happened, when someone cleared his or her throat. You never know when the trivial piece of information will become important or what will be needed to put the story into context. Soak up everything. Did they stutter? Did they laugh? Why?

7. *Limit the use of "off- the record."* Remember "off the record" is up to you. If the chief of staff, the president, or anyone else in the administration wants to go "off the record," I will refuse to do so. I will agree to "on background," meaning the information is reportable but attributed to a "senior White House source" or something similar, but on matters of public policy, I will never agree to allowing elected officials off-the-record comments. Those comments always get reported anyway. And since I went to jail to protect a confidential source, I do not use these things as arbitrarily as some.

8. *Do not become friends with those you cover.* Both Sam Donaldson and Dan Rather warned of this phenomenon more than a quarter of a century ago. Be cordial, friendly, and amicable, but at the end of the day, you compromise your ability to report on someone when you count him or her as your friend.

9. *Treat them all the same.* If you voted for them, give them even more grief.

10. *Be honest.*

11. *Always support your colleagues.* The press covering the president should represent the melting pot of America and indeed the world. Whatever you think of someone personally, professionally you should always support them whether or not you actually agree with them. Do *not* allow the president or anyone else to cleave away reporters from the herd one by one with a variety of complaints that have nothing to do with why we are there.

12. *You're not important. The question is important.* As I've often said, every one of us covering the president is replaceable. At the end of the day, what we ask is far more important than who we are. The administration wants to make it personal. They will accuse you of being inappropriate, rude, self-aggrandizing, and much more. That doesn't matter. You're not on the White House tour. You're there to cover the president. The president will have his people try to put the president's best foot forward. That is natural and correct, again as Donaldson often said. That's their job. Our job is finding out what's really going on. In that quest, you will

anger those who wish their secrets and, in some cases, inconvenient facts be kept in the dark.

There is more. One of the things I held on to for the past forty years is a pamphlet from Investigative Reporters and Editors called "Sourcery—A Reporter's Guide to Finding the Truth."[8]

The guidelines were written by James Polk, formerly of NBC News and a 1974 Pulitzer Prize winner, along with the advice and assistance of David Hayes of the *Kansas City Times* (1982 Pulitzer), Professor Carl Stepp of the University of Maryland, and Professor Steve Weinberg of the University of Missouri. Full disclosure: Weinberg was also one of my mentors and is a good friend to this day.

The guidelines are a valuable insight into how to get people to tell you the truth and how to recognize what the truth is:

1. Ask for help.
2. Be prepared.
3. Listen.
4. Be honest.
5. Talk to everyone.
6. See people face-to-face—probably one of the most important guidelines in the age of information, the internet, and social media.
7. Go back. Check again and again to see if the information is correct.
8. Be pleasant.
9. Remember the obvious question.
10. Challenge your sources.
11. Never trust your source.
12. Don't socialize with other reporters all the time.
13. If you want to protect your sources, keep them to yourself.
14. You set the rules.
15. Give your worst enemy a fair shake.
16. Let the facts fall where they may. You have no friends now. You are a reporter—tell the truth. But don't pass judgment. You're a reporter, not God. Let people's deeds speak for themselves.
17. Always say thank you.
18. Keep trying.

As for truth? Never assume. Check everything. A Chicago adage: "You say your mother loves you? Check it out."

People will tell you what they only think they know. Few people distinguish between what they actually know and what they only assume. A handy test to use: ask your source—and yourself—"How do you know that?"

Use common sense. Develop a logical mind. Try to look at things as they are—not as you hope them to be. One warning: a story that sounds too good to be true often is just that—not true.

People rarely tell 100 percent lies. Usually, there is a kernel of truth in every tale. It is the reporter's job to painstakingly strip away the layers to find what is true.

Look for what is missing. Develop a sense for what doesn't quite add up—and always look for the holes. Don't rush the truth. Success does come with being both first and right. But it's still better to be second than wrong.

Finally:

Run scared. If you are a reporter who is worried about being wrong, you have a much better chance of getting the story right.

At the end of the day, as a reporter, you want to know the truth. As I said at the beginning of this book, wanting to know as much as possible is my own personal story arc. I want to know everything I can, and to do that, I have to be able to communicate effectively and accept that my preconceived notions are up for revision on further analysis. I've managed young reporters who have come to me saying, "This is what I think." And I reply, "I don't care what you think. I barely care what I think. What do you know?"

Journalism, more than anything else, is the application of the scientific method to the art of communication. Thus, it is one of the most difficult things to do effectively. Applying science to human communication—which is full of emotion and nuance and often is anything but logical—can be a lifelong endeavor, and you'd better have a passion for it.

There are those who will vilify you and those who won't understand you. Part of that is ultimately your fault. You are both the transmitter and the receiver. What you transmit people may misunderstand. What you receive may not be what people are transmitting. How many times have I seen people on Twitter write, "I wish there was a sarcasm font"? How many times have all of us heard people say, "That's not what I meant." Communication is inexact, can be frustrating, and carries with it the ultimate consequences. "Don't shoot the messenger" is a cliché because it's happened often enough that people understand the meaning.

But being a reporter doesn't mean you are the only one who carries that burden. Scientists, artists, and anyone who endeavors to communicate to others has, through the history of mankind, suffered "cancel culture," death, isolation, excommunication, and a slap in the face at the very least. What's your choice? Give up?

Dr. Anthony Fauci is a good example of how to proceed. During the coronavirus pandemic, I first met him as he walked into the White House briefing room to explain to Americans (and the world at large to some extent) the dangers of the coronavirus and how to protect ourselves from it. As more information emerged, sometimes his direction changed, and sometimes it did not. Often, it was about using common sense to deal with a pandemic. At first, President Trump supported him and then later turned on him as Dr. Fauci refused to back Trump's growing insanity. Members of the public and even some members of Congress, particularly those of the QAnon variety, began to disparage, threaten, and vilify Dr. Fauci. Here the man was trying to help out his fellow human beings, and some of them accused him of causing the problem he was trying to solve. It had to be frustrating, so one day in a news conference that had been reduced to a Zoom meeting with perhaps hundreds of reporters, I got the opportunity and asked Dr. Fauci how he deals with it. How can you handle being vilified by those you are trying to help?

"You asked me how I deal with it. I deal with it by trying, to the best of my ability, to not pay attention to it. I have a very serious and important job now as the chief medical adviser on COVID-19 to President Biden, and I really want to use all my energy to focus on how—together with the medical team, which is an extraordinary team here—how I can be part of that team and function with value added. If I start worrying about the slings and the arrows that get thrown at me, it would be a distraction. And I tend to not want to be distracted. That's how I deal with it."

His advice is well worth adhering to—even if you're just a reporter.

All of these actions wouldn't need to be taken and this book wouldn't need to be written if the horrifyingly despotic dreams of Richard Nixon hadn't been made real by the actions of Ronald Reagan and every president since him.

Government actions during the past forty years that were taken to free us have enslaved us and destroyed the free press. Sometimes it appears the actions were taken with the best intentions, and on other occasions— especially in the misuse of the Espionage Act—there is little doubt the actions were self-serving. Even if we weren't called the "enemy of the people," before Donald Trump, each president treated the press—in some regard—as the enemy of their self-interest. Not that the press is perfect. It's tragically flawed as all humans are. The only necessary thing for a democratic government to do is to put up with the imperfections. You can't shut it down because you don't like it.

Make no mistake, there's never been a perfect "golden age" of journalism in the United States. That's the biggest lie ever told about journalism. But could there be? I have faith there could. The American people at least deserve a chance to obtain the facts and use them as they see fit.

The most disturbing and frustrating events of the past forty years are the cynical members of Congress, the executive branch, lobbyists, large media conglomerates, and now "vulture" capitalists manipulating the media to their own ends and pitting the viewing, reading, and listening public against those in the business who are simply trying to do their jobs.

It is even more frustrating watching young reporters struggle with the need to write a "clickbait" story for the boss who answers to another boss who answers to a business executive who answers to a board of directors—which only wants to make more money. No one in that chain ever sees a higher goal—except, perhaps, the reporter and his immediate editor, and they have little or no voice in the ability to make something better happen. Those who can make the changes don't see the need—and don't really care.

The worst? Those cynics who know what the press has become and take advantage of it to their own benefit. The anchors. The owners. The reporters. The politicians. The general public who loves "the show."

As Pogo said, "We have met the enemy and he is us."

As a result, we have news "deserts" cropping up all over the country. An uninformed public really serves only one useful purpose—to make sure that the most crooked and corrupt politicians stay in office, bilk us, and abuse us.

That way lies madness.

NOTES

CHAPTER 1: JUSTICE TO ALL, PARTIALITY TO NONE

1. "Posse Comitatus Act," *Wikipedia*, https://en.wikipedia.org/wiki/Posse_Comitatus_Act.

2. Stephen L. Vaughn, *Encyclopedia of American Journalism* (New York: Routledge, 2007).

3. Helen Thomas, *Watchdogs of Democracy?* (New York: Simon and Schuster, 2006).

4. "Postal Service Act," *Wikipedia*, https://en.wikipedia.org/wiki/Postal_Service_Act.

5. Colin McEnroe, "A Page from History," *Hartford Courant*, January 7, 1998.

6. Donald H. Stewart, *The Opposition Press of the Federalist Period* (Albany: State University of New York Press, 1969).

7. Ambrose Bierce, *The Devil's Dictionary* (New York: Dover, 1993).

8. H. L. Mencken, *Prejudices*, 6th ser. (New York: Knopf, 1927).

9. "The Man with the Muck Rake," April 15, 1906, *U.S. Embassy*, https://usa.usembassy.de/etexts/speeches/rhetoric/trmuck.htm.

10. Electronic Privacy Information Center, "Statement of U.S. Senator Russ Feingold on the Anti-Terrorism Bill from the Senate Floor, October 25, 2001," https://epic.org/privacy/terrorism/usapatriot/feingold.html.

11. Mencken, *Prejudices*.

12. *United States v. N.Y. Times Co.*, 328 F. Supp. 324, 331 (S.D.N.Y. 1971).

13. *New York Times Co. v. United States*, 403 U.S. 713 (1971).

14. Robert D. McFadden, "Ben H. Bagdikian, Reporter of Broad Range and Conscience, Dies at 96," *New York Times*, March 11, 2016, https://www.nytimes.com/2016/03/12/business/media/ben-h-bagdikian-reporter-of-broad-range-and-conscience-dies-at-96.html.

15. Tanner Mirrlees, *Global Entertainment Media: Between Cultural Imperialism and Cultural Globalization* (New York: Routledge, 2013).

16. Don Hewitt, *Tell Me a Story: Fifty Years and 60 Minutes in Television* (New York: Perseus Books, 2001).

17. RTDNA, "A 'Wires and Lights' Speech for Today, 60 Years Later," https://www.rtdna.org/content/edward_r_murrow_s_1958_wires_lights_in_a _box_speech.

18. Brooks Boliek, "FCC Finally Kills Off Fairness Doctrine," *Politico*, August 22, 2011, https://www.politico.com/story/2011/08/fcc-finally-kills-off-fairness -doctrine-061851.

CHAPTER 2: HEAR THE FOOTSTEPS, SAM?

1. David Greenberg, "What Roger Ailes Learned from Richard Nixon," *New York Times*, May 18, 2017, https://www.nytimes.com/2017/05/18/opinion /roger-ailes-richard-nixon-fox-news.html?ref=todayspaper.

2. Ibid.

3. Gladwin Hill, "Nixon Denounces Press as Biased; In 'Last' News Confer- ence, He Attributes His Defeat to Crisis over Cuba Nixon, Bitter at His Defeat by Brown in California, Denounces the Press as Biased Says Cuban Crisis Cost Him Election Gives No Hint of Plans—Asserts Others Will Have to Lead Coast G.O.P. Blames Cuban Crisis Changes His Plans," *New York Times*, November 8, 1962, https://www.nytimes.com/1962/11/08/archives/nixon-denounces-press -as-biased-in-last-news-conference-he.html.

4. Ibid.

5. Stephen A. Ambrose, *Nixon: The Education of a Politician, 1913–1962* (New York: Simon and Schuster, 1988).

6. Richard Harris, "Reflections," *The New Yorker*, September 24, 1973.

7. Ibid.

8. Ibid.

9. James Reston, "The Press and the Courts," *New York Times*, September 3, 1973.

10. Private interview, January 10, 2021.

11. John Cook, "Roger Ailes' Secret Nixon-Era Blueprint for Fox News Re- vealed," *Business Insider*, June 30, 2011, https://www.businessinsider.com/roger -ailes-blueprint-fox-news-2011-6.

12. "Ohio University to Rename Newsroom for FOX News' Roger Ailes," *Associated Press*, April 22, 2008, https://www.foxnews.com/story/ohio-university -to-rename-newsroom-for-fox-news-roger-ailes.

13. Jeff Guo, "What Roger Ailes Did to America: He Changed the Way Presi- dents Get Elected," *Vox*, May 19, 2017, https://www.vox.com/2017/5/19 /15660888/roger-ailes-america-trump-television-fox-news.

14. Ibid.

15. Jack Shafer, "Fox News 1.0," *The Slate*, June 5, 2008, https://slate.com /news-and-politics/2008/06/revisiting-tvn-roger-ailes-first-stab-at-running-a-tv -news-operation.html.

16. Mitch McConnell, *The Long Game: A Memoir* (New York: Penguin, 2016).

17. Sam Donaldson, *Hold On, Mr. President!* (New York: Fawcett Crest, 1987).

CHAPTER 3: NO DIFFERENT THAN TOASTERS

1. George Garneau, "President Reagan and Disinformation," *Editor and Publisher*, October 24, 1987.

2. Ibid.

3. "Broadcasting Deregulation," *Congressional Quarterly*, https://library.cqpress .com/cqresearcher/document.php?id=cqresrre1987120400.

4. Newton N. Minow, "Television and the Public Interest," address to the National Association of Broadcasters, Washington, DC, May 9, 1961.

5. James Warren, "Never Mind the 'Vast Wasteland': Minow Has More to Say," *New York Times*, May 7, 2011, https://www.nytimes.com/2011/05/08 /us/08cncwarren.html.

6. Penny Pagano, "Reagan's Veto Kills Fairness Doctrine Bill," *Los Angeles Times*, June 21, 1987, https://www.latimes.com/archives/la-xpm-1987-06-21 -mn-8908-story.html.

7. Academy for Systems Change, "Bring Back the Fairness Doctrine," *Donella Meadows Project*, https://donellameadows.org/archives/bring-back-the-fairness -doctrine.

8. *In re Complaint of Syracuse Peach Council against Television Station WTVH Syracuse, New York*, 2 FCC Rcd 5043 (1987).

9. Thomas P. O'Neill and William Novak, *Man of the House: The Life and Political Memoirs of Speaker Tip O'Neill* (New York: St. Martin's Press, 1987).

10. William A. Niskanen, "Reaganomics," in *Concise Encyclopedia of Economics*, ed. David R. Henderson (Carmel, IN: Liberty Fund), https://hcpss.instruc ture.com/courses/53860/pages/reaganomics#:~:text=The%20four%20pillars%20 of%20Reagan's,in%20order%20to%20reduce%20inflation.&text=Ronald%20 Reagan%20outlines%20his%20plan%20for%20tax%20reduction%20legislation%20 in%20July%201981.

11. Dinesh D'Souza, *Ronald Reagan: How an Ordinary Man Became an Extraordinary Leader* (New York: Touchstone, 1997).

12. Howell Raines, "Reagan and Mondale Debate; Clash on Deficit, Social Issues," *New York Times*, October 8, 1984, https://www.nytimes.com/1984/10/08/us /reagan-and-mondale-debate-clash-on-deficit-social-issues.html.

13. *Editor and Publisher Yearbook* data reported by Pew Research, March 12, 2007.

14. Knight Foundation, "Local TV News Is Thriving but Needs to Innovate to Remain Relevant," April 5, 2018, https://knightfoundation.org/press/releases /local-tv-news-is-thriving-but-needs-to-innovate-to-remain-relevant.

CHAPTER 4: DON'T WORRY ABOUT IT

1. Ian Peter, "So, Who Really Did Invent the Internet?" *Net History*, http:// www.nethistory.info/History%20of%20the%20Internet/origins.html.

2. Carl T. Bogus, "The Death of an Honorable Profession," *Indiana Law Journal* 71, no. 4 (1996), Article 5.

3. *Editor and Publisher*, August 8, 1987.

4. Ibid.

5. *Editor and Publisher*, October 24, 1987.

6. Ibid.

7. Ibid.

8. Ibid.

9. H. L. Mencken, *The American Scene: A Reader* (New York: Knopf, 1965).

10. *Laredo News*, July 13, 1984.

11. *Laredo News*, July 16, 1984.

12. Smedley D. Butler, *War Is a Racket* (1935; repr., San Diego, CA: Dauphin Publications, 2018).

13. Ibid.

14. "Mondale Claims Polls Soon Won't Mean Anything," *Laredo News*, November 5, 1984.

15. Ibid.

CHAPTER 5: A WONDERFUL BURSTER OF BALLOONS

1. Keith Runyon, "A Former C-J Journalist Reflects on His Four-Plus Years at the Paper," *Louisville*, November 8, 2018, https://archive.louisville.com/content /keith-runyon-reflects-on-c-j.

2. Archives, *Courier-Journal*.

3. Donald B. Towles, *The Press of Kentucky: 1787–1994* (Frankfort: Kentucky Press Association, 1994).

4. Ibid.

5. Ibid.

6. Runyon, "A Former C-J Journalist Reflects on His Four-Plus Years at the Paper."

7. H. L. Mencken, *The American Scene: A Reader* (New York: Vintage Books, 1982).

8. Runyon, "A Former C-J Journalist Reflects on His Four-Plus Years at the Paper."

9. *Courier-Journal*, Neighborhoods section, 1985.

10. Mencken, *The American Scene*.

11. Library of Congress.

CHAPTER 6: WHAT YOU GOT HERE IS BRAIN BLOOD

1. University of North Texas Libraries, Denton, via the Library of Congress.

2. *Editor and Publisher*, September 19, 1987.

3. "Reporter Kicked Out of Senate," *San Antonio Express News*, May 25, 1990.

4. Brian Karem, *Shield the Source* (Far Hills, NJ: New Horizon Press, 1992).

5. H. L. Mencken, *The Diary of H. L. Mencken* (New York: Knopf, 1991).

CHAPTER 7: YOU'RE A LITTLE DOG

1. "Walter Cronkite: The Most Trusted Man in America," *UO Blogs*, https:// blogs.uoregon.edu/frengsj387/vietnam-war.

2. Dan Rather, "Rather: Bob Simon a Scholar Correspondent," *CNN*, February 12, 2015, https://www.cnn.com/2015/02/12/opinion/rather-bob-simon-death /index.html.

3. Peter Arnett, "Peter Arnett: A Look Back at Operation Desert Storm," *CNN*, January 16, 2001, http://www.cnn.com/COMMUNITY/transcripts /2001/01/16/arnett/.

4. Peter Arnett at the National Press Club, March 19, 1991, https://www.press .org/reporting-war-baghdad.

5. KMOL-TV, *Good to Go*, November 1990.

6. "Electronic Media," published by Crain Communications, April 22, 1991.

7. KMOL-TV, *Texans at War*, 1991.

CHAPTER 8: THE WAR ON DRUGS IS A JOKE

1. "Spending on Illicit Drugs in US Nears $150 Billion Annually," *Science Daily*, August 20, 2019, https://www.sciencedaily.com/releases/2019/08/190820081846 .htm.

2. Drug Policy Alliance, "The Federal Drug Control Budget: New Rhetoric, Same Failed Drug War," February 2015, https://drugpolicy.org/sites/default/files /DPA_Fact_sheet_Drug_War_Budget_Feb2015.pdf.

3. *Editor and Publisher*, September 19, 1987.

4. Ibid.

5. Joseph Menn, "There Are Two Sides to This Publisher's Story," *Los Angeles Times*, March 22, 2006, https://www.latimes.com/archives/la-xpm-2006 -mar-22-fi-singleton22-story.html.

6. Jessica Bryce Young, "Orlando Sentinel Newspaper Sold to Venture Capitalists Alden," *Orlando Sentinel*, February 19, 2021, https://www.orlandoweekly.com /Blogs/archives/2021/02/19/orlando-sentinel-newspaper-sold-to-vulture-capital ists-alden.

7. Ibid.

8. "Is Network News Crumbling?" *TV Guide*, September 1991.

9. Sam Donaldson, *Hold On, Mr. President!* (New York: Fawcett Crest, 1987).

10. Ibid.

CHAPTER 9: A TALE OF TWO CULT LEADERS

1. Gabriel Sherman, *The Revenge of Roger's Angels* (New York: New York Media).

2. Jerry Knight, "Mark Fowler Plans to Resign as FCC Chairman in Spring," *Washington Post*, January 17, 1987, https://www.washingtonpost.com/archive /politics/1987/01/17/mark-fowler-plans-to-resign-as-fcc-chairman-in-spring /0e0131e4-fe53-49c3-9f2f-917f0c74af3b/.

3. Ibid.

4. Caroline E. Mayer and Elizabeth Tucker, "The FCC According to Fowler," *Washington Post*, April 19, 1987, https://www.washingtonpost.com/archive/busi ness/1987/04/19/the-fcc-according-to-fowler/29609078-f2e9-41ac-ae72 -7f008e523be2/.

5. Helen Thomas, *Watchdogs of Democracy?* (New York: Simon and Schuster, 2006).

6. Ibid.

7. Ibid.

8. "The Hunt for Pablo Escobar," *America's Most Wanted*, 1992.

9. "Lost in the Chaos," *Waco Tribune-Herald*, February 24, 2018.

10. Ibid.

11. Ibid.

12. Ibid.

13. Ibid.

14. Human Rights Campaign, "Corporate Equality Index 2021," https://www .hrc.org/resources/corporate-equality-index.

15. PR Newswire, "McClatchy Commences Voluntary Chapter 11, While Soliciting Support for Plan of Reorganization," *PR Newswire*, February 13, 2020, https://www.prnewswire.com/news-releases/mcclatchy-commences-voluntary -chapter-11-while-soliciting-support-for-plan-of-reorganization-301004417.html.

16. Barbara Ball, "A News Comment: What Does the McClatchy Bankruptcy Really Mean?" *Blythewood Online*, February 20, 2020, https://www.blythewood online.com/2020/02/a-news-comment-what-does-the-mcclatchy-bankruptcy -really-mean/.

CHAPTER 10: OPEN THE FLOODGATES

1. Michael Corcoran, "Democracy in Peril: Twenty Years of Media Consolidation under the Telecommunications Act," *Truthout.org*, February 11, 2016, https://truthout.org/articles/democracy-in-peril-twenty-years-of-media-consoli dation-under-the-telecommunications-act.

2. Bill Clinton, "Remarks at the Signing of the Telecommunications Act," Clinton Presidential Library.

3. Corcoran, "Democracy in Peril."

4. Ibid.

5. Bernie Sanders, "Bernie Sanders on Media Ownership and Telecommunications," *Feelthebern.org*, https://feelthebern.org/bernie-sanders-on-media-owner ship-and-telecommunications.

6. "Sinclair Broadcast Group," *Wikipedia*, https://en.wikipedia.org/wiki/Sin clair_Broadcast_Group.

7. Ibid.

8. Amanda Eisenberg and Kelsey Sutton, "'It Was a Total Bloodbath': USA Today Journalists Recount Layoffs," *AJR*, September 25, 2014, https://ajr.org /2014/09/05/total-bloodbath-usa-today-journalists-recount-layoffs.

9. "The Walt Disney Company to Acquire Twenty-First Century Fox, Inc., after Spinoff of Certain Businesses, for $52.4 Billion in Stock," *Businesswire*, December 14, 2017, https://www.businesswire.com/news/home/20171214005650 /en/The-Walt-Disney-Company-to-Acquire-Twenty-First-Century-Fox-Inc. -after-Spinoff-of-Certain-Businesses-for-52.4-Billion-in-Stock.

10. Rory *Carroll*, "Disney's Blackout of *LA Times* Triggers Boycott from Media Outlets," *Guardian,* November 7, 2017, https://www.theguardian.com/film/2017 /nov/07/disney-los-angeles-times-media-boycott.

11. World Health Organization, *The WHO Recommended Classification of Pesticides by Hazard and Guidelines to Classification 2009* (Geneva: World Health Organization, 2010).

12. John J. Fried, "The Pesticide Puzzle," *Chicago Tribune*, March 20, 1996.

13. Cynthia Cotts, "Conservatives in Drag," *Village Voice*, November 21, 2000, https://www.villagevoice.com/2000/11/21/conservatives-in-drag/.

14. "U.S. EPA Denies Petition to Ban Pesticide Chlorpyrifos," *Reuters*, March 29, 2017, https://www.reuters.com/article/us-usa-pesticide-epa/u-s-epa-denies -petition-to-ban-pesticide-chlorpyrifos-idUSKBN17039F.

15. U.S. Environmental Protection Agency, "Chlorpyrifos: Preliminary Human Health Risk Assessment for Registration Review," June 30, 2011, https://archive.epa.gov/oppsrrd1/registration_review/web/html/index-299.html.

16. Eric Durr, "Dow AgroSciences Agrees to Pay $2M to State Over Pesticide Ads," *Albany Business Review*, December 15, 2003, https://www.bizjournals.com/albany/stories/2003/12/15/daily3.html?page=all.

17. EPA Press Office, "EPA Takes Action to Address Risk from Chlorpyrifos and Protect Children's Health," *Environmental Protection Agency*, August 18, 2021, https://www.epa.gov/newsreleases/epa-takes-action-address-risk-chlorpyrifos-and-protect-childrens-health.

CHAPTER 11: GIVE THE DEVIL THE BENEFIT OF THE LAW?

1. Reporters Committee for Freedom of the Press, "Dancing around the Tapping Question," *Fall 2003*, https://www.rcfp.org/journals/the-news-media-and-the-law-fall-2003/dancing-around-tapping-questi.

2. American Civil Liberties Union, "Surveillance under the USA/Patriot Act," https://www.aclu.org/other/surveillance-under-usapatriot-act.

3. Electronic Privacy Information Center, "Statement of U.S. Senator Russ Feingold on the Anti-Terrorism Bill from the Senate Floor, October 25, 2001," https://epic.org/privacy/terrorism/usapatriot/feingold.html.

4. Ibid.

5. Ibid.

6. Raphael Satter, "U.S. Court: Mass Surveillance Program Exposed by Snowden Was Illegal," *Reuters*, September 2, 2020, https://www.reuters.com/article/us-usa-nsa-spying/u-s-court-mass-surveillance-program-exposed-by-snowden-was-illegal-idUSKBN25T3CK.

7. Ibid.

8. Meg Dalton, "Hugh Hefner's *Playboy* Did a Lot of Great Journalism," *Columbia Journalism Review*, September 28, 2017, https://www.cjr.org/b-roll/hugh-hefner-playboy-journalism.php.

9. Brian Karem, "The Playboy Interview with James Carville," *Playboy*, July 1, 1996, https://www.playboy.com/read/the-playboy-interview-with-james-carville.

10. Ibid.

11. Brian Karem, "The FAA—More Frightening Than Terrorists," *Playboy*, June 2002.

12. Ibid.

CHAPTER 12: IN A ROOM WITH MADNESS—POST-9/11

1. "President Delivers State of the Union Address," *Bush White House Archives*, https://georgewbush-whitehouse.archives.gov.

2. Kate Vinton, "These 15 Billionaires Own America's News Media Companies," *Forbes*, June 1, 2016, https://www.forbes.com/sites/katevinton/2016/06/01/these-15-billionaires-own-americas-news-media-companies/?sh=7b41777e660a.

3. "Knight Ridder," *Wikipedia*, https://en.wikipedia.org/wiki/Knight_Ridder.

4. "Buying the War," *Bill Moyers Journal*, June 4, 2009, https://www.pbs.org/moyers/journal/btw/watch.html.

5. Michael R. Gordon and Judith Miller, "U.S. Says Hussein Intensifies Quest for A-Bomb Parts," *New York Times*, September 8, 2002, https://www.nytimes.com/2002/09/08/world/threats-responses-iraqis-us-says-hussein-intensifies-quest-for-bomb-parts.html.

6. Brian Karem, "The Inside Search for the D.C. Sniper," *Playboy*, March 2003.

7. Robert Hanley, "The Hunt for a Sniper: The Vehicle; F.B.I. Asks Co-Owner of Car to Come Forward," *New York Times*, October 25, 2002, https://www.nytimes.com/2002/10/25/us/the-hunt-for-a-sniper-the-vehicle-fbi-asks-co-owner-of-car-to-come-forward.html.

8. Karem, "The Inside Search for the D.C. Sniper."

9. Ibid.

10. Ibid.

11. Ibid.

12. Ibid.

CHAPTER 13: WHAT THE HELL IS THE ESPIONAGE ACT?

1. Greg Myre, "Once Reserved for Spies, Espionage Act Now Used against Suspected Leakers," *NPR*, June 28, 2017, https://www.npr.org/sections/parallels/2017/06/28/534682231/once-reserved-for-spies-espionage-act-now-used-against-suspected-leakers.

2. Jake Tapper, "The Obama Administration Has Used the Espionage Act to Go after Whistleblowers Who Leaked to Journalists . . . More Than All Previous Administrations Combined," *Politifact*, January 2, 2014, https://www.politifact.com/factchecks/2014/jan/10/jake-tapper/cnns-tapper-obama-has-used-espionage-act-more-all-/.

3. Scott Wilson, "Obama: 'No Apologies' for Leaks Investigation," *Washington Post*, May 16, 2013, https://www.washingtonpost.com/news/post-politics/wp/2013/05/16/obama-no-apologies-for-leaks-investigation/.

4. Sari Horowitz, "Under Sweeping Subpoenas, Justice Department Obtained AP Phone Records in Leak Investigation," *Washington Post*, May 13, 2013, https://www.washingtonpost.com/world/national-security/under-sweeping-subpoenas-justice-department-obtained-ap-phone-records-in-leak-investigation/2013/05/13/11d1bb82-bc11-11e2-89c9-3be8095fe767_story.html.

5. Ibid.

6. *Schenck v. United States*, 249 U.S. 47, 49–51 (1917).

7. Sheldon Novick, "The Unrevised Holmes and Freedom of Expression," *Supreme Court Review* 1991: 303–90.

8. *Abrams v. United States*, 250 U.S. 616, 630 (1919).

9. Oliver Wendell Holmes, "*Schenck v. United States* 249 U.S. 47," opinion, Legal Information Institute.

10. Spencer Ackerman and Ed Pilkington, "Obama's War on Whistleblowers Leaves Administration Insiders Unscathed," *Guardian*, March 16, 2015, https://www.theguardian.com/us-news/2015/mar/16/whistleblowers-double-standard-obama-david-petraeus-chelsea-manning.

11. "Axios Media Trends," *Axios*, June 14, 2021, https://www.axios.com/newsletters/axios-media-trends-6a729b9b-4de0-410c-9c40-c62d013fc9e1.html?chunk=0&utm_term=twsocialshare#story0.

12. Charlie Savage, "Obama Commutes Bulk of Chelsea Manning's Sentence," *New York Times*, January 17, 2017, https://www.benton.org/headlines/president-obama-commutes-bulk-chelsea-manning%E2%80%99s-sentence.

13. "Secret U.S. Embassy Cables," *Wikipedia*, https://en.wikipedia.org/wiki/United_States_diplomatic_cables_leak.

14. Tal Axelrod, "Intel Dem: Assange Is 'a Direct Participant in Russian Efforts to Undermine the West,'" *The Hill*, April 11, 2019, https://thehill.com/homenews/senate/438437-top-senate-dem-assange-is-a-direct-participant-in-russian-efforts-to.

15. Reporters Without Borders, "Two Months before Assange's Extradition Hearing, RSF Calls for His Release on Humanitarian Grounds and for U.S. Espionage Act Charges to Be Dropped," *RSF*, January 6, 2020, https://rsf.org/en/news/two-months-assanges-extradition-hearing-rsf-calls-his-release-humanitarian-grounds-and-us-espionage.

16. Aishvarya Kavi, "Trump, Who Once Called Edward Snowden 'a Spy Who Should Be Executed,' Now Says He'll Look into a Pardon," *Baltimore Sun*, August 16, 2020, https://www.baltimoresun.com/news/nation-world/ct-nw-nyt-trump-edward-snowden-pardon-20200816-yrc4grw4ejg47aryc4njd2eyne-story.html.

17. Raphael Satter, "U.S. Court: Mass Surveillance Program Exposed by Snowden Was Illegal," *Reuters*, September 2, 2020, https://www.reuters.com/article/us-usa-nsa-spying/us-court-mass-surveillance-program-exposed-by-snowden-was-illegal-idUSKBN25T3CK.

18. Eugene Kiely, "Obama, Fox News, and the Free Press," *FactCheck*, September 13, 2018, https://www.factcheck.org/2018/09/obama-fox-news-and-the-free-press/.

19. Ibid.

20. Perry Bacon Jr. and Shailagh Murray, "Opponents Paint Obama as an Elitist; Clinton, McCain Try to Score Off 'Bitter' Remark," *Washington Post*, April 12, 2008.

CHAPTER 14: ENTER THE DRAGON

1. Mark Sherman, "The 10 Instances of Possible Obstruction in Mueller Report," *AP*, April 18, 2019, https://apnews.com/article/north-america-donald-trump-ap-top-news-elections-james-comey-e0d125d737be4a21a81bec3d9f1dffd8.

2. H. L. Mencken, *The American Scene: A Reader* (New York: Vintage Books, 1982).

3. "Episode 76: Michael Cohen—What Does Trump Want?" *Just Ask the Question*, December 8, 2020, https://www.justaskthequestion.com/post/episode-76-michael-cohen-what-does-trump-want.

4. Brian Karem, "Thankfully, I Got to Interrupt Sean Spicer's Horrible Hitler Gaffe," *Playboy*, April 12, 2017.

5. Ibid.

6. Joe Concha, "New O'Keefe Video Shows CNN Producer Calling Russia Coverage 'Mostly Bull——,'" *The Hill*, June 27, 2017, https://thehill.com/home news/media/339632-new-okeefe-video-shows-cnn-producer-calling-russia-cov erage-mostly-bullshit.

7. Yashar Ali, tweet, *Twitter*, June 27, 2017, https://twitter.com/yashar/status /879785504488685569 (video of White House reporter Brian Karem pushing back against Sarah Huckabee Sanders and saying what many people have been thinking).

CHAPTER 15: EVERYONE KNOWS IT'S WENDI

1. National Endowment for the Humanities, "About the Capital," *Library of Congress*, https://chroniclingamerica.loc.gov/lccn/sn82014422.

2. Ibid.

3. Chris Benderev, Rhaina Cohen, and Claire Harbage, "'People Will Forget about Us': The *Capital Gazette* Shooting Survivors, Years Later," *NPR*, March 10, 2021, https://www.npr.org/2021/03/10/973738517/-people-will-forget-about -us-the-capital-gazette-shooting-survivors-two-years-la.

4. John Bowden, "Reporter after Newsroom Shooting: 'We Are Putting Out a Damn Paper Tomorrow,'" *The Hill*, June 28, 2018, https://thehill.com/home news/media/394746-capital-gazette-reporter-we-are-putting-out-a-damn-paper -tomorrow.

5. Editorial written for the MDDC and said live during the annual meeting, https://mddcpress.com.

6. Brian Karem, "Brian Karem Reflects on the Work of Trump's Administra-tion during America's Birthday," *Playboy*, July 5, 2018, https://www.playboy.com /read/donald-trump-annapolis-shooting.

7. Glenn Smith and Tony Bartelme, "Accountability Suffers as Newspaper Closures Grow in SC, Nation," *Post and Courier*, February 13, 2021, https://www

.postandcourier.com/uncovered/accountability-suffers-as-newspaper-closures
-grow-in-sc-nation/article_7fcf2b40-6282-11eb-8e6a-db7d9f762dc8.html.

CHAPTER 16: FAKE NEWS

1. Dave Philipps, "Reality Winner, Former N.S.A. Translator, Gets More Than Five Years in Leak of Russian Hacking Report," *New York Times*, August 23, 2018, https://www.nytimes.com/2018/08/23/us/reality-winner-nsa-sentence.html.

2. "Court Rules Reporter's White House Pass Unfairly Suspended," *Federal News Network*, June 5, 2020, https://federalnewsnetwork.com/government -news/2020/06/court-rules-reporters-white-house-pass-unfairly-suspended/.

3. Smedley D. Butler, *War Is a Racket* (1935; repr., San Diego, CA: Dauphin Publications, 2018).

CHAPTER 17: IF YOU STOP COUNTING BALLOTS

1. David Makamura, tweet, *Twitter*, February 27, 2019, https://twitter.com /davidnakamura/status/1100940240796020736?lang=en.

2. Brian Karem, "Notes from the Deserted Circus That Is the New White House," *Playboy*, April 9, 2020, https://www.playboy.com/read/grisham-press -briefings.

3. Brian Karem, "Why Can't Reporters Report? And Where Can Americans Get the Facts When the President Has Become His Own De Facto Press Secretary?" *Playboy*, April 9, 2020, https://www.playboy.com/read/grisham-press-briefings.

4. Ibid.

5. Leia Idliby, "Remembering All the Questions OAN Asked before They Were Kicked Out of White House Briefings," *Mediaite*, April 2, 2020, https:// www.mediaite.com/politics/remembering-all-the-questions-oan-asked-before -they-were-kicked-out-of-white-house-briefings/; Joe Concha, "OAN Reporter Roasted for Asking Trump If Saying 'Chinese Food' Is Racist: 'Dumbest Question' Ever," *The Hill*, March 19, 2020, https://thehill.com/homenews/media/488535 -oan-reporter-roasted-for-asking-trump-if-saying-chinese-food-is-racist-dumbest.

6. Lloyd Grove, "Trump Is 'Eroding Truth,' and CNN's Jim Acosta Plays into His Hands, Says ABC's Jon Karl," *Daily Beast*, April 1, 2020, https://www.the dailybeast.com/trump-is-eroding-truth-and-cnns-jim-acosta-plays-into-his-hands -says-abcs-jon-karl.

7. Ibid.

8. Paul Farhi, "A 'Loud-Mouth Writer' Says the White House Broke Its Own Briefing-Room Rules, so He Did the Same," *Washington Post*, August 20, 2000, https://www.washingtonpost.com/lifestyle/media/a-loud-mouth-writer-says

-the-white-house-broke-its-own-briefing-room-rules-so-he-did-the
-same/2020/08/20/1d5441b8-e25c-11ea-8181-606e603bb1c4_story.html.

9. Ibid.

CHAPTER 18: WE REALLY WANT MORE
REPORTERS COVERING US

1. Maxwell Tani, "White House Reporters: Biden Team Wanted Our Questions in Advance," *Daily Beast*, February 1, 2021, https://www.thedailybeast.com/white-house-reporters-say-biden-team-asked-them-for-questions-in-advance.

2. Matthew Hagg and Michael M. Grynbaum, "Time Names Person of the Year for 2018: Jamal Khashoggi and Other Journalists," *New York Times*, January 17, 2021, https://www.nytimes.com/2018/12/11/business/media/jamal-khashoggi-person-of-the-year-time.html.

3. Jamal Khashoggi, "Opinion: Jamal Khashoggi: What the Arab World Needs Most Is Free Expression," *Washington Post*, October 17, 2018, https://www.washingtonpost.com/opinions/global-opinions/jamal-khashoggi-what-the-arab-world-needs-most-is-free-expression/2018/10/17/adfc8c44-d21d-11e8-8c22-fa2ef74bd6d6_story.html.

4. "Trump, Jr. Spreads Right-Wing Smear That 'Murdered' Saudi Journalist Supports 'Jihadists,'" *Haaretz*, October 14, 2018, https://www.haaretz.com/us-news/trump-jr-tweets-smear-that-murdered-saudi-journalist-supports-jihadists-1.6554150.

5. Mark Mazzetti, "Year before Killing, Saudi Prince Told Aide He Would Use 'a Bullet' on Jamal Khashoggi," *New York Times*, February 7, 2019, https://www.nytimes.com/2019/02/07/us/politics/khashoggi-mohammed-bin-salman.html.

6. Samuel Osborne, "Saudi Arabia Bans Journalist for Criticising Donald Trump," *Independent*, December 5, 2016, https://www.independent.co.uk/news/world/middle-east/saudi-arabia-donald-trump-journalist-banned-criticising-us-president-elect-a7456956.html.

7. Chris Melore, "Dangerous Era for Journalists: One in Five TV News Stations Report Employees Attacked in 2020," *StudyFinds*, April 29, 2021, https://www.studyfinds.org/dangereous-era-journalism-tv-news-employees-attacked/.

8. Reporters Without Borders, "Despite Improvements, Troubling Vital Signs for Press Freedom Persist," *RSF*, https://rsf.org/en/united-states.

9. Office of the Press Secretary, "Read: Trump's Statement on Saudi Crown Prince and the Killing of Jamal Khashoggi," *CNN*, November 20, 2018, https://www.cnn.com/2018/11/20/politics/trump-statement-saudi-khashoggi.

10. *Meet the Press*, tweet, *Twitter*, June 23, 2019, https://twitter.com/MeetThePress/status/1142972626895343616.

11. Brian Karem, "Biden and Khashoggi: Justice Demands More," *Bulwark*, February 26, 2021, https://thebulwark.com/biden-and-khashoggi/.

12. Ibid.

13. Ibid.

14. "Transcript: ABC News' George Stephanopoulos Interviews President Joe Biden," *ABC News*, March 17, 2021, https://abcnews.go.com/Politics/transcript-abc-news-george-stephanopoulos-interviews-president-joe/story?id=76509669.

CHAPTER 19: A STAPLE IN YOUR NAVEL

1. *Citizen Kane* (1939).

2. Paul Farhi and Elahe Izadi, "Tribune Publishing, Owner of Major U.S. Newspapers, to Be Acquired by Hedge Fund Known for Slashing Newsroom Jobs," *Washington Post*, February 16, 2021, https://www.washingtonpost.com/lifestyle/media/tribune-publishing-owner-of-major-us-newspapers-acquired-by-hedge-fund-known-for-slashing-newsroom-jobs/2021/02/16/e732ea28-70b1-11eb-93be-c10813e358a2_story.html.

3. Glenn Smith and Tony Bartelme, "Accountability Suffers as Newspaper Closures Grow in SC, Nation," *Post and Courier*, February 13, 2021, https://www.postandcourier.com/uncovered/accountability-suffers-as-newspaper-closures-grow-in-sc-nation/article_7fcf2b40-6282-11eb-8e6a-db7d9f762dc8.html.

4. Dave Bauder, "Study Finds People Want More Than Watchdogs for Journalists," *AP*, April 14, 2021, https://apnews.com/article/politics-media-tom-rosenstiel-journalists-915025bcab8f5910381eee11b5cb9d17.

5. James Chen, "Multiple," *Investopedia*, December 7, 2020, https://www.investopedia.com/terms/m/multiple.asp.

6. Alex Haley, "Interview with Martin Luther King," *Playboy*, January 1965.

7. David Sheff, "Interview with Steve Jobs," *Playboy*, February 1985.

8. Jerry Jazz Musician, "Interview with Miles Davis," *Playboy*, September 1962.

9. Smith and Bartelme, "Accountability Suffers as Newspaper Closures Grow in SC, Nation."

10. Ibid.

11. *The Newsroom*, season 1, episode 1, HBO.

12. "Remarks by President Biden on America's Place in the World," *White House*, February 4, 2021, https://www.whitehouse.gov/briefing-room/speeches-remarks/2021/02/04/remarks-by-president-biden-on-americas-place-in-the-world/.

13. Brian Karem, "Journalists Are Not Expendable," *Playboy*, February 26, 2021, https://www.playboy.com/read/journalists-are-not-expendable.

14. "Remarks by President Biden on America's Place in the World."

CHAPTER 20: FREE THE PRESS

1. Don Henley, "Dirty Laundry," *Genius.com*, https://genius.com/Don-henley -dirty-laundry-lyrics.

2. "Axios Media Trends," *Axios*, June 15, 2021, https://www.axios.com /newsletters/axios-media-trends-6a729b9b-4de0-410c-9c40-c62d013fc9e1 .html?chunk=0&utm_term=twsocialshare#story0.

3. Tom Stites, "About 1,300 U.S. Communities Have Totally Lost News Coverage, UNC News Desert Study Finds," *Poynter*, October 15, 2018, https://www .poynter.org/business-work/2018/about-1300-u-s-communities-have-totally-lost -news-coverage-unc-news-desert-study-finds/.

4. Ibid.

5. "Victor Pickard," *Wikipedia*, https://en.wikipedia.org/wiki/Victor_Pickard _(professor).

6. Brian Stelter, "AT&T to Spin Off and Combine Warnermedia with Discovery in Deal That Would Create Streaming Giant," *CNN*, May 17, 2021, https://www.cnn.com/2021/05/17/media/warnermedia-discovery-deal/index .html?fbclid=IwAR0aN11dmFMK-YidkKFAtvcy3V9Df-00eWuFgp3Odg0y IUxKvNF_Mw4zp7g.

7. Brent Merritt, "The Rise of Attention Metrics: Can a New Digital Currency Help Sustain Journalism?" *George Washington University*, July 17, 2017, https://smpa.gwu.edu/rise-attention-metrics-can-new-digital-currency-help-sus tain-journalism.

8. Investigative Reporters and Editors, University of Missouri, "Sourcery—A Reporter's Guide to Finding the Truth" (pamphlet), 1982.